Ludwig Wittgenstein:

THE MAN AND HIS PHILOSOPHY

Ludwig Wittgenstein:

THE MAN AND HIS PHILOSOPHY

Edited by **K. T. FANN**

A DELTA BOOK

A DELTA BOOK

Published by Dell Publishing Co., Inc.
750 Third Avenue, New York, N.Y. 10017
Copyright © 1967, by Dell Publishing Co., Inc.
Delta ® TM 755118, Dell Publishing Co., Inc.
Library of Congress Catalog Number: 67-11445
All rights reserved
First printing—March, 1967
Manufactured in the United States of America

Acknowledgments

The following selections in this volume are reproduced by permission of the authors and their publishers:

GEORG H. VON WRIGHT, "A Biographical Sketch," *Philosophical Review* 64, No. 4 (1955). An extensively revised version was published along with the 1966 edition of Norman Malcolm's *L. Wittgenstein: A Memoir* by Oxford University Press; reprinted here by permission of the author, the editors of *Philosophical Review,* and Oxford University Press.

"Memoirs" includes the following selections:

BERTRAND RUSSELL, "Ludwig Wittgenstein," *Mind* 60, No. 239 (1951); reprinted by permission of the author and the editor of *Mind.* From "Philosophers and Idiots," *The Listener* (Feb. 10, 1955); reprinted by permission of the author.

RUDOLF CARNAP, from his "Autobiography," in Paul Schilpp (ed.), *The Philosophy of Rudolf Carnap;* now published by The Open Court Publishing Co., La Salle, Illinois, 1964; reprinted by permission of the publisher and the author.

G. E. MOORE, from his "Autobiography," in Paul Schilpp (ed.), *The Philosophy of G. E. Moore,* 1942, now published by the Open Court Publishing Co.; reprinted by permission of the publisher. From "Wittgenstein's Lectures in 1930–33," published in three parts in *Mind* 63–64, Nos. 249, 251 and 253 (1954–5); reprinted by permission of the editor of *Mind.*

JOHN WISDOM, "Ludwig Wittgenstein, 1934–37," *Mind* 61, No. 242 (1952); reprinted by permission of the author and the editor of *Mind.*

D. A. T. GASKING and A. C. JACKSON, "Ludwig Wittgenstein," *The Australasian Journal of Philosophy* 29, No. 2 (1951); reprinted by permission of the editor and authors.

KARL BRITTON, "Portrait of a Philosopher," *The Listener* (June 10, 1955); reprinted by permission of the author.

"Ludwig Wittgenstein: A Symposium," by Erich Heller, M. O'C. Drury, N. Malcolm, and Rush Rhees, was published in *The Listener* (January 28, and February 4, 1960); reprinted by permission of the authors.

WOLFE MAYS, "Recollections of Wittgenstein," original contribution by the author to this anthology (March, 1967).

ERICH HELLER, "Wittgenstein: Unphilosophical Notes," *Encounter* 13, No. 3 (1959). Published as "Wittgenstein and Nietzsche," © copyright 1959, 1965 by Erich Heller. Reprinted from *The Artist's Journey into the Interior* by permission of Random House, Inc., and the author.

JOSÉ FERRATER MORA, "Wittgenstein, A Symbol of Troubled Times," *Philosophy and Phenomenological Research* 14, No. 1 (1953); reprinted by permission of the editor and the author. The author has made a number of stylistic changes and replaced the old note by a new one for this volume.

GILBERT RYLE, "Ludwig Wittgenstein," *Analysis* 12, No. 1 (1951); reprinted by permission of the author and Basil Blackwell, the publisher of *Analysis*.

GEORGE A. PAUL, "Ludwig Wittgenstein," in A. J. Ayer and others (eds.): *The Revolution in Philosophy*. New York: St. Martin's Press, 1956. Reprinted by permission of St. Martin's Press, Inc., Macmillan & Co., Ltd.

MORRIS LAZEROWITZ, "Wittgenstein on the Nature of Philosophy," to appear in the forthcoming revised edition of C. A. Mace (ed.): *British Philosophy in the Mid-Century*, London: George Allen & Unwin, Ltd.; reprinted here by permission of the author, the editor, and the publisher.

O. K. BOUWSMA, "The Blue Book," *The Journal of Philosophy* 58, No. 6 (1961); reprinted in his *Philosophical Essays* by University of Nebraska Press, Lincoln, Nebraska, 1965. Reprinted here by permission of the author, the editor of *The Journal of Philosophy,* and University of Nebraska Press.

LEONARD LINSKY, "Wittgenstein on Language and Some Problems of Philosophy," *The Journal of Philosophy* 54, No. 10 (1957); reprinted by permission of the author and the editor.

NORMAN MALCOLM, "Wittgenstein's *Philosophical Investigations,*" *Philosophical Review* 63, No. 4 (1954); republished in his *Knowledge and Certainty,* © 1963, Prentice-Hall, Inc., Englewood Cliffs, New Jersey, U.S.A.; reprinted by permission of the author, the editors of *Philosophical Review,* and Prentice-Hall, Inc.

PAUL FEYERABEND, "Wittgenstein's *Philosophical Investigations,*" *Philosophical Review* 64, No. 3 (1955); reprinted by permission of the author and the editors.

RUSH RHEES, "Wittgenstein's Builders." This paper is reprinted from *Proceedings of the Aristotelian Society* 60 (1959–60); reprinted by permission of the author and the editor of The Aristotelian Society.

ALICE AMBROSE, "Wittgenstein on Some Questions in Foundations of Mathematics," *The Journal of Philosophy* 52, No. 8 (1955); collected in her *Essays in Analysis* to be published by George Allen & Unwin Ltd., London; reprinted here by permission of the author, the editor of *The Journal of Philosophy,* and George Allen & Unwin Ltd.

JOSEPH L. COWAN, "Wittgenstein's Philosophy of Logic," *Philosophical Review* 70, No. 3 (1961); reprinted by permission of the author and the editors.

ARNOLD B. LEVISON, "Wittgenstein and Logical Laws." This is the combined and enlarged version of the following two articles which the author has kindly done for this anthology: "Wittgenstein and Logical Laws," *Philosophical Quarterly* 14, No. 57 (1964); "Wittgenstein and Logical Necessity," *Inquiry* 7, No. 4 (1964); used by permission of the editors of the journals.

GEORGE PITCHER, "Wittgenstein, Nonsense and Lewis Carroll." Reprinted from *The Massachusetts Review* VI: 3, © 1965 The Massachusetts Review, Inc.; reprinted by permission of the editors and the author.

ALICE AMBROSE, "Wittgenstein on Universals," in W. E. Kennick and M. Lazerowitz (eds.), *Metaphysics: Readings and Reappraisals,* Prentice-Hall, Inc., 1966; to be included in her forthcoming *Essays in Analysis* (ibid.); reprinted here by permission of the author and George Allen & Unwin Ltd., London.

JOHN WISDOM, "A Feature of Wittgenstein's Technique." This paper is reprinted from *Proceedings of the Aristotelian Society* Supplementary Volume 35 (1961); reprinted by permission of the author and the editor of the Society.

ALBERT W. LEVI, "Wittgenstein as Dialectician," *The Journal of*

Philosophy 61, No. 4 (1964); reprinted by permission of the author and editor.

DENNIS O'BRIEN, "The Unity of Wittgenstein's Thought," *International Philosophical Quarterly* 6, No. 1 (1966); reprinted by permission of the author and the editor.

Contents

Preface   11

A Biographical Sketch
  By Georg H. von Wright   13

Memoirs of Wittgenstein
  I. *By Bertrand Russell*
     LUDWIG WITTGENSTEIN   30
     FROM "PHILOSOPHERS AND IDIOTS"   31
  II. *By Rudolf Carnap*
     FROM HIS "AUTOBIOGRAPHY"   33
  III. *By G. E. Moore*
     FROM HIS "AUTOBIOGRAPHY"   39
     FROM "WITTGENSTEIN'S LECTURES IN 1930–33"   40
  IV. *By John Wisdom*
     LUDWIG WITTGENSTEIN, 1934–1937   46

Wittgenstein as a Teacher
  By D. A. T. Gasking and A. C. Jackson   49

Portrait of a Philosopher
  By Karl Britton   56

**A Symposium: Assessments of the Man
and the Philosopher**
  I. By Eric Heller   64
  II. By M. O'C. Drury   67
  III. By Norman Malcolm   71
  IV. By Rush Rhees   74

Recollections of Wittgenstein
  By Wolfe Mays   79

Wittgenstein: Unphilosophical Notes
  By Erich Heller   89

Wittgenstein, a Symbol of Troubled Times
  By José Ferrater Mora   107

Ludwig Wittgenstein
  By Gilbert Ryle   116

Ludwig Wittgenstein
  By George A. Paul   125

Wittgenstein on the Nature of Philosophy
  By Morris Lazerowitz   131

The Blue Book
  By O. K. Bouwsma   148

**Wittgenstein on Language and Some Problems
of Philosophy**
  By Leonard Linsky   171

Wittgenstein's Philosophical Investigations
  By Norman Malcolm   181

Wittgenstein's Philosophical Investigations
  By Paul Feyerabend   214

Wittgenstein's Builders
  By Rush Rhees   251

**Wittgenstein on Some Questions in Foundations
of Mathematics**
  By Alice Ambrose   265

Wittgenstein's Philosophy of Logic
  By Joseph L. Cowan   284

Wittgenstein and Logical Laws
  By Arnold Levison   297

Wittgenstein, Nonsense and Lewis Carroll
  By George Pitcher   315

Wittgenstein on Universals
  By Alice Ambrose   336

A Feature of Wittgenstein's Technique
  By John Wisdom   353

Wittgenstein as Dialectician
  By Albert W. Levi   366

The Unity of Wittgenstein's Thought
  By Dennis O'Brien   380

Selected Bibliography   405

Preface

LUDWIG WITTGENSTEIN is without doubt one of the greatest philosophers of our time and numerous philosophers in English-speaking countries would be quite prepared to describe him as *the* greatest. His place in the history of philosophy is comparable to that of Darwin in biology and Einstein in physics. Yet, strangely enough, he is very little known outside of philosophical circles. This is partly due to the fact that he was a "philosopher's philosopher" in the strictest sense of the term. He addressed himself exclusively to philosophers and their problems. As he put it, the aim of his work is "to show the fly out of the fly-bottle"—the fly being the philosopher and the fly-bottle, the philosophical problems.

Wittgenstein's philosophy is an extremely serious and original challenge to the traditional ways of philosophizing. If traditional philosophy is characterized as different attempts at answering different philosophical questions, then Wittgenstein's philosophy may be characterized as a systematic questioning of the questions themselves. As he was fond of saying, he didn't *solve* philosophical problems, but *dissolved* them. He claimed that what he was doing was a new subject and not merely a stage in a continuous development; that there was now, in philosophy, a "kink" in the development of human thought comparable to that which occurred when Galileo and his contemporaries invented dynamics; that a new method had been discovered, as had happened when chemistry was developed out of alchemy.

Because of the revolutionary nature of his philosophy and the typically aphoristic and cryptic style of his writings, Wittgenstein's work "invites and at the same time resists our craving for clear understanding." Collected here are writings by well-known contemporary philosophers, most of whom were his friends and students. We are most fortunate to have these writings available to help us understand his thought. The purpose of this volume will have been fulfilled if it succeeds in whetting any reader's appetite for Wittgenstein's own words. As for those who are already familiar with some of his writings, I hope that they will be stimulated by these essays to reread him.

Aside from being of great human interest, some knowledge of Wittgenstein the man is quite relevant to the understanding of his philosophy. He is one of those extraordinary men who can best be described as a "passionate thinker." Philosophy was for him an activity which involved his whole being. For this reason the first part of this anthology includes most of the available biographical writings which reveal something of the intensity, honesty, and simplicity of his personality.[1] The remainder of this collection includes essays on Wittgenstein's "later" philosophy. As the reader will soon learn, Wittgenstein's intellectual life is divided into two major periods. The first is represented by *Tractatus Logico-Philosophicus* and the second, by *Philosophical Investigations*. No essays specifically on the *Tractatus* are included here, since there are a number of full-length commentaries and a collection of essays in print. Nevertheless, the main features of Wittgenstein's early philosophy can easily be gathered from the writings that are included here.

All the essays except one were previously published in various journals or books and are reprinted here in their original forms. A few editor's notes and page references to other selections in this book are added in brackets. I wish to thank the authors, the publishers, and the editors of journals for their kind permission to reprint these essays. I am grateful to Wolfe Mays for his original contribution to this anthology. Special thanks are due to the executive editor of Delta Books, Richard Huett, who has read the entire manuscript and has made a number of valuable suggestions. For assisting in the preparation of the bibliography, I thank Michael Makibe. To O. K. Bouwsma, Maurice Cranston, Alice and Morris Lazerowitz, George Pitcher and George K. Plochman I am indebted for their kind help and cooperation in various ways.

---

[1] The most interesting and informative account of Wittgenstein's life up to his return to Cambridge in 1929 which I have seen cannot, unfortunately, be published. For the greater part of the remainder of Wittgenstein's life the reader is referred to the very perceptive and immensely moving *Memoir* by Norman Malcolm.

A Biographical Sketch

BY GEORG H. VON WRIGHT

ON 29 APRIL 1951 there died at Cambridge, England, one of the greatest and most influential philosophers of our time, Ludwig Wittgenstein.

It has been said that Wittgenstein inspired two important schools of thought, both of which he repudiated. The one is so-called logical positivism or logical empiricism, which played a prominent role during the decade immediately preceding the Second World War. The other is an even more heterogeneous trend which cannot be covered by *one* name. In its early phase it was sometimes called the Cambridge School of analysis. After the war its influence came to prevail at Oxford and the movement became known as linguistic philosophy or the Oxford School.

It is true that the philosophy of Wittgenstein has been of great importance to both of these trends in contemporary thought: to the first, his early work *Tractatus Logico-Philosophicus* and discussions with some members of the Vienna Circle; to the second, besides the *Tractatus,* his lectures at Cambridge and also glimpses of the works which he did not publish in his lifetime. It is also partly true that Wittgenstein repudiated the results of his own influence. He did not participate in the worldwide discussion to which his work and thought had given rise. He was of the opinion—justified, I believe —that his ideas were usually misunderstood and distorted even by those who professed to be his disciples. He doubted that he would be better understood in the future. He once said that he felt as though he were writing for people who would think in a quite different way, breathe a different air of life, from that of present-day men. For people of a different culture, as it were.[1] That was *one* reason why he did not himself publish his later works.

Wittgenstein avoided publicity. He withdrew from every contact

[1] See the Preface to *Philosophische Bemerkungen* (1964).

13

with his surroundings which he thought undesirable. Outside the circle of his family and personal friends, very little was known about his life and character. His inaccessibility contributed to absurd legends about his personality and to widespread misunderstandings of his teaching. The data published in his obituaries have often been erroneous and the atmosphere of most biographical articles on Wittgenstein which I have read has been alien to their subject.

Ludwig Josef Johann Wittgenstein was born in Vienna on 26 April 1889. The Wittgenstein family had migrated from Saxony to Austria. It is of Jewish descent. It is not, contrary to what has often been stated, related to the house of princes of the same name. Wittgenstein's grandfather was a convert from the Jewish religion to Protestantism. His mother was a Roman Catholic. Ludwig Wittgenstein was baptized in the Catholic Church.

Wittgenstein's father must have been a man of remarkable intelligence and will power. He was an engineer who became a leading figure in the steel and iron industry of the Danubean Monarchy. Wittgenstein's mother was responsible for a strong artistic influence in the family. Both she and her husband were highly musical. The wealthy and cultured home of the Wittgensteins became a center of musical life. Johannes Brahms was a close friend of the family.

Ludwig was the youngest of five brothers and three sisters. Nature was lavish to all the children both in respect of character and of artistic and intellectual talents. Ludwig Wittgenstein was undoubtedly a most uncommon man. Though he was free from that form of vanity which shows itself in a desire to seem different, it was inevitable that he should stand out sharply from his surroundings. It is probably true that he lived on the border of mental illness. A fear of being driven across it followed him throughout his life. But it would be wrong to say of his work that it had a morbid character. It is deeply original but not at all eccentric. It has the same naturalness, frankness, and freedom from all artificiality that was characteristic of him.

Wittgenstein was educated at home until he was fourteen. For three years thereafter he was at a school at Linz in Upper Austria. It seems to have been his wish to study physics with Boltzmann in Vienna. However, Boltzmann died in 1906, the same year that Wittgenstein finished school. Wittgenstein proceeded to the Technische Hochschule in Berlin-Charlottenburg.

That he chose to study engineering was a consequence of his early interests and talents, rather than of his father's influence. Throughout his life he was extremely interested in machinery. While a small boy he constructed a sewing machine that aroused much admiration. Even in his last years he could spend a whole day with his beloved steam engines in the South Kensington Museum. There are several anecdotes of his serving as a mechanic when some machinery got out of order.

Wittgenstein remained in Berlin until the spring of 1908. Then he went to England. In the summer of 1908 he was experimenting with kites at The Kite Flying Upper Atmosphere Station near Glossop, in Derbyshire. The same autumn he registered as a research student in the department of engineering at the University of Manchester. He was registered there until the autumn of 1911, but spent substantial periods on the Continent. During those three years he was occupied with research in aeronautics. From his kite-flying experiments he passed on to the construction of a jet reaction propeller for aircraft. At first it was the engine that absorbed his interest, but soon he concentrated on the design of the propeller, which was essentially a mathematical task. It was from this time that Wittgenstein's interests began to shift, first to pure mathematics and then to the foundations of mathematics.

Wittgenstein once mentioned to me that the problems on which he worked during his Manchester years have since become very urgent. I regret that I was not curious enough to ask him more. I assume that he was thinking of the role which the reaction engine has come to play, especially in aeronautics.[2]

In Wittgenstein's life the years from 1906 to 1912 were a time of painful seeking and of final awakening to clarity about his vocation. He told me that in those years he was constantly unhappy. To his restlessness bear witness the several interruptions of work already begun and the flights to something new: the departure from Germany to England, the experiments with kites, the construction of the jet engine, the design of the propeller, the interest in pure mathematics and finally in the philosophy of mathematics.

It is said that Wittgenstein asked someone for advice about literature on the foundations of mathematics and was directed to

[2] Data about Wittgenstein's time at Manchester have been recorded by Mr. W. Eccles and Mr. W. Mays. The design of the reaction engine and a number of other documents relating to this period in Wittgenstein's life have been deposited in the University Library at Manchester. I am told that Wittgenstein had patented some of his inventions in the field of aeronautics. [See W. Mays' article in this volume.]

Bertrand Russell's *Principles of Mathematics,* which had appeared
in 1903. It seems clear that this book profoundly affected Wittgenstein's development. It was probably it which led him to study the
works of Frege. The "new" logic, which in Frege and Russell had
two of its most brilliant representatives, became the gateway
through which Wittgenstein entered philosophy.

If I remember rightly,[3] Wittgenstein told me that he had read
Schopenhauer's *Die Welt als Wille und Vorstellung* in his youth
and that his first philosophy was a Schopenhauerian epistemological idealism. Of how this interest was related to his interest in
logic and the philosophy of mathematics I know nothing, except
that I remember his saying that it was Frege's conceptual realism
which made him abandon his earlier idealistic views.

Having decided to give up his studies in engineering, Wittgenstein
first went to Jena in Germany to discuss his plans with Frege. It
was apparently Frege who advised Wittgenstein to go to Cambridge
and study with Russell. He followed the advice.[4]

This was probably in the autumn of 1911.[5] At the beginning of
the following year he was admitted to Trinity College and registered
in the University, first as an undergraduate and later as an "advanced student." He was at Cambridge for all three terms of the
year 1912 and the first two terms of 1913. At the beginning of the
autumn of 1913 he visited Norway with David Pinsent, a young
mathematician with whom he had made friends at Cambridge.
After a short visit to England in October, he returned to Norway
alone and took up residence on a farm at Skjolden in Sogn north-
east of Bergen. Here he lived for most of the time until the outbreak
of the war in 1914. He liked the people and the country very much.
Eventually he learned to speak Norwegian fairly well. In an isolated
place near Skjolden he built himself a hut, where he could live in
complete seclusion.

The decade before the first Great War was a period of exceptional intellectual activity at Cambridge. Bertrand Russell had

[3] The biographical information which I acquired from conversations with Wittgenstein I
did not record on paper until after his death. I felt very strongly that it would have been
improper to write them down following our conversations. He did not often talk about
his past and only rarely of his youth, which was to him a painful recollection. The idea
that someone was collecting data for a biography would certainly have been deeply
distasteful to him.
[4] This is how Wittgenstein related the matter to me. His account is confirmed by notes
made by his sister Hermine. Russell seems, therefore, to be mistaken when in his memorial article in *Mind*, n.s., LX (1951) [included in this volume], he says that Wittgenstein
had not known Frege before he came to Cambridge.
[5] I have not been able to fix the exact dates of Wittgenstein's first visit to Frege and
arrival at Cambridge. He was registered at Manchester for the Michaelmas term of 1911.

arrived at the summit of his powers. He and A. N. Whitehead wrote *Principia Mathematica,* a milestone in the history of logic. The most influential philosopher was G. E. Moore. Wittgenstein soon became intimate with Russell,[6] and he saw much of Moore and Whitehead. Among Wittgenstein's friends during his early years at Cambridge should also be mentioned J. M. Keynes, the economist, G. H. Hardy, the mathematician, and the logician W. E. Johnson. Wittgenstein's *Tractatus* is dedicated to the memory of David Pinsent, who fell in the war.

Besides philosophy Wittgenstein did some experimental work in psychology at Cambridge. He carried out an investigation concerning rhythm in music, at the psychological laboratory. He had hoped that the experiments would throw light on some questions of aesthetics that interested him. Wittgenstein was exceptionally musical, even if one judged by the highest standards. He played the clarinet, and for a time he wished to become a conductor. He had a rare talent for whistling. It was a great pleasure to hear him whistle through a whole concerto, interrupting himself only to draw the listener's attention to some detail of the musical texture.

An important source of our knowledge of Wittgenstein during these years is a series of his letters to Russell. Another is Pinsent's diary of their Cambridge life and their travels to Iceland and Norway. The letters and the diary help to illuminate Wittgenstein's personality, not only as a young man, but also as he appeared to his friends of the 1930's and 1940's. The letters also contain interesting information about the gradual development of the work which first established Wittgenstein's fame as a philosopher.

Wittgenstein's earliest philosophical investigations were in the realm of the problems with which Frege and Russell had dealt. Concepts such as "propositional function," "variable," "generality," and "identity" occupied his thoughts. He soon made an interesting discovery, a new symbolism for so-called truth-functions that led to the explanation of logical truth as "tautology." [7]

The oldest parts of the *Tractatus* are those dealing with logic. Wittgenstein had formed his principal thoughts on these matters before the outbreak of the war in 1914, and thus before his twenty-sixth year. Later he became engrossed in a new problem. It was

[6] Russell says, in the memorial article referred to, "Getting to know Wittgenstein was one of the most exciting intellectual adventures of my life", [p. 31].
[7] The symbolism in question is much the same as that explained in *Tractatus* 6.1203. The now familiar truth-tables (*Tractatus* 4.31, etc.) he invented later.

the question of the nature of the significant proposition.[8] There is a story of how the idea of language as a picture of reality occurred to Wittgenstein.[9] It was in the autumn of 1914, on the East front. Wittgenstein was reading in a magazine about a law suit in Paris concerning an automobile accident. At the trial a miniature model of the accident was presented before the court. The model here served as a proposition; that is, a description of a possible state of affairs. It had this function owing to a correspondence between the parts of the model (the miniature houses, cars, people) and things (houses, cars, people) in reality. It now occurred to Wittgenstein that one might reverse the analogy and say that a *proposition* serves as a model or *picture,* by virtue of a similar correspondence between *its* parts and the world. The way in which the parts of the proposition are combined—the *structure* of the proposition—depicts a possible combination of elements in reality, a possible state of affairs.

Wittgenstein's *Tractatus* may be called a synthesis of the theory of truth-functions and the idea that language is a picture of reality. Out of this synthesis arises a third main ingredient of the book, its doctrine of that which cannot be *said,* only *shown.*

At the outbreak of the war, Wittgenstein entered the Austrian army as a volunteer, although he had been exempted from service because of a rupture. He served first on a vessel on the Vistula and later in an artillery workshop at Cracow. In 1915 he was ordered to Olmütz, in Moravia, to be trained as an officer. Later he fought on the East front. In 1918 he was transferred to the South front. Upon the collapse of the Austro-Hungarian army in October, he was taken prisoner by the Italians. It was not until August of the following year that he could return to Austria. During the major part of his captivity, he was in a prison camp near Monte Cassino in south Italy.

When Wittgenstein was captured he had in his rucksack the manuscript of his *Logisch-philosophische Abhandlung,* which is generally known by the Latin title proposed for it by G. E. Moore, *Tractatus Logico-Philosophicus.* He had completed the work when

[8] "My *whole* task consists in explaining the nature of the proposition," he wrote in one of the philosophical notebooks that he kept during the war.
[9] There exist several, somewhat different versions of it. The story as told here is based on an entry in Wittgenstein's philosophical notebooks in June 1930.—It would be interesting to know whether Wittgenstein's conception of the proposition as a picture is connected in any way with the Introduction to Heinrich Hertz's *Die Prinzipen der Mechanik.* Wittgenstein knew this work and held it in high esteem. There are traces of the impression that it made on him both in the *Tractatus* and in his later writings.

on a leave of absence, in August 1918. While still in captivity he got in touch with Russell by letter and was able to send the manuscript to him, thanks to the aid of one of his friends of the Cambridge years, Keynes. He also sent Frege a copy and corresponded with him.

It was Wittgenstein's habit to write down his thoughts in notebooks. The entries are usually dated, thus they compose a sort of diary. The contents of an earlier notebook are often worked over again in a later one. Sometimes he dictated to colleagues and pupils. In the spring of 1914 he dictated some thoughts on logic to Moore in Norway. In the late '20's and early '30's he dictated to Schlick and Waismann. The so-called Blue Book was dictated in conjunction with lectures at Cambridge in the academic year 1933–34. The so-called Brown Book was dictated privately to some pupils in 1934–35.[10]

Some of the notebooks which led up to the *Tractatus* have been preserved.[11] These sketches and fragments of earlier versions are of great interest, partly because they show the development of his thoughts, partly bcause they illuminate many difficult passages in the extremely compressed final version. I have been especially impressed by a notebook of the year 1916. It deals chiefly with the ego, the freedom of the will, the meaning of life, and death. Thus the somewhat aphoristic remarks on these topics in the *Tractatus* are sifted from a quantity of material. The notes show how strong were the impressions that Wittgenstein had received from Schopenhauer. An occasional Spinozistic flavor is also recognizable.

In the earliest notebooks a considerable part of the content is written in a code. Wittgenstein continued to use this code throughout his life. The notes in code are for the most part of a personal nature.

The period of the war was a crisis in Wittgenstein's life. To what extent the turmoil of the time and his experiences in war and captivity contributed to the crisis, I cannot say. A circumstance of great importance was that he became acquainted with the ethical and religious writings of Tolstoy. Tolstoy exercised a strong influence on Wittgenstein's view of life, and also led him to study the Gospels.

After the death of his father in 1912 Wittgenstein was in posses-

[10] These two books were published in 1958 under the title *Preliminary Studies for the "Philosophical Investigations," Generally known as The Blue and Brown Books.*
[11] Published in 1961 under the title *Notebooks 1914–1916.*

sion of a great fortune. One of his first steps after his return from
the war was to give away all his money.[12] Henceforth a great simplicity, at times even an extreme frugality, became characteristic of
his life. His dress was unconventional; it is impossible to imagine
him with necktie or hat. A bed, a table, and a few deck-chairs
were all of his furniture. Ornamental objects of whatever kind
were banished from his surroundings.

After the war Wittgenstein took up the vocation of schoolmaster.
In 1919–20 he was trained at a college for teachers in elementary
schools (*Lehrerbildungsanstalt*) in Vienna. From 1920 to 1926 he
taught in various remote villages in the districts of Schneeberg and
Semmering in Lower Austria. This suited his wish for a simple and
secluded life. In other ways it did not suit him well. It appears that
he was in constant friction with the people around him. Finally
there was a serious crisis. Wittgenstein resigned his post and quitted
for ever the career of schoolmaster. He went to work as a gardener's
assistant with the monks at Hütteldorf, near Vienna.

In this period, Wittgenstein contemplated entering a monastery.
The same thought occurred to him at other times in his life too.
That it never came true was, partly at least, because for him the
inner conditions of monastic life were not satisfied.

His service with the monks soon came to an end. In the autumn
of 1926 Wittgenstein accepted a task that absorbed his time and
his genius for two years. He built a mansion in Vienna for one of
his sisters. In the beginning he cooperated with his friend, the
architect Paul Engelmann. But soon Wittgenstein took over alone.
The building is his work down to the smallest detail and is highly
characteristic of its creator. It is free from all decoration and
marked by a severe exactitude in measure and proportion. Its
beauty is of the same simple and static kind that belongs to the
sentences of the *Tractatus*. It does not seem to me that the building
can be classified as belonging to some one style. But the horizontal
roofs and the materials—concrete, glass, and steel—remind the
spectator of typically "modern" architecture. (In 1914 Wittgenstein
had come to know Adolf Loos, whose work he respected.)

During this same time Wittgenstein did a sculpture in the studio

[12] Before the war Wittgenstein had made a large anonymous grant for the promotion of
literature. Two poets of whom he was in this manner a benefactor were Georg Trakl
and Rainer Maria Rilke. (For more details see Ludwig Ficker's article "Rilke und der
unbekannte Freund" in *Der Brenner*, 1954.) It may be remarked in passing that Wittgenstein had a high opinion of Trakl's talent, but that later in life, at least, he did not
greatly admire Rilke, whose poetry he thought artificial.

of his friend, the sculptor Drobil. It is the head of a young woman. The features have the same finished and restful beauty one finds in Greek sculptures of the classical period and which seems to have been Wittgenstein's ideal. In general, there is a striking contrast between the restlessness, the continual searching and changing, in Wittgenstein's life and personality, and the perfection and elegance of his finished work.

The author of the *Tractatus* thought he had solved all philosophical problems. It was consistent with this view that he should give up philosophy. The publication of the book was largely due to Russell. In 1919 the two friends met in Holland to discuss the manuscript. The problem of finding a publisher caused difficulties and the matter was further complicated by Wittgenstein's strong disapproval of Russell's introduction to the book. In July 1920 Wittgenstein wrote to Russell that he himself would take no further steps to have it published and that Russell could do with it as he wished. The German text was published in 1921 in the last issue of Ostwald's *Annalen der Naturphilosophie*. In the following year it was published in London with a parallel English translation. The translation contains a number of errors which corrupt the meaning.[13] A new translation was published in 1961.

During his years as schoolmaster and architect, Wittgenstein was not completely cut off from contact with the philosophical world. In 1923 a young man from Cambridge, Frank Ramsey, visited him at Puchberg. Ramsey had assisted in the translation of the *Tractatus* and had written, at the age of twenty, a remarkably penetrating review of the book for [the periodical] *Mind*. The visit was repeated a year later. Ramsey tried to persuade Wittgenstein to come to England on a visit. He was helped in his efforts by Keynes, who even procured money for the purpose. In the summer of 1925 Wittgenstein finally did visit his English friends.

After Ramsey, Moritz Schlick, a professor in Vienna, managed to establish contact with Wittgenstein. The study of the latter's book had made a deep impression on this honest and intelligent man, who was to become famous as the founder and leader of the Vienna Circle. Wittgenstein's influence on the philosophic movement which the Vienna Circle started is thus in part due to a personal connection, lasting for a number of years, between Wittgen-

[13] The translator's note, according to which "the proofs of the translation . . . have been very carefully revised by the author himself," does not agree with what Wittgenstein later told several of his friends.

stein and Schlick. Another member of the Circle who was personally strongly influenced by Wittgenstein was Friedrich Waismann.

Wittgenstein said that he returned to philosophy because he felt
that he could again do creative work. An external circumstance of
this important step may have been that in March of 1928 he had
heard Brouwer lecture in Vienna on the foundations of mathematics. (It is rumored to have been this which stirred him to take
up philosophy again.) Early in 1929 Wittgenstein arrived at Cambridge. He was first registered as a research student, a somewhat
unusual status for a man whom many already regarded as one of
the foremost living representatives of his subject. The idea was
that he should work for the Ph.D. It turned out, however, that he
could count his pre-war residence at Cambridge as credit towards
the degree and could present his book, published eight years earlier,
as a thesis. He received his degree in June 1929. The following year
he was made a Fellow of Trinity College.

Soon after his return to Cambridge Wittgenstein began to write
down philosophical thoughts. His output in the years 1929–32 was,
as always from then on, tremendous. From the notebooks in hand-
writing he sifted remarks for two bulky typescripts. One is called
Philosophische Bemerkungen; for the other he contemplated the
names "Philosophische Betrachtungen" or "Philosophische Gram-
matik." They are virtually completed works.[14] But Wittgenstein did
not publish them.

The only philosophical writing that Wittgenstein himself published subsequent to the *Tractatus* was the paper "Some Remarks
on Logical Form."[15] This paper was supposed to have been read
by him to the annual meeting of British philosophers—the Joint
Session of the Mind Association and the Aristotelian Society—in
1929. The papers prepared for these meetings are printed and
distributed to the participants in advance, and are subsequently
collected in a Supplementary Volume to the Proceedings of the
Aristotelian Society. Wittgenstein surprised his audience by talking
to them on an entirely different topic—the notion of the infinite in

---

[14] It was in reference to *Philosophische Bemerkungen* that Bertrand Russell, in 1930, reported to the Council of Trinity College, which was considering the award of a grant to
Wittgenstein, as follows: "The theories contained in this new work of Wittgenstein are
novel, very original, and indubitably important. Whether they are true, I do not know.
As a logician, who likes simplicity, I should wish to think that they are not, but from
what I have read of them I am quite sure that he ought to have an opportunity to work
them out, since when completed they may easily prove to constitute a whole new
philosophy." (Quoted with the permission of Lord Russell and the Council of Trinity
College, Cambridge.)

[15] While he was a schoolmaster he published a German glossary for elementary schools,
Wörterbuch für Volks- und Bürgerschulen (Holder-Piehler-Tempski, Vienna, 1926).

mathematics—and not reading his paper at all. Wittgenstein himself thought this paper worthless.

Wittgenstein's writings of the period anterior to the Blue Book are of considerable interest, not least to the historian of philosophic ideas. Their intrinsic value is, I think, less than that of either the *Tractatus* or the *Investigations*. This is natural, considering that they represent a transitional stage in Wittgenstein's development.

It will probably remain a matter of future debate to what extent there is continuity between the "early" Wittgenstein of the *Tractatus* and the "later" Wittgenstein of the *Investigations*. The writings from 1929 to 1932 testify to a continuous development and struggle— out of the former work and in the direction of the later. The Blue Book of 1933–34 conveys more the impression of a first, still somewhat rough version of a radically new philosophy. I myself find it difficult to fit the Blue Book into the development of Wittgenstein's thoughts. The Brown Book is a somewhat different case. It may be regarded as a preliminary version of the beginning of the *Investigations*. In August 1936 Wittgenstein began a revision, in German, of the Brown Book which had been dictated in English one year earlier. He called the revision *Philosophische Untersuchungen*. He soon abandoned work on it as unsatisfactory, and made a fresh start in the autumn of the same year. What he then wrote is substantially identical with the first 189 sections of the *Investigations* in its printed form.

The young Wittgenstein had learned from Frege and Russell. His problems were in part theirs. The later Wittgenstein, I should say, has no ancestors in the history of thought. His work signalizes a radical departure from previously existing paths of philosophy. But his problems grew to a great extent out of the *Tractatus*. This, I think, is the reason why Wittgenstein wanted the work which embodied his new philosophy to be printed together with the work of his youth.[16]

It is sometimes said that the later Wittgenstein resembles Moore. This is hardly true. Moore's and Wittgenstein's ways of thinking are in fact utterly different. Although their friendship lasted until the latter's death, I do not believe that there is any trace of an influence of Moore's philosophy on Wittgenstein. What Wittgenstein appreciated was Moore's intellectual vitality, his love of truth and freedom from vanity.

Of great importance in the origination of Wittgenstein's new

16 See the Preface to *Philosophische Untersuchungen*.

ideas was the criticism to which his earlier views were subjected by two of his friends. One was Ramsey, whose premature death in 1930 was a heavy loss to contemporary thought. The other was Piero Sraffa, an Italian economist who had come to Cambridge shortly before Wittgenstein returned there. It was above all Sraffa's acute and forceful criticism that compelled Wittgenstein to abandon his earlier views and set out upon new roads. He said that his discussions with Sraffa made him feel like a tree from which all branches had been cut. That this tree could become green again was due to its own vitality. The later Wittgenstein did not receive an inspiration from outside like that which the earlier Wittgenstein got from Frege and Russell.

From 1929 until his death, Wittgenstein lived—with some interruptions—in England. He became a British subject when, after the "Anschluss," he would have had to give up his Austrian passport, and the choice for him was between German and British nationality. But in general he was not fond of English ways of life and he disliked the academic atmosphere of Cambridge. When his Fellowship at Trinity College expired in 1935,[17] he had plans for settling in the Soviet Union. He visited the country with a friend and apparently was pleased with the visit. That nothing came of his plans was due, partly at least, to the harshening of conditions in Russia in the middle '30's. So Wittgenstein remained at Cambridge until the end of the academic year 1935–36. Thereafter he lived for nearly a year in his hut in Norway. It was then that he began to write the *Philosophical Investigations*. In 1937 he returned to Cambridge, where, two years later, he succeeded Moore to the chair in philosophy.

From the beginning of 1930, with some interruptions, Wittgenstein lectured at Cambridge. As might be expected, his lectures were highly "unacademic."[18] He nearly always held them in his own room or in the college rooms of a friend. He had no manuscript or notes. He *thought* before the class. The impression was of a tremendous concentration. The exposition usually led to a question, to which the audience were supposed to suggest an answer. The answers in turn became starting points for new thoughts leading to new questions. It depended on the audience, to

---

[17] The Fellowship was prolonged to include the whole of the academic year 1935–36. When he became a professor, Wittgenstein was again made a Fellow of Trinity College.
[18] A vivid and true impression of Wittgenstein as a teacher is conveyed by the memorial article, signed D. A. T. G.–A. C. J., in *The Australasian Journal of Philosophy*, XXIX (1951). [Included in this volume.]

a great extent, whether the discussion became fruitful and whether the connecting thread was kept in sight from beginning to end of a lecture and from one lecture to another. Many of his audience were highly qualified people in their various fields. Moore attended Wittgenstein's lectures for some years in the early '30's.[19] Several of those who later became leading philosophers in England, the United States, or Australia heard Wittgenstein lecture at Cambridge. There exist good, more or less verbatim notes of some of his lecture courses.

Before Wittgenstein assumed his chair, the Second Great War broke out. I think one may say that he wished for the war. But, as in 1914, he did not want to watch it from an ivory tower. For some time he served as a porter at Guy's Hospital in London. Later he worked in a medical laboratory at Newcastle. It should be mentioned that Wittgenstein had been strongly attracted to the medical profession and that once in the '30's he seriously considered leaving philosophy to take up medicine. During his time at Newcastle he devised some technical innovations that proved useful.

It need not surprise us that Wittgenstein's restless genius was not happy in academic routine. It is likely that if the war had not come his tenure of the chair would have been even more brief. In the Easter term of 1947 he gave his last lectures at Cambridge. In the autumn he was away on a leave, and from the end of the year he ceased to be a professor. He wanted to devote all his remaining strength to his research. As so often before in his life, he went to live in seclusion. For the winter of 1948 he settled on a farm in the Irish countryside. After that he lived quite by himself in a hut beside the ocean, in Galway on the Irish west coast. His neighbors were primitive fishermen. It is said that Wittgenstein became a legend among his neighbors because he had tamed so many birds; they used to come every day to be fed by him. The life in Galway, however, became physically too strenuous for him, and in the autumn of 1948 he moved to a hotel in Dublin. From then until early spring of the following year he had an excellent working period. It was then he completed the second part of the *Philosophical Investigations*.

During the last two years of his life Wittgenstein was severely

[19] Moore has published a full account and an interesting discussion of these lectures in *Mind*, n.s., LXIII–LXIV (1954–55). Moore's articles can be said to be a commentary on some of the views which Wittgenstein held in the "period of transition" (1929–33) preceding the Blue Book. [See "Memoirs" in this volume.]

ill. In the autumn of 1949 it was found that he suffered from
cancer. Wittgenstein was then on a visit to Cambridge after his
return from a short stay in the United States. He did not go back
to Ireland, but remained with friends in Oxford and in Cambridge.
In the autumn of 1950 he visited Norway with a friend and even
had plans of settling there again at the beginning of the following
year. During part of his illness he was incapable of work. But it is
remarkable that during the last two months he was not in bed and
was apparently in the best of spirits. As late as two days before his
death he wrote down thoughts that are equal to the best he
produced.

Wittgenstein's very unusual and forceful personality exerted a
great influence over others. No one who came in touch with him
could fail to be impressed. Some were repelled. Most were attracted
or fascinated. One can say that Wittgenstein avoided making
acquaintances, but needed and sought friendships. He was an incomparable, but demanding, friend. I believe that most of those
who loved him and had his friendship also feared him.

Just as there were many groundless legends concerning Wittgenstein's life and personality, so there grew up much unsound
sectarianism among his pupils. This caused Wittgenstein much
pain. He thought that his influence as a teacher was, on the whole,
harmful to the development of independent minds in his disciples.
I am afraid that he was right. And I believe that I can partly understand why it should be so. Because of the depth and originality of
his thinking, it is very difficult to understand Wittgenstein's ideas
and even more difficult to incorporate them into one's own thinking. At the same time the magic of his personality and style was
most inviting and persuasive. To learn from Wittgenstein without
coming to adopt his forms of expression and catch words and even
to imitate his tone of voice, his mien and gestures, was almost
impossible. The danger was that the thoughts should deteriorate
into a jargon. The teaching of great men often has a simplicity and
naturalness which makes the difficult appear easy to grasp. Their
disciples usually become, therefore, insignificant epigones. The his-
toric significance of such men does not manifest itself in their
disciples but through influences of a more indirect, subtle and,
often, unexpected kind.

Wittgenstein's most characteristic features were his great and
pure seriousness and powerful intelligence. I have never met a man
who impressed me so strongly in either respect.

It seems to me that there are two forms of seriousness of character. One is fixed in "strong principles"; the other springs from a passionate heart. The former has to do with morality and the latter, I believe, is closer to religion. Wittgenstein was acutely and even painfully sensitive to considerations of duty, but the earnestness and severity of his personality were more of the second kind. Yet I do not know whether he can be said to have been "religious" in any but a trivial sense of the word. Certainly he did not have a Christian faith. But neither was his view of life un-Christian, pagan, as was Goethe's. To say that Wittgenstein was not a pantheist is to say something important. "God does not reveal himself *in* the world," he wrote in the *Tractatus*. The thought of God, he said, was above all for him the thought of the fearful judge.

Wittgenstein had the conviction, he sometimes said, that he was doomed. His outlook was typically one of gloom. Modern times were to him a dark age.[20] His idea of the helplessness of human beings was not unlike certain doctrines of predestination.

Wittgenstein was not, strictly speaking, a learned man. His temperament was very different from that of the typical scholar. "Cool objectivity" and "detached meditation" are labels which do not suit him at all. He put his whole soul into everything he did. His life was a constant journey, and doubt was the moving force within him. He seldom looked back on his earlier positions, and when he did so it was usually to repudiate them.

Knowledge, for Wittgenstein, was intimately connected with doing. It is significant that his first studies were in the technical sciences. He had a knowledge of mathematics and physics not derived from extensive reading, but from a working familiarity with mathematical and experimental techniques. His many artistic interests had the same active and living character. He could design a house, make a sculpture, or conduct an orchestra. Perhaps he would never have achieved mastery in those fields. But he was no "dilettante." Every manifestation of his multidimensional spirit came from the same earnest drive to create.

Wittgenstein had done no systematic reading in the classics of philosophy. He could read only what he could wholeheartedly assimilate. We have seen that as a young man he read Schopenhauer. From Spinoza, Hume and Kant he said that he could get only occasional glimpses of understanding. I do not think that he could have enjoyed Aristotle or Leibniz, two great logicians before him.

[20] See the Preface to *Philosophical Investigations:* "the darkness of these times."

But it is significant that he did read and enjoy Plato. He must have recognized congenial features, both in Plato's literary and philosophic method and in the temperament behind the thoughts.

Wittgenstein received deeper impressions from some writers in the borderland between philosophy, religion, and poetry than from the philosophers, in the restricted sense of the word. Among the former are St. Augustine, Kierkegaard, Dostoievsky, and Tolstoy. The philosophical sections of St. Augustine's *Confessions* show a striking resemblance to Wittgenstein's own way of doing philosophy. Between Wittgenstein and Pascal there is a trenchant parallelism which deserves closer study. It should also be mentioned that Wittgenstein held the writings of Otto Weininger in high regard.

An aspect of Wittgenstein's work which is certain to attract growing attention is its language. It would be surprising if he were not one day ranked among the classic writers of German prose. The literary merits of the *Tractatus* have not gone unnoticed. The language of the *Philosophical Investigations* is equally remarkable. The style is simple and perspicuous, the construction of sentences firm and free, the rhythm flows easily. The form is sometimes that of dialogue, with questions and replies; sometimes, as in the *Tractatus,* it condenses to aphorisms. There is a striking absence of all literary ornamentation, and of technical jargon or terminology. The union of measured moderation with richest imagination, the simultaneous impression of natural continuation and surprising turns, leads one to think of some other great productions of the genius of Vienna. (Schubert was Wittgenstein's favorite composer.)

It may appear strange that Schopenhauer, one of the masters of philosophic prose, did not influence Wittgenstein's style. An author, however, who reminds one, often astonishingly, of Wittgenstein is Lichtenberg. Wittgenstein esteemed him highly. To what extent, if any, he can be said to have learned from him I do not know. It is deserving of mention that some of Lichtenberg's thoughts on philosophic questions show a striking resemblance to Wittgenstein's.[21]

It is fairly certain that both the work and personality of Wittgenstein will provoke varying comments and different interpretations in the future. The author of the sentences "The riddle does not exist" and "Everything that can be said can be said clearly" was himself an enigma, and his sentences have a content that often lies deep beneath the surface of the language. In Wittgenstein

[21] See my paper, "Georg Christoph Lichtenberg als Philosoph," *Theoria*, VIII (1942).

many contrasts meet. It has been said that he was at once a logician and a mystic. *Neither* term is appropriate, but each hints at something true. Those who approach Wittgenstein's work will sometimes look for its essence in a rational, matter-of-fact dimension, and sometimes more in a supra-empirical, metaphysical one. In the existing literature on Wittgenstein there are examples of both conceptions. Such "interpretations" have little significance. They must appear as falsifications to anyone who tries to understand Wittgenstein in his rich complexity. They are interesting only as showing in how many directions his influence extends. I have sometimes thought that what makes a man's work *classic* is often just this multiplicity, which invites and at the same time resists our craving for clear understanding.

Memoirs of Wittgenstein

I. BY BERTRAND RUSSELL

Ludwig Wittgenstein

WHEN I MADE THE ACQUAINTANCE of Wittgenstein, he told me that he had been intending to become an engineer, and with that end in view had gone to Manchester. In the course of his studies in engineering he had become interested in mathematics, and in the course of his studies in mathematics he had become interested in the principles of mathematics. He asked people at Manchester (so he told me) whether there was such a subject, and whether anyone worked at it. They told him that there was such a subject and that he could find out more about it by coming to me at Cambridge, which he accordingly did.

Quite at first I was in doubt as to whether he was a man of genius or a crank, but I very soon decided in favor of the former alternative. Some of his early views made the decision difficult. He maintained, for example, at one time that all existential propositions are meaningless. This was in a lecture room, and I invited him to consider the proposition: "There is no hippopotamus in this room at present." When he refused to believe this, I looked under all the desks without finding one; but he remained unconvinced.

He made very rapid progress in mathematical logic, and soon knew all that I had to teach. He did not, I think, know Frege personally at that time, but he read him and greatly admired him.

I naturally lost sight of him during the 1914–18 war, but I got a letter from him soon after the armistice, written from Monte Cassino. He told me that he had been taken prisoner, but fortunately with his manuscript, which was the *Tractatus*. I pulled strings to get him released by the Italian Government, and we met at the Hague, where we discussed the *Tractatus,* line by line.

I cannot say very much about his opinions before 1914, as they were in a state of formation and flux. He was thinking very intensely and very fruitfully, but was not yet arriving at anything very definite. While I was still doubtful as to his ability, I asked G. E. Moore for his opinion. Moore replied, "I think very well of him indeed." When I enquired the reason for his opinion, he said that it was because Wittgenstein was the only man who looked puzzled at his lectures.

Getting to know Wittgenstein was one of the most exciting intellectual adventures of my life. In later years there was a lack of intellectual sympathy between us, but in early years I was as willing to learn from him as he from me. His thought had an almost incredible degree of passionately intense penetration, to which I gave wholehearted admiration.

He was in the days before 1914 concerned almost solely with logic. During or perhaps just before, the first war, he changed his outlook and became more or less of a mystic, as may be seen here and there in the *Tractatus*. He had been dogmatically anti-Christian, but in this respect he changed completely. The only thing he ever told me about this was that once in a village in Galicia during the war he found a bookshop containing only one book, which was Tolstoy on the Gospels. He bought the book, and, according to him, it influenced him profoundly. Of the development of his opinions after 1919 I cannot speak.

From "Philosophers and Idiots"

A much more important philosophical contact was with the Austrian philosopher Ludwig Wittgenstein, who began as my pupil and ended as my supplanter at both Oxford and Cambridge. He had intended to become an engineer and had gone to Manchester for that purpose. The training for an engineer required mathematics, and he was thus led to an interest in the foundations of mathematics. He inquired at Manchester whether there was such a subject and whether anybody worked at it. They told him about me, and so he came to Cambridge. He was queer, and his notions seemed to me odd, so that for a whole term I could not make up my mind whether he was a man of genius or merely an eccentric. At the end of his first term at Cambridge he came to me and said: "Will you please tell me whether I am a complete idiot or not?" I replied, "My dear fellow, I don't know. Why are you asking me?"

He said, "Because, if I am a complete idiot, I shall become an aeronaut; but, if not, I shall become a philosopher." I told him to write me something during the vacation on some philosophical subject and I would then tell him whether he was a complete idiot or not. At the beginning of the following term he brought me the fulfilment of this suggestion. After reading only one sentence, I said to him: "No, you must not become an aeronaut." And he did not.

He was not, however, altogether easy to deal with. He used to come to my rooms at midnight and, for hours, he would walk backwards and forwards like a caged tiger. On arrival, he would announce that when he left my rooms he would commit suicide. So, in spite of getting sleepy, I did not like to turn him out. On one such evening, after an hour or two of dead silence, I said to him, "Wittgenstein, are you thinking about logic or about your sins?" "Both," he said, and then reverted to silence. However, we did not only meet at night. I used to take him long walks in the country round Cambridge. On one occasion I induced him to trespass with me in Madingley wood where, to my surprise, he climbed a tree. When he had got a long way up, a gamekeeper with a gun appeared and protested to me about the trespass. I called up to Wittgenstein and said the man had promised not to shoot if Wittgenstein got down within a minute. He believed me, and did so.

In the First World War he fought in the Austrian army and was taken prisoner by the Italians two days after the armistice. I had a letter from him from Monte Cassino, where he was interned, saying that fortunately he had had his manuscript with him when he was taken prisoner. This manuscript, which was published and became famous, had been written while he was at the front. He inherited a great fortune from his father, but he gave it away on the ground that money is only a nuisance to a philosopher. In order to earn his living, he became a village schoolmaster at a little place called Trattenbach, from which he wrote me an unhappy letter saying, "The men of Trattenbach are wicked." I replied, "All men are wicked." He rejoined, "True, but the men of Trattenbach are more wicked than the men of any other place." I retorted that my logical sense rebelled against such a statement; and there the matter rested until residence elsewhere enlarged his view as to the prevalence of sin. In his later years he was Professor of Philosophy at Cambridge, and most philosophers both there and at Oxford became his disciples. I myself was much influenced by his earlier doctrines, but in later years our views increasingly diverged. I saw little of him in his later years, but at the time when I knew him well he was immensely impressive as he had fire and penetration and intellectual purity to a quite extraordinary degree.

II. BY RUDOLF CARNAP

From his "Autobiography"

In the Vienna Circle, a large part of Ludwig Wittgenstein's book *Tractatus Logico-Philosophicus* was read aloud and discussed sentence by sentence. Often long reflections were necessary in order to find out what was meant. And sometimes we did not find any clear interpretation. But still we understood a good deal of it and then had lively discussions about it. I had previously read parts of Wittgenstein's work when it was published as an article in Ostwald's *Annalen der Natur- und Kulturphilosophie*. I found in it many interesting and stimulating points. But at that time I did not make the great effort required to come to a clear understanding of the often obscure formulations; for this reason I had not read the whole treatise. Now I was happy to see that the Circle was interested in this work and that we undertook to study it together.

Wittgenstein's book exerted a strong influence upon our Circle. But it is not correct to say that the philosophy of the Vienna Circle was just Wittgenstein's philosophy. We learned much by our discussions of the book, and accepted many views as far as we could assimilate them to our basic conceptions. The degree of influence varied, of course, for the different members.

For me personally, Wittgenstein was perhaps the philosopher who, besides Russell and Frege, had the greatest influence on my thinking. The most important insight I gained from his work was the conception that the truth of logical statements is based only on their logical structure and on the meaning of the terms. Logical statements are true under all conceivable circumstances; thus their truth is independent of the contingent facts of the world. On the other hand, it follows that these statements do not say anything about the world and thus have no factual content.

Another influential idea of Wittgenstein's was the insight that many philosophical sentences, especially in traditional metaphysics, are pseudo-sentences, devoid of cognitive content. I found Wittgenstein's view on this point close to the one I had previously developed under the influence of anti-metaphysical scientists and philosophers. I had recognized that many of these sentences and questions originate in a misuse of language and a violation of logic. Under the influence of Wittgenstein, this conception was strengthened and became more definite and more radical.

In 1927 Schlick became personally acquainted with Wittgenstein. Schlick conveyed to him the interest of our Circle in his book and his philosophy and also our urgent wish that he meet with us and explain certain points in his book which had puzzled us. But Wittgenstein was not willing to do this. Schlick had several talks with him; and Wittgenstein finally agreed to meet with Waismann and me. Thus the three of us met several times with Wittgenstein during the summer of 1927. Before the first meeting, Schlick admonished us urgently not to start a discussion of the kind to which we were accustomed in the Circle, because Wittgenstein did not want such a thing under any circumstances. We should even be cautious in asking questions, because Wittgenstein was very sensitive and easily disturbed by a direct question. The best approach, Schlick said, would be to let Wittgenstein talk and then ask only very cautiously for the necessary elucidations.

When I met Wittgenstein, I saw that Schlick's warnings were fully justified. But his behavior was not caused by any arrogance. In general, he was of a sympathetic temperament and very kind; but he was hypersensitive and easily irritated. Whatever he said was always interesting and stimulating, and the way in which he expressed it was often fascinating. His point of view and his attitude toward people and problems, even theoretical problems, were much more similar to those of a creative artist than to those of a scientist; one might almost say, similar to those of a religious prophet or a seer. When he started to formulate his view on some specific philosophical problem, we often felt the internal struggle that occurred in him at that very moment, a struggle by which he tried to penetrate from darkness to light under an intense and painful strain, which was even visible on his most expressive face. When finally, sometimes after a prolonged arduous effort, his answer came forth, his statement stood before us like a newly created piece of art or a divine revelation. Not that he asserted his views dogmatically. Although some of the formulations of the *Tractatus* sound as if there could not be any possibility of a doubt, he often expressed the feeling that his statements were inadequate. But the impression he made on us was as if insight came to him as through a divine inspiration, so that we could not help feeling that any sober rational comment or analysis of it would be a profanation.

Thus there was a striking difference between Wittgenstein's attitude toward philosophical problems and that of Schlick and myself. Our attitude toward philosophical problems was not very different from that which scientists have toward their problems. For us the discussion of doubts and objections of others seemed the best way of testing a new idea in the field of philosophy just as much as in the fields of science; Wittgenstein, on the other hand, tolerated no critical examination by others, once the insight had been gained by an act of inspiration. I sometimes had the impression that the deliberately rational and unemotional attitude of the scientist and likewise any ideas which had the flavor of "enlightenment" were repugnant to Wittgenstein. At our very first meeting with Wittgenstein, Schlick unfortunately mentioned that I was interested in the problem of an international language like Esperanto. As I had expected, Wittgenstein was definitely opposed to this idea. But I was surprised by the vehemence of his emotions. A language which had not "grown organically" seemed to him not only useless but despicable. Another time we touched the topic of parapsychology, and he expressed himself strongly against it. The alleged messages produced in spiritualistic séances, he said, were extremely trivial and silly. I agreed with this, but I remarked that nevertheless the question of the existence and explanation of the alleged parapsychological phenomena was an important scientific problem. He was shocked that any reasonable man could have any interest in such rubbish.

Once when Wittgenstein talked about religion, the contrast between his and Schlick's position became strikingly apparent. Both agreed of course in the view that the doctrines of religion in their various forms had no theoretical content. But Wittgenstein rejected Schlick's view that religion belonged to the childhood phase of humanity and would slowly disappear in the course of cultural development. When Schlick, on another occasion, made a critical remark about a metaphysical statement by a classical philosopher

(I think it was Schopenhauer), Wittgenstein surprisingly turned against Schlick and defended the philosopher and his work.

These and similar occurrences in our conversations showed that there was a strong inner conflict in Wittgenstein between his emotional life and his intellectual thinking. His intellect, working with great intensity and penetrating power, had recognized that many statements in the field of religion and metaphysics did not, strictly speaking, say anything. In his characteristic absolute honesty with himself, he did not try to shut his eyes to this insight. But this result was extremely painful for him emotionally, as if he were compelled to admit a weakness in a beloved person. Schlick, and I, by contrast, had no love for metaphysics or metaphysical theology, and therefore could abandon them without inner conflict or regret. Earlier, when we were reading Wittgenstein's book in the Circle, I had erroneously believed that his attitude toward metaphysics was similar to ours. I had not paid sufficient attention to the statements in his book about the mystical, because his feelings and thoughts in this area were too divergent from mine. Only personal contact with him helped me to see more clearly his attitude at this point. I had the impression that his ambivalence with respect to metaphysics was only a special aspect of a more basic internal conflict in his personality from which he suffered deeply and painfully.

When Wittgenstein talked about philosophical problems, about knowledge, language and the world, I usually was in agreement with his views and certainly his remarks were always illuminating and stimulating. Even at the times when the contrast in *Weltanschauung* and basic personal attitude became apparent, I found the association with him most interesting, exciting and rewarding. Therefore I regretted it when he broke off the contact. From the beginning of 1929 on, Wittgenstein wished to meet only with Schlick and Waismann, no longer with me or Feigl, who had also become acquainted with him in the meantime, let alone with the Circle. Although the difference in our attitudes and personalities expressed itself only on certain occasions, I understood very well that Wittgenstein felt it all the time and, unlike me, was disturbed by it. He said to Schlick that he could talk only with somebody who "holds his hand." Schlick himself was very strongly influenced by Wittgenstein both philosophically and personally. During the subsequent years, I had the impression that he sometimes abandoned his usually cool and critical attitude and accepted certain views and positions of Wittgenstein's without being able to defend them by rational arguments in the discussions of our Circle.

Waismann worked on a book in which he not only explained Wittgenstein's ideas but also developed a detailed systematic representation on this basis. We regarded it as very important that Wittgenstein's ideas should be explained to many who would not be able to read his treatise. Because Waismann had frequently talked with Wittgenstein and had a great ability for lucid representation, he seemed most suitable for this task. He actually wrote the book, which was for several years announced under the title, *Logik, Sprache, Philosophie; Kritik der Philosophie durch die Logik; mit Vorrede von M. Schlick,* and was to appear as Volume I of the collection, "Schriften zur Wissenschaftlichen Weltauffassung." Unfortunately, the book never appeared. Several times when Wittgenstein came to Vienna, he requested thoroughgoing changes and Waismann undertook the task of comprehensive and time-consuming revision. Finally, after Waismann had written and rewritten the book over a period of years, Wittgenstein suddenly declared that he did not want to see his thoughts represented in a "popularized" form. Waismann consequently could never make up his mind to have the book published. Since Schlick was convinced that the publication of the book could soon be expected, he had his Preface printed and gave proof copies of it to his friends.

The thinking of our Circle was strongly influenced by Wittgenstein's ideas, first because of our common reading of the *Tractatus* and later by virtue of Waismann's systematic exposition of certain conceptions of Wittgenstein's on the basis of his talks with him. At the same time, in the course of our discussions through the years, some divergencies became more and more apparent. Neurath was from the beginning very critical of Wittgenstein's mystical attitude, of his philosophy of the "ineffable," and of the "higher things" *(das "Höhere")*. I shall now briefly indicate the most important points of difference, especially with reference to my own conceptions.

All of us in the Circle had a lively interest in science and mathematics. In contrast to this, Wittgenstein seemed to look upon these fields with an attitude of indifference and sometimes even with contempt. His indirect influence on some students in Vienna was so strong that they abandoned the study of mathematics. It seems that later in his teaching activities in England he had a similar influence on even wider circles there. This is probably at least a contributing factor to the divergence between the attitude represented by many recent publications in analytic philosophy in England and that of logical empiricism in the United States.

Closely related is Wittgenstein's view of the philosophical relevance of constructed language systems. Chiefly because of Frege's influence, I was always deeply convinced of the superiority of a carefully constructed language and of its usefulness and even indispensability for the analysis of statements and concepts, both in philosophy and in science. All members of the Vienna Circle had studied at least the elementary parts of *Principia Mathematica*. For students of mathematics Hahn gave a lecture course and a seminar on the foundations of mathematics, based on the *Principia*. When I came to Vienna I continued these courses for students both of mathematics and of philosophy. In the Circle discussions we often made use of symbolic logic for the representation of analyses or examples. When we found in Wittgenstein's book statements about "the language," we interpreted them as referring to an ideal language; and this meant for us a formalized symbolic language. Later Wittgenstein explicitly rejected this view. He had a skeptical and sometimes even a negative view of the importance of a symbolic language for the clarification and correction of the confusions in ordinary language and also in the customary language of philosophers which, as he had shown himself, were often the cause of philosophical puzzles and pseudo-problems. On this point, the majority of British analytic philosophers share Wittgenstein's view, in contrast to the Vienna Circle and to the majority of analytical philosophers in the United States.

Furthermore, there is a divergence on a more specific point which, however, was of great importance for our way of thinking in the Circle. We read in Wittgenstein's book that certain things show themselves but cannot be said; for example the logical structure of sentences and the relation between the language and the world. In opposition to this view, first tentatively, then more and more clearly, our conception developed that it is possible to talk meaningfully about language and about the relation between a sentence and the fact described. Neurath emphasized from the beginning that language phenomena are events *within* the world, not something that refers to the world from outside. Spoken lanhave never been able to understand clearly enough to use it myself.

guage consists of sound waves; written language consists of marks of ink on paper. Neurath emphasized these facts in order to reject the view that there is something "higher," something mysterious, "spiritual," in language, a view which was prominent in German philosophy. I agreed with him, but pointed out that only the structural pattern, not the physical properties of the ink marks, were relevant for the function of language. Thus it is possible to construct a theory about language, namely the geometry of the written pattern. This idea led later to the theory which I called "logical syntax" of language.

III. BY G. E. MOORE

From his "Autobiography"

In 1912 I became acquainted with Wittgenstein. During the first year in which he was at Cambridge he attended my lectures on Psychology; but it was only during the next two years that I got to know him at all well. When I did get to know him, I soon came to feel that he was much cleverer at philosophy than I was, and not only cleverer, but also much more profound, and with a much better insight into the sort of inquiry which was really important and best worth pursuing, and into the best method of pursuing such inquiries. I did not see him again, after 1914, until he returned to Cambridge in 1929; but when his *Tractatus Logico-Philosophicus* came out, I read it again and again, trying to learn from it. It is a book which I admired and do admire extremely. There is, of course, a great deal in it which I was not able to understand; but many things I thought I did understand, and found them very enlightening. When he came back to Cambridge in 1929 I attended his lectures for several years in succession, always with admiration. How far he has influenced positively anything that I have written, I cannot tell; but he certainly has had the effect of making me very distrustful about many things which, but for him, I should have been inclined to assert positively. He has made me think that what is required for the solution of philosophical problems which baffle me, is a method quite different from any which I have ever used—a method which he himself uses successfully, but which I

I am glad to think that he is my successor in the Professorship at Cambridge.

From "Wittgenstein's Lectures in 1930–33"

In January, 1929, Wittgenstein returned to Cambridge after an absence of more than fifteen years. He came with the intention of residing in Cambridge and pursuing there his researches into philosophical problems. Why he chose Cambridge for this latter purpose I do not know: perhaps it was for the sake of having the opportunity of frequent discussion with F. P. Ramsey. At all events he did in fact reside in Cambridge during all three Full Terms of 1929, and was working hard all the time at his researches.[1] He must, however, at some time during that year, have made up his mind that, besides researching, he would like to do a certain amount of lecturing, since on 16th October, in accordance with his wishes, the Faculty Board of Moral Science resolved that he should be invited to give a course of lectures to be included in their Lecture List for the Lent Term of 1930.

During this year, 1929, when he was researching and had not begun to lecture, he took the Ph.D. degree at Cambridge. Having been entered as an "Advanced Student" during his previous period of residence in 1912 and 1913, he now found that he was entitled to submit a dissertation for the Ph.D. He submitted the *Tractatus* and Russell and I were appointed to examine him. We gave him an oral examination on 6th June, an occasion which I found both pleasant and amusing. We had, of course, no doubt whatever that his work deserved the degree: we so reported, and when our report had been approved by the necessary authorities, he received the degree in due course.

In the same month of June in which we examined him, the Council of Trinity College made him a grant to enable him to continue his researches. (They followed this up in December, 1930, by electing him to a Research Fellowship, tenable for five years, which they afterwards prolonged for a time.)

In the following July of 1929 he attended the Joint Session of the Mind Association and Aristolelian Society at Nottingham, presenting a short paper entitled "Some Remarks on Logical Form."

[1] The statement in the Obituary notice in *The Times* for 2nd May, 1951, that he arrived in Cambridge in 1929 "for a short visit" is very far from the truth. Fortunately I kept a brief diary during the period in question and can therefore vouch for the truth of what I have stated above about his residence in 1929, though there is in fact other evidence.

This paper was the only piece of philosophical writing by him, other than the *Tractatus,* published during his lifetime. Of this paper he spoke in a letter to *Mind* (July, 1933) as "weak"; and since 1945 he has spoken of it to me in a still more disparaging manner, saying something to the effect that, when he wrote it, he was getting new ideas about which he was still confused, and that he did not think it deserved any attention.

But what is most important about this year, 1929, is that in it he had frequent discussions with F. P. Ramsey—discussions which were, alas! brought to an end by Ramsey's premature death in January, 1930.[2] Ramsey had written for *Mind* (October 1923, p. 465) a long Critical Notice of the *Tractatus;* and subsequently, during the period when Wittgenstein was employed as a village schoolmaster in Austria, Ramsey had gone out to see him, in order to question him as to the meaning of certain statements in the *Tractatus*. He stayed in the village for a fortnight or more, having daily discussions with Wittgenstein. Of these discussions in Austria I only know that Ramsey told me that, in reply to his questions as to the meaning of certain statements, Wittgenstein answered more than once that he had forgotten what he had meant by the statement in question. But after the first half of the discussions at Cambridge in 1929, Ramsey wrote at my request the following letter in support of the proposal that Trinity should make Wittgenstein a grant in order to enable him to continue his researches:

> In my opinion Mr. Wittgenstein is a philosophic genius of a different order from any one else I know. This is partly owing to his great gift for seeing what is essential in a problem and partly to his overwhelming intellectual vigor, to the intensity of thought with which he pursues a question to the bottom and never rests content with a mere possible hypothesis. From his work more than that of any other man I hope for a solution of the difficulties that perplex me both in philosophy generally and in the foundations of Mathematics in particular.
>
> It seems to me, therefore, peculiarly fortunate that he should

[2] In the Preface to his posthumously published *Philosophical Investigations,* where Wittgenstein acknowledges his obligations to Ramsey (p. x), Wittgenstein himself says that he had "innumerable" discussions with Ramsey "during the last two years of his life," which should mean both in 1928 and in 1929. But I think this must be a mistake. I imagine that Wittgenstein, trusting to memory alone, had magnified into a series of discussions continuing for two years, a series which in fact only continued for a single year. It will be noticed that in the letter from Ramsey himself which I am about to quote, and which is dated 14th June, 1929, Ramsey states that he had been in close touch with Wittgenstein's work "during the last two terms," *i.e.* during the Lent and May terms of 1929, implying that he had not been in close touch with it in 1928. And though I do not know where Wittgenstein was in 1928, he certainly was not resident in Cambridge where Ramsey was resident, so that it is hardly possible that they can have had in that year such frequent discussions as they certainly had in 1929.

have returned to research. During the last two terms I have been in close touch with his work and he seems to me to have made remarkable progress. He began with certain questions in the analysis of propositions which have now led him to problems about infinity which lie at the root of current controversies on the foundations of Mathematics. At first I was afraid that lack of mathematical knowledge and facility would prove a serious handicap to his working in this field. But the progress he has made has already convinced me that this is not so, and that here too he will probably do work of the first importance.

He is now working very hard and, so far as I can judge, he is getting on well. For him to be interrupted by lack of money would, I think, be a great misfortune for philosophy.

The only other thing I know about these discussions with Ramsey at Cambridge in 1929 is that Wittgenstein once told me that Ramsey had said to him, "I don't like your method of arguing."

Wittgenstein began to lecture in January, 1930, and from the first he adopted a plan to which he adhered, I believe, throughout his lectures at Cambridge. His plan was only to lecture once a week in every week of Full Term, but on a later day in each week to hold a discussion class at which what he had said in that week's lecture could be discussed. At first both lecture and discussion class were held in an ordinary lecture room in the University Arts School; but very early in the first term Mr. R. E. Priestley (now Sir Raymond Priestley), who was then University Registrar and who occupied a set of Fellows' rooms in the new building of Clare, invited Wittgenstein to hold his discussion classes in these rooms. Later on, I think, both lectures and discussion classes were held in Priestley's rooms, and this continued until, in October, 1931, Wittgenstein, being then a Fellow of Trinity, was able to obtain a set of rooms of his own in Trinity which he really liked. These rooms were those which Wittgenstein had occupied in the academic year 1912–13, and which I had occupied the year before, and occupied again from October, 1913, when Wittgenstein left Cambridge and went to Norway. Of the only two sets which are on the top floor of the gateway from Whewell's Courts into Sidney Street, they were the set which looks westward over the larger Whewell's Court, and, being so high up, they had a large view of sky and also of Cambridge roofs, including the pinnacles of King's Chapel. Since the rooms were not a Fellow's set, their sitting room was not large, and for the purpose of his lectures and classes Wittgenstein used to fill it with some twenty plain cane-bottomed chairs, which at other times were stacked on the large landing outside. Nearly from the beginning the discussion classes were liable to last at least two hours, and from the time when the lectures ceased to be given in the Arts School they also commonly lasted at least as long. Wittgenstein always had a blackboard at both lectures and classes and made plenty of use of it.

I attended both lectures and discussion classes in all three terms of 1930 and in the first two terms of 1931. In the Michaelmas term of 1931 and the Lent term of 1932 I ceased, for some reason which I cannot now remember, to attend the lectures though I still went to the discussion classes; but in May 1932, I resumed the practice of attending the lectures as well, and throughout the academic year 1932–33 I attended both. At the lectures, though not at the discussion classes, I took what I think were very full notes, scribbled in notebooks of which I have six volumes nearly full. I remember Wittgenstein once saying to me that he was glad I was taking notes, since, if anything were to happen to him, they would contain some record of the results of his thinking.

My lecture notes may be naturally divided into three groups, to which I will refer as (I), (II), and (III). (I) contains the notes of his lectures in the Lent and May terms of 1930; (II) those of his lectures in the academic year 1930–31; and (III) those of lectures which he gave in the May term of 1932, after I had resumed attending, as well as those of all the lectures he gave in the academic year 1932–33. The distinction between the three groups is of some importance, since, as will be seen, he sometimes in later lectures corrected what he had said in earlier ones.

The chief topics with which he dealt fall, I think, under the following heads. First of all, in all three periods he dealt (A) with some very general questions about language, (B) with some special questions in the philosophy of Logic, and (C) with some special questions in the philosophy of Mathematics. Next, in (III) and in (III) alone, he dealt at great length, (D) with the difference between the proposition which is expressed by the words "I have got toothache," and those which are expressed by the words "You have got toothache" or "He has got toothache," in which connection he said something about Behaviorism, Solipsism, Idealism and Realism, and (E) with what he called "the grammar of the word 'God' and of ethical and aesthetic statements." And he also dealt, more shortly, in (I) with (F) our use of the term "primary color"; in (III) with (G) some questions about Time; and in both (II) and (III) with (H) the kind of investigation in which he was himself engaged, and its difference from and relation to what has traditionally been called "philosophy."

. . . .

(H) I was a good deal surprised by some of the things he said about the difference between "philosophy" in the sense in which what he was doing might be called "philosophy" (he called this "modern philosophy"), and what has traditionally been called "philosophy." He said that what he was doing was a "new subject," and not merely a stage in a "continuous development"; that there was now, in philosophy, a "kink" in the "development of human thought," comparable to that which occurred when Galileo and his contemporaries invented dynamics; that a "new method" had been discovered, as had happened when "chemistry was developed out of alchemy"; and that it was now possible for the first time that there should be "skilful" philosophers, though of course there had in the past been "great" philosophers.

He went on to say that, though philosophy had now been "reduced to a matter of skill," yet this skill, like other skills, is very difficult to acquire. One difficulty was that it required a "sort of thinking" to which we are not accustomed and to which we have not been trained—a sort of thinking very different from what is required in the sciences. And he said that the required skill could not be acquired merely by hearing lectures: discussion was essential. As regards his own work, he said it did not matter whether his results were true or not: what mattered was that "a method had been found."

In answer to the question why this "new subject" should be called "philosophy" he said in (III) that though what he was doing was certainly different from what, e.g., Plato or Berkeley had done, yet people might feel that it "takes the place of" what they had done—might be inclined to say "This is what I really wanted" and to identify it with what they had done, though it is really different, just as . . . a person who had been trying to trisect an angle by rule and compasses might, when shown the proof that this is impossible, be inclined to say that this impossible thing was the very thing he had been trying to do, though what he had been trying to do was really different. But in (II) he had also said that the "new subject" did really resemble what had been traditionally called "philosophy" in the three respects that (1) it was very general, (2) it was fundamental both to ordinary life and to the sciences, and (3) it was independent of any special results of science; that therefore the application to it of the word "philosophy" was not purely arbitrary.

He did not expressly try to tell us exactly what the "new method" which had been found was. But he gave some hints as to its nature. He said, in (II), that the "new subject" consisted in "something like putting in order our notions as to what can be said about the world," and compared this to the tidying up of a room where you have to move the same object several times before you can get the room really tidy. He said also that we were "in a muddle about things," which we had to try to clear up; that we had to follow a certain instinct which leads us to ask certain questions, though we don't even understand what these questions mean; that our asking them results from "a vague mental uneasiness," like that which leads children to ask "Why?"; and that this uneasiness can only be cured "either by showing that a particular question is not permitted, or by answering it." He also said that he was not trying to teach us any new facts: that he would only tell us "trivial" things—"things which we all know already"; but that the difficult thing was to get a "synopsis" of these trivialities, and that our "intellectual discomfort" can only be removed by a synopsis of *many* trivialities—that "if we leave out any, we still have the feeling that something is wrong." In this connection he said it was misleading to say that what we wanted was an "analysis," since in science to "analyse" water means to discover some new fact about it, e.g., that it is composed of oxygen and hydrogen, whereas in philosophy "we know at the start all the facts we need to know." I imagine that it was in this respect of needing a "synopsis" of trivialities that he thought that philosophy was similar to Ethics and Aesthetics.

I ought, perhaps, finally to repeat what I said in my first article, namely, that he held that though the "new subject" must say a great deal about language, it was only necessary for it to deal with those points about language which have led, or are likely to lead, to definite philosophical puzzles or errors. I think he certainly thought that some philosophers nowadays have been misled into dealing with linguistic points which have no such bearing, and the discussion of which therefore, in his view, forms no part of the proper business of a philosopher.

IV. BY JOHN WISDOM

Ludwig Wittgenstein, 1934–1937

I HAVE no notes worth speaking of about what Wittgenstein was saying in the years 1934, 1935, 1936 and 1937, when I attended his lectures and he talked to me about philosophical questions. I am relying on memory. As I remember, when I first went to a lecture by him, he was talking about the question, "What is it to understand a general term, such as 'plant'?" (See the first pages of the Blue Book.) He studied the cases in which we say of someone, "He understands," "He knows the meaning," "He is being taught the meaning," "After all he doesn't know the meaning," "I know the meaning," and so on. This led to his emphasizing the point he expressed by, "We have the idea that the several instances of a general concept all have something in common." (See the Blue Book.) (The concepts of "understanding" and of "having a meaning" are no exception.) He said that in applying the same word to several instances we mark a family resemblance—not the possession of something in common (as all ticket holders possess something in common—a ticket which matches a ticket I may hold in my hand as a sample, or as all alcoholic drinks possess something in common, in that from all of them may be distilled the essence of an alcoholic drink—alcohol).

This remark of his—that in applying the same word to several instances we mark a family resemblance and not the possession of something in common—was connected with a point which on one occasion at the Cambridge Moral Sciences Club he expressed in the words, "We have the idea that the meaning of a word is an object." This is connected with his saying "Don't ask for the meaning, ask for the use," recommended at the Moral Sciences Club as a supplement to "The meaning of a statement is the method of its verification." And all this is connected with the question "What happened when you understood?," and thus with his study of "What happened while I was expecting so-and-so from 4 to 4:30?," and so with how much a question as to what happened when someone understood, believed, remembered, was reading, was coming to a decision, felt frightened, etc., is a matter of what happened before, and what will or would happen after, he understood, believed, etc., and with how our recognition of this is hindered by "the idea of a mental mechanism," the hidden movements in which are these activities of the mind.

"We have the idea that the meaning of a word is an object" is also connected with "The application (every application) of every word is arbitrary." And this is connected with the question "Can you play chess without the queen?." (If I were asked to answer, in one sentence, the question "What was Wittgenstein's biggest contribution to philosophy?," I should answer "His asking of the question 'Can one play chess without the queen?.' ") And all this about understanding is connected with his study of what it is to prove a thing, with the fact that people were often exasperated by his ending the discussion of a philosophical puzzle with "Say what you like," with his saying to me on one occasion when I spoke of an unsuccessful philosophical discussion, "Perhaps you made the mistake of denying what he said," with his saying, "I hold no opinions in philosophy," and with his saying that he didn't *solve* philosophical problems, but *dissolved* them. At the same time he was always anxious to make people feel the puzzle—he was dissatisfied if he felt they had not done this.

The idea that the several instances of a general concept all have something in common is connected with the craving for a definition, "the idea of an exact calculus," the model, the analogy, of an exact calculus. The fascination of this model for our language is connected with the fascination of models suggested in our language—the idea that the soul is a little man within, the model for our minds of the closed picture gallery, the model for causation of the wire connection.

The substitution of the family-resemblance model for the property-in-common model, and the substitution of "Ask for the use" for "Ask for the meaning" is linked with the procedure of explaining meaning by presenting not a definition but cases, and not one case but cases and cases. And this is linked with dealing with the philosophical, metaphysical, *can't* by presenting cases and cases.

Thus Wittgenstein said that if someone says "One can't know the mind of another," one may ask "Would you call this knowing the mind of another, or that, or that?" For example, one may ask,

"Suppose a nerve of your body was joined to a nerve of Smith's, so that when someone stuck a pin into Smith you felt pain, would that be knowing, having, Smith's pain?" By this procedure, *either* (1) it is made clear what we would call "knowledge of the mind of another," and hence what it would be to know the mind of another, *or* (2) it appears that we can't imagine what it would be to know the mind of another, and that not merely in the sense in which few people can form an image of a creature with twenty-two legs on one side and twenty-one on the other, but in the sense in which there is nothing the speaker would call "knowing the mind of another" or "feeling the pain of another." If (1) is the case, then the person who says, "One can't know the mind of another" is saying of something which conceivably could happen, that it doesn't. Pigs don't fly. But if (2) is the case, then he has taken away the use of "know what is in the mind of another" which we have been taught, and not provided us with a new use. And this makes meaningless his question "Are other people automata?."

I do not mean that such a procedure constituted Wittgenstein's whole treatment of the puzzle about knowledge of the mind of another. By no means. On the contrary, he emphasized the fact that in teaching the child the use of "in pain" we not only point to others who are moaning, perhaps, but also pinch the child until it hurts, and say, "That's pain." And with this two-fold teaching and learning goes a two-fold method of verification which makes "He has toothache" very different from "It goes in jerks."

If one says that Wittgenstein showed metaphysical questions to be meaningless, one must remember that he also said that what the Solipsist *means* is right. One must remember if one asks, "Can one attach a meaning to 'Can one ever know that Smith is in pain, that there isn't a white rabbit between any two articles of furniture in this room?' " that one also asks, "Can one play chess without the queen?."

Wittgenstein as a Teacher

BY D. A. T. GASKING AND A. C. JACKSON

LUDWIG WITTGENSTEIN, sometime Professor of Philosophy at Cambridge and Fellow of Trinity College, is dead. His only published work, apart from a short address to the Aristotelian Society in 1929, was his celebrated *Tractatus Logico-Philosophicus,* the English version of which appeared in 1922. To have written that book, accepted as it is on all sides as novel, profound and influential, would have been enough to make him one of the most important philosophers of this century. Many others have since developed and reacted against the numerous obscurely expressed but fruitful suggestions with which that book is packed. But in the last twenty or so years of his life Wittgenstein turned his back on the *Tractatus* and went on to produce and to teach at Cambridge a whole new way of philosophizing. None of this later work has been published. Yet its effect on Australasian and American philosophy and its enormous effect on philosophy in Britain is apparent to anyone familiar with it who compares the sort of thing philosophers used to write twenty years ago with what very many of them write today. It is perhaps even more evident if one compares the technique of oral discussion then and now. This effect Wittgenstein produced by teaching, each year, a small group of students at Cambridge. It was natural, therefore, that to those outside his immediate environment he should seem to be a mysterious figure.

This short notice does not attempt to give an account of Wittgenstein's philosophy, merely to say something about the surroundings of that philosophy: to give, while memories are fresh, something that would partly answer such questions as "What sort of man was Wittgenstein and how did he teach?" It is possible that these personal impressions may be misleading; the man and his philosophy were complex.

There was nothing mysterious about Wittgenstein. He was a

49

University figure and there was plenty of uninformed personal gossip about him; this was fluff. What mattered was the work to which he gave his energy. He used to lecture two afternoons a week during term, starting usually at two. In recent years the lectures used to last for two hours, but in the thirties they went on longer— sometimes for more than four hours. Some years they were held in Wittgenstein's room, high over the gate of Whewell's Court, some- times in a small classroom in Trinity or in someone else's rooms. When you entered his room for a lecture you found some fifteen or twenty wooden chairs and one deck chair facing the fireplace, be- fore which stood a black iron anthracite stove. To the right below the window a trestle table with papers. On the mantelpiece a low- powered bulb on a retort stand. Behind you a small bookcase with two or three books. Wittgenstein stood waiting, occasionally glanc- ing at a watch which he pulled out of his breast pocket. A short, slightly built man in grey trousers, open-necked shirt and suede golfing jacket. His face was ruddy and very deeply lined, the eyes sharp blue and the hair (in the thirties) brown and curly. The audi- ence would consist of all those who were taking the Moral Sciences tripos seriously, about the same number of those who had recently taken the tripos, one or two other undergraduates, a philosophy don, perhaps a maths don, one or two research students from overseas.

Each year the lectures were on some philosophical problem— on the "other minds" puzzle, for example, or on the status of mathematical propositions. But whatever the problem, such was Wittgenstein's technique, by the end of the year most of the main philosophical issues would have been touched on and illuminated, directly or by implication. The technique was at first bewildering. Example was piled up on example. Sometimes the examples were fantastic, as when one was invited to consider the very odd linguistic or other behavior of an imaginary savage tribe. (E.g., "Suppose the members of the tribe decorate the walls of their houses by writing on them rows of Arabic numerals—and suppose that what they write is exactly what would be written by someone doing arith- metical calculations. They do it *exactly* right every time, but they never use it except for internal decoration—never use it in com- puting how much wood they need to build a hut or how much food they need for a feast, and so on. Would you say they were doing mathematics?") Sometimes the example was just a reminder of some well-known homely fact. Always the case was given in concrete detail, described in down-to-earth everyday language. Nearly every single thing said was easy to follow and was usually not the sort of thing anyone would wish to dispute. ("I shan't say anything that you won't all immediately agree with," said Wittgenstein once, "and if you do dispute something I'll drop it and go on to something else.")

The considerable difficulty in following the lectures arose from the fact that it was hard to see where all this often rather repetitive concrete detailed talk was leading to—how the examples were interconnected and how all this bore on the problem which one was accustomed to put oneself in abstract terms. The story of the tribe was interesting enough; one could agree that in real life one mostly did arithmetic as part of such operations as making a chair or buying groceries, and that for pure mathematicians the great thing about mathematical calculations was often their *charm*. But one often felt like making such a protest as: "What I want to know is, *are* mathematical propositions synthetic *a priori?*—and what has all this to do with my problem?"

Wittgenstein once, in lectures, gave the following sort of description of his procedure. (Here and elsewhere what appears as a long quotation is not a transcription of something taken down at the time but is a reconstruction from memory of approximately what was said.) "In teaching you philosophy I'm like a guide showing you how to find your way round London. I have to take you through the city from north to south, from east to west, from Euston to the embankment and from Piccadilly to the Marble Arch. After I have taken you many journeys through the city, in all sorts of directions, we shall have passed through any given street a number of times— each time traversing the street as part of a different journey. At the end of this you will know London; you will be able to find your way about like a born Londoner. Of course, a good guide will take you through the more important streets more often than he takes you down side streets; a bad guide will do the opposite. In philosophy I'm a rather bad guide. . . ."

Usually at the beginning of the year Wittgenstein would warn us that we would find his lectures unsatisfactory, that he would go on talking like this for hours and hours and we would get very little out of it. Plainly he was sensitive to the sort of audience he had. He wanted a small group of people who, knowing what was in store for them, were prepared to put in a full strenuous year with him learning philosophy. Visitors, even distinguished visitors, who wanted to attend a few lectures to "find out what sort of thing Wittgensein is doing" were not welcome, but anyone was welcome who seriously wanted to learn *philosophy* (and not just to hear Wittgenstein). And, if we had to work hard, Wittgenstein worked tremendously hard. He spoke without notes. Each lecture was obviously carefully prepared—its general strategy planned and numerous examples thought up. But in the lectures he thought it all through again, aloud. Members of the class would chip in briefly from time to time, though usually to make a suggestion in response to some question which was posed. At times Wittgenstein would break off, saying, "Just a minute, let me think!" and would sit for minutes on end, crouched forward on the edge of a chair, staring down at his upturned palm. Or he would exclaim with vehement sincerity: "This is as difficult as *hell!*"

At first one didn't see where all the talk was leading to. One didn't see, or saw only very vaguely, the point of the numerous examples. And then, sometimes, one did, suddenly. All at once, sometimes, the solution to one's problem became clear and everything fell into place. In these exciting moments one realized something of what mathematicians mean when they speak of the beauty of an elegant proof. The solution, once seen, seemed so simple and obvious, such an inevitable and simple key to unlock so many doors so long battered against in vain. One wondered how one could possibly fail to see it. But if one tried to explain it to someone else who had not seen it one couldn't get it across without going through the whole long, long story. Wittgenstein once described the situation in philosophy thus: "It is as if a man is standing in a room facing a wall on which are painted a number of dummy doors. Wanting to get out, he fumblingly tries to open them, vainly trying them all, one after the other, over and over again. But, of course, it is quite useless. And all the time, although he doesn't realize it, there is a real door in the wall behind his back, and all he has to do is to turn around and open it. To help him get out of the room all we have to do is to get him to look in a different direction. But it's hard to do this, since, wanting to get out, he resists our attempts to turn him away from where he thinks the exit must be."

Wittgenstein held that no answer to a philosophical question was any good unless it came to a man when he needed it. This invloved an attempt to make you see that you really did need such an answer.

Add to this that he "hoped to show that you had confusions you never thought you could have had." It would be fair to say that he tried to work his way into and through a question in the natural order and in the nontechnical way in which any completely sincere man thinking to himself would come at it. ("You must say what you really think as though no one, not even you, could overhear it." "Don't try to be intelligent; say it; then let intelligence into the room.") Whether this ideal is realizable in the form of a book is, in the opinion of many, not yet known; whether, if it were, the book would look much like what we think of as a philosophy book is discussable.

Wittgenstein was not, it seems clear, in any conventional sense a religious man. He never gave any extended presentation of his views on religion, nor, if he had done so, would it have been possible to summarize them without being misleading. The following may, however, give some clue to his attitude: A student in a mood of deep depression, for which he felt that Wittgenstein's philosophy was in some way responsible, went to Wittgenstein and explained: "Life seems to me pretty pointless and futile. In a few years I shall have ceased to exist. And it's no consolation that human life will go on. It may be millions of years yet, but in time the sun will cool down, life will become extinct, and it will all be as if life had never been." Wittgenstein replied: "Suppose you were sitting in a room, facing a door which was completely black. You sit and stare fixedly at it, impressing on your mind its total blackness, and saying to yourself sombrely over and over again, 'That door is black! That door is *black!*' After a bit you could easily begin to feel miserable about it, and to feel that it was the blackness of the door that was the melancholy fact which had produced your gloom."

He had complete respect for religious people, and for those non-philosophers who do their chosen job and follow their chosen way of life as well as they can. At times he would even try to persuade students who hoped to become professional philosophers to give it up and take a "decent" job, such as that of a mine manager or a farmer. He felt, apparently, that the life of a philosopher was a very strenuous and a very, very exacting one, not to be entered upon lightly but soberly and advisedly. He had a horror of slickness—of philosophical opinions arrived at by any process other than an honest wholehearted strenuous endeavor to find out the truth for oneself. He had no time for those who held philosophical opinions because they were fashionable, or because some eminent philosopher had advanced them—especially no time for those who held opinions for the reason that Wittgenstein had advanced them. (In a similar way he spoke with great respect of Freud, whom he described as a great man, but had little time for most of Freud's followers.) For example, at a time when the "Verification Principle" was fashionable in many quarters, he remarked at the Moral Sciences Club: "I used at one time to say that, in order to get clear how a certain sentence is used, it was a good idea to ask oneself the question: 'How would one try to verify such an assertion?' But that's just one way among others of getting clear about the use of a word or sentence. For example, another question which it is often very useful to ask oneself is: 'How is this word learned?' 'How would one set about teaching a child to use this word?' But some people have turned this suggestion about asking for the verification into a dogma—as if I'd been advancing a *theory* about meaning."

As a philosopher Wittgenstein seemed to work in almost complete independence of other philosophers other than the members and past members of his class. In lectures he hardly ever mentioned anyone else by name, nor did he quote or discuss what anyone else had written, except that once or twice he would discuss a point from someone's writings which he said he had been told of. He chose his friends and companions from among those around him who, judged by his own austere standards, seemed to him to be serious in their devotion to philosophy. He was known to speak against those whose conversation "came neither from the heart nor from the head."

It cannot be said that Wittgenstein was happy about the effect of his work. Rightly or wrongly, he appeared to believe that philosophical questions were very much harder than, in his view, many philosophers thought. He spoke about the "lack of deep puzzlement" in the work of a well-known philosophical movement. Some other philosophers whose work was plainly influenced by some of his teaching he was heard to describe (on slight evidence) as "more linguists than philosophers": in his view they did not come at problems in a natural way but rather fitted situations into prepared linguistic boxes. Which of these ways of philosophizing is preferable, and whether they should be as sharply distinguished as Wittgenstein appeared to distinguish them, will, no doubt, be keenly debated for some time.

It is not the purpose of this memoir to speak of Wittgenstein's activity outside philosophy. He was a man of great aesthetic sensibility. His lectures were delivered in spare and vivid prose. His occasional comments on pictures were those of a man who had an insight into what the artist was trying for. For a short time he had considered music as a career. About a don who criticized Blake he said, "He can't understand philosophy; how could you expect him to understand a thing like poetry?."

There are many sorts of human excellence. Not least among them is the excellence of one who devotes his whole life, giving up all else, to the attempt to do one single thing supremely well. That Wittgenstein did. How far he succeeded, those who come after us will tell.

Portrait of a Philosopher

BY KARL BRITTON

I FIRST SAW WITTGENSTEIN at G. E. Moore's Saturday-morning discussion class, at Cambridge in 1931. He came in late and unexpected, but soon he was doing all the talking; Moore, who had already lectured for a difficult hour on metaphysics, sprawled disconsolately over his desk and said very little. Many months later, I wrote to Wittgenstein asking his permission to attend his own discussion class which met in his rooms in Trinity from 5 to 7 P.M. on Fridays. He wrote giving that permission, and I attended regularly throughout the year. As far as I can recollect there were usually about twenty people present: visitors could be introduced only by permission. Moore used to come to these seminars: he occupied the only comfortable chair and was the only one permitted to smoke. We felt that Wittgenstein addressed himself chiefly to Moore, although Moore seldom intervened and often seemed to be very disapproving. Sometimes the lecturer appealed to him, but my recollection is that Moore's replies were usually very discouraging indeed. At all events we had the impression that a kind of dialogue was going on between Moore and Wittgenstein, even when Moore was least obviously being "brought in."

Wittgenstein spoke without notes but knew very well what he wanted to discuss and what he wanted to "put across," though sometimes he seemed to change his mind on some point while he was speaking. Sometimes the proceedings began with a short paper in which one of the senior members would attempt to sum up the conclusions reached at the end of the previous meeting: and it was characteristic of the situation that Wittgensein would be terribly dissatisfied with the statement produced. In discussion he would ask questions: and the one who volunteered an answer was liable to be his interlocutor throughout much of the two hours. On the whole, Wittgenstein was tremendously impatient in his discussion: not impatient of the raw newcomer to philosophy, but of the man who had developed philosophical views of his own. Wittgenstein talked often standing up and walking excitedly about—writing on the blackboard, pointing, hiding his face in his hands. But the most characteristic of all his attitudes was a very quiet, very intense stare —suddenly adopted and leading to a slow deliberate utterance of some new point. Very often he got thoroughly "stuck": appealed in vain to his hearers to help him out: he would walk about in despair murmuring: "I'm a fool, I'm a fool." And such was the difficulty of the topics he discussed, that all this struggle did not seem to us to be in the least excessive.

It was certainly an exciting and exacting session; and some, who came to it after a long afternoon in the open air, would be found fast asleep. In fact I myself normally reckoned to have at least a few minutes' nap and to wake up somewhat refreshed and a little better able to follow what was being said. My impression is that often one came away feeling that a tremendous effort had been made and little if anything achieved. But of course, looking back on the series, one can see how much had been achieved. For my own part, my views on philosophy completely changed during the time I was attending these lectures and during the following two years, when I discussed them and the *Tractatus* at Harvard, with others who had met Wittgenstein. Moreover, Wittgenstein's absolutely single-minded devotion to the investigation of philosophical problems, his high seriousness and absolute honesty—these came to be one of the most important "absolutes" in my life. I well remember thinking: What would it be like to be really disillusioned with philosophy? It would be to think that Wittgenstein's attempt was not worth while; that it is not worth while trying to think things out to the bitter end—as Wittgenstein was trying to do. Wittgenstein made us think it was worth while, and it has always seemed to me very bizarre that his philosophy should be regarded by some as trivializing, or not taking philosophy seriously enough.

Wittgenstein looked what he had once been, an artillery officer, but of course a very remarkable one. He was not tall, but slim and athletic with curly hair, extremely piercing and deep-set blue eyes and fine features. He spoke very quickly and had incorporated into his vocabulary a good deal of rather schoolboyish English slang. He had a most engaging smile and could laugh as he talked sometimes. Wittgenstein always wore the same workmanlike clothes: I particularly remember a watch on a leather strap which he wore attached to the lapel of his tweed jacket—a watch he frequently consulted. He removed after Christmas into a new (and even barer) room in Whewell's Court. I believe there was one armchair (occupied by Moore); the rest of us sat on cane chairs, or deck chairs, or on the floor. There was some kind of trestle table or writing bench on one side, covered with notebooks and papers; a new and rather elaborate coffee apparatus; and a small and beautiful silhouette in an elaborate gilt frame of a young woman: this was said to be an ancestress of his. There were seldom any philosophical books to be seen. And indeed Wittgenstein in those days often warned us against reading philosophical books. If we took a book seriously, he would say, it ought to puzzle us so much that we would throw it across the room and think about the problem for ourselves. Wittgenstein almost never referred to books in his lectures; seldom to the views of any philosopher not actually present. I once complimented a friend and disciple of his on his fine collection of philosophical books. He looked frankly shame-faced and told me that these all belonged to a past notion of how to do philosophy.

One Friday afternoon in February, at the end of one of his classes, I saw Wittgenstein in the Union Library. I need hardly say that his visits to the Union had nothing to do with the debates. I think he used to go there to read the German newspapers, but that afternoon he was taking tea and looking at journals upstairs. Wittgenstein got hold of me and showed me an article in *Mind* by Schiller on "The Value of Formal Logic." He said I ought to look at it because it was a good illustration of what he had been talking about that same afternoon—that is, "Nonsense" in the philosophical sense. And he insisted that his remark was meant seriously. I rather foolishly asked him about his own paper in the *Proceedings of the Aristotelian Society,* and he hastened to tell me that he had never read that paper to the society, having realized before he came to the meeting how terribly mistaken it was: it was apparently too late then to prevent its being published, but he insisted that I was to ignore it altogether.

On March 2, 1932, I went to tea with him in Whewell's Court. He talked to me in a fatherly and very serious way: probing my sincerity and my interest in philosophical problems: saying that I *could* not take philosophy seriously so long as I was reading for a degree, i.e., the Moral Sciences Tripos. He asked me if I could not give up the Tripos; and when I showed no eagerness to do so, he said he only hoped that it would not kill my interest in philosophy.

The Moral Science Club met regularly during the year but Wittgenstein never attended while I was there. I was told that he had come during the previous year but that his disagreements with other members had made it too uncomfortable for everyone. But although Wittgenstein did not attend the meetings of the Moral Science Club, his ideas were constantly put forward there. I myself constructed a short paper on "Boundaries" based on what Wittgenstein had said about the visual field and about death, in his book *Tractatus Logico-Philosophicus*. Not one of the dons turned up to hear it. A few undergraduate and graduate students were gathered round the fire in somebody's rooms: they listened, they criticized, and then began a discussion on another subject: and at the end of the meeting my paper was burning merrily on the back of the fire.

Wittgenstein's last discussion was held on May 27, 1932—I mean the last one I attended as an undergraduate. After that came the Tripos examinations and I took a walking holiday in the Lake District. It must have been early in June that I once again met Wittgenstein and was invited to tea. I arrived on the appointed day but he was not expecting me. He rushed out to the buttery to collect his ration of "pikelets" and tea but upset the whole lot into the grate and rushed off again for a second supply. However, when the tea was poured, he showed a touching interest in my plans for a career, advised me most strongly not to go straight into the teaching of philosophy—if I must become a teacher of philosophy I should at all events do something else first. During the discussion I ventured the suggestion that I might become a journalist, and at this he was both angry and alarmed. I must at all costs do a real job and not a secondhand one: he would much rather have heard that I intended to become a thief.

I think it was at this meeting that he expressed a very strong dislike of academic life in general and of Cambridge in particular. When he returned from London, he said, he would overhear one undergraduate talking to another in conversation saying "Oh really!" and he would know that he was back in Cambridge. He had, he said, only once been to high table at Trinity and the clever conversation of the dons had so horrified him that he had come out with both hands over his ears. The dons talked like that only to score: they did not even enjoy doing it. He said his own bedmaker's conversation, about the private lives of her previous gentlemen and about her own family, was far preferable: at least he could understand why she talked that way and could believe that she enjoyed it. Rumor said that Wittgenstein lived a very abstemious life, that he lived on cornflakes. Perhaps he did—and coffee.

That was the last time I saw him before I left Cambridge in the summer of 1932. In fact it was some years before we met again. Later, during the war, in 1942–47, Wittgenstein used to pay regular visits to Swansea, to see a friend of his there who was also a friend and colleague of mine. I returned to Swansea in April 1945 and saw the two of them together on the Mumbles train. Wittgenstein seemed not to know me, but afterwards he sent his apologies to me, explaining that the two were having a conversation which could not be interrupted. In April 1946 he came to discuss with a small group at college on "Motives and Causes." Once again I felt that he did not get where he wanted: although now I could see that he did get somewhere. When he was going I persuaded him to come again next week; and my students said: "We have never *seen* a man thinking before."

So on April 17 I called on Wittgenstein in his lodgings. It was his fifty-sixth birthday and he was proud of the fact that he looked a good deal younger than that. He had been reading *Pride and Prejudice* and found the mannered conversation of Elizabeth Bennet very hard to accept. He asked me to explain why Jane Austen wanted to pretend that a girl could talk like that. I did not attempt to do so. His landlord was a nonconformist minister and here the book question came up again. Wittgenstein had been making fun of him for having his walls lined with books he never opened—to impress his flock. He also told me how an old man who was visiting the minister had said that Jesus Christ was the world's greatest philosopher. Wittgenstein said that he had tried to explain that Jesus Christ was not a philosopher at all; but evidently he understood why the man wanted Jesus Christ to be the greatest of everything.

We spent the whole of that April morning walking and talking. As we passed Swansea's immense new Guildhall, Wittgenstein expressed horror and disgust. The magnificent stairway in particular annoyed him: he said it was the architecture of a religion which nobody now professed. I have never understood what he meant. During the walk Wittgenstein assured me (laughing) that no assistant lecturer in philosophy in the country had read fewer books on philosophy than he had. He said he had never read a single word of Aristotle, although he had lately read much of Plato and with much profit. As for Hume and Kant, it was all very well for me to read them because I was not yet as experienced in philosophical thinking as he was: but he could not sit down and read Hume—he knew far too much about the subject of Hume's writings to find this anything but a torture.

On this occasion he described how, when he first came to Cambridge from Manchester, puzzled about logical questions, he had W. E. Johnson as a supervisor: so he went and fired off all his questions at Johnson. This produced nothing but frustration on both sides, and they soon had to agree that Wittgenstein should not attend any more supervisions. But (to his surprise and pleasure) Johnson asked him to come to his Sunday tea-parties, which he did regularly. He said how very much he liked and admired Johnson and how well they got on as soon as they had decided to give up the philosophical questions.

He also told me how wonderful Bertrand Russell was in those days; how they both abandoned everything else and gave themselves up to discussions about logic and mathematics. For a long time they could agree about nothing, but at last they both came to see that the "assertion sign" which Whitehead and Russell took over from Frege, had *no meaning whatever*. This they both regarded as a great triumph and happy augury, which, of course, it was.

Some remarks that I recall seem to belong to this same morning in 1946. He said: Everyone has a simple test to discover whether or not a cobbler makes good shoes. There is no test of this sort to discover whether a philosopher does his job or not, and as long as this is the case, So-and-so (whom I had praised) is quite rightly thought of as a good philosopher. He said that many of his pupils merely put forward his own ideas: and that many of them imitated his voice and manner; but that he could easily distinguish those who really understood.

That same afternoon there was a small discussion group in college: and it went rather well. After it was over Wittgenstein was very lighthearted and took me out to a grand tea in a cafe. Then another long walk and talk in the park and by the sea: we parted at the gates just before nine o'clock. The conversation had partly been most serious: he had become convinced that a new war was being planned and that atomic weapons would put an end to everything. "They mean to do it," he repeated. But later we discussed Napoleon and Bismarck and talked about the Prince Consort and various diplomatic and other personalities of the nineteenth century. He had a great admiration for Bismarck and obviously enjoyed talking about him.

One day in July of that same year Wittgenstein rang me up and explained that his friend was away and that he wished me to take him out. However, he seemed, on the whole, very hostile. The journal *Mind* had just published two papers on "Therapeutic Positivism" and (as I afterwards found out) this had much annoyed and upset him. With me he was angry too for going to the Joint Session of the Mind Association and the Aristotelian Society, the annual jamboree of philosophers: he took it as a sign of frivolity and of ulterior interests. He railed aginst professional philosophers, mourned the present state of philosophy in England and asked: "What can one man do alone?" When I told him that the next jamboree was to be held at Cambridge in 1947 and that I was to read a paper, he said: "Very well, to me it is just as if you had told me that there will be bubonic plague in Cambridge next summer. I am very glad to know and I shall make sure to be in London." (And so he was.) However, I managed to ask him a series of questions about the nature of arithmetic and this led him to a long and extremely valuable exposition of the subject, most of it delivered while we stood, some paces apart, stock-still in the heart of Clyne woods.

It may have been on this occasion that I told him I had reviewed a book by Dr. C. E. M. Joad called *Teach Yourself Philosophy*. Wittgenstein assumed it would have been a bad book and hoped I had not lost the opportunity of saying so. I said that I had said so; but that I had lent the book to a policeman of my acquaintance who had read it aloud to his wife cover to cover. They had both been greatly charmed: "It opened up a new world to me," the policeman said. This very much interested Wittgenstein and after a moment he said: "Yes, I understand how that is. Have you ever seen a child make a grotto with leaves and stones and candles—and then creep in out of the world into a kind of world he has made for himself? It was the grotto that your policeman friend liked to creep into."

Later on he came home with me to tea: he took little notice of the children, and talked to my wife about Wales and the north of England. He spoke highly of Swansea, which he knew as a holiday place: the people might be "easygoing" (as I said) but he thought he should like them because they were friendly. "I am sorry for you," he said to me with genuine compassion, "I see how it is: you have a tidy mind." He liked the north of England, too: when he asked the bus conductor on a Newcastle bus where to get off for a certain cinema, the conductor at once told him it was a bad film there and he ought to go to another. And this started a heated argument in the bus as to which film Wittgenstein ought to see and why. He liked that: it was the sort of thing that would have happened in Austria. He also told me about his war work: at Guy's Hospital mixing ointments, and then acting as a research assistant at the Royal Victory Infirmary in Newcastle. He loved the feel of the ointments, and the smells. He often spoke as though he disliked London, and especially Cambridge.

The last time I encountered him was quite by chance. He was endeavoring unsuccessfully to cash a small check at my bank. I introduced him to the cashier: and I am afraid that was the only time I ever helped Wittgenstein to solve a problem.

A Symposium: Assessments
of the Man and the Philosopher

I. BY ERICH HELLER

A CHINESE SAGE of the distant past was once asked by his disciples
what he would do first if he were given power to set right the affairs
of the country. He answered: "I should certainly see to it that language is used correctly." The disciples looked perplexed. "Surely,"
they said, "this is a trivial matter. Why should you deem it so important?" And the Master replied: "If language is not used correctly, then what is said is not what is meant; if what is said is not
what is meant, then what ought to be done remains undone; if this
remains undone, morals and art will be corrupted; if morals and
art are corrupted, justice will go astray; if justice goes astray, the
people will stand about in helpless confusion."

There is in Wittgenstein's philosophical concern with language
a moral *élan* which puts him closer in spirit to that sage than to the
mere technicians of linguistic analysis. He was convinced of the
most intimate connection between the quality of our speech and
the quality of our living. He knew that the forms of language were
deeply rooted in our nature, and spoke of "deep disquietudes"
caused by their misuse. Once he even said that the whole aim of
his philosophy was to "clear up the ground of language." To him,
as to the Chinese sage, this mattered above everything.

Wittgenstein came from Austria—as do the mottoes he chose
for both his books, the *Tractatus Logico-Philosophicus* and *Philosophical Investigations*. Strange to think that through Wittgenstein's
mottoes at least one sentence each of the almost forgotten Austrian
essayist Ferdinand Kürnberger and the profoundly domestic Johann
Nestroy has become prescribed reading in most of the Anglo-Saxon
departments of philosophy—of the very Nestroy who had no
thought of tomorrow when night after night he amused the Viennese

with his comic turns and verbal twists, and who once warded off
the friendly advice to write something that would last, to do something for posterity: "Why," he exclaimed, "what has posterity done
for me?" From Austria too came the satirist and poet Karl Kraus,
who performed Nestroy on his one-man stage, revived the memory
of Kürnberger, and published among many other books a volume
called *Language*. Wittgenstein admired Karl Kraus as he admired
no other writer of his time. It was a case of elective affinities. Like
Karl Kraus, he was seldom pleased by what he saw of the institutions of men, and the idiom of the passersby mostly offended his ear
—particularly when they happened to speak philosophically; and
like Karl Kraus he suspected that the institutions could not be but
corrupt if the idiom of the race was confused, presumptuous and
vacuous, a fabric of nonsense, untruth, deception, and self-decep-
tion.

Wittgenstein belonged to that astonishing generation of minds
who, with all their differences, bear yet a common stamp: the
indefinable but unmistakable mark of the end of the Austrian monarchy. It happened once before that the dissolution of a great empire
brought forth men possessed of extraordinary spiritual energies;
and at that time too, when the days of Rome were numbered, these
men were largely Jews. Highly sophisticated minds seemed yet to
be driven by a primitive passion of salvation. Think of Friedrich
Adler. He appeared to all the world as if he had been born to be the
intelligent, well-educated, good-mannered and efficient parliamen-
tarian of a party of radical reform; but one day he turned political
assassin, and, having killed the Minister of the Interior, delivered
before his judges a prophetic indictment of Austrian politics. Or
Otto Weininger, of whom Wittgenstein spoke with great respect: at
twenty he was an immensely learned man and wrote his book *Sex
and Character*. Its calm and lucid prose suggested that it was an
essay in psychology. Yet it developed the messianic ethics of asceticism to that extreme point where consistency borders on insanity; and its author shot himself soon afterwards.

Or remember Schönberg: rudely he broke off the ever-more
strained conversation between personal sentiment and musical convention, and tried to save the integrity of the composer as well as
the integrity of music by subjecting both to an exceedingly rigid
mental discipline. Or Adolf Loos, the arcihtect, whose teaching and
example is clearly discernible in the mansion that Wittgenstein de-

signed and built in Vienna: he conducted his campaign against the ornamental in architecture on behalf of the same truth.

To cure the mind of the disease by shocking it into accepting the uncomfortable truth about itself: it seems unnecessary to say that also Sigmund Freud lived at that time, and in a place where the confusion of decline and fall filled the elect with the desire to lift the world into a sphere of final clarity. "Only this could give me happiness"—it is an entry in Franz Kafka's diary. He, too, was a citizen of the Austrian monarchy.

The attainment of final clarity—for Wittgenstein this meant: to produce the philosophy to end all philosophy. There was a time when he thought he had achieved it with his *Tractatus Logico-Philosophicus*. He had built a system of the greatest logical subtlety, to emerge from it with a staggeringly simple solution: "The riddle does not exist." How not? Because there is, at least theoretically, an answer to every question: "If a question can be put at all, then it can also be answered." Was this an assertion of spiritual arrogance? Not in the slightest. It simply meant that unanswerable questions were no questions. The *Tractatus* had abolished philosophy by denying all questions of ethics and aesthetics and transcendental intuition the status of questions, leaving only those which to answer was in the theoretical power of science. And, assuming that science was to answer one day every possible question, how much would this do for us? Not much; for "even if every possible scientific question were answered, the problems of our living would still not have been touched at all"; and they would not have been touched because they were and remain untouchable by science. And if all answerable questions had found their answers, what would be left? The vast realm of the "unquestionable" and therefore unanswerable—the unsayable, "of which one must be silent." Does it exist? "There is indeed the unsayable," says the *Tractatus*. How can we be sure? "It shows itself, it is the mystical." And philosophy will in the end "mean the unsayable by clearly showing what can be said"; and having shown it, it will have reached its end.

It was Wittgenstein's hope that his work might bring some light into "the darkness of our time." For when language is not used correctly, the people will stand about in helpless confusion. Karl Kraus showed how this happened; and Wittgenstein, too, was an Austrian.

II. BY M. O'C. DRURY

ANYONE WHO KNEW Wittgenstein at all well will appreciate the hesitation I feel in speaking about him. He would have found a panegyric extremely distasteful. But since his death there have grown up so many false legends about him and his teaching that I think it necessary for some of us who knew him well to try to give them their quietus.

Some people seem to think that Wittgenstein was a rather cantankerous, arrogant, tormented genius; content to dwell aloof in the profundity of his own speculations. That was not the man at all. During the twenty years or so I knew him he was the most warmhearted, generous, and loyal friend anyone could wish to have. Friendship meant a great deal to him. Two incidents come to my mind out of a host of similar memories. Wittgenstein looking for a birthday present for a friend and saying: "You don't need a lot of money to give a nice present but you do need a lot of time." Wittgenstein saying goodbye to me as I boarded a troopship for the Middle East, giving me a silver cup and saying: "Water tastes so much nicer out of silver; there is only one condition attached to it—you are not to worry if it gets lost."

He was a delightful companion. His conversation and interests extended over an immense range of topics. After I left Cambridge we seldom discussed specific philosophical problems. He preferred me to tell him about books I was reading or the medical problems I was at present engaged with. He had the ability to make one see a question in an entirely new light. For instance, I was telling him of some psychiatric symptoms that puzzled me greatly. Wittgenstein said: "You should never cease to be amazed at symptoms mental patients show. If I became mad the thing I would fear most would be your common-sense attitude. That you would take it all as a matter of course that I should be suffering from delusions."

Sometimes he liked me to read out loud to him, and he would comment on what we were reading: Frazer's *Golden Bough*, Prescott's *Conquest of Mexico*, Morley's *Life of Cromwell*, Boswell's *Life of Johnson* (he loved and revered old Dr. Johnson).

To watch Wittgenstein listening to music was to realize that this was something very central and deep in his life. He told me that this he could not express in his writings, and yet it was so important to him that he felt without it he was sure to be misunderstood. I will never forget the emphasis with which he quoted Schopenhauer's dictum: "Music is a world in itself."

Wittgenstein had a difficult temperament to contend with. No one knew this better than he himself. Nothing that has been said since about him has been half so scathing as his own self-criticism. Once when I was discussing a personal problem with him, he said to me: "One keeps stumbling and falling, stumbling and falling, and the only thing to do is to pick oneself up and try and go on again. At least that is what I have had to do all my life."

We were discussing the philosopher William James (Wittgenstein had a great admiration for James, and *The Varieties of Religious Experience* was one of the few books he insisted I must read). I said of James that I always enjoyed reading anything by him, he was so human in all he wrote. Wittgenstein replied: "That is what makes him a good philosopher. He was a real human being." And that is the first thing I want to say about Wittgenstein. He was a great philosopher because he was a very human person indeed.

I find people writing and talking as if Wittgenstein knew little and cared less about the history of philosophy: as if he regarded his own work as abrogating all that had gone before him, and he confined all previous metaphysics to the limbo of the meaningless. This is a misunderstanding. In one of the earliest conversations I had with him he said: "Don't think I despise metaphysics or ridicule it. On the contrary, I regard the great metaphysical writings of the past as among the noblest productions of the human mind." I told him that what had first attracted me to study philosophy was seeing the title of Alexander's book, *Space, Time and Deity*. He understood at once. "Of course, that is where the great problems of philosophy lie, space, time and Deity."

We were discussing a suitable title for the book which later he called *Philosophical Investigations*. I foolishly suggested he should just call it "Philosophy." He was indignant. "How could I take a word like that which has meant so much in the history of mankind; as if my writings were anything more than a small fragment of philosophy?" I do not think Wittgenstein would ever have spoken of his work as a "revolution in philosophy." It was a way of thinking for which he knew he had a special talent and which threw light on all the traditional problems of philosophy. He told me that he thought of using as a motto for the *Philosophical In-vestigations* a quotation from King Lear: "I'll teach you differences."

Wittgenstein constantly urged his pupils not to take up an academic post and become teachers of philosophy. Though later he did admit to me that with regard to a few of his pupils he had been wrong; they had turned out to be excellent teachers. But certainly in my own case and in that of many others he was most emphatic that we must earn our livelihood in some other way. This advice of his has been misinterpreted. Wittgenstein never advised anyone to give up philosophy, if by that is meant thinking about first principles and ultimate problems. When I said goodby to him for the last time at Cambridge and we both knew he had not long to live, he said to me with great seriousness: "Drury, whatever becomes of you, don't stop thinking."

Why, then, did he so strongly discourage pupils from becoming teachers of philosophy? I think it was because Wittgenstein knew from his own experience that in philosophical thinking there are long periods of darkness and confusion when one just has to wait. In philosophy above all things there is a time to speak and a time to keep silent. Wittgenstein had a great horror of what Schopenhauer once described as "professorial philosophy by philosophy professors": people having to go on talking when really they knew in their own heart that they had nothing of value to say.

When I was at Cambridge a friend of mine was studying for a doctorate in philosophy. After some period of research he decided that he had found nothing new to say on his chosen subject, and that the only honest thing to do was not to write a thesis. I remember how Wittgenstein's face lit up with pleasure when I told him of this decision. "For that action alone," he said, "they should give him his Ph.D." On several occasions Wittgenstein said to me: "My father was a businessman and I am a businessman too; I want my philosophy to be businesslike, to get something done, to get something settled."

Kant said that a great deal of philosophy reminded him of one person holding a sieve while the other tried to milk the he-goat. Wittgenstein wanted above all things to make an end of sieve holding and he-goat milking. I remember, after one particularly fatuous paper at the Moral Sciences Club, Wittgenstein exclaiming: "This sort of thing has got to be stopped. Bad philosophers are like slum landlords. It's my job to put them out of business." Talking about Spinoza, Wittgenstein said to me: "Spinoza ground lenses, that must have been a great help to him in his thinking. I wish I had some purely mechanical skill like that by which I could earn my livelihood. Something I could do when I can't get on with my writing." These were the considerations which made him advise his pupils not to become professional philosophers.

The final point I want to make about Wittgenstein is the one I find hardest to get across. It is concerned with the idea which for me is central in all his teaching. The idea which for me binds together in one volume the *Tractatus* and the *Philosophical Investigations*. Perhaps the best way to put it shortly would be this. Once Wittgenstein said to me of a certain writer that he was by far the greatest philosopher of the nineteenth century: he meant Soren Kierkegaard. Here are two short extracts from Kierkegaard's writings that seem to me to state this central idea in the best possible way. The first passage is taken from the *Journals:*

> The majority of men in every generation, even those who, as it is described, devote themselves to thinking, live and die under the impression that life is simply a matter of understanding more and more, and that if it were granted to them to live longer, that life would continue to be one long continuous growth in understanding. How many of them ever experience the maturity of discovering that there comes a critical moment when everything is reversed, after which the point becomes to understand more and more that there is something which cannot be understood. This is Socratic ignorance and that is what the philosophy of our time requires as a corrective.

For me the whole weight of Wittgenstein's teaching is directed towards this corrective: "We show the unspeakable by clearly displaying the speakable." There is, I need hardly say, nothing obscurantist, woolly, or mystical about Wittgenstein's method. It is as hard and incisive a piece of thinking as is to be found anywhere. But the whole driving force of the investigation is missed if it is not seen continually to point beyond itself.

The second passage from Kierkegaard is taken from one of the short discourses:

> It is true as the understanding says that there is nothing to wonder at, but precisely for this reason is wonder secure, because the understanding vouches for it. Let the understanding condemn what is transitory, let it clear the ground, then wonder comes in in the right place, in ground that is cleared in the changed man. Everything appertaining to that first wonder the understanding can consume; let it do so, in order that enigmatically it may help one to wonder.

That was the secret of Wittgenstein. He made wonder secure. No one had such power to awaken again that primitive wonder from which all great philosophy begins. No one had such power to shake the pillars of one's complacency. It was this that made a discussion with Wittgenstein such a refreshment. One evening not long before his death Wittgenstein quoted to me the inscription that Bach wrote on the title page of his *Little Organ Book*.

> To the glory of the most high God, and that my neighbor may be benefited thereby.

Pointing to his own pile of manuscript, he said: "That is what I would have liked to have been able to say about my own work."

"To the glory of the most high God, and that my neighbor may be benefited thereby." I think that wish was granted him.

III. BY NORMAN MALCOLM

IN A RECENT BOOK Lord Russell remarks: "The later Wittgenstein" (meaning the author of the *Philosophical Investigations* as contrasted with the author of the *Tractatus*) "seems to have grown tired of serious thinking and to have invented a doctrine which would make such an activity unnecessary." I find this observation amusing, because it is 180 degrees from the truth. The intensity and the completeness with which Wittgenstein was occupied by the problems of the *Investigations* could hardly be exaggerated. I say "occupied by the problems" advisedly, for they truly took possession of him. G. E. Moore was a deeply serious philosopher, but even he was not, I think, pursued and tormented by philosophical difficulties to the degree that Wittgenstein was. I imagine that after a few hours of work Moore could stop and turn his attention to other matters. Wittgenstein sometimes had to resort to a violent distraction, such as going to a "flick," where he would sit in the front row with his field of vision filled up by the screen, so that the scenes and incidents of the film would hold off the thoughts that pressed upon him.

In the *Investigations* he says, somewhat enigmatically: "The real discovery is the one that makes me able to break off doing philosophy when I want to," but I do not believe he ever made that discovery. I am inclined to say that philosophy was somehow *inside* Wittgenstein, giving him no rest. It was not a pursuit to which he could turn his attenion or not as he chose. With him there was an investment of energy and feeling in philosophical questions on a scale that one might expect a man to have only in connection with intimate problems of family and friends, of personal ambition, or of private conscience. His attitude towards philosophical truth was passionate rather than objective. He did not want to contemplate truth but to subjugate it.

It is perhaps a common impression that the *Philosophical Investigations* is a collection of aphorisms that are sometimes individually brilliant but which do not combine into a coherent system of thought. There is artistry in the style but the reasoning is rigorous and deep. The book is composed of a series of remarks, yet the impression of vagueness or looseness is merely superficial.

I should find it impossible to describe the literary art of Wittgenstein's philosophical writings, but an obvious component of it is the metaphors that sometimes astonish one. Commenting on the familiar solipsistic doctrine that a person can know only what he himself, and not anyone else, is thinking, Wittgenstein says: "It is correct to say I know what you are thinking," and wrong to say "I know what I am thinking." Then he adds: "A whole cloud of philosophy condensed into a drop of grammar."

In a work apparently written about 1930 and not yet published,* Wittgenstein asks: "Why is philosophy so complicated? It ought to be *entirely* simple. Philosophy unties the knots in our thinking that we have, in a senseless way, put there. To do this it must make movements as complicated as these knots are. Although the *result* of philosophy is simple its method cannot be, if it is to succeed. . . . The complexity of philosophy is not its subject matter, but our knotted undersanding."

In these remarks the metaphors are not mere adornments. They serve to provide perhaps the clearest statements of Wittgenstein's conception that philosophy cannot produce a *foundation* for mathematics or anything else; that it "simply puts everything before us, and neither explains nor deduces anything"; that it "leaves everything as it is."

For Wittgenstein it was natural to think in striking images. These might appear in his conversation on any topic. He had read an account by Dickens of a visit to a shipload of Mormons about to emigrate from England to America, and Wittgenstein was much

---

* Editor's note: It has now been published as *Philosophische Bemerkungen*. See: selected bibliography. The passage quoted here appears on page 52.

impressed by the picture of the simple resolution of those people in the face of hardship. He thought they were an excellent illustration of what religious faith can do. But he went on to remark to a friend that in order to understand them (I think he meant to understand their religious conceptions) one must have a certain "obtuseness." Then came this smile: like needing big shoes to walk across a bridge that has holes in the flooring!

Wittgenstein's conversation made an overwhelming impression because of the united seriousness and vivacity of his ideas, and also because of the expressive mobility of his beautiful face, the piercing eyes and commanding glance, the energetic movements and gestures. In comparison, someone has remarked, other people seemed only half alive.

Wittgenstein disliked teaching teachers of philosophy. Partly this was because of a repugnance for academic philosophy and a vivid awareness of the temptations to dishonesty that press upon a university lecturer. But he had another reason. If someone came to his lectures for two or three years he would be introduced to only a small part of the inquiries that Wittgenstein had found it necessary to carry out, and when this student began to teach on his own he would find it impossible to sustain himself merely on what he had learned from Wittgenstein, and he would either give up or else cultivate some affectation of originality. It pleased Wittgenstein to know that among his students there were men who would become doctors or mathematicians.

He once remarked that since this is the age of popular science it cannot be a time for philosophy. He thought that perhaps the most useful work a man trained in philosophy could do nowadays would be to present a popular but clear and decent account of some science, and he mentioned as an example of such a work, Faraday's *The Chemical History of a Candle.*

With respect to philosophical work his standards were inexorable. Of a young friend who was preparing a paper to read to the Moral Science Club of Cambridge he remarked that he ought to write it for a hundred years from now and not just for next week. This he said of a paper that was intended merely for a discussion group, not for publication.

Wittgenstein was not attracted by money or fame. While a young man he gave away the large fortune he inherited so that, as he said, he would not have friends for the sake of his money. Some time after he resigned his chair at Cambridge, and had no income and little left in savings, he was invited to give the John Locke lectures at Oxford. This would have paid him £200 as well as contributing to his reputation, for he was still unknown to the public. I recall his asking me at the time, quite unaffectedly: "Can you think of any reason why I should do it?" The reasons that would have struck another man as obvious did not interest him. This is not to say that he did not have a concern for what would happen to his name and his work in a later time. About this he was pessimistic. Of the ideas of the *Investigations* he says in his preface: "I make them public with doubtful feelings. It is not impossible that it should fall to the lot of this work, in its poverty and in the darkness of this time, to bring light into one brain or another—but, of course, it is not likely." He believed it improbable that his work would survive to another age, one that would be more favorable for philosophy.

Once I was asked whether Wittgenstein had a sense of humor. Often he smiled or laughed at a remark or incident. In my experience his laughter was moderate and brief: I could hardly conceive of him laughing to the point of tears. Sometimes he put on a charming mood of mock seriousness in which he said nonsensical things with the utmost gravity.

He did not have "a sense of humor" if one means by this a humorous view of the world and of oneself. His outlook was grim. He was always troubled about his own life and was often close to despair. He was dismayed by the insincerity, vanity, and coldness of the human heart. He thought that all of us greatly needed help (and perhaps himself most of all) if we were to become more honest and more loving. That feeling is reflected in these characteristic sentences that conclude different letters: "I wish you a better head and a better heart than I have"; "I wish you *lots* of good luck, and I know you wish me the same; and *do I need it!*"

IV. BY RUSH RHEES

WITTGENSTEIN CHANGED HIS VIEWS and his way of discussing problems in the last twenty years of his life. Some people seem to think there must be a strange drama behind this. Bertrand Russell thinks it is evidence of the "singular man" that Wittgenstein was, and he suggests that he threw away his great talent for philosophy in order to debase himself before common sense—rather as Pascal had "abandoned mathematics for piety" and "Tolstoy sacrificed his genius as a writer to a kind of bogus humility which made him prefer peasants to educated men."

But there was nothing strange in what Wittgenstein did. He returned again and again to the question which had occupied him from the beginning. Like anyone else who does this, he came to see difficulties in many of the ideas he had once accepted. In certain respects he came to see the problems differently. And as he did so he saw that other methods were needed for the study of them. In all this, I must repeat, he was going more deeply into the problems he had studied at the time when Russell admired him. If there was anything "singular" about the changes he made, it was in the penetration he showed—the way in which he would recognize difficulties which no one else would have noticed—and in the persistence with which he discussed the same things.

But neither is it strange that Russell could not follow him, or even recognize what Wittgenstein was doing at the end of his life, or recognize that it was serious philosophy at all. When Russell speaks of serious philosophy, I suppose he thinks first of the philosophy of logic. And this was first in Wittgenstein's interests too; to the end of his life. But for Russell the questions in the philosophy of logic—were often different from those which other logicians had recognized. I should want to qualify this if I were taking the matter further, since for much of the time he was discussing the work of those logicians. But to Russell it must have seemed like raising matters foreign to everything he thought of as the hard work of logic. And Wittgenstein did not expect that Russell would see what he was getting at.

I would emphasize only that he did have reasons for developing as he did. They may be criticized, and Russell might have criticized them. But we cannot understand his later work, or how it differed from his earlier work and from Russell's, unless we try to understand them. And it is wrong—I must say this flatly, and I wish I might underline it—it is wrong to suggest that Wittgenstein ever turned away from the interests and the questions which had occupied him particularly in his early days.

We might try to understand the changes he did make by speaking of the ways in which he discussed and criticized the notions of logical necessity, or logical proof, of logic and mathematics, of mathematical proof, of "insight," "self-evidence," or the relations of logic and grammar, or logical statements and empirical statements, and so on. But any of these brings others with it; and anyway we could not show what he was doing unless we could show what his discussions were like.

I might mention two matters where he has been misunderstood especially, though I doubt if a short reference can clarify much. (1) He no longer thought that a special logical symbolism had the importance he once gave it; and (2) he no longer thought that we must be able to show how the whole of logic follows from a single principle. Now many logicians speak of "formalized languages" and "natural languages." A formalized language is really a formal system or calculus; and a natural language is a language which we ordinarily speak, like French or English. These logicians emphasize that the natural languages have grown up to meet practical needs, and they are not suited for the solution of logical problems; they have too many vaguenesses and ambiguities. On the other hand the formalized languages may be so designed that they will lead us to new logical insights which we could never have come to if we had kept to the language of ordinary speech. Wittgenstein would have agreed that natural languages are not suitable for logical investigations—if by logical investigations you mean solving the problems and the difficulties in the development of a calculus. But whether such a calculus can yield important new "logical insights" is another question; and it calls for an examination of the whole idea of logical insights. This was the question to which Wittgenstein devoted himself. And for this a calculus is no help. Such questions may not interest mathematical logicians. But the philosophy of logic —the question, for instance, of whether the rules of logic are just arbitrary—is devoted to them.

Wittgenstein used sometimes to protest against the dogmatic assumption that all questions can be solved in one way; and against the assumption that if you cannot guarantee the principles of logic by showing them in a connected system then you are virtually throwing logic away. His criticisms of the idea of the "truth of logic" were something similar: when he would say that a contradiction between logical principles need not vitiate logic. But I must emphasize again that any such remark would be part of a long and complicated discussion—about contradictions altogether, about logical necessity, about the relations of logical principles to one another. A contradiction to the principles of logic would not mean that there was a logical blunder anywhere. These discussions were difficult, and he would return to them from different angles. Perhaps someone who has followed them will say that they are wrong in some way. But he cannot say that Wittgenstein was ignoring the question.

That is what Russell does seem to say when he criticizes Wittgenstein for "a suave evasion of paradoxes." Put in that way this almost suggests that Wittgenstein did not mind contradictions in an argument. But this is not what Russell means. He is thinking of what are called "the logical paradoxes"—contradictions which seem to result from recognized principles of reasoning. Certainly Wittgenstein did not look on these paradoxes in the way Russell did, and I suppose it seemed to Russell that he was not being serious about logic—almost as though he were saying that logic did not matter. Here I can only say that Wittgenstein came to the views he did because he *was* being serious about logic; because he was trying to bring out the character of logical necessity and show where it lies: and he gave serious reasons for the view he took.

This view affected what he might have said about the relation of logic and the world. Russell thinks that Wittgenstein's later philosophy had turned away from any concern with the world and our relation to it. Once again I do not think this is true. But this is an even larger question than any I have mentioned, and it would be hopeless to try to explain it here. Perhaps it seemed to Russell that, for Wittgenstein, philosophy had become a matter of clearing up linguistic muddles and curing people's headaches. And there would be no concern with the world in that; but only, as Russell puts it, "with the different ways in which silly people can say silly things."

Philosophy as therapy: as though the philosopher's interest were in the personal disabilities of the perplexed: and as though he were not perplexed himself—as though philosophy were not discussion. Some remarks which Wittgenstein himself made are partly responsible for this. But he was suggesting an analogy with therapy; and he was doing this in an attempt to bring out certain features in the method of philosophy: to show the difference between what you have to do here and what you would do in solving a problem in mathematics or in science. It was not a suggestion about what it is that philosophy is interested in. If Wittgenstein spoke of "treatment," it is the problem, or the question, that is treated—not the person raising it. It is not the personal malaise of the "patient" which makes the perplexity or question important. What has led me to this perplexity is not my personal stupidity. Rather it is a tendency in the language which could lead *anyone* there, and keeps leading people there. This is why Wittgenstein or anyone doing philosophy can understand the difficulty and the discussion of it. In this respect it is no more personal than the problems of science are.

If it were a silly question—then I suppose it *would* be personal. What makes the questions deep and important is just that they are not this. And for this reason you do learn something from the discussion: it is not as though you were simply being restored to a normal state of mind. What makes you ask questions in philosophy is not a personal misfortune. And what can "cure" you is philosophy, is discussion, is understanding. If you do not understand, then you will not have benefited in any way. And this shows that the benefit cannot rightly be described as a "cure."

I think someone has asked: "Why does Wittgenstein think language so important? Why does he think the truth is to be found there?" He did not think so. He thought language was important first of all because of its obvious connections with logic—because logic has to do with propositions, if you like. But he also said sometimes that philosophical difficulties arise because we cannot get an overall view of the grammar of the language we are using. I am not sure he would have put it exactly like this at the end, but in any case it does not mean that an overall view of the grammar would give you the *answer* to philosophical questions. For they are not questions about language. The man who is puzzled about the nature of thought is not puzzled about language; he is puzzled about thought: and similarly if he is puzzled about chance and necessity, or about the relation between sensations and physical objects, or whatever it may be. Wittgenstein was aware of this, and he emphasized it in his lectures.

And these questions about thought or about things and sensations have to be discussed. The difficulties in understanding what thought is, for instance, have to be met in some way. If we say that the discussion helps us to get an overall view of the grammar of the word "thought," this does not mean that if you had had the grammar set out before you in a kind of map, you would have seen everything you want to know. The grammar is not something that could be set out in a map, anyway. It is something that appears *in* discussion. And the only way of helping anyone to understand is by the kind of discussion that is given in philosophy.

Recollections of Wittgenstein

BY WOLFE MAYS

I FIRST WENT TO WITTGENSTEIN'S LECTURES in Cambridge early in 1940, and I attended them regularly until he left to work as a hospital orderly a year or two later. World War II had recently broken out and there were not too many philosophy students at Cambridge. I must admit that I went to his lectures not because I was a Wittgenstein enthusiast, but because it seemed a pity when in Cambridge not to do so.

The number of people present at his lectures was never more than a dozen. The lectures took place in two-hour sessions twice a week from 4 to 6 P.M. in his rooms at the top of Whewell's Court in Trinity. As biographers of Wittgenstein have by now made well known, the room (his study) in which he held his lectures was sparsely furnished, with a black cylindrical stove in the center from which a chimney pipe went up to the ceiling. He must have had the stove installed himself; having lived on the Continent he apparently did not appreciate the English open fire. During his lectures he sat by the stove in a deck chair, sometimes warming a hand near it. Close to the window there was a small bookshelf on which I noticed, among other things, the plays of Hebbel, a textbook of anatomy and some Wild West magazines.

There was a pile of deck chairs outside the room, and you took one in with you on entering, seating yourself a respectful distance from Wittgenstein. He usually wore a fawn wind cheater, open shirt, grey flannel trousers and heavy brown shoes. His face was lined and, although gaunt, still had a youthful appearance despite his crop of iron-grey hair. He was a little deaf in one ear. This he told me was the result of an explosion when he was in the Austrian Army in World War I. His English was fairly racy and he did not speak with much of a foreign accent. When annoyed he would quite commonly use expletives such as "damn."

Wittgenstein would not let you attend his class unless you agreed

to come regularly. On your first appearance he gave you something like a screening, and tried to dissuade you from coming if
he thought you were not a serious student. Some of the members
of the class during this period were Robert Thouless, Timothy
Moore (G. E. Moore's son), Mardiros, Smythies, Körner, Elizabeth Anscombe, Lewy and Rose Rand. Wittgenstein did not like
people coming late, and he got very tense when he heard someone
coming up the stairs five minutes past the hour. He put up his
head and stared into the distance as if he was looking past the wall,
at the same time drawing in his breath as the footsteps came nearer.

At first I found the man and his manner somewhat strange, and
I felt a little scared of him. His prominent staring eyes, intensity of
manner, and irritability, which no doubt showed that he was usually at a high level of anxiety, heightened this. Basically, he seemed
to be an extremely decent sort of person; I can well imagine that
he could be a loyal and pleasant companion with his intimate
friends. I was once invited to have tea with him in his room. He
was just returning from buying buns at a nearby cake shop, when
I arrived. He did not have any tea himself, but poured out some
for me in a mug. While I ate the buns and drank the tea, he talked
to me and asked questions. On another occasion I had supper with
him at a Chinese restaurant.

I could not help feeling that his academic situation as a professor of philosophy made life difficult for him. One could imagine
Wittgenstein as a musician, an artist or an architect, but certainly
not as an academic. He did not have the pedantic or legalistic
type of mind which is the trademark of some philosophers. His
approach to philosophical problems was essentially aesthetic in the
widest sense. He had a very strong, almost abnormal imagery, and
this came out in the bizarre examples he used to produce in class
to illustrate his arguments. For example, he likened his soul to a
yellow spot over his shoulder. In the manner of Dean Swift he once
tried to draw an analogy between the faces of men and those of
animals. You can often, he said, see in one man the resemblance
of a horse, in another that of a pig and in another that of a dog.
To illustrate the expressionist character of language he suggested
that we try swearing at a dog in an affectionate tone of voice, and
to bring out the arbitrary nature of naming, he argued that we
might christen the piece of chalk he was holding in his hand
"Jack."

It is doubtful whether Wittgenstein had anything like a lecturing technique, as he never gave what ordinarily could be called lectures. He used to sit in his deck chair and discuss particular topics in an informal way. Since he did not use notes he frequently had mental blocks, when he ran dry both of words and ideas, and there were then embarrassing silences. When this happened he usually asked members of the class to put questions to him in order to stimulate his thinking. During these pauses he remained seated, jaw in hand, eyes closed, shaking his bent head slowly, an attitude copied by some of his disciples. He certainly gave the impression that thinking was a difficult business. On such occasions I was never quite sure whether he had run out of material, was off color, or was using these pauses for effect. Wittgenstein would become distressed if the class was unable to continue, and we had to finish at 5 or 5:30 P.M.

It has been said that Wittgenstein was a living example of the Socratic method, since often his lectures simply consisted of an interchange of question and answer between himself and the class. It did seem that he had difficulty in producing a connected lecture. He obviously tried to think out philosophical problems afresh and did not rely for inspiration on the most recent articles in *Mind*. I was told that he would lie awake at night thinking seriously what he was going to say. Despite this, he gave the impression at times that his lectures were inadequately prepared, although he must have frequently spoken about the same topics over the years. In evaluating Wittgenstein as a teacher, it must be remembered that during his Cambridge period from 1929 to 1947, he only lectured on the topics of his choice, without needing to do routine teaching. He also did not seem to supervise graduate students and did not, as far as I know, invigilate at examinations or mark examination papers.

Wittgenstein disliked us to take notes during his classes, and he would prevent anyone who was foolhardy enough to try. He did, however, allow Smythies to take notes. It never occurred to me then that these notes were destined to become parts of the *Philosophical Investigations*. I was told that Wittgenstein also used to dictate in German to a shorthand typist parts of a book he was writing, presumably the *Investigations*. At that time I was unaware of the surreptitious circulation of the Blue and Brown books, and that Wittgenstein strongly objected to the pirating of his ideas. Nothing that I heard in the class would seem to indicate that he was at all religiously inclined. He also seemed to be distinctively apolitical, despite his desire to live in Russia.

Wittgenstein rarely took part in official university ceremonies. I was told that he once appeared wearing a gown at the formal admission of the eminent historian G. M. Trevelyan as Master of Trinity. Apart from Wittgenstein's musical interests—he played, I believe, the violin—he was in many ways a lowbrow. There was a crop of stories dealing with his avid reading of Wild West stories, and how he often used to sit in the front row of a cinema in the Chesterton Road seeing Wild West films.

Wittgenstein, who had a certain flair for the dramatic, liked to show off during a discussion. I was told, although I cannot vouch for the truth of this, that the rule excluding faculty members from starred meetings (at which students read papers) of the Moral Sciences Club, was largely directed against Wittgenstein. When attending a meeting he tended to monopolize the discussion and students were somewhat intimidated by him. At one nonstarred meeting of the Club held in Braithwaite's rooms in King's, both Moore and Russell were present. I forget the nature of the topic being discussed, but although Moore did not stand up to Wittgenstein in discussion, Russell certainly did and gave as good as he got. At another meeting in Broad's rooms in Trinity, when G. F. Hardy was reading a paper based on his book *A Mathematician's Apology,* Hardy mentioned that he did not accept Wittgenstein's view that mathematics consisted of tautologies. Wittgenstein denied that he had ever said this, and pointed to himself saying in an incredulous tone of voice, "Who, I?"

When Wittgenstein discussed philosophical questions, he did so with zest and intensity. He poked fun at traditional modes of philosophizing, and he used the bed-maker (i.e., female college servant) as a measuring rod when traditional philosophical arguments were raised in the class. "What," he would ask, "would my bed-maker say of this kind of abstract talk?" He once likened himself to Kant in a puckish sort of way, and he used to emphasize that philosophy was an activity rather than a subject. Wittgenstein invariably advised students not to become philosophers, but rather undertake some honest toil. Few of us liked to make objections during Wittgenstein's classes, as he had a tendency to deflate anyone critical of his views.

Wittgenstein's lectures were mainly devoted to questions of meaning, belief and the foundations of mathematics. When he was lecturing on belief he read extracts from James' *Principles of Psychology,* and discussed them critically. I was not at that time very sympathetic to Wittgenstein's behavioristic approach to the theory of meaning. I can now see that Wittgenstein was stressing in his lectures much more the expressive side of communication, through gesture, etc., rather than the cognitive aspects which tend to give meaning an essentialist character. When his disciples took over this approach, they emphasized the speech act as a form of behavior rather than the gesture. Was this I wonder because it is bad form for English speakers to talk with their hands?

Wittgenstein's discussion of meaning, and his criticism of the essentialist position, had something in common wth the approach of the functional anthropologist. His comparison of words to tools having different uses, i.e., meanings, in different contexts, reminded me strongly of the views of Malinowski. Malinowski noted that a cultural object such as a fish hook could have different functions according to its context of use. It could, for example, be used in one context for fishing and in another for ritual purposes. As far as I know, Wittgenstein did not actually regard words as cultural objects, but talked much more of the use of words in a fairly abstract way.

Wittgenstein often indulged in what I can only call speculative anthropology. This was particularly to be seen in the way he illustrated his arguments by reference to the behavior of hypothetical tribes. This seemed to be a variation of his method of using extreme cases, when he used striking examples to shake one out of an established philosophical position, a much more sophisticated approach than his use of the bed-maker as the "measure of all things." He might, for example, say, "Imagine how a particular tribe having a different culture could use such an expression to mean something different from what we mean." This method of philosophizing, namely, the use of the extreme or abnormal case, has been independently exploited by Sartre and Merleau-Ponty in their writings. Wittgenstein's own followers have largely concentrated on ordinary usage as the mark of philosophical respectability, although the usage referred to has been that of the university don and not that of the bed-maker.

In his lectures Wittgenstein made valiant efforts to quote examples to show that psychological data could be externalized.

He talked a good deal about the criteria for deciding whether a person was in pain or not. Suppose, he said, so and so was on the operating table and surgeons were sticking knives into him; if he showed no signs of reacting, could he therefore be said to be in pain, or was he shamming? In these examples Wittgenstein sometimes tended to regard other people as if they were inanimate objects or automata, as when he said, "Suppose I cut off Mr. X's arm thus," at the same time striking his own left arm with the edge of his right hand. I sometimes felt that this way of looking at other people covered something more than a philosophical position. It is, of course, possible that Wittgenstein's engineering background made him attempt to externalize psychological states and also to look upon people as automata.

Wittgenstein seemed to have little reading in the history of philosophy, although he had read St. Augustine, Pascal and Kent. One seldom heard the names of the great classical philosophers mentioned in his class. If he had been more conversant with the views of past philosophers, he might perhaps have used their positions as starting points for his discussions. Perhaps in some ways this was all to the good, since he did not get involved in making glosses on other philosophers' texts. Apart from his acquaintance with Frege and the Vienna Circle, Wittgenstein's knowledge of contemporary philosophers seemed restricted to those he met in Cambridge. Indeed, some of the philosophical positions he criticized in his *Philosophical Investigations,* bear a marked resemblance to positions accepted by some of his eminent Cambridge contemporaries.

There are aspects of Wittgenstein's philosophizing which are strongly reminiscent of certain tendencies in present-day existentialist thought. There could not have been any direct influence. If Wittgenstein did not read British philosophers, he certainly did not read Continental ones, with the possible exception of Kierkegaard. And yet there are some interesting points of resemblance: the emphasis in both kinds of philosophizing on the expressive aspects of language, the comparison of linguistic expression to musical expression, and the stress on behavior and social context as determiners of meaning. Wittgenstein's interest in the particular case rather than the general one has also something in common with the existentialist position, with its dislike of general principles and norms.

What has lingered in my mind over the years, as far as Wittgenstein's lectures were concerned, has been the stuffiness of the room in which they were held, the intellectual fog generated, and the puzzled look on the faces of his listeners. The awkward feeling you had Wittgenstein was going to pounce on you and ask a question to which you would give what he would consider to be a silly reply. Whether one agreed with Wittgenstein or not, there was certainly something about the man which distinguished him from the ordinary run of philosophers, if only for the fact that he did not look or behave like an academic. He had a charismatic quality which strongly attracted some students and put others off. Wittgenstein's writings get an added dimension if one knew him as a person. They are not, I think, of the sort of which it can be said that the personality of the writer is irrelevant to their understanding.

After Wittgenstein's death I found myself in touch with von Wright and von Hayek, who were interested in learning what Wittgenstein had been doing in Manchester before he first went to Cambridge. By a happy accident I met Mr. Eccles, who was just on the point of retiring from the staff of the engineering works of Metropolitan Vickers in Manchester. He was able to give me valuable information about Wittgenstein's Manchester period.

Before he went to Cambridge for the first time, Wittgenstein lived for some years in Manchester, and until recently little was known about this period of his life. The only information available was that at the age of nineteen he came to Manchester from the Technische Hochschule Charlottenburg, Berlin, where he had studied engineering, and that he had left Vienna about a year earlier. He registered as a student doing research in the Engineering Laboratory in the autumn of 1908, where according to the records he remained from 1908 to 1910.

I was interested in discovering something about Wittgenstein's Manchester period, and a letter in the *Guardian* produced a telephone call the next day from a very old friend of Wittgenstein's, Mr. W. Eccles ("W.E.") an engineer who had been a fellow-student when Wittgenstein had worked in the Engineering Laboratory. He was able to give me valuable information about this period, and additional information was also given by Mr. J. Bamber, former steward of the Engineering Laboratory, and Mr. C. M. Mason, the former Assistant Director. The university records showed that Wittgenstein was elected by the Senate to a research studentship in 1910 and again in 1911, and it is also known that in 1911 he lived at 104 Palatine Road, Withington.

It seems clear that Wittgenstein came to Manchester to do research in aeronautics; he brought with him some prints of early balloons which are now in "W.E.'s" possession. They have recently been identified by the Royal Aeronautical Society and do not seem to have been as important as Wittgenstein thought them to be.

W.E. first met Wittgenstein at the Grouse Inn on the Glossop-Hayfield road in the summer of 1908, where the latter had come to try out some experimental kites using the equipment of the upper atmosphere research station which was being run under the direction of Dr. Schuster, Professor of Physics at the University of Manchester. A photograph taken about 1908 at Glossop shows them both holding an experimental kite, with the Grouse Inn in the background.

They stayed together at the Grouse Inn, while each carried on with his own experimental work. Wittgenstein had arrived some time before, and "W.E." found him in the common living-room surrounded with books and papers on the table and also on the floor. As it was impossible to move about the room without disturbing books he set to and tidied the place up, much to Wittgenstein's amusement and subsequent appreciation—the beginning of a very close friendship.

When he first came to Manchester, Wittgenstein was very wealthy, and though he never lived ostentatiously he did not hesitate to get anything he wanted. One Sunday morning in Manchester in 1910, for example, he decided that he would like to go to Blackpool. He and "W.E." therefore went off together to the railway station and when told that there was no suitable train he said he would try to hire a special train—still possible in those days. He was finally dissuaded by "W.E." and instead they took a taxi to Liverpool, a distance of nearly forty miles, and had a trip on the Mersey ferry before returning to Manchester.

Wittgenstein's experimental work with kites did not last long, as he soon realised that until some form of engine was available it was not much use developing an aeroplane. By a stroke of good fortune the plans still exist of his experimental engine, and are in "W. E.'s" possession. Wittgenstein hit on the idea of having a reaction jet at the tip of each blade of a propeller powered by hot gases coming from a combustion chamber. It is not known how he came to have this idea, although the principle underlying his engine is a simple one, found in antiquity in the model steam turbine constructed by

Hero of Alexandria. Hero's device consists of a chamber containing water from which steam is generated by the application of heat; the chamber is surmounted by rotating arms. The steam under pressure forces itself through the channels in the arms, and in escaping it causes them to rotate. A more familiar illustration of this principle is to be found in the rotating water-sprinklers which we use to water our lawns.

Wittgenstein soon realised that the design of the combustion chamber with its discharge nozzle for the hot gases was all important. Accordingly he transferred his interests from the moors at Glossop to the laboratory of the Engineering Department. He had a variable volume combustion chamber constructed by Messrs. Cook near by, and had it arranged for a variety of fuel spray and gas discharge nozzles. The whole assembly was workmanlike and practical for its purpose. The jet of hot gas from the discharge nozzle on top was arranged to impinge on a deflector plate where its reaction could be measured. This apparatus was operated successfully, but before much experimental work was done with it Wittgenstein became interested in the design of the propeller. As this lent itself to a completely mathematical treatment his interests in mathematics developed, and eventually in turn the propeller was forgotten. No doubt it was these newly found mathematical interests which led him to migrate to Cambridge, and there to study mathematical logic with Russell.

It is of some interest to note that Wittgenstein's idea of a combustion chamber together with a tangential reaction nozzle at the tip of a propeller blade did get a practical application at a much later date. It was brought into practical use for the rotor blade of a helicopter by the Austrian designer Doplhoff during the Second World War. It has now been adopted by Fairey's for their Jet Gyrodyne, as well as by other aviation firms.

Mr. Mason reports that he clearly remembers helping Wittgenstein to set up some heavy apparatus in the laboratory, presumably the combustion chamber, and that he did not appear very adept in handling the apparatus at that time. Mr. Bamber, with whom Wittgenstein was very friendly, says that he did not think that Wittgenstein's nervous disposition helped him in his work on the combustion chamber. When anything went wrong with the apparatus he used to stamp, throw his arms about, and swear volubly in German. As far as his work and leisure activities were concerned, Mr. Bamber tells us: "He used to ignore the midday meal break and carry on till evening, and in his lodgings in Fallowfield his pastime was to relax in a bathful of *very* hot water. . . . He had great musical appreciation, and only for the more profound composers: Wagner, Beethoven, Brahms, &c. I used to attend the Hallé concerts with him occasionally and he used to sit through the concert without speaking a word, completely absorbed."

A number of letters and postcards from Wittgenstein to "W.E." are still in the possession of the latter. Most of them deal with family and personal matters, and also with Wittgenstein's election to a Research Fellowship at Trinity College, Cambridge in 1930, and in 1939 to the Professorship of Philosophy. One or two letters dated 1925 speak of a change which had come over him. He fears that the great events, external and internal, that lie between him and his English friends might prevent them from understanding one another. In answering an invitation from "W.E." to come to England, he says: "England may not have changed since 1913 but I have. However, it is no use writing to you about that as I could not explain to you the exact nature of the change (although I perfectly understand it). You will see it yourself when I get there."

Mrs. Eccles remembers being surprised by the great change in Wittgenstein, when he eventually did come to stay with them in Manchester. As a young man he had always been immaculately dressed, and as might be expected somewhat of a favourite with the ladies. When they met him at the railway station he was dressed fairly shabbily and in what seemed to be a Boy Scout uniform. She also remembers that during his stay he asked her to obtain a copy of his book *Tractatus Logico-Philosophicus,* which he had apparently not yet seen. However, no Manchester bookseller had one in stock. Finally the university library lent him their copy. The whole episode seems rather strange, as the publisher would most probably have sent him copies, although it is possible that they may not have reached him, as at that time he was teaching in a small Austrian mountain village.

Wittgenstein:
Unphilosophical Notes [1]

BY ERICH HELLER

1

WHAT MANNER OF MAN was Ludwig Wittgenstein? One answer which is easy to come by, vague, large, and true, is: a man of rarest genius. Of all words that defy definition—which may be, simply, all words—genius is the most defiant. But how else describe a man who was a logician of the first order; a writer of German prose abundant in intellectual passion and disciplined clarity (perhaps only talent is needed for writing such prose in any other language, but certainly genius for writing it in German); an engineer of great promise and some achievement; the architect of a modern mansion; a gifted sculptor; a musician who very probably would have become, had he chosen this career, a remarkable conductor; a hermit capable of enduring for long periods the utmost rigors of mind and loneliness; a rich man who chose poverty; a Cambridge professor who thought and taught but neither lectured nor dined?

He was also an Austrian who conquered British philosophy; but this, as befits Austrian conquests, was due to a misunderstanding.

[1] The original occasion of this essay was the appearance of Ludwig Wittgenstein's *The Blue and Brown Books* (Oxford: Basil Blackwell, 1958; New York: Harper, 1958), and Norman Malcolm's *Ludwig Wittgenstein, A Memoir*, with a biographical sketch by Georg Henrik von Wright (London and New York: Oxford University Press, 1958). *The Blue and Brown Books*, prefaced by Mr. Rush Rhees, were dictated by Wittgenstein to some of his pupils between 1933 and 1935. They are indispensable for any study of the intellectual history that led, within the lifetime of the mature generation of Anglo-Saxon philosophers, to a change in philosophical opinion—a break outwardly less dramatic but probably more significant than that which occurred when Bertrand Russell and G. E. Moore banished the very much post-Hegelian metaphysics of F. H. Bradley and Bernard Bosanquet from the academic scene; and it was the most strange characteristic of that new "revolution" that it was the same man, Ludwig Wittgenstein, who both perfected the "old system" (in the *Tractatus Logico-Philosophicus*, finished by 1918, first published in 1921) *and* initiated its destruction (with *Philosophical Investigations*, completed by 1949, posthumously published in 1953). Mr. Malcolm's *Memoir*, greatly assisted by Professor Wright's informative sketch, is a noble biographical document, the more moving by virtue of its simplicity and affectionate restraint. It is from this book that the biographical references of my notes are taken.

At least he himself believed that it was so. When the pages of the journal *Mind* were filled with variations on his philosophical themes, he praised a certain American magazine of detective stories, and wondered how, with the offer of such reading matter, "anyone can read *Mind* with all its impotence and bankruptcy"; [2] and when his influence at Oxford was at its height, he referred to the place as "a philosophical desert" and as "the influenza area." [3] These were ironical exaggerations, but undoubtedly serious expressions of Wittgenstein's discontent.

Why should he have been so displeased with the role his thought played in contemporary philosophical circles? What was the source of his suspicion that a misunderstanding was viciously at work in the proliferation of his views and methods throughout the departments of philosophy? And if it was a misunderstanding, was it avoidable? These questions raise a bigger one: What is the nature of philosophical opinion?

There are philosophies which, however difficult they may be, are in principle easy to teach and to learn. Of course, not everyone can teach or learn philosophy—any more than higher mathematics; but the philosophies of certain philosophers have this in common with higher mathematics: they present the simple alternative of being either understood or not understood. It is, in the last analysis, impossible to *mis*understand them. This is true of Aristotle, or St. Thomas Aquinas, or Descartes, or Locke, or Kant. Such philosophies are like mountains: you climb to their tops or you give up; or like weights: you lift them or they are too heavy for you. In either case you will know what has happened and "where you are." But this is not so with the thought of Plato, or St. Augustine, or Pascal, or Kierkegaard, or Nietzsche. Their philosophies are like human faces on the features of which are inscribed, disquietingly, the destinies of souls; or like cities rich in history. "Do you understand Nietzsche?" is like asking "Do you know Rome?" The answer is simple only if you have never been there. The trouble with Wittgenstein's thinking is that it sometimes looks like Descartes': you believe you can learn it as you learn logic or mathematics; but it almost always is more like Pascal's: you may be quite sure you cannot. For to understand it on its own level is as much a matter of imagination and character as it is one of

---

[2] Norman Malcolm, *Ludwig Wittgenstein, A Memoir* (London and New York, 1958), p. 35 f.
[3] *Ibid.*, p. 98.

"thinking." Its temperature is of its essence, in its passion lies its seriousness, the rhythm of the sentences that express it is as telling as is that which they tell, and sometimes a semicolon marks the frontier between a thought and a triviality. How can this be? Are we speaking of an artist or a philosopher? We are speaking of Ludwig Wittgenstein. *"Der Philosoph behandelt eine Frage; wie eine Krankheit."* It is a profound semicolon, and not even a philosophically initiated translator could save the profundity: "The philosopher's treatment of a question is like the treatment of an illness" is, by comparison, a flat *aperçu.*[4]

Philosophy, for Wittgenstein, was not a profession; it was a consuming passion; and not just "a" passion, but the only possible form of his existence: the thought of losing his gift for philosophy made him feel suicidal. He could not but have contempt for philosophers who "did" philosophy and, having done it, thought of other things: money, lists of publications, academic advancements, university intrigues, love affairs, or the Athenaeum—and thought of these things in a manner which showed even more clearly than the products of their philosophical thought that they had philosophized with much less than their whole person. Wittgenstein had no difficulty in detecting in their style of thinking, debating, or writing the corruption of the divided life, the painless jugglery with words and meanings, the shallow flirtation with depth, and the ear deaf to the command of authenticity. Thinking for him was as much a moral as an intellectual concern. In this lay his affinity with Otto Weininger, for whom he had great respect. The sight of a thought that was detachable from a man filled him with loathing and with an anger very much like that with which Rilke in the Fourth of the *Duino Elegies* denounced, through the image of the dancer, the cursed nonidentity between performer and performance:

> . . . How gracefully he moves!
> And yet he is disguised, a dressed-up philistine,
> Who will come home soon, entering through the kitchen.
> I cannot bear these masks, half-filled with life.

Had Wittgenstein ever cared to write about himself, this apparently most "intellectual" of philosophers might have said:

> I have at all times thought with my whole body and my whole life. I do not know what purely intellectual problems are. . . ,

[4] Ludwig Wittgenstein, *Philosophical Investigations,* tr. by G. E. M. Anscombe (Oxford, 1953), §255.

You know these things by way of thinking, yet your thought is not your experience by the reverberation of the experience of others; as your room trembles when a carriage passes. I am sitting in that carriage, and often am the carriage itself.

This, however, was written by Nietzsche.[5] And it was Nietzsche whom he resembled in many other ways: in his homelessness, his restless wanderings, his perpetual search for the exactly right conditions in which to work, his loneliness, his asceticism, his need for affection and his shyness in giving it, his intellectual extremism which drove thought to the border of insanity, the elasticity of his style, and (as we shall see) in one philosophically most important respect. Like Nietzsche, then, he knew that philosophical opinion was not merely a matter of logically demonstrable right or wrong. This most rigorous logician was convinced that it was above all a matter of authenticity—and thus, in a sense, not at all of negotiable opinions. What assumed with him so often the semblance of intolerable intellectual pride, was the demand, which he made upon himself still more than upon others, that all utterances should be absolutely authentic. The question was not only "Is this opinion right or wrong?" but also "Is this or that person *entitled* to this or that opinion?" At times this lent to his manner of debating the harsh tone of the Old Testament prophets: he would suddenly be seized by an uncontrollable desire to mete out intellectual punishment. He reacted to errors of judgment as if they were sins of the heart, and violently rejected opinions, which in themselves—if this distinction were possible—might have been harmless enough or even "correct," and rejected them because they were untrue in the self that uttered them: they lacked the sanction of the moral and intellectual pain suffered on behalf of truth.

Wittgenstein once said, using a comparison with swimming, that "just as one's body has a natural tendency towards the surface and one has to make an exertion to get to the bottom—so it is with thinking." And in talking about the stature of a philosopher, he remarked "that the measure of a man's greatness would be in terms of what his work *cost* him." [6] This is Kantian ethics applied to the realm of thought: true moral goodness was for Kant a victory over natural inclination, the costlier the better. By character and insight, Nietzsche too was such a Kantian moralist of the intellectual life.

---

[5] Nietzsche, *Gesammelte Werke*, Musarion-Ausgabe (Munich, 1926–29), Vol. XXI, p. 81.
[6] Malcolm, *op. cit.*, p. 55.

Yet he, who was never more ingenious than in producing the devastating argument against himself, could also say this:

> The labor involved in climbing a mountain is no measure of its height. But where knowledge is concerned, it is to be different; at least this is what we are told by some who consider themselves intiates: the effort which a truth costs, is to decide its value! This crazy morality is founded upon the idea that "truths" are like the installations in a Swedish gymnasium, designed to tire one out—a morality of the mind's athletics and gymnastic displays.[7]

Perhaps it is a pity that Wittgenstein was not the man to say *also* things of this kind. It might have lightened the burden of earnest irritability carried by many a contemporary philosophical debate.

2

The appreciation of Wittgenstein as a person and thinker (and how misleading is this "and"!) is bedeviled by a persistent optical delusion: the high moral pathos of his life (in which his "legend" has already taken firm roots) *seems* at first glance to be unconnected with the drift and trend, the content and method of his philosophical thought. Every page of Pascal, or Kierkegaard, or Nietzsche, at once conveys, however impersonal may be the subject matter, a sense of urgent personal involvement; but it is possible for anyone but the most sensitively predisposed to read many pages of Wittgenstein's without suspecting that the ruthless precision and often apparently eccentric virtuosity of this thinking, which has neither models nor parallels in the history of philosophy, is anything but the result of the utmost intellectual detachment. Its first emotional effect upon the reader may well be one of exasperation or melancholia—the effect which Robert Musil (not for nothing an Austrian contemporary of Wittgenstein's) ascribes in *The Man without Qualities* to a certain thinker:

> He had drawn the curtains and worked in the subdued light of his room like an acrobat who, in an only half-illuminated circus tent and before the public is admitted, shows to a select audience of experts his latest break-neck leaps.[8]

Yet Wittgenstein's work is none the less suffused with authentic pathos, and it will one day be seen as an integral part of the tragically self-destructive design of European thought.

[7] Nietzsche, *op. cit.*, Vol. IX, p. 183.
[8] Robert Musil, *Der Mann ohne Eigenschaften* (Hamburg, 1952), p. 114.

If by some miracle both European history and thought continue, then the future historians of thought will be not a little puzzled by Wittgenstein. For nothing could be less predictable than that a work which more deeply than any other affected contemporary Anglo-Saxon philosophy, Wittgenstein's *Philosophical Investigations,* should have as its motto a sentence from the classical comic playwright of Austria, Nestroy, or that its philosophical author should have experienced a kind of religious awakening thanks to a performance of *Die Kreuzelscheiber* by Anzengruber, a considerably lesser Austrian dramatist.[9] However, these will be minor surprises, less important, certainly, than the discovery of the affinities between Wittgenstein's manner of thinking and writing and that of the great eighteenth-century German aphorist Lichtenberg.[10] But of greater weight still would be the realization that the name of Wittgenstein marks the historical point at which, most unexpectedly, the cool analytical intellect of British philosophy meets with those passions of mind and imagination which we associate first with Nietzsche and then, in manifold crystallizations, with such Austrians as Otto Weininger, Adolf Loos, Karl Kraus, Franz Kafka, and Robert Musil.

Like Otto Weininger, Wittgenstein believed in the surpassing ethical significance of thinking, and in thought as both a deeply personal and almost religiously suprapersonal dedication; with Adolf Loos he shared the rejection of all ornamental comforts and decorative relaxations of the mind, and the concentration on the purest lines of intellectual architecture; with Karl Kraus, he had in common the conviction that there is an inescapable bond between the forms of living, thinking, feeling, and the forms of language (Wittgenstein's dictum "Ethics and aesthetics are one and the same" [11] may serve as a perfect characterization of Karl Kraus's artistic *credo*). As far as Kafka and Musil are concerned, a comparison between their styles of writing (and therefore their modes of perception) and Wittgenstein's would certainly be as fruitful as that between his and Lichtenberg's, and the more revealing because there can be no question of influence beyond the anonymous and peculiarly Austrian dispensations of the *Zeitgeist*. There even is a

[9] Malcolm, *op. cit.*, p. 70.
[10] Professor Wright was, to my knowledge, the first to draw attention to this; a fuller discussion of this intellectual kinship can be found in J. P. Stern's book on Lichtenberg, *A Doctrine of Occasions* (Bloomington, Ind., 1959).
[11] Ludwig Wittgenstein, *Tractatus Logico-Philosophicus*, tr. by D. F. Pears and B. F. McGuiness (London and New York, 1961), §6.421.

family resemblance between the logical structures, motives, and intentions of Wittgenstein's *Tractatus* and those of Schönberg's musical theory: for Schönberg too is guided by the conviction that the "language" of his medium, music, has to be raised to that level of logical necessity which would eliminate all subjective accidents. It is in such a constellation of minds that Wittgenstein is truly at home, whereas in the history of British philosophy he may merely "hold an important position." This, at least, is one way of accounting for the discomforts he suffered from the British philosophical climate and from a philosophical company which so deceptively appeared to consist largely of his own disciples.

What are the motives and intentions behind Wittgenstein's philosophy? What is, beyond and above its own philosophical declarations, the historical meaning of that "revolution" which changed the face of Anglo-Saxon philosophy in the course of Wittgenstein's gradual modification and final abandonment of some of the principles laid down in his *Tractatus Logico-Philosophicus?*

In his book *My Philosophical Development,* Bertrand Russell engages in a bitter attack on the author of *Philosophical Investigations,* a broadside which, if it is not damaging, is yet illuminating. The man who was one of the first to recognize Wittgenstein's *Tractatus* as a work of philosophical genius (even if he interpreted it too exclusively as the culmination of his own doctrine of Logical Atomism) says of the *Philosophical Investigations* that he has not found in it "anything interesting"—"I cannot understand why a whole school finds important wisdom in its pages." He abhors the suggestion, which he believes to be implied in Wittgenstein's later work, "that the world of language can be quite divorced from the world of fact," and suspects that such a view must render philosophical activity trivial ("at best, a slight help to lexicographers, and at worst, an idle tea-table amusement") by insidiously giving to "language an untrammelled freedom which it has never hitherto enjoyed." He disagrees most emphatically with the disciples of Wittgenstein when they tend to regard "as an outdated folly the desire to understand the world"—a desire, it would seem, very different from their own to understand the working of language. If incomprehension can ever be significant, then this can be said of Lord Russell's estimate of *Philosophical Investigations.* For he certainly knew what he attacked when once upon a time he victoriously fought the domineering influence of Bradley's Idealism, and also knew what he welcomed when Wittgenstein first sent him the *Tractatus;* but the later Wittgenstein is to him, he confesses, "completely unintelligible." [12] This might clearly show which of the two recent changes in philosophical outlook—Russell's dislodging of Bradley, or Wittgenstein's superseding of Wittgenstein—is the more profound.

Bertrand Russell was at ease intellectually with Bradley as well as with the Wittgenstein of the *Tractatus* because both were, like himself, philosophers thinking *within* the metaphysical tradition of European philosophy. This goes without saying in the case of Bradley; in the case of the *Tractatus* it may sound alarming. But it is true to say that in its own way—and an exceedingly subtle way it is!—the *Tractatus* participates in a pre-Kantian metaphysical faith: there is, in however small an area of human understanding, a preestablished correspondence between the cognitive faculties of man and the nature of the world. In other words: what man thinks and feels—and therefore *says*—about the world, has a chance of being true in a *metaphysical* sense. At a time when philosophers were still on intimate terms with God, this metaphysical faith found its luminously comprehensive dogma: God is no deceiver; He has created the world and planted in man the desire to understand it; He has also endowed him with perception and rationality, faculties which man cannot help taking for the servants of this desire. Could it have been God's intention to frustrate it from the outset by giving man nothing but the *illusion* of understanding? Is the creature made in His own image to be the eternal dupe of the universe? The simple faith that this cannot be lies at the heart of the complex metaphysical systems of the seventeenth century that have profoundly affected European thought. This faith is discernible behind the scholastic apparatus of Leibniz's Preestablished Harmony and Descartes' *Cogito ergo sum,* those grandiose attempts to demonstrate logically the integral accord between human thought and the true nature of Being. And it is the same faith in reason's power to "comprehend the wondrous architecture of the world," which inspires the great cosmic discoveries of that age; or as Kepler puts it at the end of the ninth chapter of the fifth book of his *Harmonices mundi:* "Thanks be unto you, my Lord Creator! . . . To those men who will read my demonstrations, I have revealed the glory of your creation. . . ."

[12] Bertrand Russell, *My Philosophical Development* (New York, 1959), p. 216 ff.

It is a far cry from Descartes to Wittgenstein's *Tractatus;* and yet there is an angle of vision from which the *Tractatus* looks like a last victory of the traditional metaphysical faith: a Pyrrhic victory. Compared to the vast dominions that metaphysical thought had claimed in the past for its settlements of truth, there is now hardly more than a little province of "significant" speech in a vast area of silence. But within this catastrophically narrowed space, man can still confidently assert some truths about the world, utter words whose meanings are not imprisoned within themselves, and speak sentences whose significance is not wholly embedded within the flux of linguistic commerce and convention. No, there are still words and sentences which are true in an absolute sense, reflect what "is the case" and *picture Reality*. Of course, this ideal correspondence between picture and model, thought and world, language and reality, is not easily attained. Its condition is the observance of the strictest logical rules. Thus it will hardly ever occur in the actuality of human speech. Yet it is realized, nevertheless, in the *essence* of language: indeed, it is its *real meaning*. True, in order to speak "essentially" and "significantly," we must leave much unsaid; but once we respond to the "atomic facts"— the bricks of the intelligible world—with "atomic propositions" or their "truth-functional compounds"—concepts which Wittgenstein, considerably modifying and refining them, took over from Russell —our speech, and therefore our thought, is perfectly attuned to Reality: for "Logic is not a body of doctrine, but a mirror-image of the world." [13] And although Wittgenstein courageously insisted that in proposing this relationship between language and fact he himself broke the law governing meaningful propositions,[14] his *Tractatus* is yet built upon a site salvaged from the metaphysical estate of the Preestablished Harmony. The ground, however, was soon to give; and as it gave, Bertrand Russell, for one, saw nothing but total collapse. And it is true to say that from the *Blue Books* onward Wittgenstein immersed himself in a philosophical enterprise which, if set up against the traditional hopes of philosophers, looks desperate indeed. For its intention is to cure philosophers of a sickness the name of which may well be—philosophy. His aphorism of the philosopher's treating questions as if they were patients has more than epigrammatic relevance.

[13] *Tractatus,* §6.13.
[14] *Ibid.,* §6.54.

3

The break between *Tratactus* and *Philosophical Investigations* is of the same kind as that between Nietzsche's *The Birth of Tragedy* (1871) and his *Human, All-too-Human* (1879). In both cases it was brought about by the abnegation of metaphysics, the loss of faith in any preestablished correspondence between, on the one hand, the logic of our thought and language, and, on the other hand, the "logic" of Reality. In the course of those eight years stretching from *The Birth of Tragedy* to *Human, All-too-Human,* Nietzsche came to believe that he had freed himself of this "philosophical prejudice"—which he diagnosed as the prejudice vitiating the whole history of thought—by turning (to use Wittgenstein's obviously autobiographical words from *Investigations*) his "whole examination round. (One might say: the axis of reference of our examination must be rotated, but about the fixed point of our real need.)" [15] It is no exaggeration to say that Nietzsche could have written this. Indeed, it might serve as an exact description of what he claimed as his great achievement: to have turned our whole horizon 180 degrees around the point of our "real need," which was radically different from that

> which had been satisfied in forming the . . . [traditional] categories of thought; namely the need not to "recognize" but to subsume, to schematize, and, for the sake of communication and calcula- tion, to manipulate and fabricate similarities and samenesses. . . . No, this was not the work of a pre-existent "Idea"; it happened under the persuasion of usefulness: it was profitable to coarsen and level down things; for only then were they calculable and comfortable. . . . Our categories are "truths" only in so far as they make life possible for us: Euclidean space is also such a purpose- ful "truth." . . . The inner compulsion not to contradict these "truths," the instinct to reach our kind of useful conclusions is inbred in us, we almost *are* this instinct. But how naive to take this as proof of a "truth *per se.*" Our inability to contradict proves impotence and not "truth." [16]

It was Nietzsche's declared intention not to follow any longer this "instinct" and thus to cure the philosophical sickness of cen- turies, just as it was Wittgenstein's to "solve the philosophical problems" by recognizing their source in "the functioning of our

[15] *Investigations,* §108.
[16] Nietzsche, *op. cit.,* Vol XIX, p. 27 f.

language"—"*in spite* of an instinct to misunderstand it." [17] For
Nietzsche the truth about man was that he must live without Truth.
This was the "real need." The creature that would satisfy it
Nietzsche called Superman—and never mind the offensive word,
poetically begotten in a great mind by a Darwinian age. In his
letters he often used less grandiose, if not less ambitious, words in
speaking of his philosophical goal, words to the effect that "he
felt as though he were writing for people who would think in a
quite different way, breathe a different air of life from that of
present-day men: for people of a different culture. . . ." But this
is reported by Professor von Wright as a saying of Wittgenstein's.[18]

It would of course be absurd to represent Wittgenstein as a latter-
day Nietzsche, and the comparison is certainly not meant to
"manipulate and fabricate similarities and samenesses." The two
philosophers could hardly be more different in the scope and object,
the approach and humor, the key and tempo of their thought; and
yet they have in common something which is of the greatest importance: the creative distrust of *all* those categorical certainties
that, as if they were an inherited anatomy, have been allowed to
determine the body of traditional thought. Nietzsche and Wittgenstein share a genius for directing doubt into the most unsuspected
hiding places of error and fallacy: namely where, as Wittgenstein
puts it, "everything lies open to view," where everything is simple
and familiar, where, day in day out, man takes things for granted—
until suddenly one day the fact that he has habitually ignored the
most important aspects of things, strikes him as the "most striking
and most powerful." [19] This may happen on the day when suspicion reaches the notion of "meaning," that is, the idea, held however vaguely, that through some kind of cosmic arrangement, made
by God, or logic, or the spirit of language, a definite meaning had
become attached to the world, to life, to facts, or to words. When
Nietzsche discovered the "death of God," the universe of meanings
collapsed—everything, that is, that was founded upon the trans-
cendent faith, or was leaning against it, or was intertwined with it:
in fact, *everything,* as Nietzsche believed; and henceforward everything was in need of revaluation.

With Wittgenstein the decisive change of vision, which occurred
between *Tractatus* and *Investigations,* seemed centered upon an

[17] *Investigations,* §109.
[18] Malcolm, *op. cit.,* p. 2.
[19] *Investigations,* §§126, 129.

event less dramatic than the death of God; namely, the vanishing of the belief in a categorical logic of language, and hence in a categorically harmonious relationship between words and world. But the event behind the event was of the same magnitude as the Nietzchean demise of the divinity; it entailed the same crisis of metaphysical confidence that, through the metaphysical audacity of certain German and French thinkers, led to the great perversion of metaphysics: the loss of the belief in any metaphysically dependable dealings with Reality was made up by the notion that a Preestablished Absurdity determined the relationship between the intellectual constitution of man and the true constitution of the world. Nietzsche was the first to conceive of such a possibility, and after him European art and literature excelled in showing man and world laboring under the tragic, or melancholy, or grotesque, or hilarious compulsion to make nonsense of one another. And there is a historical sense in which the two extremes of contemporary philosophizing, Heidegger's tortuous metaphysical probings into language and Wittgenstein's absorption in language games (and some of the examples he chooses reveal an almost Thurberlike talent for absurd and grotesque inventions) can be seen as two aspects of the same intention: to track down to their source in language, and there to correct, the absurdities resulting from the human endeavor to speak the truth. It is an intention which was by no means alien to Nietzsche. Certainly his universal suspicion did not spare language, and some of his utterances on the subject are virtually indistinguishable from those of Wittgenstein.

Very early in his philosophical life, Nietzsche knew that he "who finds language interesting in itself has a mind different from him who only regards it as a medium of thought," and he left no doubt which of the two he regarded as the more *philosophical* mind: "Language is something all-too-familiar to us; therefore it needs a philosopher to be struck by it." [20] This is Nietzsche's way of saying what Wittgenstein said when he discovered that "the most important aspects of things are hidden from us by virtue of their simplicity and familiarity." [21] And when Nietzsche said that "the philosopher is caught in the net of *language*," [22] he meant much the same as Wittgenstein when, referring to his own *Tractatus,* he wrote: "A *picture* held us captive. And we could not get outside it, for it lay in our language and language seemed to repeat it to

[20] Nietzsche, *op. cit.*, Vol. II, p. 29.
[21] *Investigations*, §129.
[22] Nietzsche, *op. cit.*, Vol. VI, p. 45.

us inexorably." [23] Indeed, Nietzsche sounds as if he had in mind the metaphysics of the *Tractatus* when he speaks of the conclusion of a primitive metaphysical peace which once upon a time fixed "what henceforward is to be called truth": "A universally valid and compelling notation of facts is invented and the legislation of language fixes the principal rules for truth." This would seem to come close to what Wittgenstein attempted in the *Tractatus:* "To give the essence of a proposition means to give the essence of all description, and thus the essence of the world." [24] *But,* Nietzsche asked, "is language the adequate expression for all realities?" [25] And soon he was to be quite sure that it was not. On the contrary, the grammatical and syntactical order of language, its subjects, predicates, objects, causal and conditional connections, were "the petrified fallacies of reason" which continued to exercise their "seductive spell" upon our intelligence.[26]

> Philosophy is a battle against the bewitchment of our intelligence by means of language.

This last aphorism is by Wittgenstein;[27] but it would be impossible to guess where Nietzsche ends and Wittgenstein begins.

4

One of Wittgenstein's aphorisms runs as follows:

> Philosophy results in the discovery of one or another piece of simple nonsense, and in bruises which the understanding has suffered by bumping its head against the limits of language. They, the bruises, make us see the value of that discovery.[28]

And in one of the jottings of his late years Nietzsche wrote under the heading "Fundamental solution":

> Language is founded upon the most naive prejudices. . . . We read contradictions and problems into everything because we *think only* within the forms of language. . . . *We have to cease to think if we refuse to do it in the prisonhouse of language;* for we cannot reach further than the doubt which asks whether the

[23] *Investigations,* §115.
[24] *Tractatus,* §5.4711.
[25] Nietzsche, *op. cit.,* Vol. VI, p. 78.
[26] *Ibid.,* Vol. XV, p. 304 f.
[27] *Investigations,* §109.
[28] *Ibid.,* §119. This is one of Karl Kraus's aphorisms on language: "If I cannot get further, this is because I have banged my head against the wall of language. Then, with my head bleeding, I withdraw. And want to go on." (*Beim Wort genommen* [Munich, 1955], 326.)

limit we see is really a limit. . . . *All rational thought is interpreta-*
tion in accordance with a scheme which we cannot throw off.[29]

Yet neither Nietzsche nor Wittgenstein "ceased to think." In
Nietzsche's thought, the persistent misgiving that the established
conventions of philosophical language did not cater for our "real"
intellectual needs was only one facet of his central thesis: With the
death of God, with the silencing of that Word which was at the
beginning, *all* certainties of faith, belief, metaphysics, morality, and
knowledge had come to an end, and henceforward man was under
the terrible compulsion of absolute freedom. His choice was that
of either creating, with the surpassing creativity of the Creator, his
own world, or of spiritually perishing. For the world *as it is* has
neither meaning nor value. Meaning and value must be *given* to it:
by God or by man himself. If God is dead and man fails, then
nothing in this world has any value and our own language deceives
us with all its ancient intimations of higher meanings.

> In the world everything is as it is, and everything happens as it
> does happen: *in* it no value exists—and if it did, it would have no
> value.

These sentences from Wittgenstein's *Tractatus* [30] might have been
invented by Nietzsche—and many like these were in fact invented
by him in *The Will to Power,* where, as an inspired actor, indeed
as an initiate, he defined the mind of European nihilism which he
so urgently desired to overcome.

Wittgenstein's *Investigations* would be as trivial as Bertrand
Russell thinks they are, were they not, in their infinite intellectual
patience, informed with a sense of urgency not altogether unlike
that which inspired Nietzsche's prophetic impetuosity. To bring
some light into "the darkness of this time"—this was the hesitant
hope of the author of *Philosophical Investigations.* This hope, like
all true hope, was founded upon the paradox of faith: faith despite
doubt. It was, for Wittgenstein, a faith in language; and language
remained all-important for him even after it had ceased to be the
mirror of Reality. Having exposed all its dangers, shown how our
minds are held captive by its metaphors, denounced the witchcraft
with which it assails our intelligence, he was still left with the
ineradicable trust in its ultimate wisdom and its power to heal our
disease.

Nothing in Wittgenstein's work is more vulnerable to further

[29] Nietzsche, *op. cit.,* Vol. XIX, p. 84.
[30] *Tractatus,* §6.41.

questioning than this trust; indeed, its very intellectual vulnerability confirms it as his faith. Often he speaks of language with utmost vagueness:

> When philosophers use a word—"knowledge," "being," "object," "I," "proposition," "name,"—and try to grasp the *essence* of the thing, one must always ask oneself: is the word ever actually used in this way in the language in which it has its home? [31]

One may well ask: who, with language speaking in a hundred tongues through our literatures, dialects, social classes, journals, and newspapers, establishes this actual use? Shakespeare? Donne? James Joyce? the *Oxford English Dictionary?* the College Porter? the habitual reader of *The News of the World?* And when Wittgenstein says, "What *we* do is to bring words back from their metaphysical to their everyday usage," [32] or "When I talk about language, . . . I must speak the language of every day," [33] one is struck by the homely imprecision of this program and wonders why he does not wish to bring language back to Lichtenberg's or Gottfried Keller's usage, or speak the language of Karl Kraus, which is in fact much closer to Wittgenstein's than is the speech of a Vienna or London "every day"?

Wittgenstein said:

> Philosophy may in no way interfere with the actual use of language; it can in the end only describe it. . . . It leaves everything as it is. [34]

> We must do away with all explanation, and description alone must take its place. [35]

But might we not be "held captive" by a picture "actually used" in language, and can we be sure that "actual usage" will never "bewitch our intelligence"? And if it does, how are we to loosen its grip without "explaining" its nature? (And I am using "explain" here as it is "actually used.") Or is Schopenhauer, who so indignantly "interfered" with the corrupt use made of language by those who thoughtlessly speak or print it day in day out, guilty of errors of judgment *because* he wrote a prose inspired by a literary tradition which indeed he believed was being more and more betrayed by the everyday traffic in words? And what is the "everything"

---

[31] *Investigations*, §116. Was it the vagueness of this which induced the translator to use "language game" where the German has simply *"Sprache"*?
[32] *Ibid.*
[33] *Ibid.*, §120.
[34] *Ibid.*, §124.
[35] *Ibid.*, §109.

that philosophy "leaves as it is"? Not, surely, the manner of thinking and uttering thoughts. Many philosophers, like all great poets,
have deeply affected our perception, and therefore our language,
and thus have changed our world: Plato, for instance, or Descartes,
or Rousseau, or Kant, or Nietzsche, or indeed Wittgenstein.

When Wittgenstein speaks of the language of every day, he does
not mean what "actual usage" suggests he means. In fact, he means
Language—means something that is of surpassing importance as
the repository of our common humanity, of understanding, knowledge, and wisdom. Why then does he describe what he means with
the words "actual usage" or "the language of every day"? Is this
merely an uneasy concession made by a believer to an empiricist?
Or a way of denouncing the violations of language of which many
a philosopher has been guilty in his pursuit of spurious heights
and depths? This may be so. But he may have been prompted even
more by a Tolstoyan belief in the virtue of the simple life, a
belief that he applied to the life of language. Tolstoy indeed was
one of the very few writers of the nineteenth century who deeply
interested him; and thus it was perhaps a kind of linguistic Rous-
seauism that led Wittgenstein to insist upon "natural" language,
a language unspoiled by the dubious refinements of a philosophical
"civilization" which, having uprooted words from the ground of
their origin, had made them serve "unnatural" demands.

In *Investigations* there are, above all, two aphorisms that allow
the reader to observe how Wittgenstein avoids, in the manner of
an empiricist fighting shy of metaphysics, the open declaration of
his all-but-metaphysical faith in Language. This is the first:

> The problems arising through a misinterpretation of our forms
> of language have the character of *depth*. They are deep disquie-
> tudes; their roots are as deep in us as the forms of our language,
> and their significance is as great as the importance of our
> language.[36]

How true! And yet how disquieting is the word "misinterpretation"!
It seems to suggest that there is, or can be, an absolutely reliable
"rule" for deciding, philosophically or philologically, what is a
correct and what is a wrong "interpretation" of every particular
"form of language." But no such standard can apply. For to a
higher degree than is dreamt of in linguistic philosophy, language
has in common with other forms of human expression that it often
evades unambiguous "interpretation": it can be as purely allusive

[36] *Ibid.*, §111.

as are dance and gesture, as evanescent in meaning as is music, as ungrammatically extravagant as is life itself. No sooner have we left the field of logic, grammar, and syntax, than we have entered the sphere of aesthetics where we do not ask whether a writer "interprets" [37] words correctly, but whether he uses them well or badly: and whether or not he uses them well, depends not upon his ability to "interpret" them, but upon something more adequately described as a feeling for language, as sensibility, or as genius. However original such genius may be, tradition has helped to form it—tradition or, to use Wittgenstein's words, the particular "form of life" within which alone, according to him, language has its meaning: "to imagine a language means to imagine a form of life." [38] That this is so, is one of Wittgenstein's most striking realizations; and indeed it not only renders the "rules of language," as he well knew, logically unmanageable but also makes their "description," which he hoped for, a task that could not be fulfilled by even a legion of Prousts and Wittgensteins: for what is *the* "form of life" which, in one language, is shared by Goethe and Hitler, or, in another, by Keats and the *Daily News?*

With the "deep disquietudes" caused by a "misinterpretation of our forms of language," the quoted aphorism suggests something even more misleading than is the word "misinterpretation" itself. For the suggestion is that depth is a by-product of error. But if words like "depth" or "truth" or "error" are meaningful at all, then truth is deeper than falsehood; and indeed the suggestion is, as it were, withdrawn by the aphorism's very form and rhythm, which unmistakably intimate that language itself, not only its misinterpretation, has the character of depth, and that the disquietudes which arise from it are as deep as is the peace it may bring: through a great writer and even, rarely, through a philosopher whose thought is rooted in the mystery of words—or, to use the terms of the second aphorism we have had in mind, "in the ground of language." This second aphorism does indeed come close to revealing Wittgenstein's metaphysical secret. "What is it that gives to our investigation its importance," he asks with the voice of an imaginary interlocutor, "since it seems only to destroy everything interesting? (As it were all the buildings, leaving behind only bits of stone and rubble.)" And he replies: "What we are destroying is nothing but houses of cards and we are clearing up the ground of

[37] *Ibid.,* §§106, 107.
[38] *Ibid.,* §19.

language on which they stand." [39] The ground of language—it is a transparent metaphor; and what shines through it is a mystical light, even if there is nothing left for it to illuminate but a philosophical landscape most thoughtfully cleared of all the fragile and disfiguring edifices built throughout the ages by the victims of linguistic delusion, such as Plato, St. Thomas Aquinas, Spinoza, or Immanuel Kant, those "ancient thinkers" who, wherever they "placed a word," believed

> they had made a discovery. Yet the truth about it is quite different!
> —they had touched upon a problem and, deluding themselves they had solved it, put up an obstacle to its solution.—To come to know means now to stumble over petrified words that are as hard as stone, and to break one's leg rather than a word.

Wittgenstein? No, Nietzsche.[40]

It is an ending a little like that of Goethe's *Tasso* where a man, a poet, with all his certainties shattered, holds fast to his last possession: language. And it has remained an open question of literary interpretation whether that ending promises an ultimately happy consummation or a tragedy. Be this as it may, Wittgenstein was not a poet but a philosopher. And philosophy enters with Wittgenstein the stage which has been reached by many another creative activity of the human mind—by poetry, for instance, or by painting: the stage where every act of creation is inseparable from the critique of its medium, and every work, intensely reflecting upon itself, looks like the embodied doubt of its own possibility. It is a predicament which Nietzsche uncannily anticipated in a sketch entitled "A Fragment from the History of Posterity." Its subject is "The Last Philosopher." Having lost faith in a communicable world, he is imprisoned within his own self-consciousness. Nothing speaks to him any more—except his own speech; and, deprived of any authority from a divinely ordered universe, it is only about his speech that his speech can speak with a measure of philosophical assurance.[41]

In *Philosophical Investigations* Wittgenstein said: "What is your aim in philosophy?—To show the fly the way out of the fly-bottle." [42] But who asks? Who answers? And who is the fly? It is an unholy trinity; the three are one. This way lies no way out. This way lie only fly-bottles, and more and more fly-bottles.

[39] *Ibid.*, §118.
[40] Nietzsche, *op. cit.*, Vol. X, p. 49.
[41] *Ibid.*, Vol. VI, p. 36.
[42] *Investigations*, §309.

Wittgenstein, a Symbol of Troubled Times

BY JOSÉ FERRATER MORA

WITTGENSTEIN WAS A GENIUS. This contention will hardly be denied by professional philosophers. Logicians will recognize that he was fertile in enunciating profound logical insights. Metaphysicians, on the other hand, will admit that all of Wittgenstein's sentences quoted as meaningless by Carnap in the latter's *Logical Synax of Language* deserve close attention. It is also well known that the *Tractatus Logico-Philosophicus* had a tremendous influence on the epistemological doctrines of the Vienna Circle and on the Logico-Positivistic School. But my contention that Wittgenstein was a genius has a wider scope. It means that he was more than a *philosophical* genius. He was, in fact, a genius of our age, a symbol of troubled times. If this has been acknowledged neither by English-speaking philosophers nor by Continental European philosophers, it is due to a sad circumstance. English-speaking philosophers, who are thoroughly familiar with Wittgenstein's deeds, pay almost no attention to such expressions as "troubled times." It is not easy to understand its meaning when you devote the best hours of your life to teaching philosophy in beautiful university campuses. You begin to catch a glimpse of it only when you nose into the world. The average Continental European knows more about it than the cleverest of the English-speaking philosophers. Continental European philosophers, on the other hand, have taken scarcely any notice of Wittgenstein's work. Those who studied it were a handful of logicians or positivists, exclusively interested in the fields of Logic and Epistemology. As a consequence, those who know what the words "troubled times" mean, do not know Wittgenstein; those who know Wittgenstein do not know what the words "troubled times" mean. Thus, it was improbable that anybody should maintain

107

that Wittgenstein was something more than an acute analyst of philosophical puzzles.

I do not know whether Wittgenstein himself was aware of this or not, although I suspect that he was. I have heard Professor Paul Schrecker say that Wittgenstein was a "mystery man." That is true. It is also understandable. Wittgenstein did not seek popularity. One even wonders whether he was afraid of the world and tried to follow the ancient dictum *láthe biosas,* live hidden! At any event, he abandoned the main doctrines of the *Tractatus* and became more and more interested in what we are now going to deal with: Therapeutic Philosophy. But he never seemed to have lost sight of two of the statements contained in the *Tractatus.* One is: *Philosophy is not a theory but an activity.* The other is: *Whereof one cannot speak, thereof one must be silent.* Together they form the cornerstone of his unique *Wille zum Geheimnis*—of his "Will to remain secret." His obstinate loyalty to the two-mentioned apothegms is, in my opinion, due to this reason: at the same time as Wittgenstein worked out his "thoughts," he was compelled to eliminate them. *The ultimate tendency of Wittgenstein's "thought" was the suppression of all "thought."* He seemed to understand quite well that thought is the most perturbing factor in human life. It is not a mark of health, but of illness. That is why it cannot be properly expressed. Wittgenstein discovered that "general ideas" cannot be said. Neither can they be thought. It is true that, according to his recommendation, you can say anything you like—provided you are careful. But, in fact, you *say* nothing whatever. Your talk is a "yes-but-no," or a "this-you-can-say-if" attitude. *What* you "say," is indifferent. In fact, it would be better to stop talking. If you cannot do it right now, it is because you are still sick, haunted by all sorts of verbal ghosts: the ghost of "general ideas," the ghost of "meaningful thought." All this is sickness. Of course, you want to be cured. How? There is only one way: Therapeutic Positivism. Instead of the psychiatrist, you should call the philosopher. He will be more amusing and, perhaps, less expensive.

What does it all mean? Let me try to clarify this point. Of course, it all depends upon a proper understanding of Wittgenstein's "latest" method.

The trouble is that such a method cannot be "explained." It is *not* a philosophical method; it is a therapeutics. Besides, it is a nonsystematic therapeutics. Logical Positivists, who worshipped

Wittgenstein in their time, were baffled by the incredible "looseness" of the new method. But Logical Positivists have always been more or less "systematic." They also have been quite dogmatic and have shown no sympathy for human anxieties. All they have cared for has been to rebuke metaphysicians. How foolish! As a matter of fact, you can rebuke nobody. You can only *cure,* if you are willing to. In order to do it properly, you do not need to be "systematic." You do not need rules. All you need is to be an intelligent guesser, a really clever fellow. This shows that Wittgenstein's method cannot be explained, but only *followed.* Wittgenstein's Therapeutic Positivism was not a theory; it was a series of "recommendations." It scarcely appeals to our intellect; it rather appeals to our *still subsisting* consciousness, stirred by worries, undermined by anxieties. For many centuries this consciousness was considered the typical mark of human nature. Socrates tried to convince people that man not only has problems, but *is* a problem. To a large extent, he succeeded. Many philosophers have since claimed that man's greatness is a function of his permanent problematicism. No one disputed this view until recent times, when many people suddenly began to wonder whether problematic consciousness helps you very much in facing the problems of existence. After all, you are in danger of travelling indefatigably around your own consciousness and of forgetting that there is something outside you—let us call it "reality." There comes, therefore, a moment when you need urgently to restore your connection with reality. Socrates was all right; he was willing to drink the hemlock, and he did. But most people are not willing to. They are afraid that too much emphasis on philosophical irony is the surest way to drive you to tragedy.

Wittgenstein's "recommendations" had apparently nothing to do with this subject. Neither he nor his disciples wasted time talking about human nature, or about the problems of "unhappy consciousness." After all, these were philosopher's talk. For many years Wittgenstein was worried by just one problem: the problem of language. The analysis of language, its traps, what have they to do with the eradication of human anxieties? They have much to do with it. Man does not always voice his fears through such acts as screaming, howling, or gesticulating. He often reveals them by raising such questions as: "Why the deuce did I come into this world?," or, less provocatively but no less dismayingly: "Is

'7 + 5 = 12' an *a priori* synthetic judgment?." These seem to be philosophical questions or, as Wittgenstein and his disciples would put it, philosophical puzzlements. Since they are expressed by means of language, the best way to prove that they ought not to puzzle anybody is to remove the traps laid by language. It would seem, indeed, that language is the root of all philosophical puzzlements. The worst of it is that such puzzlements are responsible not only for raising memorable and unanswerable questions, but also for causing violent disagreements. People do not realize how many human beings have been delicately scorched only because they happened to disagree with some hardhearted dogmatist about such burning issues as whether the world is one or plural, finite or infinite, existent or inexistent. It is true that many questions of this kind have been dismissed by Logical Positivists, helped, incidentally, by Wittgenstein's *Tractatus*. But Logical Positivists have been unable to keep pace with Wittgenstein. As a matter of fact, they have disagreed with classical philosophers only in ascertaining *what* you can say. They have assumed that if you want to be a philosopher you can scarcely say anything. But after many claims to rigor, they have relapsed into laxness. Their regime has been liberalized. You can now say a pretty good quantity of things, some of them even not entirely trivial. You will always find some decadent Logical Positivist, softened by tolerance, willing to uphold your claims. In any event, you will always be permitted to become a "systematic" philosopher and, hence, a follower of philosophical tradition. Perhaps you will be forced to deny that man must devote his life to contemplation and you will have to declare that he must give himself to action. Perhaps that which was formerly called "consciousness" will have to be renamed "behavior." It does not matter. Having accepted restrictions, you will be allowed to do something suspiciously anti-Wittgensteinian: to solve questions.

For every non-Wittgensteinian philosopher, from Thales to Carnap, man has been an entity capable of solving questions. Even when the range of solvable questions has been conspicuously narrowed, nobody has denied that there *are* questions. Therefore, all non-Wittgensteinian philosophers play their game on a common ground. I will call it "humanism." It means that, come what may, you will always have an inalienable right: the right of raising questions. Now, this is precisely what Socrates had declared to be specifically "human." Provided this right be upheld, man will never cease to be what Leibniz called *un petit Dieu*.

Wittgenstein was for some time a staunch defender of this "not-much-but-still-something" attitude. He was, besides, the father of many valuable restrictions. But he soon went farther than his descendants. These men were full of prejudices. They considered themselves capable of possessing "general ideas." They called themselves, accordingly, "logical" or "systematical." They spent much time in discussions trying to forge logical rules, modes of speech, language forms of all kinds and shapes. They became enraged over distinctions between meaningless and meaningful questions and fought memorable battles to establish dividing lines between the former and the latter. Suddenly some of them reached the conclusion that *all* philosophical questions are verbal questions. It seems that they approached Wittgenstein's Therapeutic Positivism. They did not. To begin with, a real Therapeutic Positivist would not be so fussy about the distinction between meaningless and meaningful questions, between verbal and nonverbal questions. He would feel entirely freed from the worries caused by all questions as such. To be sure, he would still follow the rules of the game and would occasionally use the term "question"—meaning, of course, "puzzlement." But he would deny that questions must be solved. *Questions are not to be solved; they are to be dissolved.* Therefore, you must stop arguing about languages and metalanguages. You must clear away the illusion that you can discover an "ideal language." All this is, according to Wittgenstein, a mirage. It is a remnant of "humanism." If you let yourself be drawn by it, you will never get rid of interminable *unfruitful* discussions. It is even possible that you might become tolerant—*too early.* One of these days you will discover that there are some real philosophical questions embodied in the language of Aristotelians or even Thomists. Instead of accepting their tenets for what they are—expressions of philosophical puzzlement—you will assume that they express philosophical problems and that, therefore, they can *to some extent* be solved.

Now, philosophical problems are not to be solved, but *unmasked.* I said before that if you do not pay attention to your verbal behavior, you run the risk of becoming tolerant "too early." I meant what I said. It would be unjust to consider that a Therapeutic Positivist is intolerant. As a matter of fact, he is more tolerant than anybody else. But he is tolerant only *in due time,* when questions *have been* shown to be puzzlements, and puzzlements *have been* unmasked as intellectually inconsistent worries. *Before* this has been done, you will be terrorized; *afterwards,* you will be freed. Once questions are dissolved, you will be allowed to do what you wish; you will be permitted to talk any language: the language of the Aristotelians, of the Heracliteans, of the Milesians. *It will not matter.* Philosophical questions become puzzlements and cause worries only when you believe that they are rooted in man, when you fail to realize that they are floating around us and that we can take or leave them. They cause anxiety only when we are enslaved by them. They will cease to worry us as soon as we realize that the best weapon against them is "freedom," that is to say, detachment.

That weapon is precisely Wittgenstein's method. It is not so much a "method" as a "scalpel"—a "mental scalpel." The trouble is that it cannot be described. It is not "universally valid"; it cannot be used in the same way by everybody. If it could, it would raise again questions of method. Sterile nonliberating questions would be renewed and traditional philosophy reestablished. It is, therefore, preferable to decide once and for all that instead of facing questions you have to cope with worries, puzzlements, perplexities. Therefore, if you are by chance a philosopher, you will have to abstain from such things as giving classes, writing books, attending meetings. You will be unable to utter any "general proposition." General propositions, being verbal functions, do not propose anything. The usual escape—the submission of questions to logical analysis—will also soon prove untenable. Such an analysis is based upon the unconvincing and "dangerous" predominance of general statements over particular cases, examples, instances. Thus, it will soon be discovered that "theories" or logical devices are incapable of freeing us from any "question-worry." No "theory," no "generalized method," will be capable of competing with a simple therapeutic activity whose end will no longer be to solve questions but to cure souls.

For a Therapeutic Positivist, trained in Wittgenstein's supersubtle school of analysis, "method" is, then, a personal activity, intended radically to clarify the reasons of philosophical puzzlements and to pull out the roots of disagreement. This changes completely not only the nature of philosophical analysis, but also the nature of the philosophical profession. The Professor of Philosophy will have to become a *sui generis* "psychiatrist." The student will have to become a "patient." Burdened sometimes with the sense of intellectual sin, he will knock at the door of the Professor's office.

He will not ask: "Do you believe that 'Hannibal and Plato' is a good topic for a term paper?." This is not an intellectual puzzlement. It is a purely practical question. He will rather ask such questions as: "Do you *really* believe that Being and Value are interchangeable?." I presume, however, that the best way to introduce one's self to a Therapeutic Positivist is to state bluntly the *whole* of your worries. The "patient" would do better if he decided to say, for instance, "I am a Hegelian; I firmly believe that Being-in-itself will never become Being-in-and-for-itself, unless it spends some time out-of-itself." The Therapeutic Positivist likes difficult cases. Of course, the "patient" might very well not be worried in the least by believing in the truth or in the meaningfulness of such a philosophical statement. He might even assert that since becoming a Hegelian he has felt freed from all worries. This seems to pose a big problem for Therapeutic Positivists. If their activity is justified only in so far as they can disentangle philosophical puzzlements, it seems that they should discreetly retire when the so called "patient" is not puzzled at all. But let us not be deceived by what the Therapeutic Positivist says he purports to do. After all, *he* never *intended* to say that the task of Therapeutic Positivism is to "cure" patients. As a matter of fact, the Therapeutic Positivist never intends to *say* anything at all; he merely purports to *act* in certain ways which require the use of words. Therefore, even if the patient himself is not puzzled, he will exhibit philosophical puzzles. Of course, the most frequent cases are those in which patients have puzzles *and* are puzzled by them. These cases justify the comparison of the Therapeutic Positivist with a *sui generis* psychiatrist. The words *"sui generis"* express the fact that the Therapeutic Positivist deals only with *intellectual* puzzlements. Hence he cannot invite the patient to lie down on a sofa and suggest that he mumble something about the dreams he had forty-five years ago. Neither can he administer a drug to him. A drug would perhaps clear up an abscess, but not a question. The Therapeutic Positivist, however, wants to clear up, to solve—or, again, dissolve—the problem itself held by the patient. He is not an empiricist worry-catcher, but a pure analyst. He does not need sofas, drugs and, of course, books; he just needs brains.

There are many *ways* of removing philosophical puzzlements, but only one method can be really trusted: skill. It is difficult to demonstrate to a philosopher that analogies between different kinds of expressions do not hold. If we believe some of his followers, this is, however, what Wittgenstein tried to do. He showed in a masterful way that if such an analogy existed, it would have been useless. It would have ceased to be an analogy and would have become a unique expression. He showed many other things, all of them wrapped in a peculiar mixture of clarity and mystery. Some of these things may be doubtful. But one at least is certain: that only with the help of a great mental skill can you demonstrate to a philosopher—not a "handy patient," indeed—that he *has* expressed philosophical questions—that are inexpressible. In order to perform this deed, it is probably not enough to remove language traps; you need, besides, to pick up subtly all kinds of intellectual myths and hold them smilingly up in the face of the patient. Together with a great logical skill, you will assuredly need psychological *finesse*. Concealed in the various layers of languages and sublanguages, an incredible number of obscure motivations are scattered. They must be sifted out by *purely intellectual* means, analyzed and, last but not least, *pulverized*. Only at this final stage will the patient recognize *willingly* that his puzzlements lacked foundation, that his *questioning* was meaningless. He will acknowledge, in addition, that *all* questioning is meaningless. Relieved from this burden, he will no longer talk—or if he does, he will talk *as if* he did not—and will devote himself to "activity" and to "life." His "mental complex" will vanish altogether. I do not know what Wittgenstein called this "complex"—or even whether he really named it at all. Let me coin a name for it: the "Socratic complex." Socrates, in fact, had taught men to behave in a manner strictly opposed to the one recommended by Wittgenstein. To be sure, the great Greek philosopher also wanted to relieve us from "complexes." But, contrary to Wittgenstein, his "method" consisted in creating, in suggesting, in stirring up problems. In a certain way, Wittgenstein could be called the "Anti-Socrates." Now, if Socrates and Wittgenstein are extreme opposites, they are extreme opposites of the *same* historical line. Like all extremes, they touch each other: *extrema se tangunt*. No wonder they resemble each other in so many respects. They both used an individual method. They both hated writing. Socrates did not write books. Wittgenstein regretted having written one. They both were geniuses: the genius of construction, Socrates; the genius of destruction, Wittgenstein.

Yes; Wittgenstein was a genius. Knowingly or not, he mirrored our times more faithfully than most of the professional pessimists. Heidegger has tried to stress nothingness; Sartre, nausea; Kafka and Camus, absurdity. All these writers have described a world where reality itself has become questionable. They have, however, left unshaken the right of asking questions. In Wittgenstein's Therapeutic Positivism, on the other hand, that which becomes questionable is *the question itself*. Nothing has been left, not even the ruins. No wonder we can consider Wittgenstein to be a penetrating reflection of the gloomy aspects of our age. He did "describe" this "age of anxiety," this "age of longing," better than anybody else; better than poets, better than novelists. Is it surprising, then, that an obscure professor at Cambridge symbolizes more exactly our troubled times than a famous playwright in Paris? [1]

[1] This article was written in 1951, at a time when Wittgenstein's philosophic activities were a mystery wrapped in an enigma to all but a handful of faithful followers. "Wittgenstein," Gilbert Ryle wrote, "attended no philosophical conferences; gave no lectures outside Cambridge; corresponded on philosophical subjects with nobody and discouraged the circulation even of notes of his Cambridge lectures and discussions" (See Ryle's article below). As a consequence, Ryle himself confessed that he was able to offer only "a set of impressions, partly, of mere echoes of echoes." Nevertheless, since 1951 we have witnessed the publication of Wittgenstein's posthumous works and notes, which, as it so often happens, have proved to be quite abundant for a man who seemed to dislike writing. Furthermore, an extensive literature on Wittgenstein's thoughts and afterthoughts may now be offered to whom it may concern. Therefore, when we deal with Wittgenstein today we are interested in such themes as "use versus meaning," "linguistic games," "family resemblances," "bewitchment of intelligence by means of language," and so on. The mystery of Wittgenstein's philosophic excogitations has been dissolved even more quickly and thoroughly than philosophic problems. On the other hand, as Norman Malcolm has pointed out, Wittgenstein seemed to be distressed, not to say infuriated, when the latter's philosophy was looked at from a therapeutic viewpoint.

Thus, it seems only fair to contend that this article is *not* on Wittgenstein's philosophy. I have simply taken the at one time elusive and mysterious Wittgenstein as a symbol of some of our age's anxieties. This article, therefore, remains what it originally was intended to be: "a sociohistorical interpretation of a human attitude."

Ludwig Wittgenstein [1]

BY GILBERT RYLE

AN ORIGINAL AND POWERFUL PHILOSOPHER, Ludwig Wittgenstein, an Austrian who finally became a naturalized British subject, came to England shortly before the first World War to study engineering. In 1912, bitten by logical and philosophical problems about the nature of mathematics, he migrated to Cambridge to work with Bertrand Russell. During that war, he was in the Austrian army and ended up a prisoner of war. In this period he wrote his one book, the famous *Tactratus Logico-Philosophicus,* of which a not quite reliable English translation was published in 1922. He taught in an Austrian village school for some time, during which he came into close philosophical touch with a few of the leading members of the Vienna Circle. In 1929 he came to Cambridge, where the importance of his ideas had been quickly recognized. In 1939 he became Professor. For part of the last war he was a hospital orderly at Guy's Hospital. In 1947 he resigned his Chair. Besides the *Tractatus,* he published only one article.

In the last twenty years, so far as I know, he published nothing; attended no philosophical conferences; gave no lectures outside Cambridge; corresponded on philosophical subjects with nobody and discouraged the circulation even of notes of his Cambridge lectures and discussions. But with his serious students and a few colleagues, economists, mathematicians, physicists and philosophers, he would discuss philosophical matters unwearyingly. Yet from his jealously preserved little pond, there have spread waves over the philosophical thinking of much of the English-speaking world. Philosophers who never met him—and few of us did meet him—can be heard talking philosophy in his tones of voice; and students who can barely spell his name now wrinkle up their noses at things which had a bad smell for him. So what is the difference that he has made to philosophy?

[1] A B.B.C. Third Programme talk, given on May 26, 1951.

It is vain to try to forecast the verdict of history upon a contemporary. I have to try to do this for one who has for about 30 years avoided any publication of his ideas. So what I offer is a set of impressions, interpretations, partly, of mere echoes of echoes.

From the time of Locke to that of Bradley philosophers had debated their issues as if they were psychological issues. Certainly their problems were, often, genuine philosophical problems, but they discussed them in psychological terms. And if they asked themselves, as they seldom did ask, what they were investigating, they tended to say that they were investigating the workings of the mind, just as physical scientists investigate the working of bodies. The sorts of "Mental Science" that they talked were sometimes positivistic, sometimes idealistic, according, roughly, as they were more impressed by chemistry than by theology or *vice versa*.

However, fifty years ago philosophers were getting their feet out of these psychological boots. For psychology had now begun to be done in laboratories and clinics, so armchair psychology became suspect. But even more influential was the fact that logical quandaries had recently been exposed at the very roots of pure mathematics. The mathematicians needed lifelines, which they could not provide for themselves. Logicians had to work out the logic of mathematics, and they could not base this logic on the findings of any empirical science, especially of so hazy a science as psychology. If logic and philosophy were not psychological enquiries, what were they?

During the first twenty years of this century, many philosophers gave another answer to this question, a Platonic answer. Philosophy studies not the workings of minds or, of course, of bodies either; it studies the denizens of a third domain, the domain of abstract, or conceptual entities, of possibilities, essences, timelessly subsisting universals, numbers, truths, falsities, values and meanings. This idea enabled its holders to continue to say that philosophy was the science of something, while denying that it was the science of any ordinary subject matter; to champion its autonomy as a discipline, while denying that it was just one science among others; to give it the standing of a science while admitting its unlikeness to the sciences. Thus the question "What are philosophy and logic the sciences of?" received a new answer, though one with a disquietingly dreamlike ring. It was the answer given by Frege and by Russell.

In Vienna thinkers were facing much the same question, though from an opposite angle. Whereas here it had been widely assumed that philosophy was Mental Science, and therefore just a sister science to physics, chemistry, zoology, etc., in the German-speaking world it was widely assumed that philosophy stood to the other sciences not as sister but as mother—or even governess. Somehow professors of philosophy there enjoyed such a pedagogic domination that they could dictate even to the scientists. *Of course* philosophers were the right people to decide whether the teachings of Darwin, Freud and Einstein were true.

Late in the nineteenth century Mach had mutinied against this view, that metaphysics was a governess science. By the early 1920's this mutiny became a rebellion. The Vienna Circle repudiated the myth that the questions of physics, biology, psychology or mathematics can be decided by metaphysical considerations. Metaphysics is not a governess science or a sister science; it is not a science at all. The classic case was that of Einstein's Relativity principle. The claims of professors of philosophy to refute this principle were baseless. Scientific questions are soluble only by scientific methods, and these are not the methods of philosophers.

Thus, in England the question was this: What are the special virtues which the natural and the mathematical sciences lack but logic and philosophy possess, such that these must be invoked when the former find themselves in quandaries? In Vienna the question was this: Given that philosophers cannot decide scientific questions, what are the logical virtues which scientific procedures possess, but philosophical procedures lack? The contrast between philosophy and science was drawn in both places. In Vienna, where the autonomy of the sciences was actually challenged, the object was to expose the pretensions of philosophy as a governess science. Here, where, save for psychology, the autonomy of the sciences was not seriously challenged, it was drawn in order to extract the positive functions of logic and philosophy. Philosophy was regarded in Vienna as a blood-sucking parasite; in England as a medicinal leech.

To Wittgenstein the question came in its English form. And so he could not be called one of the Logical Positivists. Their polemics were not his; and his quest for the positive function of logic and philosophy was not, until much later, theirs. He was influenced by Frege and Russell, not by Mach. He had not himself felt the dead hand of professorial philosophy which cramped, and still cramps, even scientific thought in Germany and Austria. He, conversely, himself helped to fix the logical lifelines for the mathematicians.

I want to show how Wittgenstein transformed and answered what was all the time his master question, "What can philosophers and logicians do, and how should they do it?"

I have said that, after a long imprisonment in psychological idioms, philosophy was, for a time, re-housed in Platonic idioms. But this was only a temporary asylum. For after a short period during which philosophers tried not to mind the dreamlike character of the new asylum, something awoke them from the dream. Russell, in his enquiries into the logical principles underlying mathematics, found that he could not well help constructing statements which had the logically disturbing property that they were true only on condition that they were false, and false only on condition that they were true. Some of these self-subverting statements seemed to be inherent in the very basis which was to make mathematics secure. There was a major leak in the dry dock which Frege and he had built for mathematics.

Russell found a patch for the leak. Underlying the familiar distinction between truth and falsehood, there is a more radical distinction between significance and meaninglessness. True and false statements are both significant, but some forms of words, with the vocabulary and constructions of statements, are neither true nor false, but nonsensical—and nonsensical not for reasons of wording or of grammar, but for logical reasons. The self-subverting statements were of this sort, neither true nor false, but nonsensical simulacra of statements. Notice, it is only of such things as complex verbal expressions that we can ask whether they are significant or nonsense. The question could not be asked of mental processes; or of Platonic entities. So logic is from the start concerned, not with these but rather with what can or cannot be significantly said. Its subject matter is a linguistic one, though its tasks are not at all those of philology.

In Wittgenstein's *Tractatus* this departmental conclusion is generalized. All logic and all philosophy are enquiries into what makes it significant or nonsensical to say certain things. The sciences aim at saying what is true about the world; philosophy aims at disclosing only the logic of what can be truly or even falsely said about the world. This is why philosophy is not a sister science or a

parent science; that its business is not to add to the number of
scientific statements, but to disclose their logic.

Wittgenstein begins by considering how a sentence, a map, a
diagram or a scale model can represent or even significantly misrepresent the facts. The isolated words "London" and "south" are
not true or false. Nor can a single dot on a sheet of paper be an
accurate or inaccurate map. The sentence "London is north of
Brighton" is true. The same words, differently arranged as
"Brighton is north of London" make a false statement. Arranged
as "South is London of Brighton" they make a farrago which is
neither true nor false, but nonsense. For dots on paper to represent
or misrepresent the direction of Brighton from London, there must
be a dot for each town and they must be set out in accordance with
some convention for points of the compass. For a statement, map
or diagram to be true or false, there must be a plurality of words
or marks; but, more, these bits must be put together in certain
ways. And underlying the fact that the truth or falsity of the statement or map partly depends upon the particular way in which its
bits are arranged, there lies the fact that whether a significant statement or map results at all, depends wholly on the general way in
which the bits are put together. Some ways of jumbling them together are ruled out. What rules rule them out?

In the *Tractatus* Wittgenstein came to the frustrating conclusion
that these principles of arrangement inevitably baffle significant
statement. To try to tell what makes the difference between significant and nonsensical talk is itself to cross the divide between significant and nonsensical talk. Philosophizing can, indeed, open our
eyes to these structural principles, but it cannot issue in significant
statements of them. Philosophy is not a science; it cannot yield
theories or doctrines. None the less it can be skilful or unskilful,
successful or unsuccessful. It is in pursuing the activity itself that
we see what we need to see. Rather like learning music or tennis,
learning philosophy does not result in our being able to tell what
we have learned; though, as in music and tennis, we can show
what we have learned.

Now it is true that philosophical clarity is achieved in the acts
of appreciating arguments rather than in propounding theorems.
But it is false that all philosophical talk is nonsensical talk. Wittgenstein had himself said very effective things, and talking effectively is
not talking nonsensically. What had brought him to this frustrating

conclusion? When he wrote the *Tractatus,* he was, I think, over-influenced by his own analogies between saying things and making maps, diagrams and scale models. Certainly, for marks on paper to constitute a temperature chart, or for spoken words to constitute a significant statement, the dots and the words must be arranged according to rules and conventions. Only if the zigzag of dots on the nurse's graph paper is systematically correlated with the thermometer readings taken at successive moments of a day, can it represent or even misrepresent the alterations in the patient's temperature. Only if words are organized according to a number of complex general rules does a true or false statement result.

Suppose we now asked the nurse to depict on a second sheet of graph paper, not the course of the patient's temperature, but the rules for representing his temperature by dots on graph paper, she would be baffled. Nor can the rules and conventions of map-making themselves be mapped. So Wittgenstein argued in the *Tractatus* that the philosopher or logician is debarred from saying what it is that makes things said significant or nonsensical. He can show it, but not tell it. After the *Tractatus* he realized that, though saying things does resemble depicting things or mapping things in the respect for which he originally drew the analogy, it does not resemble them in all respects. Just as the nurse can tell, though not depict, how the temperature chart represents or misrepresents the patient's temperature, so the philosopher can tell why, say, a scientist's statement makes or does not make sense. What alone would be absurd would be a sentence which purported to convey a comment upon its own significance or meaninglessness.

The *Tractatus* has two distinct but connected aims. The first, which I have crudely sketched, is to show both what philosophy is not, namely any sort of a science, and what it is, namely an activity of exploring the internal logic of what is said, for example, in this or that scientific theory. The second, which I shall not even try to sketch, is to show what sort of an enquiry Formal Logic is. This brings me to a general point about the *Tractatus*. Wittgenstein's first interest had been in the logic of mathematics and thence in the logical paradoxes which were the big leak in the dry dock that Frege and Russell had built. He was, therefore, equipped and predisposed to squeeze whatever can be significantly said into the few statement patterns with which the logic of mathematical statements operates. He used its terminology, its codes, and its abacus operations in his task of exploring various philosophical issues, and, above all, his own master issue, that of the nature of philosophizing itself. In consequence, the *Tractatus* is, in large measure, a closed book to those who lack this technical equipment. Few people can read it without feeling that something important is happening; but few experts, even, can say what is happening.

But this is not the end of the story. Maybe it is only the preface. For, after lying fallow for some years, Wittgenstein returned to philosophy. His teaching in this period differs markedly from that of the *Tractatus*; it even repudiates parts of the *Tractatus*.

First, he no longer forces all expressions into the favored few patterns of the logic of mathematics. With this goes a revolt against molds of any sorts. The rubrics of logical systems and the abstract terms of philosophical schools are like the shoes of Chinese ladies, which deformed their feet and prevented them from walking on them. Philosophical elucidation is still inspection of expressions, but it is no longer inspection through the slots of a logician's stencil or through the prisms of a scholastic classification system. His diction has reverted from that of a Russell discussing esoteric matters with mathematicians to that of a Socrates discussing everyday ideas with unindoctrinated young men. Nor does he now elucidate only the propositions of the sciences. Like Moore, he explores the logic of all the things that all of us say.

Next, though I think that his master problem is still that of the nature, tasks and methods of the philosophical activity, he no longer thinks that philosophers are condemned to trying to say the unsayable. But he now avoids any general statement of the nature of philosophy, not because this would be to say the unsayable, but because it would be to say a scholastic and therefore an obscuring thing. In philosophy, generalizations are unclarifications. The nature of philosophy is to be taught by producing concrete specimens of it. As the medical student learns surgery by witnessing and practicing operations on dead and live subjects, so the student of philosophy learns what philosophy is by following and practicing operations on particular quandary-generating ways of talking. Thus Wittgenstein would rove, apparently aimlessly because without any statement of aim, from one concrete puzzle to its brothers, its cousins, its parents and its associates, demonstrating both what makes them puzzling and how to resolve them—demonstrating, but not telling; going through the moves, but not compiling a manual of them; teaching a skill, not dictating a doctrine.

One favorite procedure of his might be called the "tea-tasting method." Tea-tasters do not lump their samples into two or three comprehensive types. Rather they savor each sample and try to place it next door to its closest neighbors, and this not in respect of just one discriminable quality, but along the lengths of various lines of qualities. So Wittgenstein would exhibit the characteristic manner of working of a particular expression, by matching it against example after example of expressions progressively diverging from it in various respects and directions. He would show how striking similarities may go with important but ordinarily unremarked differences, and how we are tempted to lean too heavily on their similarities and hence to be tripped up by their latent differences.

For philosophers do not examine expressions at random. The quest for their internal logic is forced upon us by the fact that we find ourselves already caught up in unforeseen entanglements. Why do we slide into quandaries? Let me invent an example. We find ourselves talking as if like a train, so time itself might one day slow down and stop. We divide a train into coaches and coaches into compartments. We divide a month into weeks and weeks into days. When a train is passing me, some coaches are beyond me, some are still to come, and one compartment of one coach is directly abreast of me. I look at its occupants through the window. Surely time is like this. Last week has gone, next week is still to come, but I can exchange glances with the occupants of Now. So, as trains always slow down and stop somewhere, what makes time puff on so tirelessly? Might not Now be the last compartment of the last coach? Yet surely not; there would still be something behind it, if only the empty wind. You see that it is tempting, but also that it smells like nonsense to speak of the last compartment of time. Why may we say some things about time which are very much like some things that we legitimately say about trains, when to some of the proper corollaries of what we say about trains there correspond no proper corollaries about time? To answer this question, we should have to examine the functioning of whole ranges of things that we say about trains, rivers and winds; about moving shadows, rainbows and reflections; about perpetual-motion machines, stars, clocks, sundials, and calendars; about the series of numbers, days of the week and minutes of the day. And then we may see why we slid and no longer incline to slide from the proper corollaries of familiar dictions about trains to corresponding corollaries of somewhat similar dictions about time. We see that we had overpressed certain analogies between ways of talking; and that we were so dominated by a favorite model, that we had gone on using it where it could no longer work. And now we know, in a way, what time is, though there is no shorter or better way of saying what time is than by going through again the same sort of process of linguistic tea-tasting.

I must conclude. Wittgenstein has made our generation of philosophers self-conscious about philosophy itself. It is, of course, possible for a person to be very thoughtful about the nature and methods of an activity, without being made any the better at performing it. The centipede of the poem ran well until he began to wonder how he ran. Maybe we have been made a bit neurotic about the nature of our calling. But Wittgenstein's demolition of the idea that philosophy is a sort of science has at least made us vigilant about our tools. We no longer try to use for our problems the methods of arguing which are the right ones for demonstrating theorems or establishing hypotheses. In particular we have learned to pay deliberate attention to what can and cannot be said. What had, since the early days of this century, been the practice of G. E. Moore has received a rationale from Wittgenstein; and I expect that when the curtain is lifted we shall also find that Wittgenstein's concrete methods have increased the power, scope and delicacy of the methods by which Moore has for so long explored in detail the internal logic of what we say.

Ludwig Wittgenstein

BY GEORGE A. PAUL

Wittgenstein's second book, *Philosophical Investigations,* presents some of the ideas on which he worked from about 1929 onwards. It was written in German and published in 1953, some two years after his death, with a translation into English by Miss Anscombe. Part I was complete by 1945, and in the Preface Wittgenstein described it as "the precipitate of philosophical investigations which have occupied me for the last 16 years," i.e., since about 1929.

HE FOLLOWS Moore in the defense of common sense and in a regard for our ordinary language; but criticizes the notion of *analysis* in a way that has quite changed philosophy. He writes of every sentence in our language as being " 'in order as it is' "[1], claims that "philosophy may in no way interfere with the actual use of language," and declares that "what *we* do" in philosophy "is to bring words *back* from their metaphysical to their everyday usage." That is, "when philosophers use a word—'knowledge,' 'being,' 'object,' 'I,' 'proposition,' 'name'—and try to grasp the *essence* of the thing, we must always ask: is the word ever *actually* used in this way in the language which is its original home?" In such cases "we must stick to the subjects of our everyday thinking, and not go astray and imagine that we have to describe extreme subleties";[2] we must "look into the workings of our language." The confusions which occupy us arise not when our language is "doing work" but when it is "like an engine idling."

[1] Cf. Moore, *Defence of Common Sense*, p. 198: "I am maintaining that all the propositions . . . are *wholly* true."
[2] Cf. Moore, "I am not using the expressions in any such *subtle* sense. I meant by them precisely what any reader in reading them will have understood me to mean."

125

With Moore, Wittgenstein shared also a sympathy for metaphysical philosophers. Where there exists a prejudice which stands in the way of seeing how a word is actually used, it is often "not a *stupid* prejudice," for "the problems arising through a misinterpretation of our forms of language have the character of *depth*: they are deep disquietudes; their roots are as deep in us as the forms of our language, and their importance is as great as the importance of our language." These philosophers have, when at their best, "run their heads up against the limits of language."

And Wittgenstein emphasized, with Moore, "our strange position" that we know what many words and phrases mean even though "no philosopher hitherto," or anyone else, has succeeded in setting out in detail what they mean; we are constantly failing to see *our* use of this and that word clearly; but in our philosophical investigations we are trying to understand the functions and structures of *our* language; we are trying to look into the workings of *our* language in such a way as to make us recognize those workings. Compare Moore's formulation: "My main object here has been to try to *make* the reader see it" [§ 304].

Here, at this point, Wittgenstein parts wholly from Moore. We must "make a radical break with the idea that language always functions in *one* way, always serves the *same* purpose: to convey thoughts—which may be about houses, pains, good and evil, or anything that *"stands in the way of our seeing* the use of the word as it is" [§ 305].

Moore had, in 1903, written of certain difficulties in philosophy as if they were like difficulties in vision, in seeing something clearly; of a philosophical investigation as like a visual investigation, a visual scrutiny. Moore had thought: it is like trying to discern something of a kind difficult to see, such as air or clear water in a stream. (I may see it all of a sudden by a fleeting ripple.) Or it is like coming to see by a careful scrutiny that what in an X-ray plate I took for one shadow is two. Moore wrote, for example, "the other element 'consciousness' is extremely difficult to fix . . . seems to escape us . . . seems transparent; we look through it"; [3] and (to take an example of the other kind of difficulty) the Idealist "fails to see that *esse* and *percipi* are *distinct,* are *two* at all."

Naturally enough Moore's remedy for a philosophical difficulty *so* described was this: to look still more attentively at what is *before his mind* just *at the time when* he asks the question. "If we

[3] Moore, *Refutation of Idealism*, p. 20.

look *attentively* enough, it can be distinguished"; "whoever will *attentively* consider with himself *what is before his mind*" can "come to recognize" that he has there not one object but two. Of such an account Wittgenstein wrote: we imagine "that we have to describe extreme subtleties."

Yet Moore admits that "the moment we try to fix our attention on consciousness, to see what *distinctly* it is, it seems to vanish." On which Wittgenstein notes that "it is as if one had altered the adjustment of a microscope"; or "we feel as if we had to repair a torn spider's web with our fingers."

Moore's kind of picture of a philosophical problem is characterized by Wittgenstein as follows: It is as if in our usual forms of expression there were "something *hidden* that has to be brought to light," and we often go so far as to "think we already see it there." The picture is of "something that lies *within,* which we *see* when we look into the thing; something that lies *beneath the surface,* and which an analysis *digs out.*"

But, says Wittgenstein, the attempt at "scrutiny" results not in a digging up of something from beneath, but in our coming only on things which we think of as mere surface phenomena, and not refined enough to be what we are looking for. Take as an example scrutiny of an intention: "For a moment I intended to . . ." That is, I had a particular feeling, an inner experience; and I remember it. But I am urged, "And now remember quite precisely!" At this the *"inner* experience of intending seems to vanish again. *Instead* one remembers thoughts, feelings, movements, and also connections with earlier situations"; what, in this context, one had the inclination to treat as mere superficial accompaniments.

Wittgenstein describes this part of Moore's position as "that *dead-end* in philosophy, where one believes that the difficulty of the task consists in this: our having to describe phenomena that are *hard to get hold of,* the present experience that slips quickly by, or something of that kind. Where we find ordinary language too crude, and it looks as if we were having to do not with phenomena of everyday but with ones that *'easily elude us.'* "

But the fact is that "the picture of the inner process," so far from "giving us the correct idea of the *use*" of the word "intend," *"stands in the way*" of our seeing the use of the word as it is." Concentrated on looking for the hidden which we think is there, we have no attention to spare for what lies openly around us.

We are bewitched too by an inadequate conception of what it is for something "to be hidden." What we are looking for is indeed "hidden"; but not by being behind something else, or difficult to dig out, or difficult to discriminate sharply from something else, or transparent. What is hidden in that way is of no interest to us. We have overlooked a no less common way in which a thing, or movement, may be concealed from us. "The decisive movement in the conjuring trick has been made, and it was *the very one that we thought quite innocent.*"

The things we are looking for "already lie open to view," and have "escaped remark only because they are always before our eyes." Expecting something queer, we go in pursuit of chimeras; looking for something with a halo, we miss the humble; dazzled by the thought of the ideal, we fail to see clearly the actual. "Philosophy is a battle against the *bewitchment* of our intelligence," not, as Moore and other analysts thought, against defective vision or wandering attention. It is a poor conjurer who has to have the lights turned low.

Just as, in Moore's views, Idealists had failed to realize how complex is the concept of *spirit,* so Moore, in Wittgenstein's view, has failed to realize how complex is such a concept as *consciousness.*[4] Moore and others have purified it, refined it, "sublimed" it, looking at it only when it is "idling"; have failed to "be struck by" what no doubt they already clearly see, the complex and varied use of the phrase "conscious of," taking these, the true circumstances of its use, to be merely "its coarser accompaniments." "The criteria which we accept for 'being able to,' 'understanding' are much more complicated than might appear at first sight. The role of these words in our language is other, *more involved, than we are tempted to think.*" But "this *role* is what we have to understand in order to resolve philosophical paradoxes. And hence *definitions* usually fail to resolve them; so, a fortiori does the assertion that a word is '*indefinable.*' "

Moore is again a target of Wittgenstein's account of the philosopher who, pointing to an object in front of him, says "This is here," and claims that the sentence makes sense to him: "he should ask himself in what *special* circumstances this sentence is *actually* used," for there it does make sense.

Analytic philosophers, in short, no less than metaphysical ones, must be made to bring words back from philosophical to actual

4 *Refutation of Idealism,* p. 20.

everyday usage, to their use in the language which is their original home.

Everything we need for our problems lies open to view, and philosophy simply puts everything before us. It aims to give the wide presentation we need of the facts of usage, and "may in no way interfere with the actual usage of language; it can in the end only describe it. It leaves everything as it is." A man (perhaps myself) may be "unable to look and see how, for example, *propositions* work," or the word "conscious," or "this." Very well, then, we must make him (make myself) look and see it. "We must do away with all explanation, and *description alone* must take its place."

Yet philosophy is not just any description of uses of language, however extensive, various, and exact. Such a description only "gets its purpose *from the philosophical problems.*" It is not enough to turn our attention away from the sublimed, indiscernible essence and accommodate our sight to the multitudinous ordinary; or to loosen our too concentrated gaze from what is at this moment immediately in front of our mind, and spread our attention so that we see also circumstances before and after. In the crowd of circumstances thus seen, I may still remain every bit as lost as before. "A philosophical problem has the form: 'I don't know my way about.'" I may be lost even when I see clearly everything that is around me.

As we learn our language and employ it we do not thereby acquire any wide, extensive view of the uses which make it up, and how they stand to one another. But for every problem it is of basic importance to *acquire* such a wide-ranging familiarity with some regions of usage; to assemble many facts of usage, and command a wide view. "The work of the philosopher consists in *assembling reminders* for a particular purpose"; but not only in that, for though I should assemble a multitude I might become even more lost than before, I might even less "know my way about."

Besides *assembling* reminders, sketches, I must *select* and *arrange* them, in such a way that I come to get some *picture* of the landscape. The very nature of philosophical investigation compels a man to travel over a wide region of uses, criss-cross in every direction, the same use being approached again and again, each time from a different direction, from a different point of view, from a different use. These various sketches do not of themselves fall together to form a picture, or even a map, of a place or region; they have to *be* arranged "so that if you looked at them you could *get* a picture" of the landscape there, and so to some extent get to "know your way about."

"Hence the importance of *finding* and *inventing* intermediate cases." Only by this *finding, inventing,* and *arranging* of views, not by an inactive observation of all equally that happens to come before my eye, do I get to know my way about and "out of the fly-bottle." The "essence," so to speak, becomes "surveyable," not by "digging out," "analysis," and not by passive watching of what "already lies open to view," but "by a rearrangement," or several, which I have to make.

Instead of concentrating into a gaze, I am to make a wide survey; and it is not that cases just come before me in their arrangement, for there are cases to be invented by me and arrangements of them to be made by me. Here is why Wittgenstein presents no method in philosophy; there is no method for inventing cases, no method for arranging them.

And there is no method for *"being struck by"* one fact rather than another. Yet no matter how much detail about a use we may methodically assemble, we may, and commonly do, "fail to be struck by what, once seen, is *most* striking and most powerful." The fly in the fly-bottle may countless times eye the way out—and not be particularly struck by it.

Wittgenstein did not think that all philosophical problems must arise only from ordinary language. He says merely that the most widespread ones do. But he knew well that the specialized language of any subject is liable to give rise to philosophical problems. In such a case, to bring a word back to its actual use, is to bring it back to its actual use in that specialized language, however unordinary, that is its original home. He himself worked on philosophical problems which arise in mathematics, not much of which enters into ordinary language.

Wittgenstein on the Nature of Philosophy

BY MORRIS LAZEROWITZ

> I shall light a candle of understanding in your heart
> which shall not be put out.
>
> —II ESDRAS.

LUDWIG WITTGENSTEIN was one of the most original philosophers of this century and there can be no doubt that the impact of his perceptions into the nature of philosophical problems will radically and permanently change the course of philosophy in the future. Unfortunately, the influence of his thought has been retarded. Apart from a paper in the *Proceedings of the Aristotelian Society* and his famous *Tractatus Logico-Philosophicus,* he did not permit any of his work to be published during his lifetime, although some of his lectures were privately circulated in mimeographed form among a selected group of his students. According to all accounts Wittgenstein was a man of compelling personality and tended to gather a circle of favored students around himself. An aura of mystery, not untinged with religion, was thus created around his work as well as around the special group of students. Understandably, such an atmosphere might well, and in fact did, have consequences less than desirable from an intellectual point of view. Fortunately time has already begun to disperse the emotional mists and clear up the air; and now that Wittgenstein's work is being made publicly available, now that it belongs to the public domain, so to speak, it should make itself felt widely and objectively in the doing of philosophy. Without stretching a metaphor unfairly, philosophy up to the present may be described as an expanding museum of exhibits, a sort of Madame Tussaud's to which new figures are constantly being added but from which no figures are ever removed. But some things that Wittgenstein said will plant a seed in the minds of philosophers

131

which will in time develop into an improved understanding of the workings of philosophy, enable us to look at it in a new way. And the explanations of theories and arguments flowing from this understanding will not become just further exhibits: they will instead place the exhibits in a light which will enable us to see them for what they are.

Philosophy, over the years, presented itself in a number of different guises to Wittgenstein, some of them the usual ones all of us know, others not. It is, of course, the later ways in which he saw philosophy that are so enlightening and helpful, but to realize how enlightening these are, some of the earlier ways need to be looked at. Before considering these, however, it is important to notice a connection between some things G. E. Moore did and insights into philosophy Wittgenstein arrived at later. As is well known, Moore brought philosophical theories (or some of them, at least) down to earth from the Platonic "heaven above the heavens" where they were protected against our understanding. Placed in the light of the ordinary sun they could be scrutinized under less distorting conditions. Such a general philosophical view as Bradley's, that physical things are not real, or are mere appearance, which casts a spell over the intellect, he would translate into (and perhaps it would not be far off to say, *deflate* into) its concrete implications, for example, that he was not really wearing a waistcoat or that he was mistaken in believing that there was a sheet of paper on which he was writing with a fountain pen. Moore's ostensible purpose in effecting his translations into the concrete was to force on our attention the consequences of an abstract philosophical theory, consequences which we apparently tend to avoid noticing. The point of doing this was, frequently if not always, to refute a theory by subjecting it to "trial by example." But what could not fail to emerge, whether grasped consciously or unconsciously, was that construed as having Moore's translations, the theories were altogether too plainly false for anyone to have failed to see *for himself* that they were false. A further puzzling feature attaching to Moore's translations is that many philosophers who became acquainted with them did not give up their views. The idea which inevitably suggests itself is that a philosophical view like "Physical things are unreal" is not what it has been taken to be. The question could not but arise whether the view is actually *incompatible with* a factual proposition such as that Moore is wearing a waistcoat and is writing with a fountain pen.

Surprising as it might seem, Moore's translations into the concrete, if they show anything, tend to show that the theories are not open to his translations. The problem then becomes one of understanding rightly how a philosopher is using language when he says, "Physical things are not real," or "Physical things exist but are mere appearance." Wittgenstein's later work shows us the way to a correct understanding of such statements.

In one place Moore observed that it would seem that language, ordinary everyday language, was "expressly designed to mislead philosophers." [1] With the same complaint apparently in mind Wittgenstein said that "philosophy is a battle against the bewitchment of our intelligence by means of language," [2] and "a philosophical problem has the form 'I don't know my way about.' " [3] Moore resorted to one procedure, that of careful analysis of the meanings of words, to free philosophers from their bewitchment. Wittgenstein also used this procedure to help them find their way through the maze of language. According to him "A main source of our failure to understand is that we do not *command a clear view* of our use of words—our grammar is lacking in this sort of perspicuity." [4] To express the matter with the help of a metaphor of his that has captured the imagination of many philosophers, what will help the fly escape from the fly-bottle is analysis of usage, getting straight about how we ordinarily use words. There is, however, a difference in their procedures which it will be useful to look at. This difference might very well have led Wittgenstein to say that a philosopher of Common Sense ("and that, *n.b.,* is not the common-sense man" [5]) is himself captive in the fly-bottle but favors a special corner in it, that in trying to refute positions which go counter to Common Sense he also "does not know his way about." For Moore's disagreements with other philosophers result in *philosophical* stalemates, stalemates as old as those between Parmenides and his opponents.

It will be recalled that Moore's defence of Common Sense against the attacks of philosophers, attacks sustained throughout the long history of philosophy, has been rejected as begging the question, and Moore has been criticized as being dogmatic about the "truisms"

[1] *Philosophical Studies* (London: Routledge and Regan Paul, 1922), p. 217.
[2] *Philosophical Investigations*, p. 47.
[3] *Ibid.,* p. 49.
[4] *Ibid.*
[5] L. Wittgenstein, *Preliminary Studies for the Philosophical Investigations.* Generally known as *The Blue and Brown Books*, p. 48. Subsequent references to this work will be designated *The Blue Book.* Subsequent references to *Philosophical Investigations* will be abbreviated to *Investigations.*

he lays down. And in bringing them, unsupported by chains of reasoning, against the counterclaims of philosophers who back their own propositions with analytical arguments, he has, in the opinion of many thinkers, begged the very questions that are in debate. Moore's familiar expletives, "nonsense," "absurd," "obviously false," etc., may momentarily silence a philosopher who goes against Common Sense, but it does not affect the way he continues to think about the "errors" of Common Sense. Long ago Parmenides said, "Heed not the blind eye, the echoing ear, nor yet the tongue, but bring to this great debate the test of reason." We might restate this philosophical recipe to the following effect, without antecedent prejudice to the question as to whether our senses are reliable sources of information or not: Disregard the eye, the ear, and the tongue (for we all pretty much hear the same, taste the same, and see the same), but bring only reasoning to a philosophical investigation. Moore's defence does not do this. Thus, e.g., Moore allows that he neither gives nor attempts to give an argument for *the premises* of what he puts forward as proofs for the existence of external things; and a philosopher who does give arguments against the Common Sense claim that we have knowledge of the existence of things like waistcoats and pens might, with the appearance of justification, charge that Moore is dogmatic and begs the question. And, indeed, Moore does need to explain why calling philosophers' attention to truths of Common Sense does not bring them back to it nor make them give up their wayward attacks on it. But perhaps an explanation can be found only by looking at philosophy from a vantage point outside it. It may be that only from an external standpoint will it be possible to see the nature of philosophical stalemates.

It can with justice be said that Wittgenstein has been read with too much haste recently and that some of his ideas have been slid over and others have been put into the service of the private needs of philosophers, with consequent gaps and distortions in our understanding of his later work. In the present connection it is important to read with particular care one of his passages on what happens when we philosophize and how we are to be brought back from philosophy to Common Sense without at the same time being brought back to philosophy. The passage also shows how his procedure differs from Moore's. Moore, on the whole, represents the philosopher who departs from Common Sense as having made an error of language, and identifies the mistake, with the aim of effecting a cure. The following is the passage:

When we think about the relation of the objects surrounding us to our personal experiences of them, we are sometimes tempted to say that these personal experiences are the material of which reality consists. How this temptation arises will become clearer later on.

When we think in this way we seem to lose our firm hold on the objects surrounding us. And instead we are left with a lot of separate personal experiences of different individuals. These personal experiences again seem vague and seem to be in constant flux. Our language seems not to have been made to describe them. We are tempted to think that in order to clear up such matters philosophically our ordinary language is too coarse, that we need a more subtle one.

We seem to have made a discovery—which I could describe by saying that the ground on which we stood and which appeared to be firm and reliable was found to be boggy and unsafe.—That is, this happens when we philosophize; for as soon as we revert to the standpoint of common sense this *general* uncertainty disappears.

This queer situation can be cleared up somewhat by looking at an example; in fact a kind of parable illustrating the difficulty we are in, and also showing the way out of this sort of difficulty: We have been told by popular scientists that the floor on which we stand is not solid, as it appears to common sense, as it has been discovered that the wood consists of particles filling space so thinly that it can almost be called empty. This is liable to perplex us, for in a way of course we know that the floor is solid, or that, if it isn't solid, this may be due to the wood being rotten but not to its being composed of electrons. To say, on this latter ground, that the floor is not solid is to misuse language. For even if the particles were as big as grains of sand, and as close together as these are in a sandheap, the floor would not be solid if it were composed of them in the sense in which a sandheap is composed of grains. Our perplexity was based on a misunderstanding; the picture of the thinly filled space had been wrongly *applied*. For this picture of the structure of matter was meant to explain the very phenomenon of solidity.

As in this example the word "solidity" was used wrongly and it seemed that we had shown that nothing really was solid, just in this way, in stating our puzzles about the *general vagueness* of sense-experience, and about the flux of all phenomena, we are using the words "flux" and "vagueness" wrongly, in a typically metaphysical way, namely, without an antithesis; whereas in their correct and everyday use, vagueness is opposed to clearness, flux to stability.[6]

Looking at a philosophical utterance in this way is enormously helpful, but it is not enough. And Wittgenstein did go beyond this point of view to deeper insights into the way philosophy works, as

[6] *The Blue Book*, pp. 45–6.

is shown, for example, by his characterizing a philosophical problem as one which arises "when language goes on holiday," [7] or "when language is like an engine idling, not when it is doing work." [8] The plain implication of these observations and of many other things he has said is that a philosophical problem is not a mere verbal muddle to be cleared up by analysis of usage, but is rather the expression of a special kind of game that can be played with language. On this construction of what doing philosophy consists in, to solve a philosophical problem is just to understand the game that is being played with terminology.

To go back to his earlier work, in the *Tractatus* Wittgenstein states a number of views about the nature of philosophy or of some of its parts. The following statements give the most important of the views he advanced:

> (1) Most of the propositions and questions to be found in philosophical works are not false but nonsensical. Consequently we cannot give any answer to questions of this kind, but can only establish that they are nonsensical. . . . And it is not surprising that the deepest problems are in fact *not* problems at all. [4.003]

> (2) Philosophy is not a body of doctrine but an activity. A philosophical work consists essentially of elucidations. Philosophy does not result in "philosophical propositions," but rather in the clarification of propositions. [4.112]

> (3) All philosophy is a "critique of language." . . . [4.0031]

> (4) The totality of true propositions is the whole of natural science (or the whole corpus of the natural sciences). [4.11] Philosophy is not one of the natural sciences. (The word "philosophy" must mean something whose place is above or below the natural sciences, not beside them.) [4.111] [9]

The inconsistencies among these different things that Wittgenstein said about philosophy are not inconspicuous, and their going unnoticed must have an explanation. But bringing out inconsistencies is not important in the present connection. What is important to see is that philosophy could present such different faces to him. About his own statements in the *Tractatus,* presumably those which concern philosophy, he said: "My propositions serve as elucidations in the following way: anyone who understands me eventually recog-

[7] *Investigations*, p. 19.
[8] *Ibid.*, p. 51.
[9] From the translation by D. F. Pears and B. F. McGuinness.

nizes them as nonsensical, when he has used them—as steps—to climb up beyond them. (He must, so to speak, throw away the ladder after he has climbed up it.) He must transcend these propositions, and then he will see the world aright" [6.54].

This pronouncement, which many people have found exciting, is odd, and the excitement it arouses must derive from some sort of hidden message it conveys. Perhaps, like the Delphic oracle, it "neither speaks nor conceals, but gives a sign." On the surface the pronouncement seems to imply that his own statements are nonsensical *elucidations,* and also, according to his own words, that nonsensical elucidations can lead to one's seeing the world aright. The underlying implication would seem to be that philosophers do not see the world aright, and that they can be led by nonsense to see it aright. It must be granted that nonsense seems at times to have remarkable curative powers, but it is hard to think that it could be a "specific" for philosophers. However that may be, the series of views he advanced, either explicitly or by implication, about philosophy are the following. (*a*) Most philosophical utterances are devoid of literal intelligibility, in the way in which "The good is more identical than the beautiful" is without literal intelligibility. (*b*) No philosophical proposition is true. This follows directly from (4), and parallels something he said at a later time: "What the philosophers (of whatever opinion) say is all wrong, but what the bedmaker says is all right." [10] He seems to have held, (*c*), that some philosophical propositions are true. Thus, he came out for one of Hume's views about causation: "Belief in the causal nexus is *superstition*" [5.1361]; and he also came out for the view that a proposition about the future is an hypothesis: "It is an hypothesis that the sun will rise tomorrow: and this means that we do not *know* whether it will rise" [6.36311]. (*d*) He held, furthermore, that in philosophy no propositions are advanced. According to one way philosophy presented itself to him, it was just clarification analysis and had no propositions of its own to put forward: there are no "philosophical propositions" as there are scientific ones.

The claim, (*a*), that most philosophical utterances are devoid of literal intelligibility is usually linked with the so-called Verifiability Principle, which requires some comment. Moritz Schlick formulated in the following words the principle for determining whether an

[10] From notes taken by A. Ambrose and M. Masterman in the intervals between dictation of *The Blue Book*. These notes will be referred to subsequently as *The Yellow Book*. [Note. A "bedmaker" is a domestic who services rooms in a Cambridge college: Ed.]

indicative sentence which does not express an *a priori* proposition has or lacks literal significance. "Stating the meaning of a sentence amounts to stating the rules according to which the sentence is to be used, and this is the same as stating the way in which it can be verified (or falsified). The meaning of a proposition is the method of its verification." [11] This version of the principle is usually attributed to Wittgenstein and probably it originated with him. It has commonly been understood by those who have rejected it, to eliminate metaphysical sentences from the class of literally meaningful sentences constructible in a language, and in this way to rid philosophy of its most spectacular if also its most unsatisfactory branch. This understanding of what the job of the criterion is fits in with a number of statements in the *Tractatus,* but a careful reading of the wording of the criterion brings to light the curious fact that it does not eliminate metaphysics and certainly contains within itself the possibility of the return of the rejected. For the criterion, as it is worded, does not preclude the possibility of there being supersensible verification, which would be the kind of verification appropriate to a statement referring to a nonsensible reality. That is, as phrased (and the phrasing cannot be supposed the result of a merely accidental lapse), the criterion is open to the specification, "The meaning of a metaphysical proposition is the method of its verification." The criterion does not rule out of court the claims of a philosopher like Husserl, who wrote: "Under the title of *A Pure or Transcendental Phenomenology* the work here presented seeks to found a new science—though, indeed, the whole course of philosophical development since *Descartes* has been preparing the way for it—a science covering a new field of experience, exclusively its own, that of 'Transcendental Subjectivity.' " [12]

In the present connection, it is particularly interesting to notice that one idea about philosophy expressed in the *Tractatus* (4.113) is that it "settles controversies about the limits of natural science." This would seem to imply the view that at least one task of philosophy is to settle territorial disputes between science and religion. The underlying idea, from which perhaps Wittgenstein never completely freed himself, is that the metaphysician is able to survey reality in all of its parts, supersensible as well as sensible, and, like the guide at the maze in Hampton Court, is able to help those who get lost

---

[11] *Gesammelte Aufsätze, 1926–36* (1938), p. 340.
[12] Edmund Husserl, *Ideas, General Introduction to Pure Phenomenology,* trans. by W. R. Boyce Gibson (1931), p. 11.

in the cosmic maze. This idea may have considerable connection with the fact that a number of Wittgenstein's later students have returned to metaphysics. It should be mentioned, however, that some followers of Wittgenstein have taken a different course, also consonant with the criterion. According to him one task of philosophy, perhaps its only task, is to bring to light modes of verification appropriate to different sorts of propositions. Interestingly enough, logic has a similar function, according to Aristotle. Ross describes Aristotle's conception of logic as not being "a substantive science, but a part of general culture which everyone should undergo before he studies any science, and which alone will enable him to know for what sorts of proposition he should demand proof and what sorts of proof he should demand for them." [13]

To return to the four different and incompatible views of philosophy to be found in the *Tractatus:* (a) Most philosophical utterances are senseless; (b) Philosophical propositions are not truths; (c) Some philosophical propositions are truths; (d) There are no philosophical propositions. These lie comfortably enough alongside each other, and there is no evidence that Wittgenstein ever attempted to sort them out and select from among them. Nevertheless, it cannot be supposed that in Wittgenstein's active and original mind they could continue indefinitely to live in amity with each other. And their existence shows unmistakably that one of his main preoccupations, perhaps his central one, was to get clear about the nature of philosophy. In his later thinking Wittgenstein did not completely free his mind from his earlier views about philosophy. A few examples will be enough to show this. In *Philosophical Investigations* he writes: "The results of philosophy are the uncovering of one or another piece of plain nonsense and of bumps that the understanding has got by running its head up against the limits of language" [14] and also, "My aim is: to teach you to pass from a piece of disguised nonsense to something that is patent nonsense." [15] In *The Blue Book* he sometimes seems to represent philosophers as making false empirical claims, although in this connection he disagrees with Moore as to how they are to be corrected. He wrote:

> There is no common-sense answer to a philosophical problem. One can defend common sense against the attacks of philosophers only by solving their puzzles, i.e., by curing them of the tempta-

---

[13] W. D. Ross, *Aristotle* (1930), p. 20.
[14] p. 48.
[15] p. 133.

tion to attack common sense, not by restating the views of common sense. A philosopher is not a man out of his senses, a man
who doesn't see what everybody sees; nor on the other hand is his
disagreement with common sense that of the scientist disagreeing
with the coarse views of the man in the street.[16]

At times he represents philosophers as making mistaken claims
about the uses of terminology, claims which his own investigations
are designed to correct. He describes what he does in the following
words:

> Our investigation is therefore a grammatical one. Such an
> investigation sheds light on our problem by clearing misunder-
> standings away. Misunderstandings concerning the use of words,
> caused, among other things, by certain analogies between the
> forms of expression in different regions of language.—Some of
> them can be removed by substituting one form of expression for
> another; this may be called an "analysis" of our forms of expres-
> sion, for the process is sometimes like one of taking a thing
> apart.[17]

He also wrote:

> When philosophers use a word—"knowledge," "being," "ob-
> ject," "I," "proposition," "name"—and try to grasp the *essence*
> of the thing, one must always ask oneself: is the word ever
> actually used in this way in the language game which is its original
> home?—
> What *we* do is to bring words back from their metaphysical to
> their everyday usage.[18]

At times he seems to represent the philosopher as making two
different kinds of mistake simultaneously, one a factual mistake, to
be removed by looking or introspection, the other a linguistic mistake, to be removed by noting what an expression is normally
applied to. Thus in *The Blue Book* he said: "Examine expressions
like 'having an idea in one's mind,' 'analyzing an idea before one's
mind.' In order not to be misled by them see what really happens
when, say, in writing a letter you are looking for the words which
correctly express the idea which is 'before your mind.' " [19] We may
gather from this that the Platonist, for example, is led by a common
form of words into holding a false factual belief about what is
before one's mind; he is misled by a linguistic analogy into forming

[16] pp. 58–59.
[17] *Investigations*, p. 43.
[18] *Ibid.*, p. 48.
[19] p. 41.

a wrong notion of the actual application of the expression, "analyzing an idea before one's mind" (compare with "analyzing a substance before one's eyes"). This in turn results in a false belief regarding what *is* before one's mind when one conducts an analysis. The impression gained is that both errors are to be corrected by looking at the facts, both the erroneous idea about usage and the erroneous idea about what takes place when we "have an idea before our mind." But plainly the "linguistic mistake" of the Platonist, who appears to think that there are special refined objects designated by the phrase "idea before one's mind," is not like that of a person who thinks the word "horse" is normally used to apply to cows or like that of a person who sees a horse but thinks he sees a cow or thinks he sees what in fact does not exist. Wittgenstein could not have failed to realize this, and, indeed, a new insight into philosophy had begun to develop in his mind.

The direction of his thinking became more and more oriented toward the notion that philosophical problems are muddles, verbal tangles which are to be straightened out by recourse to ordinary usage, with the help of a special device he called "language games." A philosopher develops a "mental cramp," and the therapy for removing it is to bring him back to ordinary usage. The following passage from *The Blue Book* will make this clear. In considering the question whether I can know or believe that someone else has a pain, he wrote:

> But wasn't this a queer question to ask? *Can't* I believe that someone else has pains? Is it not quite easy to believe this? . . . Needless to say, we don't feel these difficulties in ordinary life. Nor is it true to say that we feel them when we scrutinize our experiences by introspection. . . . But somehow when we look at them in a certain way, our expression is liable to get into a tangle. It seems as though we had either the wrong pieces, or not enough of them, to put together our jig-saw puzzle. But they are there, only all mixed up; . . .[20]

The thing to do to get straightened out, to cure our verbal malady, is "to look how the words in question *are actually used in our language*."[21] When Wittgenstein observed that to call what he did "philosophy" was perhaps proper but also misleading, and that what he did was one of the "heirs" of philosophy, he certainly had in mind the technique of examining the actual usage of expressions

[20] p. 46.
[21] *The Blue Book*, p. 56.

in the language for the purpose of "dissolving" philosophical problems. It is worth noticing, in passing, that he conceived his work as beneficially destructive: "Where does our investigation get its importance from, since it seems only to destroy everything interesting, that is, all that is great and important? (As it were all the buildings, leaving behind only bits of stone and rubble.) What we are destroying is nothing but houses of cards and we are clearing up the ground of language on which they stand." [22]

To return to the question whether what he did might appropriately be called philosophy, he had in mind not only the procedure of attempting to settle controversies by examining usage—so as to bring philosophers down to the linguistic realities—but also, possibly, the new notion that was beginning to take form. It must be allowed that he did not give very much expression to the insight into the linguistic structure of philosophical theories which gave rise to this notion, nor did he elaborate and develop it; but he did give *some* expression to it and he did make some application of it. In *The Blue Book* there occurs this important paragraph:

> The man who says "only my pain is real," doesn't mean to say that he has found out by the common criteria—the criteria, i.e., which give our words their comon meanings—that the others who said they had pains were cheating. But what he rebels against is the use of *this* expression in connection with *these* criteria. That is, he objects to using this word in the particular way in which it is commonly used. On the other hand, he is not aware that he is objecting to a convention. He sees a way of dividing the country different from the one used on the ordinary map. He feels tempted, say, to use the name "Devonshire" not for the county with its conventional boundary, but for a region differently bounded. He could express this by saying: "Isn't it absurd to make this a county, to draw the boundaries *here?*" But what he says is: "The *real* Devonshire is this." We could answer, "What you want is only a new notation, and by a new notation no facts of geography are changed." It is true, however, that we may be irresistibly attracted or repelled by a notation. (We easily forget how much a notation, a form of expression, may mean to us, and that changing it isn't always as easy as it often is in mathematics or in the sciences. A change of clothes or of names may mean very little and it may mean a great deal.) [23]

The idea that quite unmistakably comes through from this passage is that a philosophical theory is a misleadingly phrased intro-

[22] *Investigations*, p. 48.
[23] p. 57.

duction of an altered piece of terminology. The form of sentence in which a philosopher presents his remodelling of conventional language is the form of sentence ordinarily used to state a matter of fact; and in presenting his renovated terminology in this way he makes himself dupe to what he does, as well as anyone who either sides with him or opposes him. The philosopher imagines himself to be expressing a matter of fact or a theory, i.e., to be delivering himself on what really is the case or on what exists or on what cannot exist; and his mistake lies in the construction he places on what he is doing, not in his understanding of the actual use of terminology. He is mistaken about what he does with conventions of usage and is not mistaken about what the accepted conventions are:

> The fallacy we want to avoid is this: when we reject some form of symbolism, we're inclined to look as it as though we'd rejected a proposition as false. It is wrong to compare the rejection of a unit of measure as though it were the rejection of the proposition, "The chair is 3' instead of 2' high." This confusion pervades all philosophy. It's the same confusion that considers a philosophical problem as though such a problem concerned a fact of the world instead of a matter of expression.[24]

This view as to the nature of philosophical statements and of what might be called the "fallacy of philosophy" quite plainly has great explanatory power. The position that philosophical utterances are about states of affairs, about reality, does not, for one thing, square with the analytical arguments with which philosophers support their theories; neither does it explain, for another thing, how a philosopher can hold his views while not being, to use Wittgenstein's words, "a man out of his senses, a man who doesn't see what everybody sees." The position that philosophical utterances use language improperly or are misdescriptions of actual usage does not explain why a philosopher is not corrected by bringing terminology back to its "original home." It does not explain why a philosopher who is made to feel embarrassed by being shown the correct use of language nevertheless does not give up his claim, or if he does give it up is able to return to it later. The view which makes philosophical utterances out to be pronouncements embodying covertly revised criteria for the use of expressions explains both these things, and it also explains other eccentricities

---

[24] *The Yellow Book.*

attaching to philosophical theories. To use Wittgenstein's imaginative metaphor, it explains why the fly cannot be shown the way out of the fly-bottle. The fly cannot be led out because it does not want to be led out. The fly-bottle is only superficially its prison. At a deeper level, the fly-bottle is its home which it has built for itself out of language.

A somewhat extended passage from *The Yellow Book* would seem plainly enough to indicate that this was the direction his thinking took about the nature of philosophical theorizing, i.e., about what goes on when we think in a "philosophic moment," to use Moore's expression. It should be remarked immediately that the passage does not indicate this direction unambiguously and in so many plain words, without indications of other directions. But Wittgenstein's mind does not seem to have worked in straight lines. The following is the passage, and it is well worth a careful reading:

> Suppose now I call my body by the name of Wittgenstein. I can now say, "Wittgenstein has toothache," just as I can say, "Shaw has toothache." On the other hand I should have to say, "I feel the pain," and I might feel it at a time when Wittgenstein had not toothache; or when Shaw had. It is only a matter of fact that Wittgenstein has the toothache when I feel the pain.
>
> If I use "I" and "Wittgenstein" thus, "I" is no longer opposed to anything. So we could use a different kind of notation. We could talk of pain in the one case and of behavior in the other. But does this mean the same as saying that I have real toothache and the other person has not? No, for the word "I" has now vanished from the language. We can only now say, "There is toothache," give its locality and describe its nature.
>
> In doing this we are keeping the ordinary language and beside it I am putting another. Everything said in the one can, of course, be said in the other. But the two draw different boundaries; arrange the facts differently. What is queer about an ordinary notation is that it draws a boundary round a rather heterogeneous set of experiences. This fact tempts people to make another notation, in which there is no such thing as the proprietor of a toothache. But without the people realizing it, or even realizing that there are two, the two notations clash.
>
> Put it another way. To the person who says, "Only I can have real toothache," the reply should be, "If only you can have real toothache there is no sense in saying, 'Only I can have real toothache.'" Either you don't need 'I' or you don't need 'real.' Your notation makes too many specifications. You had much better say, 'There is toothache,' and then give the locality and the description. This is what you are trying to say and it is much clearer

without too many specifications. 'Only I have real toothache' either has a common-sense meaning, or, if it is a grammatical (philosophical) proposition, it is meant to be a statement of a rule; it wishes to say, 'I should like to put,' instead of the notations, 'I ache.' Thus the rule does not allow 'only I have real toothache' to be said. But the philosopher is apt to say the thing which his own rule has just forbidden him to say, by using the same words as those in which he has just stated the rule.

"I can't know whether another person has toothache" seems to indicate a barrier between me and the other person. I want to point out to you that this is a pseudo-problem. It is our language which makes it seem as though there were a barrier.

I talked before of the differences which our language stresses, and the differences it hushes up. Here is a wonderful example of a difference hushed up. It is not entirely hushed up; for of course all the notations must have the same multiplicity. Nothing can be said in the one which can't also be said in the others. But a notation can stress, or it can minimize; and in this case it minimizes.[25]

Even a cursory reading of these words exposes a number of different tendencies in Wittgenstein's thinking about philosophy. Thus, he describes the question as to whether it is possible to know that another person has a pain as a "pseudo-question." There is also the hint that a philosophical problem is some sort of mix-up, the linguistic symptom of a mental cramp. There is, further, the notion that philosophical theories, or anyway some philosophical theories, introduce alternative forms of expression which translate into expressions in ordinary use, i.e., "keeping the ordinary language and beside it . . . putting another," the difference between the two being that they "arrange the facts differently." It may be remarked, to bring into connection what Wittgenstein says here with other things he says about philosophy, that it is hard to see how an alternative notation could in any way be an attack on common sense, to be cured by bringing philosophers back to ordinary language. And it is equally hard to see how a notation which uses "the words 'flux' and 'vagueness' wrongly, in a typically metaphysical way, namely, without an antithesis" could translate into ordinary language where "in their correct and everyday use vagueness is opposed to clearness, flux to stability." Indeed, it is not hard to see that a notation which translates into the language of common sense cannot be an attack on common sense; and it is not hard to see that a notation in which ordinary words occur without their antitheses cannot trans-

[25] *The Yellow Book.*

late into, have "the same multiplicity" as, a language in which they occur with their antitheses. All this only goes to show that on different occasions and in somewhat different connections Wittgenstein tried out different ideas to explain the enigma that is philosophy.

If we do not let ourselves be diverted by the different ideas in the above passage as to what a philosopher does and how he gets himself into difficulties, we are led to the notion, not that the philosopher fails to "command a clear view of our use of words," but that the perception he has into the uses of words makes him wish to modify or in some way alter those uses. It is evident that the alterations he institutes do not have any of the jobs alternative forms of expression usually have, e.g., to say the same thing with greater economy or with improved efficiency for calculating or with greater vividness or just to avoid monotony of expression. The picture of the philosopher which begins to come into focus is that of someone who scans the intricate map of language, and, unlike the grammarian and the thesaurus compiler, is not satisfied merely to report rules imbedded in the language, but in various ways changes the rules. Differences in the uses of expressions which ordinary language does not perspicuously display, differences which it "hushes up," he is sometimes impelled to try to bring out in sharp relief; and differences in the uses of expressions ordinary language "stresses" he is sometimes inclined to mute. The reasons, in the form of arguments, that he gives for the changes he introduces quite obviously make negligible or no connection with the everyday kinds of work language does for us. The conclusion which is at least latent in a good many things he said is that a philosopher alters ordinary language or "puts another language beside it" for the remarkable effects doing this creates. In the passage above, ordinary language is represented as responsible for the idea that a barrier exists between people which prevents one person from knowing that another has a pain. But it should be realized at once that the sentence "I cannot know whether another person has a toothache," i.e., the sentence which creates the idea of a barrier, is *not* an ordinary sentence. Wittgenstein was, of course, aware that ordinary language does not put this idea in the mind of "the man in the street": in his words, "we don't feel these difficulties in ordinary life." The sentence is a philosophical production whose job is not at all like that of a sentence such as "I cannot know whether Socrates has a toothache; he endures pain with stoicism." To describe what is happening in Wittgenstein's way, a philosopher who says, "I cannot know whether another has a pain" is objecting to the conventional use of "has a pain" but is not aware that he is objecting to a convention. His sentence announces the academic deletion from the language of such phrases as "knows that another person has a pain," "knows that another person sees red," and in this way he brings out the great difference between the use of "has a pain" and the use of "has a tooth." But he introduces his reediting of language conventions in a way which creates the idea that there is some sort of barrier between people. It is not everyday language but the manner in which he announces changes in everyday language which is responsible for the inappropriate idea.

When Wittgenstein said, "What we are destroying is nothing but houses of cards and we are clearing up the ground of language on which they stand," quite possibly what he intended to convey was that, like the pretence use of cards as building materials, a philosophical theory is constituted by a pretence use of language. Quite possibly he wanted to convey that to give utterance to a philosophical theory is not to use language to express a theory but is only to use language to create the false idea that a theory is being expressed. And when he observed that "we may be irresistibly attracted by a notation," he may have been referring to deeper things in our minds that philosophical utterances link up with. It is not easy to know where one is reading too much and where too little into the mind of an original thinker.

The Blue Book

BY O. K. BOUWSMA

WHEN I FIRST BEGAN THINKING about writing this paper on *The Blue Book,* I thought it might be helpful and interesting to find out something about the history of this book. Accordingly I wrote to Miss Alice Ambrose, with whose generous permission I am including the following note from her letter in response.

This is the note:

> The history of *The Blue Book* is as follows: Wittgenstein was listed in the Cambridge *Reporter* as giving two courses of lectures in 1933–34, one being called "Philosophy for Mathematicians." To this, as I remember, 30 or 40 people turned up, which distressed him. After three or four weeks of lecturing he turned up at lecture and told the class he couldn't continue to lecture. I remember the occasion and remember how amazed I was that an announced course of lectures could be abandoned in this way. Of the people in that class he chose five of the rest of us to dictate *The Blue Book* to: H. M. S. Coxeter and R. L. Goodstein, mathematicians, also Francis Skinner (who might have been on a Trinity Grant to do math. though he actually left off doing math. in order to devote himself to Wittgenstein's work), Margaret Masterman Braithwaite and myself. About a month later, I see by a reference to my diary that the five of us had increased to seven, and I know one of them was Mrs. Helen Knight but for the life of me I can't remember the other one. Wittgenstein quarreled with Coxeter because Coxeter quite innocently ran off on a mimeograph the material for the first term's dictation and discussion. So Coxeter didn't continue in the second term. Mrs. Braithwaite also dropped out during the year in the third term. I've forgotten what the unpleasantness was in her case. She and I took down discussion that he wasn't including in *The Blue Book* and we called this *The Yellow Book*. He once flew at her for doing so, but as he was also distressed when something he thought good was not taken down because he wasn't dictating—and she pointed this out to him at the time—this practice on our part was allowed to continue. I believe I continued with it after she left. *The Blue*

Book dictation and discussion went on during all three terms along with the other set of lectures—which were evidently attended by quite a large group since I refer to them in my diary as "big" (12 members I see from one entry). The small group met for *The Blue Book* each week as regularly as for a class. I can't remember whether this was the year Moore attended his lectures, but I suspect it was. Can't remember how many terms he attended. I have notes from these lectures. But *The Blue Book* was dictated. I believe I typed some of the dictated material and later on Wittgenstein had it mimeographed—but not a few pages at a time. When he had the material compiled into *The Blue Book* I don't remember but I suppose after the year was over. Yes, there was discussion during the dictation but what he did at each meeting was not greatly determined by our comments, as I remember it. I believe that what he talked about in the lectures and what he gave us for *The Blue Book* was pretty different.

The Brown Book, like *The Blue Book,* was dictated throughout the three terms along with his regular lecture course. For that Skinner and I were the only ones and we met him 2–4 hours per day, 4 days a week. That was in 1934–35. We sometimes went on beyond term for a few days of the vacation.

In a later note she wrote:

As for your question about how *The Blue Book* was dictated, as far as I remember he never had even notes with him. I think I remember but once, and I think this was a lecture when he seemed to have a card with him to which he referred once or twice at the beginning of the lecture. It was in general unlike him to write out things ahead. His custom was to dictate, stop for discussion, and continue dictation.

A reviewer is expected to have read and to understand the book he reviews. Accordingly, since I am about to review this book, or something of that sort, naturally I expect that I understand it. And if I understand it, and there are some readers who do not, perhaps I can help them to understand it, or at least help them not to misunderstand in certain ways or help them to misunderstand it in a certain preferred way. This is rather strange since it seems to involve that the author himself failed to help them to understand it or failed to help them enough, and so some reader comes forward to do what the author did not do. In some cases this seems to be how it is. Think of all the helps over hard places for boys and men in reading Kant, for instance, supplied by helpers. Kant couldn't do it. So here are all Kant's little helpers. Very well, then, I too am a little helper. But if I am such a little helper I am going to help myself generously to the helpmost helper, namely, the author himself. I will help the reader to the help offered by the author, reminding the reader of those helps.

This book, notes, discussions, investigations, dictations, contains no introduction, no conclusion, no chapters, no chapter headings, no helpful title. So at the outset there is no guide, no warning, no preparation, no cautionary remark. Perhaps the students to whom these dictations were dictated were better prepared. I doubt it, however. The author may very well have considered and said that a bump is also education, a bump of the right sort, of course—bumping one's head, for instance, against such a question as "What is the meaning of a word?" If accordingly the reader has pretty well absorbed the shock of that question and has gone on reading, since all the words are familiar enough—there are scarcely any strange words,—he may nevertheless soon feel as though he were being turned round and round and then as though this world of words were whirling past him. There seems to be no increment, nothing upon which one can fix his grasp and tell his friends, "This I have found." And if now he tries again, reading more slowly, intent upon this paragraph and then upon the next one, then even though he may seem to understand this paragraph and the next one, he will not understand how they are connected. He may ask himself: And what about that question: "What is the meaning of a word?" And what have "toves" and the "red flower" of the field to do with it? What is the individuality of a number? How long is a piece of string? And as he pages through the book, the contents may strike him as more and more distressing. Such incoherence! "Bring me a red flower," "We observe certain actions of the amoeba," thinking "performed by the hand," "the visual image two inches behind the bridge of my nose," "Imagine a yellow patch," "Can a machine have toothache?," "Bright's disease," "unconscious toothache," "Do you know the ABC?," "How can we hang a thief who doesn't exist?," "Is your imagination so absolutely exact . . . ?" One may certainly wonder as to how those students learned anything from these dictations and may quit trying oneself. Madness, perhaps, but little method! Of course, one may still go on reading since these pages are studded with scenery, startling and sometimes amusing. So one may go along for the ride.

The impression of incoherence is, I suspect, common to nearly all readers. And there are reasons other than the formal ones I've

noticed to account for this. This book is a book in philosophy.
And it is read chiefly by readers of philosophy. And with what
expectations would such readers read? Obviously they will expect
what they are accustomed to getting when they read philosophy.
Their disappointment and the measure of incoherence will be determined in the same way. And what are they used to? They are used
to proofs, to arguments, to theories, to evidences, refutations, to
infallibles, to indubitables, to foundations, to definitions, to analyses, etc. And if in these terms any reader should, having read,
seek to turn his reading to some profit and ask himself: "What has
the author proved, for what has he presented arguments, what is
his theory, what has he refuted, and what are his infallibles?," he is
certain to be disappointed. The author has neither proved nor refuted anything. And he has presented nothing as infallible, nor a
theory. What is such an author doing in philosophy? A skeptic one
might admit. He understands the questions and understands what
ignorance and knowledge are. He has busied himself about the questions. He has said: "We do not and we cannot know," presumably
a respectable answer. The skeptic has tried and failed and investigated the nature of his failure. Man cannot know as he cannot fly.
He is not an angel. And this author? This author spends seventy
and more pages lolling. He does not, of course, say that he is lolling,
which seems anyway obvious enough, since he does it so strenuously, nor that he lolls evading. So he's no angel either. In any
case it does strike some readers that this book is the work of a
strangely articulate and irresponsible author. He doesn't say "Yes"
and he doesn't say "No." The flexible man! Was Descartes right
in his statement of the *Cogito* or not? What we want is an answer:
Yes, or: No. And what do we get? Not even a weak answer such
as "Probably" or "Not at all likely." Surely a straight-forward
question deserves a straight-forward answer. No wonder that man
stomped out and slammed the door.

I have been trying in these paragraphs to represent a certain
source of misunderstanding, an obstacle to understanding. It may
also be represented in this way: Philosophers are people who investigate what sorts of things there are in the universe. They are, of
course, scrupulous in these investigations beyond the scrupulosity
of any other investigator. They stand at the gate and wait, fearing
to tread where angels rush in. And what do they ask? They ask
such questions as: Are there angels, universals, pure possibilities,

uncrusted possibilities, possibilities with a little mud on them, fairies, creatures made of beautiful smoke, relations, the Lost Atlantis, real equality among toothpicks, sense data, ghosts, selves in prison with two feet, everlasting shoemakers, heaven, thinking horses, pure uncontaminated acts, absolutely independent tables, the minds of stars, the spirits of an age, perfect circles, the geometrical point of a joke, the devil, floating impressions, categorical don'ts, one simple called Simon, perspectives waiting to take their places as the penny turns, gods, any ding-dong an sich with a bell so one can find it in the dark, trees, houses, and mountains in the mind, itches of necessary connection, two impossibilities before breakfast, blue ideas, enghosted pieces of furniture, etc.?

And if now anyone comes to the reading of this book expecting the author, for instance, to say: "Yes, yes, God exists," and then to show him a new and knockout proof that is guaranteed for a thousand years or to help him to an old one, long buried in a Kant heap, but now freshly washed and polished, well, the author is more likely to remind him that though Nietzsche some years ago read an obituary notice to the effect that God is dead, he, the author, had not even heard that God was sick. "The living God!" And as for inventing any new *a priori* synthetic, a new drug to cure this or that, or any and all, sorts of incertitude, though he seems at one time to have been interested in inventing a new type of airplane propeller and showed a keen interest in all sorts of gadgets, a milk bottle, for instance, from which, with the use of a spoon, one could pour off the cream—"Now, there's America for you!"—this particular form of invention he seems not to have been interested in. He was more inclined to recommend a few old home remedies and common herbs, garden-variety simples which he was insistent one should not confuse. And as for those readers in general who want answers to their questions and who, if they already have answers, want better reasons, the author gives neither better reasons for the old answers nor any answers, and those readers who keep their questions may be considered either fortunate or unfortunate, as the case may be.

I have tried to show how it is that this book should disappoint some readers, supposing that they had expectations in reading it. I have suggested that the reason why such readers have such expectations is that it is, or is read as, a book in philosophy. And it is a book in philosophy surely? Well, it is and it isn't. It is certainly obvious that the author is busy about philosophical problems.

The first sentence in the book is the sentence: "What is the meaning of a word?" and that is a philosophical staple, a sort of thorn which all philosophers carry about with them. And there are others: What is thinking? What is locality? What is a rule? What is expectation? What is time? What is knowledge? So if one were to show someone that this is a book in philosophy and that those readers who were disappointed in it were justified in expecting what they have been led to expect from it, one might point out to him the presence in the book of these questions. Of course, these readers might still be misled. For the question is: Are these questions treated philosophically in the book? and if this means: Are they treated in the way in which such questions are treated by Descartes or Hume or Plato? who either give answers to such questions or at least try to—they certainly are not men of whom one might be tempted to say that they once did good work and then said to themselves, "I have done enough, now I'll rest; let George do it, while I fiddle with words,"—the answer is that they are not treated philosophically. So if some reader complains, "But I thought that the author was another Descartes," we can understand what he was looking for and what led him to this.

And now it would be natural to say that since the author is manifestly aware of these questions, and must know that these questions cry out and have been crying out for centuries for answers, that he does not answer is a bad sign. For either he does not understand these questions and spends his words and his thoughts in evasions, or he understands but cannot answer these questions and now spends his words and thoughts in other evasions. In either case what we seem to have—modesty mercifully tempering judgment—is seventy and more pages of evasion, diversionary tactics, a whole school of red herrings. (Red herring and straw men and a few dead ducks are most common among the fish, flesh, and fowl in these woods.) It seems in any case that in the midst of these pressing and worrying questions—and what questions could be more urgent?—the author skips about in what strikes some as a kind of philosophical surrealism, juxtaposing the most distantly related ideas such as machines and toothaches, and questions and cramps, and mental processes and fidgeting with teacups. There are realists, naive realists, sophisticated realists, neo-realists, critical realists, semi-critical realists, and now surrealists. "The cow jumped over the moon."

I have certainly made it plain that the author has not altogether

abandoned those questions with which we have been so much occupied. It isn't as though he quite bluntly said that these are not
questions, which on the face of it they obviously are—in fact it is
precisely the face of it that leads us on. The questions look like
questions, sound like questions, and are labored over as questions.
There are, in fact, answers too, many answers, and it is said that
there are so many answers shows that the questions are difficult
and if askers complain that answerers do not understand answerers,
this shows it all the more. And now it isn't as though the author
said that someone first began trying to find the answers to exclamations and then others joined in and they asked and they answered
and did not understand one another's answers and then all talked
about what difficult questions the exclamations are. If someone in
such a situation had said, "But these aren't questions, they're
exclamations," one can imagine the hubbub that would have ensued.
They would have exclaimed and questioned and protested and
held up each other's favorite exclamations to show that they were
questions and they would have deferred to one another's questions,
if not to one another's answers. But this is all foolishness. It isn't
at all like that. Still, ...

Whatever these questions are they certainly aren't exclamations.
Are they nothing? Well, if so, they are an especially interesting
sort of nothing which can be heard, seen, worried about, respected,
etc. We can be sure, too, that these questions are not rhetorical
questions, nor pretended questions as though someone made them
up to look like and sound like questions. Nor are they to be explained as slips of the tongue or pen, though someone might
suggest, jokingly, of course, that when your thinking slips, questions like this might happen. And your thinking slipping is rather
like your tongue slipping, an educated tongue, that is. And if,
by the way, in this book the word "muddle" should come in it
should not be understood that the author intends to *tell* you that
these questions are muddles. In what follows I should like to try
to explain what he does do.

And now I want to try to help myself to keep a certain perspective of what the author is doing. It may not be the only one nor the
most profitable one but it suits me. I say what the author is *doing*
rather than what the author is saying in order to prevent the misunderstanding that one could be told what he says and if one then

remembered this, that would be what the author aimed at. This would be as though the author aimed to put something in the reader's pocket. But what he does is unlike that. What, then, is he doing? Remember to begin with that these are dictations. They are dictated to a few students. And now I want to say that these dictations are designed in connection with other oral discussions to help in teaching these students an art. Obviously these students must also exercise themselves in practicing this art. "Now you do it." This art has been described in a variety of ways. *It is the art of attacking those questions* we noticed earlier. Attacking is not answering. If this description should give a wrong impression, let us say that it is the gentle art of attacking. *It is the art of disentangling.* Disentangling what? Meanings. If it should come as a surprise that meanings can be entangled, be assured, then, that it is a part of the teaching to show how meanings can be entangled and disentangled. *It is the art of cure.* This is, perhaps, the description of the art which is best known. There is physical therapy. There is mental therapy. And here is a specialty. There are mental cramps. Perhaps it will be better to disassociate it from the expression "mental therapy." Let us call it intellectual therapy of a certain sort. *It is the art of finding one's way when lost.* And who is lost? Who isn't? And where? In the woods. In a labyrinth. Without Ariadne threads of discourse which one must learn to use—everyone has his head full of them—one cannot find his way. *It is the art of removal, of riddance.* And what does one get rid of? Of temptations. What temptations? Not bottles, except on occasion and then it is not the bottle which is the temptation, which any fly would like to be in a position to tell you. "I have been trying in all this to remove the temptation to think that there must be . . ." [p. 41]. *It is the art of discussion.* For what purpose? To show differences. One might be inclined to say that, whereas Socrates practiced and taught the art of discussion for the sake of seeking what is common, this author practiced and taught the art of discussion in order to restore the balance, to correct distortion, stressing differences. And what is the art of discussion? It is the art of presenting meaning. *It is the art of exposure.* Exposing what? Hidden analogies. As there are hidden motives, not hidden by but hidden even from those whose motives they are, and these are helpful in explaining what people do when they are themselves persuaded, so too there are hidden analogies which are not noticed by those on whose behalf they are appealed to to explain what they say. *It is the art of helpful reminders.* For what purpose? When your words seem to carry you along so that you seem to have lost the reins and you lose your head to the words, then, if you pause, reminding yourself of how words are harnessed together to do the speaker's work, then you regain control. Runaway language.

It is the art of working-puzzles. Crossword puzzles? No, not crossword puzzles but word puzzles. The author's analogy is with jig-saw puzzles. "It's no use trying to apply force in fitting pieces together. All we should do is to look at them carefully and arrange them" [p. 46]. Presumably there are sentences or rather arrangements of words which puzzle us because the words are jumbled, though not in such a way as immediately to strike us as jumbled. So we may ask: Are they jumbled? And then we rearrange them and get them in order. *It is the art of scrutinizing the grammar of a word.* Naturally this is to serve a purpose. If we recall that it is in terms of the grammar of a word, some particularly relevant part of the context of a word, that we present to ourselves that aspect of the meaning of a word we need in order to bring to light some deviation from the grammar of the word, into which we may have drifted or fallen, we can understand the service of such scrutiny. *It is the art of freeing us from illusions.* Illusions? Yes, illusions of a special sort, illusions of sense where there is no sense. And how are we freed from illusions? By looking more closely. So in this case we look more closely at the sentence or sentences with respect to which we are deceived. And how, then, do we look more closely? Obviously it is not a matter of looking more closely at the words on the page. What we are to see looking more closely is that the words as they are put together here, perhaps not only in this sentence but in these surroundings, cease to have the meaning which they have in the surroundings in which they have meaning. And no other meaning has been given. *It is the art of the detective.* The author also describes what he does as "investigations." "In fact one may say that what in these investigations we were concerned with . . ." [p. 70]. A detective is one who surveys the scene, notices details, picks up scraps, fragments, piecing them together in order to get some idea, a picture of what happened. With every new clue he gets a new picture or a completer picture. He abandons clues, and seizes upon new ones. He is frequently like a man groping in the dark. And the art of the investigator taught in these dictations also surveys the language scene, looking for clues, hitting on this, guessing here, in order to explain the deviation, the unwitting deviation, from sense. "So this is what misled me." But what he must hit upon is the explanation which will satisfy the thinker who was himself misled. Until he has done this he is not freed. This analogy is intended to stress that there is no straight line of investigation. Cases here may be as baffling and complicated as cases which the detective investigates. It would, however, be misleading to say that the investigator also tries to get a picture of what happened. He has nothing to investigate but the language. And that is not a happening. *It is the art of clarification, of relief from the toils of confusion.* What confusion? Grammatical confusion. There is strife among these words that will not lie down together and that keep up this turmoil in our heads. And there will be no rest until we put each word into its own bed.

That fly that was let out of the fly-bottle understands how he got in there, since the condition of his being let out is that he should understand that. And now he can fly in and out as he likes. It is no longer a fly-bottle for him. He can now buzz in and out enjoying the structure of the bottle. A fun-bottle, then? Yes, until he finds himself in another bottle with a different opening. Eternal vigilance is the price of buzzing freely.

The variety among these descriptions may suggest to us something of the complexity of the art which the author set out to teach. It is, however, unlikely that, apart from the practice of it in the examination of particular cases which constitutes the main body of *The Blue Book,* these descriptions will be helpful. For it is the author himself who introduced these descriptions in order to help these students to get the point of what he was doing. So the presence of these descriptions for that purpose also suggests how difficult he must have found trying to teach this to others. Now, however, I should like to give an account, perhaps misleadingly simple, of what the author does in this book. On page 16 is the sentence: "I shall propose to you to look closely at particular cases . . . ," and what I want to give an account of is what the author does looking closely. If what I now go on to say is simple, this should not lead one to suppose that to do what he does is either simple or easy.

One may, as I think, distinguish in the art I have been describing three phases or moments. I hesitate to say that there are

three things which he does. And I do not mean to say that in looking closely at any particular case all three phases can be distinguished or that there is this systematic arrangement, one, two,
three, which he follows. There is not. I mean rather that whenever
he is looking closely at some particular case he will be engaged
in one of these three phases or moments. And I have intentionally
used the words "phases" or "moments" to avoid the mistake of supposing that some exact line could be drawn between them. The
three phases I have in mind are these: First, the author seeks to
quicken the sense of the queer. Second, the author is concerned
to present the meaning of those expressions which are involved in
the particular case, and especially those which are relevant to exhibiting not the queerness but the sources, the roots of it. Third,
the author seeks to uncover the "misleading analogy." These
phases or objectives are not pursued in any such order, though they
may be, but it may well be that one's sense of the queer is quickened
by the presentation of the meaning and even more by the uncovering of "the misleading analogy."

I want to explain each of these.

It is quite obvious that, except for a few extraordinary cases,
philosophical questions do not strike us as queer. Perhaps to begin
with a question like: Do I exist? or Do I alone exist? or Do forests
murmur? may strike a young ear or an untutored ear as queer, but
such questions as What is knowledge? or Does God exist? or How
is science possible? are not likely to strike either a young ear or an
old ear as queer. Accordingly, if the beginning of intelligence lies
here, it is obvious that a great deal of work must be done with
spoiled ears. They do not hear the queer. The queerness of the
questions must be made to ring. And so the author must make it
ring. There are presumably a number of ways. Sometimes it is
sufficient or at least helpful to draw attention to the queerness.
"Now, listen to the question: What is the meaning of a word?
Can't you hear that's queer?" And then, if someone strains to hear,
he will hear it queer like a shadow passing over the question.
There are other ways. If there are questions which have already
struck one as queer and these questions are heard now side by
side with the other question, the queerness of these questions may,
as it were, be communicated to the other question, like vibrations.
And if there are no familiar questions which one may employ to
bring out the queerness of the first one, then one may invent some

questions in which the queerness is as loud as a bang. "What is the color of the number three?" Does unconscious toothache hurt in the unconscious more, or less, than conscious toothache hurts in consciousness? Of course, one must exercise a nice judgment here, inventing only what is adapted to the necessities of the case. It may be a mistake to invent a question whose queerness is loud as a bang. One may need queerness that whispers, barely audible, sufficient to provide the right nuance. There are other ways, such as giving an answer intended to echo the form of queerness in the question. "Thinking is a process which goes on invisibly in your feet while you are busy making words at the other end of the line." "Why in the feet?" "Well, why not?" But one may also accentuate the queerness by the contrast with the unqueer. You ask: What is the meaning of a word? and do not know what to say. But when I ask you: What is the meaning of the word "ogre"?, you tell me. So you do know what the meaning of a word is, namely, the word "ogre." So what is it you do not know? It should be obvious that what is done in such cases is to play with the similarities and differences among whatever forms of sense and sentences may serve the purpose.

And now I want to go on to the second phase, the presentation of meaning. If we regard the queerness discussed in the preceding paragraph as an impression of a sometimes scarcely perceptible deviation from sense, then we may appreciate the author's interest in presenting the sense. For in that case what is involved is a contrast between what is regarded as a deviation and some sense or other also of course heard or seen. Something is not quite right. Perhaps the word "difference" is a better word than "contrast." What accordingly we have is either sense in the guise of nonsense or nonsense in the guise of sense. It sounds like sense and it sounds like nonsense. It cannot in any particular case be both. If a question sounds queer, then it will not be surprising if it turns out to be nonsensical. And if it turns out to make sense, then some special explanation will be needed to show this sense. There may be some analogy one has missed. "The child is father of the man," "Go and catch a falling star." In any case if this is how the queerness is to be regarded, then in order to understand it, it will be necessary to exhibit the sense from which the sentence or sentences are a deviation. The principle involved is simple. Some words together in a certain order, taken together with other words, etc., make sense and the same words taken together with certain other words in a certain order do not make sense. So what we need is to remind ourselves of the sense of the words which make up the queer sentence in order to see precisely what the deviation, what the difference is.

And how now does one present the sense?

Presenting the sense must not be confused with giving the meaning. If someone does not know the meaning of a word, then you explain the meaning to him. But presenting the sense is not like that. If you know the meaning, then you can present the sense. And this consists in reminding oneself of what one says, the lay of the lingo in the surroundings of this or that word, what words, sentences, go together with the word or expression about which one is concerned. I consider it absolutely magnificent that a man should have conceived of the idea that you can present to yourself the meaning of a word. And yet, it turns out to be so simple. That one is able to do this provides the perspective which makes possible the comparisons and contrasts by means of which similarities and differences are discernible. For what holds of the delineation of sense holds also of the delineation of nonsense. The point in presenting the meaning is not to present the meaning complete—even in a dead language meaning is not complete—but to present so much of the meaning as is required for whatever the purpose may be.

The third phase is that of uncovering the "misleading analogy." If it is allowed that the queerness which the author is concerned with is that of nonsense in the guise of sense, then we may conceive of the task involved as two-fold, namely, to exhibit the nonsense, the deviation from sense, and to explain the illusion of sense. How is it that one should have come to ask this or to say this in the first place, and that one should hold on so tenaciously? There are a number of analogies we may notice in the book: "We try to find a substance for a substantive" [p. 1]; "The contradiction which here seems to arise could be called a conflict between two different usages of a word, in this case, the word 'measure' " [p. 26]; "the existence of the words 'thinking' and 'thought' along side of the words denoting (bodily) activities, such as writing, speaking, etc., makes us look for an activity, different from these but analogous to them, corresponding to the word 'thinking,' " [p. 7] etc. Uncovering the misleading analogy helps one to explain the hold of these questions upon us. Hector was dragged around the city of Troy by a horse. But we are dragged around by hidden analogies and most of all if we think. This is how it comes about that some-times the best advice is: "Don't think. Look." And it may be hard not to think.

The author has the following explanation of the misleading analogy: "The cases in which particularly we wish to say that someone is misled by a form of expression are those in which we would say: 'He wouldn't talk as he does if he were aware of this difference in the grammar of such-and-such words, or if he were aware of this other possibility of expression'" [p. 28]. It may be helpful to add that if today he wouldn't, then tomorrow when he is aware, he won't. The point is that the object is not a science of misleading expressions from which one can now figure out what is misleading some stranger. The object is to assist some individual, always an individual, to help him discover what misleads and has misled him. And what misled him is to be seen only when he is no longer misled. When he says: "Now, I see" and breathes a sigh of relief, even though it may be a bit sheepishly, that is the moment to which the art is directed.

Here we may take notice of the analogy with psychoanalysis. We might say in connection with psychoanalysis: "He wouldn't do as he does if he were aware of what it is in his past that he has forgotten that now drives him to do this." And the art in this case is devoted to refreshing his memory and to bringing him round to where he says, "That is it," and now he doesn't do it anymore. This is cure. In the case of both those who talk as they do and those who do as they do, the explanation is not to be sought in asking them. They find out only as by cure they also cease to talk so and to do so. Beyond this the analogy does not go. In the case of psychoanalysis it is the past, the materials of memory, both lost but retrievable, and not lost, which one tries to bring back, to discover the moving cause, something hidden. But in the case of "He wouldn't talk as he does," one does not investigate anyone's past. One investigates the language and a particular area of that, and that is much more like investigating a familiar part of one's environment, which is also the environment of all of us. There is nothing sticky about this investigation, no private dirty linen shook and washed in private or in public.

There is one further point. The misleading analogy is hidden. It is present in the language and not hidden there. It is, however, hidden from the person who is misled by it. Hence it isn't as though he attended carefully to the analogy and went on from there with his eyes open. In that case he could tell us that he was following an analogy. But he knows nothing about it. All the same he keeps bumping his head against it. Relieving him consists in getting him to recognize the analogy that has misled him. And what are the clues? His question, and what he goes on to say in explaining and answering the question, will bear the marks of the analogy. There are forms of bewilderment too.

I have now given an account of the art which, as I conceive it, the author of this book teaches in three phases. It is carried on by discussion, either in writing or orally. There is commonly a helper and a helped, though obviously several people may help one another. The queer is seen to be queerer and queerer. Ideas mingled throw up a mist and when by way of discussion, catalytic agent, the ideas fall apart, the mist is cleared away.

I have already referred to the complexity and the difficulty of teaching this art. And how does one go about teaching an art? No doubt, by practicing it and in such a way that the learner can observe what the teacher is doing. In teaching someone to use his hands, in carpentry for instance, the learner observes how the teacher holds the tools and what he does with each. He learns by doing what the teacher does. The teacher also observes what the learner does and now and then corrects him. Of course the learner understands that he is building a house and why he does what he does. He did not have to be told what carpentry is. Didn't he come to the carpenter and say, "Teach me to be a carpenter"? How different it is with these students! They could have had no idea what the art was that he would teach them and perhaps had no idea that he was to teach them an art. They had more likely come to him expecting that he would answer their questions. Perhaps they asked him: "What is the meaning of a word?" or "What is thinking?" So he, unlike the carpenter, had not simply to teach them an art with which they were well acquainted, but he had to introduce them to an art of which they had not heard and for which they could have felt no need. Hence, even if he had stood before them and said: "Now, pay close attention to what I am doing" and had then gone on to practice his art as he does in those early pages, is it likely that they would have understood? He is, remember, teaching an art which is new. He is the author, the inventor, the first teacher. But why should an art which is new be so difficult to teach? It isn't like working with new materials, plastics, for instance, supposing that were difficult. Why cannot the teacher tell them plainly what he is going to teach and then teach it? The art is a language art and there is nothing new about that. Nevertheless, anyone who reads this book can see with what diligence and patience the author tried to get these students to understand him. This explains his varied attempts by analogy to tell them. And it explains, too, his attempts to show them and to help them over the difficulties which he realized hindered them.

I want now to emphasize the difficulties, taking notice of them in each of the phases.

There are in the first phase two sorts of difficulties, those involved in following what the author does and those involved in doing what he does. Consider the case in which the author considers: "How can one think what is not the case?" He introduces for comparison the sentence: "How can we hang a thief who doesn't exist?" He does this to startle one into an appreciation of the queerness of the first question and to show, too, what sort of queerness is involved. There is a part of this which seems not difficult. The sentence which is introduced certainly is a queer one. Another one which is queer is: "Can a machine have toothache?" And most readers are likely to be amused by such antics. But this, of course, is not the point. It isn't the queerness of those sentences which interests the author. The question is as to whether the queerness of these sentences helps to bring to light the queerness of the sentences considered. For those sentences are regarded as grammatically confused, and the sentences with which they are compared are intended to stress this confusion. The question "Can a machine have toothache?" is grammatically confused in the same way that "Can a machine think?" is. And yet one might very well retort: "Perhaps a machine cannot have toothache, but it seems a machine can think." And this may be alarming. Who wants to be mechanical and to have toothache? So, too, the question "How can we hang a thief who doesn't exist?" (It seems we can hang a thief who doesn't exist—in effigy, and that suits people, too, who figure out a way of thinking what is not the case. They think the effigies.) is intended to show the queerness of "How can we think what is not the case?" But in order to get the full impact of this, one must have some nice sense of the grammar and of the confusions involved, which one may come by naturally, being meaning-

keen, or may come by with special instruction. It is only with special
instruction that one can understand what is being done. And that
will involve those difficulties one meets in the other two phases.

As for the difficulties involved in doing what the author does,
inventing such devices, I scarcely know what to say. If you are
something of a poet you may certainly learn from the poets, though
even this does not mean that writing poems will be easy. And if
you are nothing of a poet, then though you may love poems, you
cannot do as the poets do with or without difficulties.

Consider difficulties involved in understanding what Wittgenstein
does under the second phase. It would seem that anyone can do
in this case what is required. For all that one needs to do is to
remember what people as a matter of fact do say. You speak
English. You understand English. You know what goes with what,
the continuities of sense. Of course. But what at the outset is
difficult is to take this, these words, these sentences, as the presentation of sense. For one has, as it were, for years been looking
through the words, into the darkness, the *hinein,* where no man can
follow, for the meaning. That is what stirs in the question "What
is the meaning of a word?" Hence, even though someone now
emphasizes, "But this is the meaning," this may not help. It may
all pass before one like a blur. Let us suppose, however, that one
has finally overcome this difficulty, not that it does not return, but
one does have one's moments. All this is done for a purpose. The
presentation of meaning, of such aspects as are required, serves in
at least two ways, to accentuate the queerness and to provide the
area within which the misleading analogy is to be identified. None
of this, remember, is a matter of rules, or of self-evidence, so
beloved of many, foundations of security. No one proves that this
question is queer, or that in the sentence "But you can look for
a thief who isn't there" or "But you can be afraid of a little man
who isn't there" meaning is presented, or that if it is presented it
does serve in the ways described. Let us suppose, however, that
when the author has now done this in some cases, one also understands this, can follow what he has done. Does this, however,
involve that one can now on one's own do likewise? Obviously not.
What do we lack?

And now the third phase, identifying "the misleading analogy."
If the first ideas involved here are strange, new, and difficult, the
third is, too, and is unintelligible apart from them. For the mis-

leading analogy explains the hold which the queer has upon us. And I think that this is fearfully difficult and from another point of view fantastically simple. Suppose I say that the meaning of a word is a sort of something, vegetable, animal, or mineral, no, but not a gas either, nor a liquid; but why should it not be something paraphysical, for instance, if you call a word physical, mineral or a gas, in which case you might say that it is either para-mineral or para-gas? This sentence makes it much too clear that I am thinking of meaning as a thing for even me to have the illusion of thinking it. Let us disregard that. Let us suppose further that someone is startled by this. He exclaims: "Why, he is thinking of meaning as a thing!" and now comes the question: "But what leads him to do this?" It is no answer to say: "Everybody does." For here is at least one person who for the moment does not. And now comes the answer: Naturally enough because the expression "the meaning of a word," is like the expression "the king of a country," and the king of a country is a thing, animal, has weight, lives on air, meat, vegetables, noise, etc., so the question arises: What sort of thing is the meaning of a word, no animal, imponderable, neither living nor dead? Now I do not know whether it is difficult to tumble to so simple an explanation of what seems, when one is involved in it, so fearfully intricate. It almost seems as though something like a change of heart is required for this. It is well nigh miraculous, like opening ten-ton doors with a feather. For isn't it ridiculously simple? You think of meaning in a certain way and you find yourself all fenced in ("Don't fence me in"), and how now did you come to do this? There was an expression which looked like another expression, and misled by this you went on as though their meanings, too, were analogous. How does one tumble in a case like this? Perhaps one can set oneself in readiness. "Relax. Don't resist." And is that so easy? Haven't we inherited the tensions of all those generations before us? Original (the inherited) knots and besides original knots, original knots. One's nature is knots. In any case it is that simple. If only there were some complicated explanation, ladders and ladders of explanation, an architectural mystery-piece of calculation, that would suit our natural bent.

Learning to do what the author teaches may in some respects be compared to learning to walk. There are certain to be bumps and falls. One must want to learn. But there are no special resources required. Nearly everyone can and does learn to walk. So, too, in this case. One must try when one can't do. One must risk stupidities and clumsiness and misunderstandings. One must be patient and diligent. Above all one must want to do the doing of which is here taught. And no special resources are required. What is required is an acquaintance with the language, an eye and an ear for sense. This is a requirement and may be compared to the musical ear in the case of music. This man can scarcely make out differences in tone. He has never heard a melody. So he can't study music. And there does seem to be something comparable in the case of reading philosophy. To some readers everything makes sense. What the author of this book does may be described in this way. The students lend him their eyes and ears for sense and he tries to sharpen them, tries to make them keen. "I will show you how to see and hear sense." And are no special talents required? It seems that there are.

The one obvious and pervading difficulty in reading this book and one against which one must struggle continually as soon as he understands the danger is the temptation to misunderstanding the very book which is designed to help us to remove temptation to misunderstandings in other circumstances. I try to persuade you not to steal at the grocery store and in doing so tempt you to steal from me. The hankering for orderliness, for system, for summaries is a general aspect of this. (What is the man doing? He's putting three books together on the shelf [p. 44].) But it may also be remarked in the way in which certain sentences are widely misunderstood. The temptation here arises from one's coming upon a sentence the like of which one had perhaps met in some other context and one goes on to read it now in terms of that context, utterly oblivious of the immediate context in which it is found. There are two such sentences which I should like to point out.

The first of these sentences is the one at the bottom of page 4: "But if we had to name anything which is the life of the sign, we should have to say that it was its use." This sentence apart from the "if we had to" and "we should have to," looks like a definition. "The life of the sign" is, of course, the meaning. So, how convenient this is that the author, in spite of himself, should have yielded and given us what we so much want: The meaning of a word is its use. No sentence has more powerfully formed the jargon of contemporary discussion in philosophy. Nearly everyone these days speaks and writes in this new fashion. And yet nothing has been changed. If before we were puzzled with "What is the meaning of a word" now we are puzzled with "What is the use of a word?" (I think I paced up and down in this cage for years.) Having made a puzzle out of this we ask such further questions as how the author came upon such a definition. What English teacher would ever allow the interchange of the words "meaning" and "use"? As a definition the sentence is indefensible and if it is defensible, what good comes of it? Locke speaks of "use" but to what advantage? Some people have even been misled into identifying the statement with some old or new Pragmatism.

But what then?

The author on page 67 writes: "Think of words as instruments characterized by their use, and then think of the use of a hammer, the use of a chisel, the use of a square, of glue-pot, and of the glue." One can see from this how the sentence on page 4 is to be understood. It is intended not as a definition but as an analogy or if as a definition, then as a definition of a special sort. In the latter case it comes to something like this: If you will say "use" and write "use" instead of "meaning" in writing and speaking of words, and can manage to think accordingly, that will help. Help what? It will help you to rid yourself of the temptation to think of the meaning as something in the dark which you cannot see very well. The idea is that, if your thinking is dominated in this case by one misleading analogy, then you may be led right by another leading analogy. If, of course, that second analogy also misleads one, not much may be gained. But as long as one is well aware of the analogy and what it is for, it should do its work. And it should now help one to see what the role of a word is in the various circumstances of our lives in which we speak and write that word together, of course, with other words. And if we allow that we understand the word, are acquainted with the meaning, then this is where it is to be found, since this is all we know. So we may understand that sentence as one which is intended to help us to a change in perspective. Once that change has come about, the sentence, like the ladder, is of no further use.

The other sentence is the sentence on page 28, "But ordinary language is all right." The same temptation which gave rise to misunderstanding in the former case gives rise to misunderstanding in this case. The immediate context of the sentence is disregarded and the sentence is understood as stating some philosophical theory, perhaps naive. And in this way it, too, has affected current jargon. There are ordinary-language philosophers. People now go on with all sorts of difficult questions. They want to know just what ordinary language is and whether it really is a language and how one can decide that without first finding out what a language is. And then, of course, there's still the question as to whether it is all right. It seems that no one with any conscience could speak so carelessly. But what now is the situation? It comes to this. Some philosophers, particularly those who love mathematics more than poetry, are struck, when they read the newspaper or listen to the conversation at dinner, with the disorder of the language. The conversation at dinner is certainly not Euclidean. Perhaps one can imagine some lovers of poetry also who when reading the newspaper or listening to conversation at dinner remark that no verse should be that free. So the mathematicians, as a first step, propose some rules. Conversational deduction is to come later. And perhaps the lovers of poetry introduce measures and some rudiments of drill, marching, leaping, sprinting, waltzing, to make the news less pedestrian. In protection against this someone comes along and reads an excerpt from the newspaper. He asks: "What is the matter with that? So the man did catch the monkey in the subway." Again he asks: "And what is the matter with trying to get the little boy who says 'wove' for 'love' and 'wanded' for 'landed' to say 'love' for 'wove' and 'landed' for 'wanded'? He now says that the airpwane wanded. A little free verse here does no harm. And more doesn't either." The mathematicians frown. The poets frown too. Now, this is approximately what the author's sentence comes to. "Ordinary language is all right." The grocer understands the boy when the boy gives him the money and asks for five apples. The grocer's bawd understands what the grocer says when he says [it] and pats her cheek. And the grocer's bawd's sister understands what the grocer's bawd says when she says: "And what are the neighbor's saying now?" And the neighbors understand one another. And so on. Ordinary language is all right? Of course, we understand one another. The question is: What are all those rules for? And the shackles on the verse? There is nothing mysterious about the author's sentence when seen against the background of prejudice which gives rise to it.

When Protagoras was consulted about what would happen to

the young Hippocrates if he associated with Protagoras, Protagoras answered: "Young man, if you associate with me, on the very first day you will return home a better man than you came, and better on the second day than on the first and better every day than you were on the day before." And if now we were to ask concerning some young Hippocrates from Harvard or Yale what would happen to him if he reads this book, we should certainly not with the courage of Protagoras' convictions say anything like what Protagoras said. Let us try a few answers. "Young man, if you read this book as you read most books nothing whatsoever will happen to you and it won't take long. On the very first day you will return home a no-better man than you came, on the second day the same, and so on." Or: "Young man, if you read this book diligently, digging as you are used to digging in the books you read, coming up with a shining truth here and a nice bristling idea there, the chances are that you will have got it all wrong. You will go home full of indigestibles, and oh, the pity of it! a worse man than you came, not much worse, but let us say, four or five misunderstandings worse." Or: "Young man, if you read this book with your mind wide open, and take time to stew in it or to let it stew in you; if with a little bit of luck, it should cling to you like a bramble and it should hurt and sting and all the while the agitations keep you alert, then inkling by inkling, glimpse by glimpse, chink by chink, on the very first day ten years later, you will return home a different man than you came."

And what now are intelligible reactions to this book? Since this book as here represented, at least, aims to teach its readers how to do a certain thing, one obvious reaction is this: "We don't want it done." I say that this is intelligible so long as no reasons are given. As a blind reaction it's fine. But how is one to give reasons? Is one to say: "Yes, yes, we admit the grammatical confusion and the misleading analogy, but what we ask and say makes sense anyhow"? Has anyone given such a reason? The other reaction is this: "We want it done. But we want it done better." It seems that it could be done better. This comment no doubt reflects the impression of incoherence referred to earlier. It may also reflect a failure to recognize the almost overwhelming obstacles involved. For one has not simply to present the particular cases, one has also to help the reader to understand the presentation and to clear away the obstacles to understanding. These different tasks, which are all necessary, make it impossible to proceed in a straight line. There is, however, something even more telling. The presentation of a case is nothing neatly defined. The grammars of different words are interwoven and the presentation of the particular case is bound to reflect the incoherence of the language. Perhaps one could express it in this way: The coherence of the language, the criss-crossing of the grammar of the words we are interested in, is quite different from the coherence of words in a certain language game, in a story or in an essay. (A good illustration of this is the discussion beginning on page 6 to the bottom of page 15.) This is not to say that the coherence of this book is loose but rather that the orderlines of this book is determined by the variety of the tasks and by the particular sort of complexity of the materials. One might also take note here of what either are or seem to be obvious mistakes in the presentation of a case, and it might be a good test of one's reading of the book that he should be able to discover those mistakes. I do not think, however, that the presence of these mistakes affects the pedagogical efficacy of the book. It may actually enhance it.

Towards the end of Moore's notes on Wittgenstein's Lectures in 1930–33, is the following paragraph:

> He went on to say that, though philosophy had now been "reduced to a matter of skill," yet this skill, like other skills, is very difficult to acquire. One difficulty was that it required a "sort of thinking" to which we are not accustomed and to which we have not been trained—a sort of thing very different from what is required in the sciences. And he said that the required skill could not be acquired merely by hearing lectures: discussion was essential. As regards his own work, he said it did not matter whether his results were true or not: what mattered was that "a method had been found."[1]

Though I came upon this passage only after I had written this piece, what I have written might be described as an elaboration of the content of this paragraph.

---

[1] G. E. Moore, "Wittgenstein's Lectures in 1930–33," *Mind*, Vol. LXIV, No. 253 (January, 1955), p. 26. (See "Memoirs" in this volume.)

Wittgenstein on Language and Some Problems of Philosophy

BY LEONARD LINSKY

IN THE PHILOSOPHICAL INVESTIGATIONS Wittgenstein asks, "Is what we call 'obeying a rule' something that it would be possible for only *one* man to do, and to do only *once* in his life?" [§ 199].[1] The question, Wittgenstein observes, is a grammatical one calling not for empirical investigation but a logical analysis of the concept of obeying a rule. Wittgenstein says that it is not possible that there should have been only one occasion on which someone obeyed a rule. Of course, we can imagine all sorts of situations in which a rule is promulgated, obeyed only once, and then withdrawn. This is not what Wittgenstein is talking about here. He is talking about the practice of obeying rules, not this or that particular rule. In the same way we may distinguish between the practice of playing chess and this particular game which falls under that practice. Of course, a case cannot fall under a practice unless the practice already exists. It is not possible that there should have been only one occasion on which a report was made, or an order given and understood. It is not possible that only once in the history of man there was such a thing as making a report. For making a report is conforming to a certain practice or use. There cannot be a practice without cases falling under the practice any more than there can be cases falling under a practice without a practice.

Suppose we are asked why we call a certain activity "giving an order." Perhaps we are asked this question because certain features of this activity were unnoticed. We might then point them out in

---

[1] All quotations are from *Philosophical Investigations* by Ludwig Wittgenstein (Oxford: Basil Blackwell, 1953). The numbers between brackets refer to numbered remarks of Part I of this work.

explaining our use of words. If this process is carried out long enough, we may finally reach the point at which we say, "But this is the way our language is used." And in doing so we appeal to the customs and uses of our language which make the expression "to give an order" apply in just this case. But now imagine the background of custom removed, and you will see that the possibility of distinguishing between a correct and an incorrect use of words has disappeared as well.

Now try to imagine a private language. Here the background of customs is also private. What would a private custom (practice) be? What would a private rule be? Well, I might call the object before me a "took" instead of a "book." And in a sense I would be speaking a private language. But Wittgenstein is not talking about this sort of thing when he says that there cannot be a private language. "Following a rule is analogous to obeying an order. We are trained to do so, we react to an order in a particular way. But what if one person reacts in one way and another in another to the order and the training? Which is right?" [§ 206]. In order to answer this question we must refer to the common behavior of the community of men who are using this language. The right way of reacting to an order must be the customary way. Without the rules embedded in these customs, there is no system of reference by which we can justify the claim that one response is the right one and another response the wrong one to a particular order.

When Wittgenstein discusses private languages, he has in mind languages which could not possibly be understood by anyone other than the speaker. Malcom has observed [2] that the idea of just such a private language is presupposed in a host of philosophical programs and theories. It is involved in the problem of our knowledge of other minds. That problem arises when we suppose that in the case of our sensations, our language is a private language. It is only from my own case that I know what is meant by pain. I experience only my own pains. But if the meaning of "pain" is known to me only from my own case, from my own private exemplar, it becomes a mystery as to how anybody else can understand me when I use the language of pains. Only I can experience my pains. Similarly, when others speak of pains they are referring to their own exemplars, which are inaccessible to me. For all I can really know, they may be referring to nothing at all!

[2] Norman Malcolm, "Wittgenstein's *Philosophical Investigations*" [included in this volume].

Let us imagine the following case. I want to keep a diary about the recurrence of a certain sensation. To this end I associate it with the sign "E" and write this sign in a calendar for every day on which I have the sensation.—I will remark first of all that a definition of the sign cannot be formulated.—But still I can give myself a kind of ostensive definition.—How? Can I point to the sensation? Not in the ordinary sense. But I speak, or write the sign down, and at the same time I concentrate my attention on the sensation—and so, as it were, point to it inwardly.—But what is this ceremony for? for that is all it seems to be! A definition surely serves to establish the meaning of a sign.—Well, that is done precisely by the concentration of my attention; for in this way I impress on myself the connexion between the sign and the sensation.—But "I impress it on myself" can only mean: this process brings it about that I remember the connexion *right* in the future. But in the present case I have no criterion of correctness. One would like so say: whatever is going to seem right to me is right. And that only means that here we can't talk about "right." [§258]

In this remark, Wittgenstein is saying that a private language would be one in which there could be no criteria for distinguishing the correct from the incorrect use of language. Our own (public) language does provide such criteria. The criteria for the correct application of words for sensation are taught and learned in many kinds of public situations. When we try to imagine such learning situations, it becomes apparent that the private exemplar is not needed at all.

It might be said that there are indeed criteria for the correct use of my private language. All I have to do is to appeal to memory to see if I have used, for example, the sign "E" in accordance with my private intention. To this Wittgenstein says:

Let us imagine a table (something like a dictionary) that exists only in our imagination. A dictionary can be used to justify the translation of a word *x* into a word *y*. But are we also to call it a justification if such a table is to be looked up only in the imagination?—"Well, yes; then it is a subjective justification."—But justification consists in appealing to something independent.—"But surely I can appeal from one memory to another. For example, I don't know if I have remembered the time of departure of a train right and to check it I call to mind how a page of the timetable looked. Isn't it the same here?"—No; for this process has got to produce a memory which is actually *correct*. If the mental image of the timetable could not itself be tested for correctness, how could it confirm the correctness of the first memory? (As if someone were to buy several copies of the morning paper to assure himself that what it said was true.) [§265]

The difficulty with the notion of a private language is that in it there is no difference between seeming to be correct and being correct. If it seems to me that I am using "E" in accordance with my remembered intention that is as far as I can go toward settling the matter. But if there is no difference between seeming and being a correct use, doesn't the notion of correctness itself, and with it the idea of language, become inapplicable?

> Let us remember that there are certain criteria in a man's behavior for the fact that he does not understand a word, that it means nothing to him; that he can do nothing with it. And criteria for his "thinking he understands," attaching some meaning to the word, but not the right one. And, lastly, criteria for his understanding the word right. [§269]

Wittgenstein's point here seems to be that the expressions "to understand a word," " to appear to understand a word," are expressions of our common language. The criteria for their correct use are public criteria. That these criteria are public and can be taught and learned, in spite of the supposed inaccessible private exemplar, is shown by the fact that all of us do in practice know how to use the expressions involved. It cannot, then, be correct to call any of these supposed private and inaccessible processes "defining" or "understanding," for these words belong to our common language and the criteria for their application are publicly taught and learned. Wittgenstein makes this point in the following remark:

> What reason have we for calling "E" the sign for a *sensation?* For "sensation" is a word of our common language, not of one intelligible to me alone. So the use of this word stands in need of a justification which everybody understands.—And it would not help either to say that it need not be a *sensation;* that when he writes "E", he has *something*—and that is all that can be said. "Has" and "something" also belong to our common language.— So in the end when one is doing philosophy one gets to the point where one would like just to emit an inarticulate sound.—But such a sound is an expression only as it occurs in a particular language game, which should now be described. [§261]

There is another side to Wittgenstein's view on the nature of language which is closely connected with these topics. This is what has been called his instrumentalist theory of language. This instrumentalist view is the center of gravity of Wittgenstein's philosophy.

We can approach it first from a consideration of the idea of a language game. A language game is a use of language for some purpose.

> Now think of the following use of language: I send someone shopping. I give him a slip marked "five red apples." He takes the slip to the shopkeeper, who opens the drawer marked "apples," then he looks up the word "red" in a table and finds a color sample opposite it; then he says the series of cardinal numbers—I assume he knows them by heart—up to the word "five" and for each number he takes an apple of the same color as the sample from the drawer.—It is in this and similar ways that one operates with words. [§1]

And consider again this example of a language game:

> The language is meant to serve for communication between a builder A and an assistant B. A is building with building stones: there are blocks, pillars, slabs, and beams. B has to pass the stones, and that in the order in which A needs them. For this purpose they use a language consisting of the words, "block," "pillar," "slab," "beam." A calls them out;—B brings the stone which he has learned to bring at such-and-such a call.—Conceive this as a completed primitive language. [§2]

In these descriptions the view of language as a tool, an instrument, is prominent. The language game is a whole "consisting of language and the actions into which it is woven." This view of language as a tool is in complete opposition to Wittgenstein's earlier view presented in the *Tractatus Logico-Philosophicus,* that language is to be regarded as a picture or mirror of reality. Much of the *Philosophical Investigations* is devoted to replacing the picture theory by the toolbox theory of language. "Language is an instrument. Its concepts are instruments" [§ 569]. Instruments may be classified according to their methods of operation and the functions which can be performed with them. The notion of the meaning of a linguistic expression is replaced by the notion of its use.

> Think of the tools in a toolbox: there is a hammer, pliers, a saw, a screwdriver, a rule, a glue-pot, glue, nails and screws.— The functions of words are as diverse as the functions of these objects. (And in both cases there are similarities.) [§11]

And again,

> It is like looking into the cabin of a locomotive. We see handles all looking more or less alike. (Naturally, since they are all supposed to be handled.) But one is the handle of a crank which can

be moved continuously (it regulates the opening of a valve); another is the handle of a switch, which has only two effective positions, it is either off or on; a third is the handle of a brake-lever, the harder one pulls on it, the harder it brakes; a fourth the handle of a pump: it has an effect only so long as it is moved to and fro. [§12]

These comparisons help to explain Wittgenstein's comment that "to imagine a language means to imagine a form of life" [§ 19]. Asking and answering questions, describing a room, cursing, complaining of pains, expressing fears or doubts, proving a theorem in geometry, all of these are language games or forms of life in which various portions of our language are woven into activities aimed at some goal. So the notion of meaning is, for Wittgenstein, largely replaced by the notion of use. "For a large class of cases—though not for all—in which we employ the term 'meaning' it can be defined thus: the meaning of a word is its use in the language" [§ 43]. Once the identification of meaning and use is made, it becomes possible to understand some very fertile sources of philosophical confusions. The meaning of an expression is the use (or uses) that it has in some actual language game (or games). If, now, we ignore the language games which give our words their significance and regard them apart from these contexts, we become puzzled as to how obvious kinds of statements such as "I know how you feel" or "I know he is in great pain" can be known to be true or even intelligible. It is part of Wittgenstein's technique to remind us constantly of the normal language games which are the homes of these statements; to remind us that in certain surroundings we do know how to use them. In one remark Wittgenstein considers the following philosophical protest: "Yes, but there is *something* there all the same accompanying my cry of pain. And it is on account of that that I utter it. And this something is what is important— and frightful." And Wittgenstein responds with a move typical of the method of the *Philosophical Investigations*. He asks: "Only whom are we informing of this? And on what occasion?" [§296]. The effect of this question is to shock us out of the mood which produced the philosophical protest by reminding us that we are puzzled because we have removed our language from the normal setting which gives it meaning. The gears of the machine of language are disengaged and the engine idles. This idling of language is characteristic of philosophical talk.

   Though in certain moods (philosophical ones) it can seem utterly
baffling that we should be able to say such things as "I know how
he feels," the puzzle never arises in any living situation in which
these words are used but only when they are separated from these
surroundings ("forms of life") and contemplated apart from any
language game. "But what are these words to be used for now?
The language game in which they are to be applied is missing"
[§ 96]. The same view of the nature of philosophy is expressed
when Wittgenstein says: "Philosophy begins when language goes
on holiday" [§ 38].

   Here we come back again to the criticism of the private inaccessible exemplar which the private-language theory requires our
sensation to be. At one point Wittgenstein considers the following
philosophical contention:

> Imagine a person whose memory could not retain *what* the
> word "pain" meant—so that he constantly called different things
> by that name—but nevertheless used the word in a way fitting in
> with the usual symptoms and presuppositions of pain. [§271]

Such a man uses the word "pain" in the same way that the rest
of us do, and Wittgenstein's comment on this case is this, "Here I
should like to say: a wheel that can be turned though nothing else
moves with it, is not part of the mechanism" [§ 271]. The private
sensation is not engaged with the rest of the mechanism of our language. It is an idle wheel. We are reminded here of the pragmatist's
dictum that the difference which makes no difference is not a
difference. The point is brought home in the striking image of the
beetle in the box.

> Now someone tells me that he knows what pain is only from
> his own case!—Suppose everyone had a box with something in it:
> we call it a "beetle." No one can look into anyone else's box, and
> everyone says he knows what a beetle is only by looking at *his*
> beetle.—Here it would be quite possible for everyone to have
> something different in his box. One might even imagine such a
> thing constantly changing.—But suppose the word "beetle" had a
> use in these people's language?—If so it would not be used as the
> name of a thing. The thing in the box has no place in the lan-
> guage game at all; not even as a something: for the box might
> be empty.—No, one can "divide through" by the thing in the box;
> it cancels out, whatever it is. [§293]

Here again a contrast is invited with the earlier *Tractatus*. There
Wittgenstein characterized philosophy in this well-known passage:

"Most propositions and questions, that have been written about philosophical matters, are not false, but senseless" [§ 4.003]. In his later *Investigations,* the terms "senseless" or "meaningless" are carefully avoided in the descriptions of philosophical theories. Instead of such wholesale treatments we get detailed descriptions of the manner in which philosophers use their language, and this is contrasted with the ordinary uses in connection with which our language acquires its meaning.

But are not these views about the mind simply behaviorism? "But doesn't what you say come to this: that there is no pain, for example, without pain-behavior?" [§ 281]. And Wittgenstein's reply is, "It comes to this: only of a living human being and what resembles (behaves like) a living human being can one say: it has sensations; it sees; is blind; hears; is deaf; is conscious or unconscious" [§ 281]. Well, how do we know that plants or rocks can't feel and that machines can't think? It isn't because we have investigated them so carefully. Certainly we haven't investigated all of them! No, it is because it is only in such human and animal surroundings that we are taught to use words like "sensation," "pain," "see." Aside from such contexts, they simply don't apply, for the criteria of their application are missing.

The topic we are dealing with carries us directly into Wittgenstein's use of the notion of criteria. The very fact that language is used and that others can be taught to use it correctly shows that there are criteria of correctness. It is in order to remind us of the criteria of application for the various parts of our language that Wittgenstein constantly tries to get us to look at the situations in which we might learn or teach to another certain language games. "How would you teach the use of such an expression?" now comes to stand beside the earlier question, "How would you verify?" In answering either we refer to criteria. And criteria must be public. How else could we share a common language? The criterion for pain is pain-behavior, at least the criterion for others' being in pain. If we are to talk about the inner at all, the criteria must be outer manifestations. "An 'inner process' stands in need of outward criteria" [§ 580]. And, of course, the concepts of the "inner," the "private," the "inaccessible" themselves belong to our common (public) language and have in their normal language games (public) criteria for their use. So we begin to see where those philosophers who have proposed an "egocentric predicament" have gone wrong. For them, each of us begins with his own private language of the mind and then the predicament is as to how we can go from this privacy to a common public language shared by a community. Of course, beginning with the dogma of privacy the passage cannot be made.

In answering the question "How would you teach the language of pain?" we are led to answer the further question "What would show that the language has been learned?" And in answering this we answer the question "What features of a situation *count* as settling the issue as to whether or not these words apply here?" and notice something must count if learning is to take place. A principal difficulty about the notion of criteria lies in the temptation to confuse it with the notion of a symptom.

> The fluctuation in grammar between criteria and symptoms makes it look as if there were nothing at all but symptoms. We say, for example: "Experience teaches that there is rain when the barometer falls, but it also teaches that there is rain when we have certain sensations of wet and cold, or such-and-such visual impressions." In defense of this one says that these sense impressions can deceive us. But here one fails to reflect that the fact that the false appearance is precisely one of rain is founded on a definition. [§354]

If we are deceived, we are deceived about rain and not something else, consequently something counts as being rain; not everything can be at most a sign or symptom of rain. This thought is continued in the next remark. "The point here is not that our sense impressions might lie, but that we understand their language" [§ 335].

In the case of pain-behavior and pain, the failure to keep clearly in mind the distinction between symptom and criteria may mislead us into thinking that somehow the pain-behavior is a symptom of pain, while the pain itself is hidden and inaccessible to us. It is important to remember that we have learned the concept "pain" in certain human surroundings (people holding parts of their bodies, crying, contorting). That is why we are so sure that a machine cannot experience pain. "But surely a machine cannot think!—Is that an empirical statement? No. We only say of a human being and what is like one that it thinks. We also say it of dolls and no doubt of ghosts too. Look at the word 'to think' as a tool" [§ 360].

But surely there can be pain-behavior without pain. People

simulate, act, or otherwise pretend. Of course, but first of all it is to be noted that it would be impossible to pretend being in pain unless something counted as being in pain. The possibility of pretending, simulating, depends upon the existence of criteria for the genuine case, and of course, there are criteria for the faked case as well. We are not saying that it is not possible to have pain-behavior without pain, but that in certain surroundings to doubt or question the presence of pain when confronted with the pain behavior is to have the very meaning of "pain" crumble away before us.

Wittgenstein's Philosophical Investigations

BY NORMAN MALCOLM

*Ein Buch ist ein Spiegel; wenn ein Affe hinein-
guckt, so kann freilich kein Apostel heraussehen.*
—LICHTENBERG

AN ATTEMPT TO SUMMARIZE the *Investigations* would be neither
successful nor useful. Wittgenstein compressed his thoughts to the
point where further compression is impossible. What is needed is
that they be unfolded and the connections between them traced out.
A likely first reaction to the book will be to regard it as a puzzling
collection of reflections that are sometimes individually brilliant,
but possess no unity, present no system of ideas. In truth the unity
is there, but it cannot be perceived without strenuous exertion.
Within the scope of a review the connectedness can best be brought
out, I think, by concentrating on some single topic—in spite of the
fact that there are no separate topics, for each of the investigations
in the book criss-crosses again and again with every other one. In
the following I center my attention on Wittgenstein's treatment of
the problem of how language is related to inner experiences—to
sensations, feelings, and moods. This is one of the main inquiries
of the book and perhaps the most difficult to understand. I am
sufficiently aware of the fact that my presentation of this subject
will certainly fail to portray the subtlety, elegance, and force of
Wittgenstein's thinking and will probably, in addition, contain positive mistakes.

References to Part I will be by paragraph numbers, e.g., [§ 207],
and to Part II by page numbers e.g., [p. 207].

Private language. Let us see something of how Wittgenstein attacks what he calls "the idea of a private language." By a "private"

181

language is meant one that not merely is not but *cannot* be understood by anyone other than the speaker. The reason for this is that
the words of this language are supposed to "refer to what can only
be known to the person speaking; to his immediate private sensations" [§ 243]. What is supposed is that I *"associate* words with
sensations and use these names in descriptions" [§ 256]. I fix my
attention on a sensation and establish a connection between a
word and the sensation [§ 258].

It is worth mentioning that the conception that it is possible and
even necessary for one to have a private language is not eccentric.
Rather it is the view that comes most naturally, to anyone who
philosophizes on the subject of the relation of words to experiences.
The idea of a private language is presupposed by every program
of inferring or constructing the "external world" and "other minds."
It is contained in the philosophy of Descartes and in the theory
of ideas of classical British empiricism, as well as in recent and
contemporary phenomenalism and sense-datum theory. At bottom
it is the idea that there is only a contingent and not an *essential*
connection between a sensation and its outward expression—an
idea that appeals to us all. Such thoughts as these are typical
expressions of the idea of a private language: that I know only
from my *own* case what the word "pain" means [§§ 293, 295];
that I can only *believe* that someone else is in pain, but I *know*
it if I am [§ 303]; that another person cannot have *my* pains [§ 253];
that I can undertake to call *this* (pointing inward) "pain" in the
future [§263]; that when I say, "I am in pain" I am at any rate
justified *before myself* [§ 289].

In order to appreciate the depth and power of Wittgenstein's
assault upon this idea you must partly be its captive. You must
feel the strong grip of it. The passionate intensity of Wittgenstein's
treatment of it is due to the fact he lets this idea take possession
of him, drawing out of himself the thoughts and imagery by which
it is expressed and defended—and then subjecting those thoughts
and pictures to fiercest scrutiny. What is written down represents
both a logical investigation and a great philosopher's struggle with
his own thoughts. The logical investigation will be understood only
by those who duplicate the struggle in themselves.

One consequence to be drawn from the view that I know only
from my *own* case what, say, "tickling" means is that "I know only
what *I* call that, not what anyone else does" [§ 347]. I have not

learned what "tickling" means, I have only called something by that name. Perhaps others use the name differently. This is a regrettable difficulty; but, one may think, the word will still work for me as a name, provided that I apply it consistently to a certain sensation. But how about "sensation"? Don't I know only from my *own* case what *that* word means? Perhaps what I call a "sensation" others call by another name? It will not help, says Wittgenstein, to say that although it may be that what I have is not what others call a "sensation," at least I have *something.* For don't I know only from my own case what "having something" is? Perhaps my use of *those* words is contrary to common use. In trying to explain how I gave "tickling" its meaning, I discover that I do not have the right to use any of the relevant words of our common language. "So in the end when one is doing philosophy one gets to the point where one would like just to emit an inarticulate sound" [§ 261].

Let us suppose that I did fix my attention on a pain as I pronounced the word "pain" to myself. I think that thereby I established a connection between the word and the sensation. But I did not establish a connection if subsequently I applied that word to sensations other than pain or to things other than sensations, e.g., emotions. My private definition was a success only if it led me to use the word correctly in the future. In the present case, "correctly" would mean *"consistently* with my own definition"; for the question of whether my use agrees with that of others has been given up as a bad job. Now how is it to be decided whether I have used the word consistently? What will be the difference between my having used it consistently? What will be the difference between my having used it consistently and its *seeming* to me that I have? Or has this distinction vanished? "Whatever is going to seem right to me is right. And that only means that here we can't talk about 'right' " [§ 258]. If the distinction between "correct" and "seems correct" has disappeared, then so has the concept *correct.* It follows that the "rules" of my private language are only *impressions* of rules [§ 259]. My impression that I follow a rule does not confirm that I follow the rule, unless there can be something that will prove my impression correct. And the something cannot be another impression—for this would be "as if someone were to buy several copies of the morning paper to assure himself that what it said was true" [§ 265]. The proof that I am following a rule must appeal to something *independent* of my impression that I am. If in the nature of the case there cannot be such an appeal, then my private language does not have *rules,* for the concept of a rule requires that there be a difference between "He is following a rule" and "He is under the impression that he is following a rule"—just as the concept of understanding a word requires that there be a difference between "He understands this word" and "He thinks that he understands this word" [cf. § 269].

"Even if I cannot prove and cannot know that I am correctly following the rules of my private language," it might be said, "still it *may* be that I am. It has *meaning* to say that I am. The supposition makes sense: you and I *understand* it." Wittgenstein has a reply to this [§§ 348–353]. We are inclined to think that we know what it means to say "It is five o'clock on the sun" or "This congenital deaf-mute talks to himself inwardly in a vocal language" or "The stove is in pain." These sentences produce pictures in our minds, and it *seems* to us that the pictures tell us how to *apply* them—that is, tell us what we have to look for, what we have to do, in order to determine whether what is pictured is the case. But we make a mistake in thinking that the picture contains in itself the instructions as to how we are to apply it. Think of the picture of blindness as a darkness in the soul or in the head of the blind man [§ 424]. There is nothing wrong with it *as a picture.* "But *what* is its application?" What shall count for or against its being said that this or that man is blind, that the picture applies to him? The *picture* doesn't say. If you think that you understand the sentence "I follow the rule that *this* is to be called 'pain' " (a rule of your private language), what you have perhaps is a picture of yourself checking off various feelings of yours as either being *this* or not. The picture appears to solve the problem of how you determine whether you have done the "checking" right. Actually it doesn't give you even a hint in that direction; no more than the picture of blindness provides so much as a hint of *how* it is to be determined that this or that man is blind [§§ 348–353, 422–426, p. 184].

One will be inclined to say here that one can simply *remember* this sensation and by remembering it will know that one is making a consistent application of its name. But will it also be possible to have a *false* memory impression? On the private-language hypothesis, what would *show* that your memory impression is false—or true? Another memory impression? Would this imply that memory is a court from which there is no appeal? But, as a matter of fact, that is *not* our concept of memory.

> Imagine that you were supposed to paint a particular color "C," which was the color that appeared when the chemical substances X and Y combined.—Suppose that the color struck you as brighter on one day than on another; would you not sometimes say: "I must be wrong, the color is certainly the same as yesterday"? This shows that we do not always resort to what memory tells us as the verdict of the highest court of appeal [§56].

There is, indeed, such a thing as checking one memory against another, e.g., I check my recollection of the time of departure of a train by calling up a memory image of how a page of the timetable looked—but "this process has got to produce a memory which is actually *correct*. If the mental image of the timetable could not itself be *tested* for correctness, how could it confirm the correctness of the first memory?" [§ 265].

If I have a language that is really private (i.e., it is a logical impossibility that anyone else should understand it or should have any basis for knowing whether I am using a particular name consistently), my assertion that my memory tells me so and so will be utterly empty. "My memory" will not even mean—my memory *impression*. For by a memory impression we understand something that is either accurate or inaccurate; whereas there would not be, in the private language, any *conception* of what would establish a memory impression as correct, any conception of what "correct" would mean here.

The same. One wants to say, "Surely there can't be a difficulty in knowing whether a feeling of mine is or isn't the *same* as the feeling I now have. I will call this feeling pain and will thereafter call the *same* thing pain whenever it occurs. What could be easier than to follow that rule?" To understand Wittgenstein's reply to this attractive proposal we must come closer to his treatment of rules and of what it is to follow a rule. (Here he forges a remarkably illuminating connection between the philosophy of psychology and the philosophy of mathematics.) Consider his example of the pupil who has been taught to write down a cardinal number series of the form "o, n, 2n, 3n . . ." at an order of the form "+n," so that at the order "+1" he writes down the series of natural numbers [§ 185]. He has successfully done exercises and tests up to the number

1,000. We then ask him to continue the series "+2" beyond 1,000; and he writes 1,000, 1,004, 1,008, 1,012. We tell him that this is wrong. His instructive reply is, "But I went on in the same way" [§ 185]. There was nothing in the previous explanations, examples and exercises that made it *impossible* for him to regard that as the continuation of the series. Repeating *those* examples and explanations won't help him. One must say to him, in effect, "That isn't what we *call* going on in the *same* way." It is a fact, and a fact of the kind whose importance Wittgenstein constantly stresses, that it is *natural* for human beings to continue the series in the manner 1,002, 1,004, 1,006, given the previous training. But that is merely what it is—a fact of human nature.

One is inclined to retort, "Of course he can misunderstand the instruction and misunderstand the order "+2"; but if he *understands* it, he must go on in the right way." And here one has the idea that "The understanding itself is a state which is the *source* of the correct use" [§ 146]—that the correct continuation of the series, the right application of the rule or formula, springs from one's understanding of the rule. But the question of whether one understands the rule cannot be divorced from the question of whether one will go on in that one particular way that we call "right." The correct use is a criterion of understanding. If you say that knowing the formula is a state of the mind and that making this and that application of the formula is merely a *manifestation* of the knowledge, then you are in a difficulty: for you are postulating a mental apparatus that explains the manifestations, and so you ought to have (but do not have) a knowledge of the construction of the apparatus, quite apart from what it does [§ 149]. You would like to think that your understanding of the formula determines in advance the steps to be taken, that when you understood or meant the formula in a certain way "your mind as it were flew ahead and took all the steps before you physically arrived at this or that one" [§ 188]. But how you meant it is not independent of how in fact you use it. "We say, for instance, to someone who uses a sign unknown to us: 'If by "$x!2$" you mean x^2, then you get *this* value for y, if you mean $2x$, *that* one!—Now ask yourself: how does one *mean* the one thing or the other by "$x!2$"?" [§ 190]. The answer is that his putting down *this* value for y shows whether he meant the one thing and not the other: "*That* will be how meaning it can determine the steps in advance" [§ 190]. How he meant the

formula determines his subsequent use of it, only in the sense that
the latter is a criterion of how he meant it.

It is easy to suppose that when you have given a person the
order "Now do the *same* thing," you have pointed out to him the
way to go on. But consider the example of the man who obtains
the series 1, 3, 5, 7 . . . by working out the formula $2x + 1$ and
then asks himself, "Am I always doing the same thing, or something different every time?" [§226]. One answer is as good as the
other; it doesn't matter which he says, so long as he continues in
the right way. If we could not observe his work, his mere remark
"I am going on in the same way" would not tell us what he was
doing. If a child writing down a row of 2's obtained "2, 2, 2," from
the segment "2, 2" by adding "2" once, he might deny that he had
gone on the *same* way. He might declare that it would be doing
the same thing only if he went from "2, 2" to "2, 2, 2, 2" in
one jump, i.e., only if he *doubled* the original segment (just as it
doubled the original single "2"). That could strike one as a *reasonable* use of "same." This connects up with Wittgenstein's remark:
"If you have to have an intuition in order to develop the series
1 2 3 4 . . . you must also have one in order to develop the
series 2 2 2 2 . . ." [§214]. One is inclinded to say of the latter
series, "Why, all that is necessary is that you keep on doing the
same thing." But isn't this just as true of the other series? In both
cases one has already *decided* what the correct continuation is,
and one calls that continuation, and no other, "doing the same
thing." As Wittgenstein says: "One might say to the person one
was training: 'Look, I always do the same thing: I . . .'" [§223].
And then one proceeds to show him what "the same" *is*. If the
pupil does not acknowledge that what you have shown him is the
same, and if he is not persuaded by your examples and explanations
to carry on as you wish him to—then you have reached bedrock
and will be inclined to say "This is simply what I do" [§217].
You cannot give him more reasons than you yourself have for
proceeding in that way. Your reasons will soon give out. And then
you will proceed, without reasons [§211].

Private rules. All of this argument strikes at the idea that there can
be such a thing as my following a rule in my private language—
such a thing as naming something of which only I can be aware,
"pain," and then going on to call the same thing, "pain," whenever

it occurs. There is a charm about the expression "same" which makes one think that there cannot be any difficulty or any chance of going wrong in deciding whether *A* is the same as *B*—as if one did not have to be *shown* what the "same" is. This may be, as Wittgenstein suggests, because we are inclined to suppose that we can take the identity of a thing *with itself as* "an infallible paradigm" of the *same* [§215]. But he destroys this notion with one blow: "Then are two things the same when they are what *one* thing is? And how am I to apply what the *one* thing shows me to the case of two things?" [§215]

The point to be made here is that when one has given oneself the private rule "I will call this same thing 'pain' whenever it occurs," one is then free to do anything or nothing. That "rule" does not point in any direction. On the private-language hypothesis, no one can teach me what the correct use of "same" is. I shall be the sole arbiter of whether this is the *same* as that. What I choose to call the "same" will *be* the same. No restriction whatever will be imposed upon my application of the word. But a sound that I can use *as I please* is not a *word*.

How would you teach someone the meaning of "same"? By example and practice; you might show him, for instance, collections of the same colors and same shapes and make him find and produce them and perhaps get him to carry on a certain ornamental pattern uniformly [§208]. Training him to form collections and produce patterns is teaching him what Wittgenstein calls "techniques." Whether he has mastered various techniques determines whether he understands "same." The exercise of a technique is what Wittgenstein calls a "practice." Whether your pupil has understood any of the rules that you taught him (e.g., the rule: this is the "same" color as that) will be shown in his practice. But now there cannot be a "private" practice, i.e., a practice that cannot be exhibited. For there would then be no distinction between believing that you have that practice and having it. "Obeying a rule" is itself a practice. "And to think one is obeying a rule is not to obey a rule. Hence it is not possible to obey a rule 'privately'; otherwise thinking one was obeying a rule would be the same thing as obeying it" [§202]; cf. [§380].

If I recognize that my mental image is the "same" as one that I had previously, how am I to know that this public word "same" describes what I recognize? "Only if I can express my recognition in some other way, and if it is possible for someone else to teach me that 'same' is the correct word here" [§378]. The notion of the private language doesn't admit of there being "some other way." It doesn't allow that my behavior and circumstances can be so related to my utterance of the word that another person, by noting my behavior and circumstances, can discover that my use of the word is correct or incorrect. Can I discover this for myself, and how do I do it? That discovery would presuppose that I have a conception of correct use which comes from outside my private language and against which I measure the latter. If this were admitted, the private language would lose its privacy and its point. So it isn't admitted. But now the notion of "correct" use that will exist within the private language will be such that if I *believe* that my use is correct, then it is correct; the rules will be only impressions of rules; my "language" will not be a language, but merely the impression of a language. The most that can be said for it is that I *think* I understand it [cf. §269].

Sensations of others. The argument that I have been outlining has the form of *reductio ad absurdum:* postulate a "private" language; then deduce that it is not *language.* Wittgenstein employs another argument that is an external, not an internal, attack upon private language. What is attacked is the assumption that once I know from my *own* case what pain, tickling, or consciousness is, then I can transfer the idea of these things to objects outside myself [§283]. Wittgenstein says:

> If one has to imagine someone else's pain on the model of one's own, this is none too easy a thing to do: for I have to imagine pain which I *do not feel* on the model of the pain which I *do feel*. That is, what I have to do is not simply to make a transition in imagination from one place of pain to another. As, from pain in the hand to pain in the arm. For I am not to imagine that I feel pain in some region of his body. (Which would also be possible.) [§302]

The argument that is here adumbrated is, I think, the following: If I were to learn what pain is from perceiving my own pain, then I should, necessarily, have learned that pain is something that exists only when *I* feel pain. For the pain that serves as my paradigm of pain (i.e., my own) has the the property of existing only when *I* feel it.[1] That property is essential, not accidental; it is nonsense to suppose that the pain I feel could exist when I did not feel it. So if I obtain my *conception* of pain from pain that I experience, then it will be part of my conception of pain that *I* am the only being that can experience it. For me it will be a *contradiction* to speak of *another's* pain. This strict solipsism is the necessary outcome of the notion of private language. I take the phrase "this is none too easy" to be a sarcasm.

One is tempted at this point to appeal to the "same" again: "But if I suppose that someone has a pain, then I am simply supposing that he has just the same as I have so often had" [§350]. I will quote Wittgenstein's brilliant counterstroke in full:

> That gets us no further. It is as if I were to say: "You surely know what 'It is 5 o'clock here' means; so you also know what 'It's 5 o'clock on the sun' means. It means simply that it is just the same time there as it is here when it is 5 o'clock."—The explanation by means of *identity* does not work here. For I know well enough that one can call 5 o'clock there "the same time," but what I do not know is in what cases one is to speak of its being the same time here and there.
>
> In exactly the same way it is no explanation to say: the supposition that he has a pain is simply the supposition that he has the same as I. For *that* part of the grammar is quite clear to me: that is, that one will say that the stove has the same experience as I, *if* one says: it is in pain and I am in pain [§350].

Expressions of sensation. Wittgenstein says that he destroys "houses of cards" [*"Luftgebäude"*: §118] and that his aim is to show one how to pass from disguised to obvious nonsense [§464].

---

[1] [This is an error. Apparently I fell into the trap of assuming that if two people, A and B, are in pain, the pain that A feels must be *numerically* different from the pain that B feels. Far from making this assumption, Wittgenstein attacks it when he says: "In so far as it makes *sense* to say that my pain is the same as his, it is also possible for us both to have the same pain" (*op. cit.*, §253). There is not some sense of "same pain" (*numerically* the same) in which A and B *cannot* have the same pain. "Today I have that same backache that you had last week" is something we say. "Same" means here, answering to the same description. We attach no meaning to the "question" of whether the backache you had and the one I have are or are not "numerically" the same.

A more correct account of Wittgenstein's point in §302 is the following: A proponent of the privacy of sensations rejects circumstances and behavior as a criterion of the sensations of others, this being essential to his viewpoint. He does not need (and could not have) a criterion for the existence of pain that he feels. But surely he will need a criterion for the existence of pain that *he* does *not* feel. Yet he cannot have one and still hold to the privacy of sensation. If he sticks to the latter, he ought to admit that he has not the faintest idea of what would count for or against the occurrence of sensations that he does not feel. His conclusion should be, not that it is a contradiction, but that it is unintelligible to speak of the sensations of others. (There is a short exposition of Wittgenstein's attack on the idea that we learn what sensation is *from our own case,* in "Knowledge of Other Minds," see *Knowledge and Certainty* [Prentice-Hall, Inc., 1963], pp. 136–138.)]

But this is not all he does or thinks he does. For he says that he changes one's *way of looking at things* [§144]. What is it that he wishes to substitute for that way of looking at things that is represented by the idea of private language? One would *like* to find a continuous exposition of his own thesis, instead of mere hints here and there. But this desire reflects a misunderstanding of Wittgenstein's philosophy. He rejects the assumption that he should put forward a *thesis* [§128]. "We may not advance any kind of theory" [§109]. A philosophical problem is a certain sort of confusion. It is like being lost; one can't see one's way [§123.] Familiar surroundings suddenly seem strange. We need to command a view of the country, to get our bearings. The country is well known to us, so we need only to be *reminded* of our whereabouts. "The work of the philosopher consists in assembling reminders for a particular purpose" [§127]. "The problems are solved, not by giving new information, but by arranging what we have always known" [§109]. When we describe (remind ourselves of) certain functions of our language, what we do must have a definite bearing on some particular confusion, some "deep disquietude" [§111], that ensnares us. Otherwise our work is irrelevant —to *philosophy*. It is philosophically pointless to formulate a general theory of language or to pile up descriptions for their own sake. "This description gets its light, that is to say its purpose —from the philosophical problems" [§109]. Thus we may not complain at the absence from the *Investigations* of elaborate theories and classifications.

Wittgenstein asks the question "How do words *refer* to sensations?," transforms it into the question "How does a human being learn the meaning of the names of sensations?," and gives this answer: "Words are connected with the primitive, the natural expressions of the sensation and used in their place. A child has hurt himself and he cries; and then the adults talk to him and teach him exclamations and, later, sentences. They teach the child new pain-behavior" [§244]. Wittgenstein must be talking about how it is that a human being learns to refer with words to his *own* sensations—about how he learns to use "I am in pain"; not about how he learns to use "He is in pain." What Wittgenstein is saying is indeed radically different from the notion that I learn what "I am in pain" means by fixing my attention on "a certain" sensation and calling it "pain." But is he saying that what I do instead is to fix my attention on my *expressions* of pain and call them "pain"?' Is he saying that the word "pain" means crying? "On the contrary: the verbal expression of pain replaces crying and does not describe it" [§244]. My words for sensations are used *in place of* the behavior that is the natural expression of the sensations; they do not *refer* to it.

Wittgenstein does not expand this terse reminder. He repeats at least once that my words for sensations are "tied up with my natural expressions of sensation" [§256] and frequently alludes to the importance of the connection between the language for sensations and the behavior which is the expression of sensation [e.g., §§288, 271]. The following questions and objections will arise:

(1) What shows that a child has made this "tie up"? I take Wittgenstein to mean that the child's utterances of the word for a sensation must, in the beginning, be frequently concurrent with some nonverbal, natural expression of that sensation. This concomitance serves as the criterion of his understanding the word. Later on, the word can be uttered in the absence of primitive expressions. ("It hurts" can be said without cries or winces.)

(2) In what sense does the verbal expression "replace" the nonverbal expression? In the sense, I think, that other persons will react to the child's mere words in the same way that they previously reacted to his nonverbal sensation-behavior; they will let the mere words serve as a *new* criterion of his feelings.

(3) I feel inclined to object: "But has the child *learned* what the words *mean*? Hasn't he merely picked up the *use* of the word from his parents?" My objection probably arises from assimilating the learning of the meaning of words to the labeling of bottles— a tendency that is easily decried but not easily resisted. "Learning *ought* to consist in attaching the right name to the right object," I should like to say [cf. §26]. The example of "the beetle in the box" is pertinent here [see §293]. The aim of this fantasy is to prove that attending to a private object can have nothing to do with learning words for sensations. Suppose you wanted to teach a child what a tickling feeling is. You tickle him in the ribs, and he laughs and jerks away. You say to him, "That's what the feeling of tickling is." Now imagine he felt something that you can't know anything about. Will this be of any interest to you when you decide from his subsequent use of the word "tickling" whether he understands it? Others understand the word too. If each one has something that only he can know about, then all the somethings may be different.

The something could even be nothing! Whatever it is, it can have no part in determining whether the person who has it understands the word. "If we construe the grammar of the expression of sensation on the model of 'object and name' the object drops out of consideration as irrelevant" [§293; cf. §304].

My previous objection could be put like this: the teaching and learning of names of sensations cannot stop at the mere expressions of sensation; the names must be brought *right up* to the sensations themselves, must be applied *directly* to the sensations! Here we can imagine Wittgenstein replying, "Like *what*, e.g?." as he replies to an analogous objection in a different problem [§191]. In *what* sense is Wittgenstein denying that names are applied directly to sensations? Do I have a model of what it would be to apply the name "directly"? No. I have this picture—that learning the meaning of "pain" is applying the sign "pain" to pain itself. I have that picture, to be sure, but what does it teach me, what is its "application"? When shall I say that what it pictures has taken place, i.e., that someone has learned the meaning of "pain"? It doesn't tell me; it is *only* a picture. It cannot conflict with, cannot refute, Wittgenstein's reminder of what it is that determines whether a child has learned the word for a sensation. (4) Wittgenstein says that the verbal expressions of sensation can take the place of the nonverbal expressions and that in learning the former, one learns "new pain-behavior." This seems to mean that the words (and sentences) for sensations are related to sensations in the same way as are the primitive expressions of sensations. I am inclined to object again. I want to say that the words are used to *report* the occurrence of a sensation and to inform others of it. The natural expressions, on the contrary, are not used to inform others; they are not "used" at all; they have no purpose, no function; they *escape* from one. But I have over-simplified the difference, because (*a*) a sentence can be forced from one, can escape one's lips ("My God, it hurts!"), and (*b*) a natural expression of sensation can be used to inform another, e.g., you moan to let the nurse know that your pain is increasing (you would have suppressed the moan if she hadn't entered the room), yet the moan is genuine. Perhaps my objection comes to this: I don't *learn* to moan; I do learn the words. But this is the very distinction that is made by saying that moaning is a "natural," a "primitive," expression of sensation.

It is a mistake to suppose that Wittgenstein is saying that the

utterance "My leg hurts" is *normally called* an "expression of sensation." (Of course it isn't. For that matter, only a facial expression,
not a groan, is called an *"expression* of pain." But this is of no
importance.) He is not reporting ordinary usage, but drawing our
attention to an *analogy* between the groan of pain and the utterance
of those words. The important similarity that he is trying to
bring to light (here I may misinterpret him) is that the verbal
utterance and the natural pain-behavior are each (as I shall express it) "incorrigible." [2] A man cannot be in *error* as to whether
he is in pain; he cannot say, "My leg hurts" by mistake, any more
than he can groan by mistake. It is senseless to suppose that he has
wrongly identified a tickle as pain or that he falsely believes
that it is in his leg when in fact it is in his shoulder. True, he may
be undecided as to whether it is best described as an "ache" or a
"pain" (one is often hard put to give satisfactory descriptions of
one's feelings); but his very indecision *shows* us what his sensation is, i.e., something between an ache and a pain. His hesitant
observation, "I'm not sure whether it is a pain or an ache," is
itself an *expression* of sensation. What expresses is an ambiguous
sensation. The point about the incorrigibility of the utterance
"I'm in pain" lies behind Wittgenstein's reiterated remark that
"I *know* I'm in pain" and "I don't know whether I'm in pain" are
both senseless [e.g., §§ 246, 408].[3] Wherever it is *meaningless* to
speak of "false belief," it is also meaningless to speak of "knowledge"; and wherever you cannot say, "I don't know . . ." you also
cannot say, "I know . . ." Of course, a philosopher can say of me
that I *know* I am in pain. But "What is it supposed to mean—
except perhaps that I *am* in pain?" [§246].[4]

There are many "psychological" sentences, other than sentences
about sensations, that are incorrigible, e.g., the *truthful* report of
a dream is a criterion for the occurrence of the dream and, unless
some other criterion is introduced, "the question cannot arise" as
to whether the dreamer's memory deceives him [pp. 222–223]. If
one who has a mental image were asked whom the image is of,

[2] [I try to explain the notion of "incorrigibility," as I understand it, in "Direct Perception" (see *Knowledge and Certainty* [Prentice-Hall, Inc., 1963], pp. 77–86). I concentrate there on the seeing of after-images, but with appropriate changes the notion carries
over to bodily sensations.]
[3] It is interesting to note that as long ago as 1930 Wittgenstein had remarked that it
has no sense to speak of *verifying* "I have a toothache." (See G. E. Moore, "Wittgenstein's Lectures in 1930–33," *Mind*, LXIII [January 1954], 14.)
[4] [In "A Definition of Factual Memory," I mention a sense in which an adult person
(but not an infant or a dog) can be said to know that he has a pain (see *Knowledge
and Certainty*, p. 239).]

"his answer would be decisive," just as it would be if he were asked whom the drawing represents that he has just made [p. 177]. When you say, "It will stop soon," and are asked whether you *meant* your pain or the sound of the piano turning, your truthful answer is the answer [§§666–684].

When Wittgenstein says that learning the words for sensations is learning "new pain-behavior" and that the words "replace" the natural expressions, he is bringing to light the arresting fact that my sentences about my present sensations have the same logical status as my outcries and facial expressions. And thus we are helped to "make a radical break with the idea that language always functions in one way, always serves the same purpose: to convey thoughts—which may be about houses, pains, good and evil, or anything else you please" [§304].

This is not to deny that first-person sentences about sensations may, in other respects, be more or less like natural expressions of sensation. Wittgenstein's examples of the use of "I am afraid" [pp. 187–188] show how the utterance of that sentence can be a cry of fear, a comparison, an attempt to tell someone how I feel, a confession, a reflection on my state of mind, or something in between. "A cry is not a description. But there are transitions. And the words 'I am afraid' may approximate more, or less, to being a cry. They may come quite close to this and also be *far* removed from it" [p. 189]. The words "I am in pain" "may be a cry of complaint, and may be something else" [p. 189]; and "it makes me shiver" may be a "shuddering reaction" or may be said "as a piece of information" [p. 174]. If we pursue these hints, it is not hard to construct a list of examples of the use of the words "My head hurts," in which the variety is as great as in Wittgenstein's list for "I am afraid." E.g., compare "Oh hell, how my head hurts!" with "If you want to know whether to accept the invitation for tonight, then I must tell you that my head hurts again." In one case the sentence "My head hurts" belongs to an exclamation of pain, not in the other. In saying that in both cases it is an "expression" of pain, Wittgenstein stretches ordinary language and in so doing illuminates the hidden continuity between the utterance of that sentence and—expressions of pain.

Criterion. That the natural pain-behavior and the utterance "It hurts" are each incorrigible is what makes it possible for each of them to be a criterion of pain. With some reluctance I will under-

take to say a little about this notion of "criterion," a most difficult region in Wittgenstein's philosophy. Perhaps the best way to
elucidate it is to bring out its connection with *teaching* and *learning* the use of words. "When I say the ABC to myself, what is the
criterion of my doing the same as someone else who silently repeats
it to himself? It might be found that the same thing took place in
my larynx and in his. (And similarly when we both think of the
same thing, wish the same, and so on.) But then did we learn
the use of the words, 'to say such-and-such to oneself,' by someone's pointing to a process in the larynx or the brain?" [§376]. Of
course we did not, and this means that a physiological process
is not our "criterion" that *A* said such-and-such to himself. Try
to imagine, realistically and in detail, how you would teach someone the meaning of "saying the ABC silently to oneself." This, you
may think, is merely psychology. But if you have succeeded in
bringing to mind what it is that would show that he *grasped* your
teaching, that he *understood* the use of the words, then you have
elicited the "criterion" for their use—and that is not psychology.
Wittgenstein exhorts us, over and over, to bethink ourselves of how
we learned to use this or that form of words or of how we should
teach it to a child. The purpose of this is not to bring philosophy
down to earth (which it does), but to bring into view those features
of someone's circumstances and behavior that *settle* the question of
whether the words (e.g., "He is calculating in his head") rightly
apply to him. Those features constitute the "criterion" of calculating
in one's head. It is logically possible that someone should have been
born with a knowledge of the use of an expression or that it should
have been produced in him by a drug; that his knowledge came
about by way of the normal process of teaching is not necessary.
What is necessary is that there should be something on the basis
of which we *judge* whether he *has* that knowledge. To undertake to
describe this may be called a "logical" investigation, even though
one should arrive at the description by reflecting on that logically
inessential process of teaching and learning.

If someone says, e.g., "I feel confident . . . ," a question can arise
as to whether he understands those words. Once you admit the
untenability of "private ostensive definition" you will see that there
must be a *behavioral* manifestation of the feeling of confidence
[§579]. There must be behavior against which his words "I feel
confident . . . ," can be checked, if it is to be possible to judge that

he does not understand them. Even if you picture a feeling of confidence as an "inner process," still it requires "outward criteria" [§580].

Wittgenstein contrasts "criterion" with "symptom," employing both words somewhat technically. The falling barometer is a "symptom" that it is raining; its looking like *that* outdoors (think how you would teach the word "rain" to a child) is the "criterion" of rain [§354]. A process in a man's brain or larynx might be a symptom that he has an image of red; the criterion is "what he says and does" [§§376, 377]. What makes something into a symptom of *y* is that experience teaches that it is always or usually associated with *y*; that so-and-so is the criterion of *y* is a matter, not of experience, but of "definition" [§354]. The satisfaction of the criterion of *y* establishes the existence of *y* beyond question. The occurrence of a symptom of *y* may also establish the existence of *y* "beyond question"—but in a different sense. The observation of a brain process may make it certain that a man is in pain—but not in the same way that his pain-behavior makes it certain. Even if physiology has established that a specific event in the brain accompanies bodily pain, still it *could* happen (it makes sense to suppose) that a man was not in pain although that brain event was occuring. But it will not make sense for one to suppose that another person is not in pain if one's criterion of his being in pain is satisfied. (Sometimes, and especially in science, we *change* our criteria: "what today counts as an observed concomitant of a phenomenon will tomorrow be used to define it" [§79].)

The preceding remarks point up the following question: Do the propositions that describe the criterion of his being in pain *logically imply* the proposition "He is in pain"? Wittgenstein's answer is clearly in the negative. A criterion is satisfied *only in certain circumstances*. If we come upon a man exhibiting violent pain-behavior, couldn't something show that he is not in pain? Of course. For example, he is rehearsing for a play; or he has been hypnotized and told, "You will act as if you are in pain, although you won't be in pain," and when he is released from the hypnotic state he has no recollection of having been in pain; or his pain-behavior suddenly ceases and he reports in apparent bewilderment that it was as if his body had been possessed—for his movements had been entirely involuntary, and during the "seizure" he had felt no pain; or he has been narrowly missed by a car and as soon as a sum for damages has been pressed into his hand, his pain-behavior ceases and he laughs at the hoax; or . . . , etc. The expressions of pain are a criterion of pain in *certain* "surroundings," not in others [cf. §584].

Now one would like to think that one can still formulate a logical implication by taking a description of his pain-behavior and con-joining it with the negation of every proposition describing one of those circumstances that would count against saying he is in pain. Surely, the conjunction will logically imply "He is in pain"! But this assumes there is a *totality* of those circumstances such that if none of them were fullfilled, and he was also pain-behaving, then he *could not but* be in pain [cf. §183]. There is no totality that can be exhaustively enumerated, as can the letters of the alphabet. It is quite impossible to list six or nine such circumstances and then to say "That is all of them; no other circumstances can be imagined that would count against his being in pain." The list of circum-stances has no "all," in that sense; the list is, not infinite, but *in-definite*. Therefore, entailment-conditions cannot be formulated; there are none.

The above thought is hard to accept. It is not in line with our *ideal* of what language should be. It makes the "rules" for the use of "He is in pain" too vague, too loose, not really *rules*. Wittgen-stein has deep things to say about the nature of this "ideal": We want to say that there can't be any vagueness in logic. The idea now absorbs us, that the ideal "must" be found in reality. Meanwhile we do not as yet see *how* it occurs there, nor do we understand the nature of this "must." We think it must be in reality; for we think we already see it there" [§101]. "The strict and clear rules of the logical structure of propositions appear to us as something in the background—hidden in the medium of the understanding" [§102]. "The more narrowly we examine actual language, the sharper becomes the conflict between it and our requirement. (For the crystalline purity of logic was, of course, not a *result of in-vestigation:* it was a requirement)" [§107]. What we need to do is to remove from our noses the logical glasses through which we look at reality [§103]. We must study our language as it is, without preconceived ideas. One thing this study will teach us is that the criteria for the use of third-person psychological statements are not related to the latter by an entailment-relation.

Wittgenstein suggests that propositions describing the fulfillment of behavioral criteria are related to third-person psychological statements in the way that propositions describing sense inpressions are related to physical-object statements [compare §486 and p. 180]. It does not *follow* from the propositions describing my sense impressions that there is a chair over there [§486]. The relation cannot be reduced to a *simple* formula (p. 180). *Why* doesn't it follow? Wittgenstein does not say, but the reason would appear to be of the same sort as in the example of "He is in pain." The propositions describing my sense impressions would have to be conjoined with the proposition that I am not looking in a mirror, or at a painted scenery, or at a movie film, or . . . ,etc. Here too there cannot be an exhaustive enumeration of the negative conditions that would have to be added to the description of sense impressions *if* "There's a chair over there" *were* to be logically implied.

The puzzling problem now presents itself: if it does not *follow* from his behavior and circumstances that he is in pain, then how can it ever be *certain* that he is in pain? "I can be as *certain* of someone else's sensations as of any fact," says Wittgenstein [p. 224]. How can this be so, since there is not a definite set of six or eight conditions (each of which would nullify his pain-behavior) to be checked off as not fulfilled? It *looks* as if the conclusion ought to be that we cannot "completely verify" that he is in pain. This conclusion is wrong, but it is not easy to see why. I comprehend Wittgenstein's thought here only dimly. He says:

> A doctor asks: "How is he feeling?" The nurse says: "He is groaning." A report on his behavior. But need there be any question for them whether the groaning is really genuine, is really the expression of anything? Might they not, for example, draw the conclusion "If he groans, we must give him more analgesic" —without suppressing a middle term? Isn't the point the service to which they put the description of behaviour [p. 179]?

One hint that I take from this is that there can be situations of real life in which a question as to whether someone who groans is pretending, or rehearsing, or hypnotized, or . . . , simply does not exist. "Just try—in a real case—to doubt someone else's fear or pain" [§303]. A doubt, a question, would be rejected as absurd by anyone who knew the actual surroundings. "But might there not be still further surroundings, unknown to you, that would change the whole aspect of the matter?" Well, we go only *so* far—and then we are certain. "Doubting has an end" [p. 180]. Perhaps we can *imagine* a doubt; but we do not take it seriously [cf. 84]. Just as it becomes certain to us that there is a chair over there, although we can imagine a *possible* ground of doubt. There is a concept of certainty in these language games only because we stop short of what is conceivable.

" 'But, if you are *certain,* isn't it that you are shutting your eyes in face of doubt?'—They are shut" [p. 224]. This striking remark suggests that what we sometimes do is draw a boundary around *this* behavior in *these* circumstances and say, "Any additional circumstances that might come to light will be irrelevant to whether this man is in pain." Just as we draw a line and say, "No further information will have any bearing on whether there is a chair in the corner—that is settled." If your friend is struck down by a car and writhes with a broken leg, you do not think: Perhaps it was prearranged in order to alarm me; possibly his leg was anesthetized just before the "accident" and he isn't suffering at all. Someone *could* have such doubts whenever another person was ostensibly in pain. Similarly: "I can easily imagine someone always doubting before he opened his front door whether an abyss did not yawn behind it; and making sure about it before he went through the door (and he might on some occasion prove to be right)—but that does not make me doubt in the same case" [§84].

The man who doubts the other's pain may be neurotic, may "lack a sense of reality," but his reasoning is perfectly sound. *If* his doubts are true then the injured man is *not* in pain. His reaction is abnormal but not illogical. The certainty that the injured man is in pain (the normal reaction) ignores the endless doubts that *could* be proposed and investigated.

And it is important to see that the abnormal reaction *must* be the exception and not the rule. For if someone *always* had endless doubts about the genuineness of expressions of pain, it would mean that he was not using *any criterion* of another's being in pain. It would mean that he did not accept anything as an *expression* of pain. So what could it mean to say that he even had the *concept* of another's being in pain? It is senseless to suppose that he has this concept and yet always doubts.

Third-person sensation-sentences. Wittgenstein assimilates first-person, not third-person, sensation sentences to *expressions* of sensation. I will say one or two things more about his conception of the use of third-person sensation sentences.

(1) "Only of a living human being and what resembles (behaves like) a living human being can one say: it has sensations; it sees; is blind; hears; is deaf; is conscious or unconscious" [§281]. The human *body* and *human* behavior are the *paradigm* to which third-person attributions of consciousness, sensations, feelings are related. (The use of first-person sensation sentences is governed by *no* paradigm.) Thus there cannot occur in ordinary life a question as to whether other human beings ever possess consciousness, and I can have this question when I philosophize only if I forget that I use that paradigm in ordinary life. It is by analogy with the human form and behavior that I attribute consciousness (or unconsciousness) to animals and fish: the more remote the analogy the less sense in the attribution. (Just as it is by analogy with our ordinary language that anything is called "language") [§494]. In order to imagine that a pot or a chair has thoughts or sensations one must give it, in imagination, something like a human body, face, and speech [§§282, 361]. A child says that its doll has stomach ache, but this is a "secondary" use of the concept of pain. "Imagine a case in which people ascribed pain *only* to inanimate things; pitied *only* dolls!" [§282; cf. §385, p. 216]. Wittgenstein means, I think, that this is an impossible supposition because we should not want to say that those people *understood* ascriptions of pain. If they did not ever show pity for human beings or animals or expect it for themselves, then their treatment of dolls would not be *pity*.

(2) My criterion of another's being in pain is, first, his behavior and circumstances and, second, his words (after they have been found to be connected in the right way with his behavior and circumstances). Does it follow that my interest is in his behavior and words, not in his pain? Does "He is in pain" *mean* behavior? In lectures Wittgenstein imagined a tribe of people who had the idea that their slaves had no feelings, no souls—that they were automatons—despite the fact that the slaves had human bodies, behaved like their masters, and even spoke the same language. Wittgenstein undertook to try to give sense to that idea. When a slave injured himself or fell ill or complained of pains, his master would try to heal him. The master would let him rest when he was fatigued, feed him when he was hungry and thirsty, and so on. Furthermore, the masters would apply to the slaves our usual dis-

tinctions between genuine complaints and malingering. So what could it mean to say that they had the idea that the slaves were automatons? Well, they would *look* at the slaves in a peculiar way. They would observe and comment on their movements *as if* they were machines. ("Notice how smoothly his limbs move.") They would discard them when they were worn and useless, like machines. If a slave received a mortal injury and twisted and screamed in agony, no master would avert his gaze in horror or prevent his children from observing the scene, any more than he would if the ceiling fell on a printing press. Here is a difference in "attitude" that is not a matter of believing or expecting different facts.

So in the *Investigations,* Wittgenstein says, "My attitude towards him is an attitude towards a soul. I am not of the *opinion* that he has a soul" [p. 178]. I do not *believe* that the man is suffering who writhes before me—for to what facts would a "belief" be related, such that a change in the facts would lead me to alter it? I *react* to his suffering. I look at him with compassion and try to comfort him. If I complain of headache to someone and he says, "It's not so bad," does this prove that he believes in something *behind* my outward expression of pain? "His attitude is a proof of his attitude. Imagine not merely the words 'I am in pain' but also the answer 'It's not so bad' replaced by instinctive noises and gestures" [§310]. The thought that behind someone's pain-behavior is the pain itself does not enter into our use of "He's in pain," but what does enter into it is our sympathetic, or unsympathetic, reaction to him. The fact that the latter does enter into our use of that sentence (but might not have) gives sense to saying that the sentence "He is in pain" does not just *mean* that his behavior, words, and circumstances are such and such—although these are the criteria for its use.

When he groans we do not *assume,* even tacitly, that the groaning expresses pain. We fetch a sedative and try to put him at ease. A totally different way of reacting to his groans would be to make exact records of their volume and frequency—and do nothing to relieve the sufferer! But our reaction of seeking to comfort him does not involve a presupposition, for, "Doesn't a presupposition imply a doubt? And doubt may be entirely lacking" [p. 180].

Form of life. The gestures, facial expressions, words, and activities that constitute pitying and comforting a person or a dog are, I think, a good example of what Wittgenstein means by a "form of life." One could hardly place too much stress on the importance of this latter notion in Wittgenstein's thought. It is intimately related to the notion of "language-game." His choice of the latter term is meant to "bring into prominence the fact that the *speaking* of language is part of an activity, or of a form of life" [§23; cf. §19]. If we want to understand any concept we must obtain a view of the human behavior, the activities, the natural expressions, that surround the words for that concept. What, for example, is the concept of *certainty* as applied to *predictions?* The nature of my certainty that fire will burn me comes out in the fact that "Nothing could induce me to put my hand into a flame" [§472]. That reaction of mine to fire shows the *meaning* of certainty in this language-game [§474]. (Of course, it is *different* from the concept of certainty in, e.g., mathematics. "The kind of certainty is the kind of language game" [p. 124].) But is my certainty justified? Don't I need reasons? Well, I don't normally think of reasons, I can't produce much in the way of reasons, and I don't feel a need of reasons [cf. §477]. Whatever was offered in the way of reasons would not strengthen my fear of fire, and if the reasons turned out to be weak I still wouldn't be induced to put my hand on the hot stove.

As far as "justification" is concerned, "What people accept as a justification—is shown by how they think and live" [§325]. If we want to elucidate the concept of justification we must take note of what people *accept* as justified; and it is clearly shown in our lives that we accept as justified both the certainty that fire will burn and the certainty that this man is in pain—even without reasons. Forms of life, embodied in language games, teach us what justification is. As philosophers we must not attempt to justify the forms of life, to give reasons for *them*—to argue, for example, that we pity the injured man because we believe, assume, presuppose, or know that in addition to the groans and writhing, there is pain. The fact is, we pity him! "What has to be accepted, the given, is—so one could say—*forms of life*" [p. 226]. What we should say is: *"This language game is played"* [§654].

From this major theme of Wittgenstein's thought one passes easily to another major theme—that "Philosophy simply puts

everything before us, and neither explains nor deduces anything"
[§126]. "It leaves everything as it is" [§124].

Strawson's criticism. Mr. Peter Strawson's critical notice [5] of the
Investigations contains misunderstandings that might obtain currency. To Strawson it appears that, for Wittgenstein, "no word
whatever stands for or names a special experience," [6] "no words
name sensations (or 'private experiences'); and in particular the
word 'pain' does not." [7] Wittgenstein "has committed himself to
the view that one cannot sensibly be said to recognize or identify
anything, unless one uses *criteria;* and, as a consequence of this,
that one cannot recognize or identify sensations." [8] His "obsession
with the *expression* of pain" leads him "to deny that sensations
can be recognized and bear names." [9] Wittgenstein is hostile to
"the idea of what is not observed (see, heard, smelled, touched,
tasted), and in particular to the idea that what is not observed
can in any sense be recognized or described or reported" [10]—although at one place in the book [p. 189] "it looks as if he were
almost prepared to acknowledge" that "I am in pain" "may be just
a report of my sensations." [11] His "prejudice against 'the inner' "
leads him to deny that it is possible for a person to report the
words that went through his mind when he was saying something
to himself in his thoughts.[12] Strawson attributes Wittgenstein's
errors not only to prejudice and, possibly, to "the old verificationist
horror of a claim that cannot be checked," [13] but also to various
confusions and muddles.[14]

It is important to see how very erroneous is this account of
Wittgenstein. The latter says, "Don't we talk about sensations every
day, and give them names" and then asks, "How does a human
being learn the names of sensations?—of the word 'pain' for example" [§244]. So Wittgenstein does not deny that we *name* sensations. It is a howler to accuse Wittgenstein of "hostility to the

[5] "Critical Notice: *Philosophical Investigations,*" *Mind,* LXII (January 1954), pp. 70–99.
(References to Strawson will be placed in footnotes, references to Wittgenstein will remain in the text.)
[6] P. 83.
[7] P. 84.
[8] P. 86.
[9] P. 87.
[10] P. 90.
[11] P. 94.
[12] P. 91.
[13] P. 92.
[14] See p. 86 and p. 98.

idea of what is not observed" ("observed" apparently means "perceived by one of the five senses") and of "hostility to the idea that what is not observed can in any sense be recognized or described or reported." [15] Dreams and mental pictures are not observed, in Strawson's sense; yet Wittgenstein discusses *reports* of dreams [p. 222; also p. 184] and *descriptions* of mental pictures [e.g., §367]. Consider this general remark: "Think how many different kinds of things are called 'description': description of a body's position by means of its coordinates; description of a facial expression; *description of a sensation of touch;* of a mood" [§24, my italics]. And at many places in the *Investigations,* Wittgenstein *gives* descriptions of various sensations, although sensations are not observed, in Strawson's sense. Strawson's belief that Wittgenstein thinks that "one cannot sensibly be said to recognize or identify anything, unless one uses criteria," [16] is proved false by the remarks about mental images: I have *no* criterion for saying that two images of mine are the same [§377]; yet there is such a thing as *recognition* here, and a correct use of "same" [§378]. How can it be maintained that Wittgenstein has a prejudice against "the inner" when he allows that in our ordinary language a man *can* write down or give vocal expression to his "inner experiences —his feelings, moods, and the rest—for his private use"? [§243]. Wittgenstein does not deny that there are *inner* experiences any more than he denies that there are *mental* occurrences. Indeed, he gives examples of things that he calls "*seelische Vorgänge,*" e.g., "a pain's growing more or less," and in contrast with which a thing like *understanding a word* is not, he argues a "*seelischen Vorgäng* [§154]. Either to deny that such occurrences exist or to claim that they cannot be named, reported, or described is entirely foreign to Wittgenstein's outlook. For what would the denial amount to other than an attempt to "reform language," which is not his concern? It may *look* as if he were trying to reform language, because he is engaged in "giving prominence to distinctions which our ordinary forms of language easily make us overlook" [§132]. For example, Wittgenstein suggests that when we think about the philosophical problem of sensation the word "describe" *tricks* us [§290]. Of course he does not mean that it is a mistake to speak of "describing" a sensation. He means that the

[15] P. 90.
[16] P. 86.

similarity in "surface grammar" [§664] between "I describe my sensations" and "I describe my room" may mislead, may cause us to fail "to call to mind the differences between the language games" [§290].

Strawson rightly avers, "To deny that 'pain' is the name of a (type of) sensation is comparable to denying that 'red' is the name of a color." [17] I suppose that, conversely, to affirm that "pain" is the name of a sensation is like affirming that "red" is the name of a color, and also that "0" is the name of a number. This classification tells us nothing of philosophical interest. What we need to notice is the *difference* between the way that "0" and "2," say, function, although both are "names of numbers" (think how easily one may be tempted to deny that 0 is a number), and the difference between the way "red" and "pain" function, although both are "names." "We call very different things 'names'; the word 'name' is used to characterize many different kinds of use of a word, related to one another in many different ways" [§38]. To suppose that the uses of "pain" and "red," as *names,* are alike is just the sort of error that Wittgenstein wants to expose. If one thinks this, one will want to bypass the *expression* of pain and will wonder at Wittgenstein's "obsession" with it. Not that Strawson does bypass it, but he seems to attach the wrong significance to it. He appears to think that the fact that there is a characteristic pain-behavior is what makes possible a *common* "language of pain," and he seems to imply that if we did not care to have a *common* language of pain each of us would still be able to name and describe his pains in "a private language game," even if there were no characteristic pain-behavior.[18] It looks as if he thinks that with his private language he could step between pain and its expression, and apply names to the bare sensations themselves [cf. §245].

For Strawson the conception of a private language possesses no difficulty. A man "might simply be struck by the recurrence of a certain sensation and get into the habit of making a certain mark in a different place every time it occurred. The making of the marks would help to impress the occurrence on his memory." [19] Just as, I suppose, he might utter a certain sound each time a cow appeared. But we need to ask, what makes the latter sound a

17 P. 87.
18 See pp. 84–88.
19 P. 85.

word, and what makes it the word for *cow*? Is there no difficulty here? Is it sufficient that the sound is uttered when and only when a cow is present? Of course not. The sound might refer to anything or nothing. What is necessary is that it should play a part in various activities, in calling, fetching, counting cows, distinguishing cows from other things and pictures of cows from pictures of other things. If the sound has no fixed place in activities ("language games") of this sort, then it isn't a word for *cow*. To be sure, I can sit in my chair and talk about cows and not be engaged in any of those activities—but what makes my words *refer* to cows is the fact that I have already mastered those activities; they lie in the background. The kind of way that "cow" refers is the kind of language game to which it belongs. If a mark or sound is to be a word for a *sensation* it, too, must enter into language games, although of a very different sort. What sort? Well, such things as showing the location of the sensation, exhibiting different reactions to different intensities of stimulus, seeking or avoiding causes of the sensation, choosing one sensation in preference to another, indicating the duration of the sensation, and so on. Actions and reactions of that sort constitute the sensation-behavior. They are the "outward criteria" [§580] with which the sign must be connected if it is to be a sign for a sensation *at all,* not merely if it is to be a sign in a *common* language. In the mere supposition that there is a man who is "struck by the recurrence of a certain sensation" and who gets into the habit of "making a certain mark in a different place every time it occurred," no ground *whatever* has been given for saying that the mark is a sign for a sensation. The necessary surroundings have not been supplied. Strawson sees no problem here. He is surprised that "Wittgenstein gives him considerable trouble over the question of how a man would *introduce* a name for a sensation into this private language." [20] It is as if Strawson thought: There is no difficulty about it; the man just *makes* the mark refer to a sensation. How the man does it puzzles Strawson so little that he is not even inclined to feel that the connection between the name and the sensation is queer, occult [cf. §38]—which it would be, to say the least, if the name had no fixed place in those activities and reactions that constitute sensation-behavior, for that, and not a magical act of the mind, is what *makes* it refer to a sensation.

[20] *Ibid.*

The conception of private language that Wittgenstein attacks is not the conception of a language that only the speaker does understand, but of a language that no other person *can* understand [§243]. Strawson thinks that Wittgenstein has not refuted the conception of a private language but has only shown that certain conditions must be satisfied if a common language is to exist. Strawson appears to believe (I may misunderstand him) that each of us not only can have but does have a private language of sensations, that if we are to understand one another when we speak of our sensations there must be criteria for the use of our sensation words, and that therefore the words with which we *refer* to our sensations must, in addition, contain "allusions" either to behavior or to material substances that are "associated" with the sensations.[21] The allusions must be to things that can be perceived by us all. By virtue of this the use of sensation words can be taught and misuses corrected, and so those words will belong to a common language. There is another feature of their use (namely, their reference) that cannot be taught. Thus sensation words will have both a public and a private meaning. Strawson's view appears to be accurately characterized by Wittgenstein's mock conjecture: "Or is it like this: the word 'red' means something known to everyone; and in addition, for each person, it means something known only to him? (Or perhaps rather: it *refers* to something known only to him.)" [§273]

But if my words, *without* these allusions, can refer to my sensations, then what is alluded to is only *contingently* related to the sensations. Adding the "allusions to what can be seen and touched" [22] will not help one little bit in making us understand one another. For the behavior that is, for me, contingently associated with "the sensation of pain" may be, for you, contingently associated with "the sensation of tickling"; the piece of matter that produces in you what you call "a metallic taste" may produce in me what, if you could experience it, you would call "the taste of onions"; my "sensation of red" may be your "sensation of blue"; we do not know and cannot know whether we are talking about the same things; we cannot *learn* the essential thing about one another's use of sensation words—namely, their reference. The language in which the private referring is done cannot be turned into a common language by hav-

21 P. 86.
22 *Ibid.*

ing something grafted on to it. Private language cannot be the under-structure of the language we all understand. It is as if, in Strawson's conception, the sensation words were supposed to perform two func-tions—to refer and to communicate. But if the reference is incom-municable, then the trappings of allusion will not communicate it, and what they do communicate will be irrelevant.

Strawson's idea that expressions like "jabbing pain," "metallic taste," mean something known to everyone and, in addition, for each person, refer to something known only to him, is responsible, I believe, for his failure to understand Wittgenstein on the topic of recognizing and identifying sensations. There is *a* sense of "rec-ognize" and "identify" with respect to which Wittgenstein does deny that we can recognize or identify our own sensations, feelings, images. Consider, for example, that although a man understands the word "alcohol" he may fail to identify the alcohol in a bottle as alcohol, because the bottle is marked "gasoline" or because the cork smells of gasoline; or, although he understands "rabbit" and is familiar with rabbits, he may fail to recognize a rabbit as a rabbit, taking it for a stump instead; or, he may be in doubt and say, "I don't know whether this is alcohol," "I'm not sure whether that is a rabbit or a stump." But can a man who understands the word "pain" be in doubt as to whether he has pain? Wittgenstein re-marks:

> If anyone said, "I do not know if what I have got is a pain or something else," we should think something like, he does not know what the English word "pain" means; and we should explain it to him.—How? Perhaps by means of gestures, or by pricking him with a pin and saying: "See, that's what pain is!" This explana-tion, like any other, he might understand right, wrong, or not at all. And he will show which he does by his use of the word, in this as in other cases.
>
> If he now said, for example: "Oh, I know what 'pain' means; what I don't know is whether *this,* that I have now, is pain"—we should merely shake our heads and be forced to regard his words as a queer reaction which we have no idea what to do with [§288].

That a man wonders whether what he has is pain can only mean that he does not understand the word "pain"; he cannot both under-stand it and have that doubt. Thus there is a sense of "identify" that has no application to sensations. One who understands the word "alcohol" may fail to identify *this* as alcohol or may be in doubt as to its identity or may correctly identify it. These possibilities have no meaning in the case of pain. There is not over and above (or underneath) the understanding of the word "pain" a further process of correctly identifying or failing to identify *this* as pain. There would be if Strawson's conception was right. But there is not, and this is why "That expression of doubt ['Oh, I know what 'pain' means; what I don't know is whether *this,* that I have now, is pain'] has no place in the language game" [§288]. (Strawson does not have, but in consistency should have, an inclination to dispute this last remark of Wittgenstein's.) [23] The fact that there is no *further* process of identifying a particular sensation is a reason why "the object drops out of consideration as irrelevant" when "we construe the grammar of the expression of sensation on the model of 'object and name' " [§293]—a remark that Strawson misunderstands as the thesis that "no words name sensations." [24] If my use of a sensation word satisfies the normal outward criteria and if I truthfully declare that I have that sensation, then I *have* it—there is not a further problem of my applying the word right or wrong within myself. If a man used the word "pain" in accordance with "the usual symptoms and presuppositions of pain" then it would have no sense to suppose that perhaps his memory did not retain *what* the word "pain" refers to, "so that he constantly called different things by that name" [§271]. If my use of the word fits those usual criteria there is not an added problem of whether I accurately pick out the objects to which the word applies. In this sense of "identify," the hypothesis that I identify my sensations is "a mere ornament, not connected with the mechanism of all" [§270].

It does not follow nor, I think, does Wittgenstein mean to assert that there is *no* proper use of "identify" or "recognize" with sensations. He acknowledges a use of "recognize" with mental images, as previously noted. It would be a natural use of language, I believe, if someone who upon arising complained of an unusual sensation were to say, "Now I can identify it! It is the same sensation that I have when I go down in an elevator." Wittgenstein, who has no interest in reforming language, would not dream of calling this an incorrect use of "identify." He attacks a philosophical use of the word only, the use that belongs to the notion of the private object. In this example of a nonphilosophical use, if the speaker employed the rest of the sensation language as we all do, and if his behavior

23 See p. 85.
24 P. 84.

in this case was approximately what it was when he was affected by the downward motion of an elevator, then his declaration that he was feeling the elevator sensation would be decisive; and also his declaration that it was *not* the elevator sensation would be decisive. It is *out of the question* that he should have made a mistake in identifying the sensation. His identification of his sensation is an *expression* of sensation (in Wittgenstein's extended sense of this phrase). The identification is "incorrigible." We have here a radically different use of "identify" from that illustrated in the examples of alcohol and rabbit.

The philosophical use of "identify" seems to make possible the committing of *errors* of identification of sensations and inner experiences. The idea is that my sensation or my image is an object that I cannot show to anyone and that I identify it and from it derive its description [§374]. But if this is so, why cannot my identification and description go wrong, and not just sometimes but always? Here we are in a position to grasp the significance of Wittgenstein's maneuver: "Always get rid of the idea of the private object in this way: assume that it constantly changes, but that you do not notice the change because your memory constantly deceives you" [p. 207]. We are meant to see the *senselessness* of this supposition: for what in the world would *show* that I was deceived constantly or even once? Do I look again—and why can't I be deceived that time, too? The supposition is a knob that doesn't turn anything [cf. §270]. Understanding this will perhaps remove the temptation to think that I have something that I cannot show to you and from which I derive a knowledge of its identity. This is what I just said to myself in my thoughts " 'what went on within me' is not the point at all" [p. 222]. He is not declaring, as Strawson thinks, that I cannot report what words went through my mind.[25] He is saying that it is a report "whose truth is guaranteed by the special criteria of truthfulness" [p. 222]. It is *that* kind of report. So it is not a matter of trying faithfully to observe something within myself and of trying to produce a correct account of it, of trying to do something at which I might unwittingly fail.

The influence of the idea of the private object on Strawson's thinking is subtly reflected, I believe, in his declaration that a metallic taste is "quite certainly recognizable and identifiable in itself" and in his remark that "if the question 'What is the criterion

25 See pp. 90, 91.

of identity here?' is pushed, one can only answer: 'Well, the taste itself' (cf. 'the sensation itself')." [26] Strawson realizes that we don't identify a sensation by means of criteria (e.g., a metallic taste by means of the metallic material that produces it). He is inclined to add that we identify it by "the sensation itself." This seems to be to misconstrue the "grammar" of "identify" here. It may be to the point to consider again the comparison of colors and sensations. Wittgenstein says, "How do I know that this color is red? —It would be an answer to say 'I have learned English' " [§381]. One thing this answer does is to deny that I have *reasons* for saying that this color before me is red. We might put this by saying that I identify it as red by "the color itself," not by anything else. The cases of red and pain (or metallic taste) so far run parallel. Equally, I don't have reasons for saying that this color is red or that this sensation is pain. But it *can* happen that I should fail to identify this color correctly, even though I have learned English (e. g., the moonlight alters its appearance). Here the parallel ends. Nothing can alter the "appearance" of the sensation. Nothing counts as mistaking its identity. If we assimilate identifying sensations to identifying colors, because in neither instance reasons are relevant, we conceal the philosophically more important difference. To insist that the parallel is perfect, that one identifies sensations in the same sense that one identifies colors, is like saying that "there must also be something boiling in the pictured pot" [§297]. Identifying one's own sensation is nothing that is either in error or *not* in error. It is not, in *that* sense, *identifying*. When I identify my sensation, I do not *find out* its identity, not even from "the sensation itself." My identification, one could say, *defines* its identity.

We use a man's identification of his sensation as a criterion of what his sensation is. But this is a *dependent* criterion. His verbal reports and identifications would not *be* a criterion unless they were grounded in the primitive sensation-behavior that is the primary and independent criterion of his sensations. If we cut out human behavior from the language game of sensations (which Strawson does in defending the "private language game") one result will be that a man's identifying a sensation as the "same" that he had a moment before will no longer be a criterion of its being the same. Not only the speaker but *no one* will have a criterion of identity. Consequently, for no one will it have any mean-

26 P. 86.

ing to speak of a man's being "struck by the *recurrence* of a certain sensation." [27] I hope that I will be forgiven if I have misunderstood Mr. Strawson.

Conclusion. I have discussed only one strand of this complex, difficult, and exciting book. Countless other riches are there: a powerful attack upon Wittgenstein's own *Tractatus;* deep inquiries into the notions of *concept* and *proposition;* investigations of *naming, thinking, meaning, intending, understanding, imagining,* a remarkable study of *seeing as,* a notion that is important to Gestalt psychology; a revolutionary account of the nature of philosophy. All this, and far more, is presented with the passion and profundity of genius, in language of never-failing force.

Miss Anscombe is to be warmly congratulated for her most skillful and sensitive translation. It is cause for rejoicing that she will translate the material for subsequent volumes of Wittgenstein's works.

27 P. 85, my italics.

Wittgenstein's Philosophical Investigations

BY PAUL FEYERABEND

I

IN DISCUSSING THIS BOOK I shall proceed in the following way: I shall first state a philosophical theory T, which is attacked throughout the book. In doing so I shall not use the usual statement of the theory (if there is any) but Wittgenstein's, which may, of course, be an idealization. Secondly, I shall show how the theory is criticized by Wittgenstein—first, using an example (which plays a considerable role in the *Investigations,* but which I have used to present arguments not presented in the book in connection with this example), then discussing in general terms the difficulties revealed by the example. Thirdly, I shall state what seems to be Wittgenstein's own position on the issue. This position will be formulated as a philosophical theory, T', without implying that Wittgenstein intended to develop a philosophical theory (he did not). Finally I shall discuss the relation between the theory stated and Wittgenstein's views on philosophy and I shall end up with a few critical remarks.[1]

For brevity's sake I shall introduce three different types of quotation marks: The usual quotation marks ("...") enclosing Wittgenstein's own words, daggers († ... †) enclosing further developments of his ideas and general remarks, asterisks (*...*) enclosing critical remarks. Text without any of these quotation marks is an abbreviated statement of what Wittgenstein is saying.

---

[1] Although many different problems are discussed in the *Investigations,* it seems to me that the criticism of T (or the assertion of T') is to be regarded as the core of the book. I shall therefore concentrate on elaborating T and T', and I shall omit all other problems (if there are any).

II

†The theory criticized is closely related to medieval realism (about universals) and to what has recently been termed "essentialism." [2] The theory, as presented by Wittgenstein, includes the following five main items:

†(1) "Every word has a meaning. This meaning is correlated with the word. It is the object, for which the word stands" [1; §§90,120].[3] Meanings exist independently of whether or not any language is used and which language is used. They are definite, single objects and their order "must be *utterly simple*" [§97].

†(2) As compared with this definiteness and purity of meanings (their order "must . . . be of the purest crystal" [§97]), "the actual use . . . seems something muddied" [§426]. That indicates an imperfection of our language.

†(3) This imperfection gives rise to two different philosophical problems: (*a*) The philosopher has to find out what a word '*W*' stands for, or, as it is sometimes expressed, he has to discover the *essence* of the object which is designated by '*W*,' when its use in everyday language is taken into account. From the knowledge of the essence of *W* the knowledge of the whole use of '*W*' will follow [§§264, 362, 449]. (*b*) He has to build an ideal language whose elements are related to the essences in a simple way. The method of finding a solution to problem (*a*) is analysis. This analysis proceeds from the assumption that "*the essence is hidden from us*" [§92] but that it nevertheless " '*must*' be found in reality" [§101]. However different the methods of analysis may be—analysis of the linguistic usage of '*W*'; phenomenological analysis of W ('deepening' of the phenomenon *W*); intellectual intuition of the essence of *W*—the answer to problem (*a*) "is to be given once for all; and independently of any future experience" [§92]. The form of this answer is the definition. The definition explains why '*W*' is used in the way it is and why *W* behaves as it does [§75; §§97, 428, 654]. The solution of (*b*) is presupposed in the solution of (*a*); for it provides us with the terms in which the definitions that constitute the solution of (*a*) are to be framed. A definite solution of (*b*) implies a certain form of problem (*a*). If it is assumed, e.g., that

[2] Cf. K. R. Popper, *The Open Society and Its Enemies* (Princeton, 1950), Vol. I, p. 31 ff.
[3] Bracketed references are to the numbered sections of Part I of the *Philosophical Investigations*, unless otherwise indicated.

sentences are word pictures of facts [§291; cf. *Tractatus Logico-Philosophicus* 2.1; 4.04] then 'What is a question?' is to be translated into 'What kind of fact is described by a question? The fact that somebody wants to know whether . . . , or the fact that somebody is doubtful as to . . . , etc.?'

†(4) Asking how the correctness of a certain analysis may be checked, we get the answer that the essence can be *experienced*. This experience consists in the presence of a mental picture, a sensation, a phenomenon, a feeling, or an inner process of a more ethereal kind [§305]. 'To grasp the meaning' means the same as 'to have a picture before one's inner eye' and "to have understood the explanation means to have in one's mind an idea of the thing explained, and that is a sample or a picture" [§73]. The essence of the object denoted, the meaning of the denoting expression (these are one and the same thing; cf. §§371, 373), follows from an analysis of this picture, of this sensation; it follows from the exhibition of the process in question (thus the essence of sensation follows from an analysis of my present headache [§314]). It is the presence of the picture which gives meaning to our words [§§511, 592], which forces upon us the right use of the word [§§73, 140, 305, 322, 426, 449], and which enables us to perform correctly an activity (reading, calculating) the essence of which it constitutes [§§179, 175, 186, 232]. Understanding, calculating, thinking, reading, hoping, desiring are, therefore, mental processes.

†(5) From all this it follows that teaching a language means showing the connection between words and meanings [§362] and that "learning a language consists in giving names to objects" [§253]. So far the description of *T*, as it is implicitly contained in the *Philosophical Investigations*.

III

†In criticizing *T*, Wittgenstein analyzes *T*4 and in this way shows the impossibility of the program *T*3 as well as the insolubility of the problems connected with this program. That implies that, within *T*, we shall never be able to know what a certain word '*W*' means or whether it has any meaning at all, although we are constantly using that word and although the question how it is to be used does not arise when we are not engaged in philosophical investigations. But did not this paradox arise because we assumed that meanings are

objects of a certain kind and that a word is meaningful if and only if it stands for one of those objects; i.e., because we assumed $T1, 2$ to be true? If, on the other hand, we want to abandon $T1, 2$, we meet another difficulty: words have, then, no fixed meaning [§79]. "But what becomes of logic now? Its rigor seems to be giving way here.—But in that case doesn't logic altogether disappear?—For how can it lose its rigor? Of course not by our bargaining any of its rigor out of it.—The *preconceived idea* of crystalline purity can only be removed by turning our whole examination round" [§108]; i.e., by changing from T to T'. It will turn out that this change cannot be described simply as the change from one *theory* to another, although we shall first introduce T' as a new theory of meaning.

†Before doing so we have to present Wittgenstein's criticism of T. This criticism is spread throughout the book. It consists of careful analyses of many special cases, the connection between which is not easily apprehended. I have tried to use *one* example instead of many and to present as many arguments as possible by looking at this example from as many sides as possible. All the arguments are Wittgenstein's; some of the applications to the example in question are mine.

IV

†The philosopher is a man who wants to discover the meanings of the expressions of a language or the essences of the things designated by those expressions. Let us see how he proceeds. Let us take, e.g., the word 'reading.' "Reading is here the activity of rendering out loud what is written or printed; and also of writing from dictation, writing out something printed, playing from a score and so on" [§156].

(A) †According to $T1$ we have to assume that the word 'reading' stands for a single object. Now, there is a variety of manifestations of reading: reading the morning paper; reading in order to discover misprints (here one reads slowly, as a beginner would read); reading a paper written in a foreign language that one cannot understand but has learned to pronounce; reading a paper in order to judge the style of the author; reading shorthand, reading *Principia Mathematica,* reading Hebrew sentences (from right to left); reading a score in order to study a part one has to sing; reading a

score in order to find out something about the inventiveness of the
composer, or to find out how far the composer may have been
influenced by other contemporary musicians; reading a score in
order to find out whether the understandings of the score is connected with acoustic images or with optical images (which might
be a very interesting psychological problem). But this variety,
without "any one feature that occurs in all cases of reading" [§168],
is only a superficial aspect. All these manifestations have something *in common* and it is this common property which makes them
manifestations of *reading*. It is also this property that is the essence
of reading. The other properties, varying from one manifestation
to the other, are accidental. In order to discover the essence we
have to strip off the particular coverings which make the various
manifestations *different* cases of reading. But in doing so (the
reader ought to try for himself!) we find, not that what is essential
to reading is hidden beneath the surface of the single case, but that
this alleged surface is one case out of a family of cases of reading
[§164].†

> Consider for example the proceedings which we call "games." I
> mean boardgames, card games, ball games, Olympic games and
> so on. What is common to them all?—Don't say: "There *must* be
> something common or they would not be called 'games' "; but *look
> and see* whether there is anything common to *all*—for if you look
> at them you will not see something that is in common to all, but
> similarities, relationships and a whole series of them at that. . . .
> And the result of this examination is: we see a complicated net-
> work of similarities overlapping and criss-crossing. . . . I can think
> of no better expression to characterize these similarities than
> "family-resemblances"; for the various resemblances between
> members of a family: build, features, colors of eyes, gait, tem-
> perament, etc., etc., overlap and criss-cross in the same way.—
> And I shall say: "games" form a family [§66 f.].

> And in the same way we also use the word 'reading' for a family
> of cases. And in different circumstances we apply different criteria
> for a person's reading [§164].

†(B) Looking at the outer manifestations of reading we could
not discover the structure suggested by *T*1. Instead of an accidental
variety centering in a well-defined core we found "a complicated
network of similarities" [§66]. Does that fact refute *T*1? Surely
not; for a philosopher who wants to defend *T*1, there are many

possible ways of doing so. He may admit that the *overt behavior* of the person reading does not disclose any well-defined center, but he may add that reading is a *physiological process* of a certain kind. Let us call this process the reading process (RP). Person P is reading if and only if the RP is going on within (the brain or the nervous system of) P. [Cf. §158]. But the difficulties of this assumption are clear. Consider the case of a person who does not look at any printed paper, who is walking up and down, looking out of the window and behaving as if he were expecting somebody to come; but the RP is going on within his brain. Should we take the presence of the reading process as a sufficient criterion for the person's reading, adding perhaps that we had discovered a hitherto unknown case of reading? [Cf. §160.] It is clear that in a case like that we should, rather, alter some physiological hypotheses. If, again, reading is a physiological process, then it certainly makes sense to say that P read 'ali' within 'totalitarianism,' but did not read before he uttered those sounds and did not read afterward either, although anybody who observed the outer behavior of P would be inclined to say that P had been reading the whole time. For it is quite possible that the RP should be present only when P is uttering 'ali' [cf. §157]. It seems, however, that it is quite meaningless to hypothesize that in the circumstances described a person was reading only for one second or two, so that his uttering of sounds in the presence of printed paper before or after that period must not be called 'reading.'

†(C) To the failure of attempts (A) and (B) to discover the essence of reading certain philosophers will answer in the folowing way: Certainly—that was to be expected.† For reading is a *mental process,* and "the one real criterion for anybody's *reading* is the conscious act of reading, the act of reading the sounds off from the letters. 'A man surely knows whether he is reading or only pretending to read' " [§159]. †The idea to which they are alluding is this: Just as the sensation *red* is present when we are looking at a red object, so a specific mental process, the reading process (MRP), is present in the mind when we are reading. The MRP is the object of our analysis of reading, its presence makes our overt behavior a manifestation of reading (etc., as already indicated in *T*4). In short, it is thought that this mental process will enable us to solve problems which we could not solve when considering material processes only: "When our language suggests a body and

there is none; there, we should like to say, is a *spirit"* [§36]. But it will turn out that mental processes are subject to the same kind of criticism as material processes that neither a material nor a spiritual mechanism enables us to explain how it is that words are meaningful and that their meanings can be known; that in pointing to mental processes we cling to the same scheme of explanation as in the physiological or the behavioristic theory of meaning (considered in the two last sections) without realizing that we are doing so.[4] That can be shown by very simple means: Consider the case of a person who does not look at any printed paper, who is walking up and down, looking out of the window, and behaving as if he were expecting somebody to come; but the MRP is going on in his mind (in his consciousness). Should we take the presence of this mental process as a sufficient criterion for the person's reading, adding, perhaps, that we had discovered a hitherto unknown case of reading? It is clear that we should alter, rather, some psychological hypotheses (the hypothesis that reading is always correlated with the MRP). But the last argument is a simple transformation of the first argument of section (B) with 'MRP' (the mental process which is supposed to be the essence of reading) substituted for 'RP' (the physiological process, which was supposed to be the essence of reading in section B). By this substitution the second argument can be used for the present purpose as well.

†(*a*) Let us now turn to a more detailed investigation of the matter. Let us first ask whether really *every act of reading is accompanied by the MRP*. A few minutes ago I was reading the newspaper. Do I remember any particular mental process which was present all the time I was reading? I remember that I was expecting a friend (actually I looked at my watch several times) and that I was angry because he did not come, although he had promised to do so. I also remember having thought of an excellent performance of *Don Giovanni* which I had seen a few days ago and which had impressed me very much. Then I found a funny misprint and was amused. I also considered whether the milk which I had put on the fire was already boiling, etc. Nevertheless, I was *reading* all the time, and it is quite certain that I was [cf. §171].† "But now notice this: While I am [reading] everything is quite simple. I notice nothing *special;* but afterward, when I ask myself what it was

---

[4] This point is elaborated in some detail in G. Ryle's *Concept of Mind* (London, 1949), which should not, however, be taken to agree completely with Wittgenstein's ideas.

that happened, it seems to have been something indescribable. *Afterward* no description satisfies me. It is as if I couldn't believe that I merely looked, made such and such a face and uttered words. But don't I *remember* anything else? No" [cf. §175; "being guided" instead of 'reading']. †The same applies to activities such as calculating, drawing a picture, copying a blueprint, etc. I *know* of course that I was reading, but that shows only that my knowledge is not based on the memory of a certain sensation, impression, or the like—because there was no such impression.† Compare now another example: Look at the mark ∾ and let a sound occur to you as you do so; utter it—let us assume it is the sound 'u.' †Now read the sentence 'Diana is a beautiful girl.' Was it in a different way that the perception of the 'eau' (in 'beautiful') led to the utterance of the sound 'u' in the second case? Of course there was a difference! For I *read* the second sentence whereas I did not read when I uttered the 'u' in the presence of the ∾. But is this difference a difference of mental content, i.e., am I able to discover a specific sensation, impression, or the like which was present in the second case, and missing in the first case, whose presence made the second case a case of *reading*?† Of course, there were many differences: In the first case "I had told myself beforehand that I was to let a sound occur to me; there was a certain tension present before the sound came. And I did not say 'u' automatically as I do when I look at the letter U. Further that mark [the ∾] was not *familiar* to me in the way the letters of the alphabet are. I looked at it rather intently and with a certain interest in its shape [§166]. But imagine now a person who has the feeling described above in the presence of a normal English text, composed of ordinary letters. Being invited to read, he thinks that he is supposed to utter sounds just as they occur to him—one sound for each letter—and he nevertheless utters all the sounds a normal person would utter when reading the text. "Should we say in such a case that he was not really reading the passage? Should we here allow his sensations to count as the criterion for his reading or not reading?" [§160]. From the negative answer to this question we have to conclude that, even if we were able to discover a difference between the way in which the perception of the ∾ leads to the utterance of the sound 'u' and the way in which, e.g., the perception of the 'eau' within 'beautiful' leads to the utterance of the 'u,' this difference—if it is a difference of mental content, of behavior, etc.—cannot be interpreted as justifying the assumption of an essential difference between cases of reading and not reading.[5]

(*b*) It may be objected to this analysis that the MRP is some-times present quite distinctly. "Read a page of print and you can see that something special is going on, something highly character-istic" [§165]. This is true especially where "we make a point of reading slowly—perhaps in order to see what does happen if we read" [§170]. Thus one could be inclined to say that the MRP is a subconscious process which accompanies *every* case of reading but which can be brought to light only by a special effort.[6]

Answer: (1) Reading with the intention of finding out what hap-pens when we are reading is a special case of reading and as such different from ordinary reading [cf. §170]. Nevertheless reading without this intention is also a case of reading, which shows that the reason for calling it a case of *reading* cannot be the presence of a sensation which—admittedly—is present only in special cases and not in the case discussed. Finally, the description of the MRP can-not be a description of reading in general, for the ordinary case is omitted. We should not be misled by the picture which suggests "that this phenomenon comes in sight 'on close inspection.' If I am supposed to describe how an object looks from far off, I don't make the description more accurate by saying what can be noticed about the object on closer inspection" [§171].

†(2) Not every kind of introspection is judged in the same way. It is possible that a person who is supposed to find the MRP by introspection, being tired, should experience and describe quite un-

[5] There are cases of mental disease where the patient talks correctly although with the feeling that somebody is making up the words for him. This is rightly regarded as a case of mental disease and not, as the adherents of the mental-picture theory of meaning would be inclined to say, as a case of inspiration: For one judges from the fact that the person in question *talks correctly*, although with queer sensations. Following Locke, a distinction is usually made between impressions of sensation and impressions of reflec-tion. When Wittgenstein talks of sensations, of feelings, of a "picture in the mind," he seems to mean both. So his investigations are directed against a primitive psychologism (concepts are combinations of impressions of sensation) as well as against a more ad-vanced psychologism (concepts are combinations of impressions of reflection). They are also directed against a presentational realism (concepts are objects of a certain kind, but *having* a concept, or *using* a concept is the same as having an idea in one's mind—i.e., although concepts are not psychological events, their representations in people are), against a theory which Wittgenstein elsewhere described as implying that "logic is the physics of the intellectual realm."

[6] A psychologist or an adherent of the phenomenological method in psychology would be inclined to judge the situation in this way. His intention would be to create a kind of "pure situation" in which a special process comes out quite distinctly. It is then sup-posed that this process is hidden in every ordinary situation (which is not pure, but) which resembles the pure situation to a certain extent. In the case of reading the pure situation would be: reading plus introspecting in order to find out what is going on. The ordinary situation is: simply reading.

usual things while thinking all the time that the task which was set him by the psychologist is being performed by giving these descriptions.[7] No psychologist will welcome such a result. Instead of thinking that new and illuminating facts about reading have been discovered, he will doubt the reliability of the guinea pig. From this we have to conclude once more that the sensations experienced in connection with reading, and even those experienced as the essence of reading by the readers themselves, have nothing whatever to do with the question what reading really is.

†(3) Let us now assume that a reliable observer whom we ask to read attentively and to tell us what happens while he is reading provides us with the following report: 'The utterance is *connected* with seeing the signs, it is as if I were *guided* by the perception of the letters, etc.' [cf. §§169, 170, 171]. Does he, when answering our question in this way, describe a mental content, as a person who is seeing red and who tells us that he is seeing red describes a mental content? Does he say, 'I am being guided by the letters' because the mental content *being guided* is present? Then one would have to conclude that every case of being guided is accompanied by *being guided,* as we assumed at the beginning of section (C) that every case of reading is accompanied by the MRP. But this last assumption has already been refuted, and the other, being completely analogous to it, can be refuted by the same arguments. We have to conclude, therefore, that the possibility of describing the process of reading as a case of being guided does not imply that reading is a mental process, because being guided is not one [cf. §172].[8]

†(c) As already indicated, people usually try to escape from argument (Ca) by assuming that the MRP is a subconscious sensation which has to be brought to light by introspection. A different

[7] An illustrative example for experiences of this kind may be found in B. Russell, *History of Western Philosophy* (New York, 1945), p. 145.

[8] The idea that reading is a single object (in spite of the variety of manifestations demonstrated in Sec. A) is apparently supported by the fact that one can give a definition like the one we gave at the beginning of Sec. IV, or that one can say that reading is a form of being guided. But let us not be misled by words. For the definition of reading in terms of being guided or the like supports the idea that reading is a single object only if being guided can itself be shown to be a single object. But an analysis similar to the one sketched in Sec. A will show that this is not the case.

One of the main reasons for the wide acceptance of the assumption that it is possible to discover the essence of reading by introspection is the fact that the great number of manifestations of reading is usually not taken into account. Beset by theory T we *think* [§§173, 66] that acute observation must disclose the essence and that what we find in acute observation is hidden in the ordinary case of reading (T4). But our knowledge of the ordinary is much too sketchy to justify that assumption "A main cause of philosophical disease—a one-sided diet: one nourishes one's thinking with only one kind of example" [§593].

form of the same escape is the following one: The arguments that have been brought forward so far assume that reading and the MRP can be separated from one another. This, however, is not the case: Reading is inseparably connected with the MRP. What occurs separably from reading is not the MRP, but only an erroneous interpretation of something as reading. But how are we to decide whether the MRP itself is present or only something else erroneously interpreted as reading; or, what comes to the same thing, how are we to decide whether we are reading or only believing that we are reading? The given content of consciousness cannot be used for deciding that question, for it is *its* reliability which is to be ascertained. The only possible alternative is to call a sensation a case of the MRP if and only if it is accompanied by reading. But now we assume, contrary to our previous assumption, that we do possess a criterion for reading other than a sensation.

† Another argument against the assumption of a hidden mental content, which may be brought to daylight by introspection or some other mental act, consists in developing the paradoxical consequences of such a view: "How can the process of [reading] have been hidden when I said 'now I am [reading]' *because* I was [reading]? ! And if I say it is hidden—then how do I know what I have to look for?" [§153; "understanding" replaced by "reading."] [9]

†(d) So far we have shown (by a kind of empirical investigation into the use of the word "reading") that there is not a mental content which is *always* present when a person is reading, and that therefore giving the criterion for a person's reading cannot consist in pointing out a particular mental content. Now we shall show that even if there were a mental content which is present if and only if a person is reading, we could not take this content to be the essence of reading. Let us assume that a mental content is the essence of reading and that a person is reading if and only if this content, namely the MRP, is present. We shall now show that the process characterized by the presence of the MRP cannot be reading.† First of all: If reading is a particular experience, "then it becomes quite unimportant whether or not you read according to some generally

---

[9] The same criticism applies to the method of the phenomenologists. How do they know which phenomenon is the 'right' one? They proceed from the assumption that the essence is not open to general inspection but must be discovered by some kind of analysis which proceeds from an everyday appearance. In the course of this analysis several phenomena appear. How are we to know which one of them is the phenomenon that we are looking for? And if we know the answer to this question, why then is it necessary to analyze at all?

recognized alphabetical rule" [§165]. One is reading if and only if he is experiencing the MRP; nothing else is of any importance. That implies, however, that no distinction can be drawn between reading and believing that one is reading [cf. §202], or, to put it in another way, that anybody who believes that he is reading is entitled to infer that he *is* reading. The important task of a teacher would, therefore, consist in schooling the receptivity of his pupils [§232], reading would be something like listening to inner voices in the presence of printed paper and acting in accordance with their advice [§233]. That different people who are reading the same text agree in the sounds they utter would be miraculous [§233]. † Our assumption that reading is a mental act leads, therefore, to the substitution of miracles for an everyday affair. It leads to a substitution for a simple process (uttering sounds in the presence of printed paper) of a more complicated one (listening to inner voices in the presence of printed paper) i.e., it misses the aim of explaining the process of *reading*.†10

(*e*) But does introducing inner voices really solve our problem—namely, to explain why people read correctly and justify our own reading of a text in a certain way? Usually we simply read off the sound from the letters. Now we want to be justified, and we think that a mental content might justify our procedure. But if we do not trust the signs on the paper—then why should we trust the more ethereal advice of the intuition, or of the mental content which is supposed to be the essence of reading? [§§232,233.]

V

† What conclusions are to be drawn from this analysis? First of all: It appears impossible to discover the essence of a thing in the way that is usually supposed, i.e., *T*4 seems to be inapplicable. But if that is the case, the correctness of the analysis can no longer be checked in the usual way. There is no criterion for deciding whether a statement like ' "*A*" stands for *a*' or 'the sentence "*p*" designates

10 In presenting the idea to be criticized we assumed, as in T_4, that the *MRP* is also the reason for our uttering the sounds we utter. The criticism developed in the text applies also to the idea that in calculating we are guided by intuitions (Descartes' theory): It is said that the perception of '2 + 2' is followed by a nonperceptual mental event which advises us how to behave in the sequel; it whispers, as it were, into our mind's ear, 'Say 4!' But the idea cannot explain why we calculate as we do. For instead of explaining the process of obeying a rule (the rule of the multiplication table) it describes the process of obeying a kind of inspiration. In the case of an inspiration I *await* direction. But I do not await inspiration when saying that 2 + 2 are four [§232].

the proposition that *p'* is true or not; and there is no way to decide whether a certain sign is meaningful, either. But usually we are not all troubled by such questions. We talk and solve (mathematical, physical, economic) problems without being troubled by the fact that there is apparently no possibility of deciding whether or not we are acting reasonably, whether or not we are talking sense. But isn't that rather paradoxical? Isn't it rather paradoxical to assume that a sign which we constantly use to convey, as we think, important information is really without meaning, and that we have no possibility of discovering that fact? And since its being meaningless apparently does not at all affect its usefulness in discourse (e.g., for conveying information), doesn't that show that the presuppositions of the paradox, in particular *T*1, 2, need reconsideration? [11]

VI

† A great deal of the *Philosophical Investigations* is devoted to this task. † The phenomena of language are first studied in primitive kinds of application "in which one can command a clear view of the aim and functioning of words" [§5; §130]. The primitive, rudimentary languages which are investigated in the course of these studies are called *"language games."* Let us consider one such language game: It is meant

> to serve for communication between a builder A and an assistant B. A is building with building stones: there are blocks, pillars, slabs and beams. B has to pass the stones, and that in the order which A needs them. For this purpose they use a language consisting of the words "block," "pillar," "slab," "beam," A calls them out;— B brings the stone which he has learned to bring at such and such a call.—Conceive this as a complete primitive language [§2].

Consider first of all how A prepares B for the purpose he is supposed to fulfill. "An important part of the training will consist in the teacher's pointing to the objects, directing the [assistant's] attention to them and at the same time uttering a word, for instance the word 'slab' as he points to that shape" [§6; "child" replaced by 'assistant']. This procedure cannot be called an ostensive definition,

---

[11] There is another presupposition as well, amely that in Sec. IV *all* possibilities of experiencing the essence have been considered. Clearly, this assumption cannot be proved. But one thing is certain: We considered all possibilities of experiencing the essence which have so far been treated by philosophers who follow theory *T*. Cf. H. Gomperz, *Weltanschauungslehre*, Vol. II, p. 140 ff., where medieval realism about concepts is criticized by arguments like Wittgenstein's. Cf. also n. 23 below.

because the assistant who at the beginning is supposed to be without any knowledge of any language cannot as yet *ask* what the name is [§6]; which shows that teaching a language can be looked at as "adjusting a mechanism to respond to a certain kind of influence" [§497; cf. §5]. Finally the assistant is able to play the game, he is able to carry out the orders given to him by the builder A. Let us now imagine that A teaches B more complicated orders—orders which contain color-names, number-words ('4 red slabs!') and even orders which contain what one would be inclined to call descriptions ('Give me the slab lying just in front of you!'), etc.

> Now, what do the words of this language *signify?*—What is supposed to show what they signify, if not the kind of use they have? And we have already described that. So we are asking for the expression "This word signifies *this*" to be made a part of the description. In other words the description ought to take the form "the word . . . signifies. . . ." . . . But assimilating the descriptions of the uses of words in this way cannot make the uses themselves any more like one another. For, as we see, they are absolutely unlike [§10].

† Compare, e.g., the way in which the word "four" is used with the way in which the word "slab" is used within the language game in question. The difference in the uses of the two words comes out most clearly when we compare the procedures by means of which their respective uses are taught. A child who is to count correctly has first to learn the series of numerals by heart; he has then to learn how to apply this knowledge to the case of counting, e.g., the number of apples in a basket. In doing so, he has to say the series of cardinal numbers, and for each number he has to take one apple out of the basket [cf. §1]. He has to be careful not to count one apple twice or to miss an apple. The numeral which according to this procedure is coordinated with the last apple is called 'the number of apples in the basket.' This is how the use of numerals is taught and how numerals are used in counting. Compare with this the use of a word like 'slab.' It is taught by simple ostension: The word 'slab' is repeatedly uttered in the presence of a slab. Finally the child is able to identify slabs correctly within the language game it has been taught. Nothing is involved which has any similarity to the counting procedure which was described above. The application of the word itself to a concrete object is much simpler than the application of a number-word to a collection whose cardinal number cannot be seen

at a glance. This application does not involve any complicated technique; a person who understands the meaning of 'slab' is able to apply this word quite immediately. †

Let us now imagine that somebody, following $T1$, should argue in this way: It is quite clear: 'slab' signifies slabs and '3' signifies 3 . . . every word in a language signifies something [cf. §3]. According to Wittgenstein, he has

> so far said *nothing whatever;* unless [he has] explained exactly *what* distinction [he] wish[es] to make. (It might be of course that [he] wanted to distinguish the words of [our] language [game] from words "without meaning" [§13].

> Imagine someone's saying: "*All* tools serve to modify something. Thus the hammer modifies the position of the nail, the saw the shape of the board and so on."—And what is modified by the rule, the glue-pot, the nails?—"Our knowledge of the thing's length, the temperature of the glue and the solidity of the board."— Would anything be gained by this assimilation of expressions? [§14].

VII

† Our example and its interpretation suggests an instrumentalist theory of language.[12] The orders which A gives to B are instruments in getting B to act in a certain way. Their meaning depends on how B is supposed to act in the situations in which they are uttered. It seems reasonable to extend this theory—which is a corollary to T' soon to be described—to language games which contain descriptive sentences as well. The meaning of a descriptive sentence would then consist in its role in certain situations; more generally, within a certain culture [cf. §§199, 206, 241, 325, p. 226]. Wittgenstein has drawn this consequence—which is another corollary of T':

> What we call "*descriptions*" are instruments for particular uses. Think of a machine-drawing [which directs the production of the machine drawn in a certain way], a cross section, an elevation with measurements, which an engineer has before him. Thinking

---

[12] Or an intuitionist (pragmatist, constructivist) theory of language—the expressions "intuitionist" or "pragmatist" being used in the way in which they serve to describe one of the present tendencies as regards foundations of mathematics. I am inclined to say—and there is strong evidence in favor of this view—that Wittgenstein's theory of language can be understood as a constructivist theory of meaning, i.e., as constructivism applied not only to the meanings of mathematical expressions but to meanings in general. Cf. Poincaré, *Derniers pensées* (German edition), pp. 143 ff., and especially Paul Lorenzen, "Konstruktive Begründung der Mathematik," *Math. Zs.,* Bd. LIII (1950), pp. 162 ff. Cf. also *Philosophical Investigations,* p. 220: "Let the *proof* teach you *what* was being proved."

of a description as a word picture of facts has something misleading about it: one tends to think only of such pictures as hang
on the walls: which seem simply to portray how a thing looks,
what it is like. (These pictures are as it were idle.) [§291]

And quite generally: "Language is an instrument. Its concepts are
instruments" [§569]. This idea has an important consequence. Instruments are described by referring to how they work. There are
different kinds of instruments for different purposes. And there is
nothing corresponding to the ethereal meanings which, according to
$T1$, are supposed to make meaningful the use of *all* instruments
alike. "Let the use of words teach you their meaning" [p. 220] is to
be substituted for $T4$—and this now seems to be the new theory, T'.
But in order to appreciate the importance of T' we have first of all
to consider the following objections, which seem to be inevitable.
In talking, ordering, describing, we certainly use words and get other
people to act in a certain way (to revise their plans which we show
to be unreasonable, to obey our wishes, to follow a certain route
which we point out to them on a map). But the description of the
meanings of the elements of a language game is not exhausted by
pointing to the way in which we use those elements and the connection of this use with our actions and other people's. For in uttering
the words and the sentences we *mean* something by them, we want
to express our thoughts, our wishes, etc. [cf. §501]. It is "our
meaning it that gives sense to the sentence. . . . And 'meaning it' is
something in the sphere of the mind" [§358; cf. $T4$]. What we mean
seems to be independent of the way we use our words and the way
other people react to our utterances [cf. §205, and again $T4$]. Moreover, the meanings of our utterances, being hidden beneath the
surface of the various ways in which we use their elements, can
only be discovered by looking at the mental pictures, the presence
of which indicates what we mean by them. A person who wants to
understand, has, therefore, to grasp this mental picture. "One would
like to say: 'Telling brings it about that [somebody else] *knows* that
I am in pain [for example]; it produces this mental phenomenon:
everything else [in particular whether "he does something further
with it as well"—e.g., looks for a physician in order to help me] is
inessential to the telling' " [§363]. "Only in the act of understanding
is it meant that we are to do *this*. The *order*—why, that is nothing
but sounds, ink marks" [§431]. Meaning and understanding are,
therefore, mental processes.

† Apparently this idea makes it necessary to give an account of meaning which is independent of the description of the way in which signs are used within a certain language game. Another great part of the *Philosophical Investigations* is devoted to showing that this is not the case. A careful analysis of the way we use phrases such as 'A intends to . . . ,' 'A means that . . . ,' 'A suddenly understands that . . . ,' shows that in trying to account for this use we are again thrown back on a description of the way we use certain elements of the language game in which those expressions occur and the connection of this use with our actions and other people's.

VIII

†(A) The meaning we connect with a certain sign is a mental picture. We do not look into the mind of a person in order to find out what he is really saying. We take his utterances *at their face value,* e.g., we assume that, when saying 'I hate you' he is in a state of hating. "If I give anyone an order I feel it to be *quite enough* to give him signs. And I should never say: This is only words. Equally, when I have asked someone something and he gives me an answer (i.e., a sign) I am content—that was what I expected—and I don't raise the objection: "But that's a mere answer" [§503]. On our present view, this attitude is easily shown to be superficial. For it might be that on looking into the speaker's soul (or mind) we discover something quite different, e.g., love in the person who said 'I hate you.'

† Now two questions arise about this procedure. First: Why trust the language of the mind (one wonders what kind of language this may be) when we do not trust the overt language, i.e., the sentence 'I hate you'? [cf., e.g., §74 and all the passages on the interpretation of rules: §§197 ff.]. For whatever appears to be found in the mind can be interpreted in various ways, once we have decided *not* to proceed as we usually do, i.e., not to take parts of a certain language game which we are playing at their face value. Secondly: Let us assume that somebody who really loves a certain person tells her that he hates her.[13] Does this fact make 'I hate you' mean the same as 'I love you'? Or imagine a person, who abounds in slips of the tongue (or is at the moment rather occupied with a difficult problem

---

[13] Psychoanalysis has made rather a misleading use of such cases. It has introduced a picture language (so-called symbols) and interpreted it in such a way that it is not conceivable how the theory could possibly be refuted.

and so not listening attentively), giving what we consider to be a wrong or an irrelevant answer. Doesn't that reaction of considering his answer as irrelevant show that what he says is thought to be meaningful independently of what he is thinking? For we don't say: 'He certainly gave the right answer; what he said was accompanied by the right thought processes,' but rather 'He gave a quite irrelevant answer; maybe he didn't understand our question or expressed himself wrongly.' Or "suppose I said 'abcd' and meant 'The weather is fine.' For as I uttered the signs I had the experience normally had only by someone who had year-in year-out used 'a' in the sense of 'the,' 'b' in the sense of 'weather' and so on. Does 'abcd' now mean 'The weather is fine' ?" [§509; cf. §665]. How does somebody else find out what I meant by 'abcd'? Of course I can explain to him that 'abcd' means 'The weather is fine'; and I can also indicate how the parts of the first string of signs are related to the parts (the words) of the second string. But it would be a mistake to assume that such an explanation reveals what 'abcd' really means. For from the few words which I intend to be an explanation one cannot yet judge whether an *explanation* has been given or not.

† Of course I *say* ' "abcd" means "The weather is fine" ' or 'By "abcd" I mean "The weather is fine," ' and I have the intention of giving an explanation. But now imagine someone's saying 'Mr. A and Mrs. B loved—I mean lived—together for a long time.' [14] In this case he does not want to give a definition or an explanation according to which 'love' is supposed to mean the same as 'live'; rather, he committed a slip of the tongue and wanted to correct himself. In certain cases this is clear enough. In other cases it follows, e.g., from the fact that 'love' is never again mentioned in connection with Mr. A and Mrs. B, etc. When, therefore, I say, 'By "abcd" I mean "The weather is fine," ' it is not yet certain what the case is, whether I intended to give an explanation, or was just awaking from a kind of trance, or whatever else might be the case. The way 'I mean' is to be interpreted follows from the context in which the whole sentence is uttered and from what we find out about the further use of the sign 'abcd' [cf. §686]. In order to find out whether 'abcd' really means 'The weather is fine' we have, therefore, to find out how 'abcd' is being used quite independently of any feelings on the part of the person who said 'abcd' and of any explanation given

---

[14] In Freud's *Vorlesungen über Psychoanalyse* one will find plenty of examples of this kind.

by him. Of course his explanation may be the starting point of a training in the use of a new language in which 'a,' 'b,' 'c,' 'd' really have the meanings indicated. But note now that "abcd" makes sense only within this language game. I cannot mean 'The weather is fine' by 'abcd' before this language game has been established. I myself could not possibly connect any sense with 'abcd' before the elements of this sign have become meaningful by being made elements of a certain language game. And even the fact "that I had the experience normally had only by someone who had year-out year-in used 'a' in the sense of 'the,' 'b' in the sense of 'weather' and so on" [§509] could not make them meaningful; I could not even *describe* this experience as I did just now, because such a description does not yet exist.

† We have to conclude that no mere mental effort of a person A can either make a string of signs mean something different from the meaning it has within a certain language game of which it is part, played by the people who come into contact with A, or justify its being said that *he* means (intends) something different from everybody else who uses it. This seems rather paradoxical. But let us assume for a moment that two people

> belonging to a tribe unacquainted with games should sit at a chess board and go through the moves of a game of chess; and with the appropriate mental accompaniments. And if *we* were to see it we should say they were playing chess. But now imagine a game of chess translated according to certain rules into a series of actions which we do not ordinarily associate with a *game*—say into yells and stamping of feet. And now suppose those two people to yell and stamp instead of playing the form of chess that we are used to; and this in such a way that their procedure is translatable by suitable rules into a game of chess. Should we still be inclined to say they were playing a game? [§200].

The decision of this question again depends on the situation. Imagine, e.g., that their yelling and stamping has an important role within a religious ceremony of the tribe. That any change of procedure is said to offend the gods and is treated accordingly (the offenders are killed). In this case neither the possibility of the translation nor the presence of the chess-feelings in the minds of the participants would turn this procedure into a game of chess (although it is also quite possible to imagine a tribe where people who lose games of chess are thought to be hated by the gods and are killed. But in this case a difference will be made between games and religious procedures by the fact, e.g., that only priests are admitted to the latter, or that different expressions are used for describing them, which is missing in our case). On the contrary, the strange mental state of those who are troubled by chess-feelings would be an indication either of insanity (cf. n. 5 above) or of lack of religious feeling.

† Now we can turn round our whole argument and look at the people who are sitting at a chess board and moving the pieces. Are they really playing chess? We see now that the inspection of their minds does not help us: they might be queer people, thinking of chess when they are performing a religious ceremony. Their assertion that they are playing chess, even, is not necessarily helpful, for it might be that they heard the words from somebody else and misinterpreted them to mean sitting in front of the board and making arbitrary moves with the pawns. The fact that they are using a chess board does not help us either, for the board is not essential to the game. What, then, is essential? The fact that they are playing according to certain *rules,* that they follow the rules of the chess game. Applying this result to the meaning of sentences in general we arrive at the idea that "if anyone utters a sentence and *means* or *understands* it he is operating a calculus according to definite rules" [§81]. Thus in analyzing the concepts of meaning, understanding, thinking, etc., we finally arrived at the concept of *following a rule.* But before turning to that concept we have to get more insight into the concepts just mentioned, and especially into the concept of *intention.* †

(B) It is the "queer thing about *intention,* about the mental process, that the existence of a custom, of a technique, is not necessary to it. That, for example, it is imaginable that two people should play chess in a world in which otherwise no games existed; and even that they should begin a game of chess—and then be interrupted" [§205]. The underlying idea is the same, as in the case of meaning: just as we can attach meaning to a sign by just connecting its use with a certain image which we voluntarily produce, we can also intend to do something by producing a certain mental picture. But how, we have to ask, is it possible to find out whether or not A, who just announced his intention of playing chess, was really intending to do so? Surely chess is defined by its rules [cf. §205]. Should we therefore conclude that the rules of chess were present in the mind of A when he uttered his intention? [§205].

† Investigation similar to that of IV C*a* above will show that not every act of intending to play chess is accompanied by a special mental picture which is characteristic of the intention of playing chess. Of course, the intention to play chess is sometimes present quite distinctly (I have not played chess for a long time, I am a keen chess player, and *now* I want to play chess and won't stop looking until I have found a chess board and a suitable partner). But this is only a *special kind* of intending to play chess (cf. IV C*b* above); therefore its characteristics cannot be the reason for calling other cases cases of intending to play chess—cases, e.g., in which these characteristics are completely absent. But if we assume, on the other hand, that A has a perfect copy of the rules of chess before his inner eye—must he necessarily follow the features of this copy in such a way that the result will be a game of chess? Is it not possible that he either interprets them in an unusual way, that in going over from the reading of his mental picture to the outer world (the chess board, his actions in front of the chess board), he automatically makes a kind of translation, so that finally he is not doing what one would be inclined to call 'playing chess' [ct. §§73, 74, 86, 139, 237]? And should we still say that he is intending to play chess just because, somewhere in the chain of events which in the end lead to his actions, a copy of the rules of chess enters in? Of course, we could *interpret* this copy as we are used to do. But is *he* interpreting it in the same way? And even if he could tell us how he is interpreting it do we know how to take his explanations? We see that "interpretations *by themselves* do not determine meaning" [§198]. We have simply to wait. And if he really acts in such a way that he regards playing chess—as we understand it—as a fulfillment of his intention, then we may say that he intended to play chess. But if it turned out that he did not know how to play chess or that, apparently intending to play chess, he sat down at the chess board and made irregular moves, we should under certain circumstances conclude that he had wrong ideas as to his intentions. Of course the phrase 'under certain circumstances' has to be inserted. For it is perfectly possible that A, intending to play chess, was introduced to a person he did not like and, with the intention of avoiding playing chess with him, acted as if he did not know the rules of chess or as if he had never intended to play chess. But what has to be criticized is the idea that such a difference might be found out by inspecting his mind (or soul) and by reading off his intention from

his mental processes. It is his further actions (talking included), as well as his personal history, which teach us how we are to take his first utterance—that he intended to play chess. But as it now turns out that our criteria for deciding whether a person, A, intends to play chess or not are "extended in time" [cf. §138], we have to conclude that intending to play chess cannot be a mental event which occurs at a certain time. *Intending is not an experience* [cf. p. 217]: it has "no experience-content. For the content (images for instance) which accompany and illustrate [it] are not the . . . intending" [p. 217].

†(C) The same applies to understanding. † Let us examine the following kind of language game [§§143 ff.]: When A gives an order, B has to write down series of signs according to a certain formation-rule. The orders are of the kind "1, 2, 3, . . . !" or "2, 4, 6, 8, . . . !" or "2, 4, 9, 16, . . . !" or "2, 6, 12, 20, 30, 42, . . . !" etc. B is supposed to continue the series in a certain way, i.e., he is supposed to write down the series of numerals in the first case, the series of the even numerals in the second case, etc. First of all, A will teach B the rules of the language game. He will then give orders to B, in order to check B's abilities. He will finally state that B has mastered the system, that he understands it. It should be clear that, when used in this way, 'understanding' cannot signify a mental phenomenon. For we also say that B understands (is master of) the language game just explained when lying on his bed and sleeping [cf. §148]. But the mental-act philosopher is ready with a new expression—he speaks of a *subconscious* mental phenomenon, i.e., he says that B, although dreaming perhaps of beautiful women, is nevertheless subconsciously thinking of the new language game and its rules.

The objections to this idea are obvious. Whether subconscious or not, the alleged thinking process may or may not determine the actual behavior of B (cf. VIII B, above); i.e., B may not be able to carry out the orders of A although a clever psychologist has found out that the thinking process which is supposed to accompany his ability to obey the orders is present. We shall not say in this case that B has mastered the game, that we have discovered a special case of mastering the game (cf. IV Cb2, above); we shall simply say that he had not mastered it although he or the psychologist thought he had. This objection being accepted, it might be said that

knowing the game is a state of the mind (perhaps of the brain) by means of which we explain the *manifestations* of that knowledge. Such a state is called a disposition. But there are objections to speaking of a state of the mind here, inasmuch as there ought to be two different criteria for such a state: a knowledge of the construction of the apparatus quite apart from what it does [§149].

What the apparatus does is in our case the actual behavior of B when he receives certain orders.

But there is a second way in which the word 'understanding' is used. Understanding in this sense is not meant to be understanding of a game as a whole (understanding the rules of chess, i.e., knowing how to play chess) but understanding the meaning of a particular move within the game, e.g., understanding the order "2, 4, 6, . . . ! "Let us imagine the following example: A writes series of numbers down, B watches him and tries to find a law for the sequence of numbers. If he succeeds, he exclaims: 'Now I can go on!' —So this capacity, this understanding is something that makes its appearance in a moment" [§151], and this suggests that 'understanding,' used in this way, might mean a mental event. But wait: *Do* we find any mental event which is common to all cases of understanding? Imagine that A gave the order 1, 5, 11, 19, 29, . . . ! to B and that, upon A's arriving at 19, B said, 'I understand.' What happened to B?

> Various things may have happened; for example, while A was slowly putting one number after the other, B was occupied with trying various algebraic formulae on the numbers which had been written down. After A had written the number 19, B tried the formula $a_n = n^2 + n - 1$; and the next number confirmed his hypothesis. Or again—B does not think of formulae. He watches A writing his numbers down with a certain feeling of tension and all sorts of vague thoughts go through his head. Finally he asks himself: "What is the series of differences?" He finds the series, 4, 6, 8, 10 and says: Now I can go on.—Or he watches and says "Yes, I know *that* series"—and continues it, just as he could have done if A had written down the series 1, 3, 5, 7, 9.—Or he says nothing at all and simply continues the series. Perhaps he had what may be called the feeling "that's easy!" [§151].

> We can also imagine the case where nothing at all occurred in B's mind except that he suddenly said "Now I know how to go on"—perhaps with a feeling of relief [§179].

> But are the processes which I have described here *understanding*? [§152].

Is it not possible that a person who has the feelings just described is not able to write down the series as it was meant by A? Should we not be inclined to say that he did not really understand? "The application is still a criterion of understanding" [§146]. It would, therefore, be quite misleading "to call the words ['Now I can go on'] a 'description of a mental state.'—One might rather call them a 'signal'; and we judge whether it was rightly employed by what he [i.e., B] goes on to do" [§180].

† Now let us use this example to discuss intention and meaning as well. What if B, in carrying out the order 2, 4, 6, 8, . . . ! wrote 1,000, 1,004, 1,008, 1,012, etc. [cf. §185]? Of course A will say: 'Don't you see? You ought to write 2, 4, 6, 8, . . . !' And if that does not lead to a change in the behavior of B, he will tell him: "What I meant was that [you] should write the next but one number after every number [you] wrote; and from this all those propositions follow in turn" [§186]. Now several conclusions may be drawn from this situation.† First of all one may be inclined to say that 2, 4, 6, 8, . . . ! was an incomplete order and that there was clearly a possibility of misunderstanding [cf. a similar argument in §19]. For this order reveals so to speak, only an external character of the series to be written down, namely the character that its first members are '2,' '4,' '6,' etc. And the training of B, too, taught him only an external character of all the series, namely, that they began in a certain way. B has therefore to *guess* how to continue, and of course he may hit upon the wrong guess. But the order "take the next but one!" seems to be of a different character. It contains so to speak the whole of the series in a nutshell. Understanding *this* order implies knowing the law of development for the whole series. But let us now investigate how the understanding of this order may be taught. Of course, A has to write down the series 2, 4, 6, 8, . . . and has to explain to B what 'next but one' means. He does so by comparing this series with 1, 2, 3, 4, . . . and by showing that '4' is the 'next but one to 2,' etc. The explanation will therefore be similar to the explanation of 2, 4, 6, 8, . . . ! Why, then, should teaching the pupil how to take 'the next but one' remove any possibility of error? On the contrary! We could imagine that B has been taught how to use 2, 4, 6, 8, . . . ! but that he does not know, what 'the next but one' means. In this case the teacher would have to explain the 'next but one' by referring to 2, 4, 6, 8, . . . ! and not the other way round. The same applies to algebraic formulae. Consider a 'difficult' series such as 1, 3, 13, 21, 31, 43, . . . It is not easily seen how this series might be continued. If we hear that its algebraic formula is $n^2 - n + 1$ we are able to write down the next members at once.

But that only shows that we already knew how to apply the algebraic expression, but did not know how to apply 1, 3, 13, 21, 31,
43, ... if the continuation of this series is ordered. It does not show
us an essential quality which, so to speak, contains the whole series
in a nutshell. For an onlooker who is unacquainted with the formula
as well as with the series will have to learn how to apply the formula
in developing series. And the methods of teaching this ability will
be similar to the methods of teaching 2, 4, 6, 8, ... ! [cf. §146].

Let us return now to intention. The existence of algebraic formulae for the description of series is misleading in one way: A cannot
write down the whole series in order to make himself understood to
B. But he can use an algebraic formula or a simple expression, such
as 'take the next but one.' He can write down the formula within a
few seconds and one is therefore inclined to assume that meaning
the series 1, 2, 3, 4, ... *ad infinitum* can be a mental act which
occurs within a few seconds.

> Here I should first of all like to say: Your idea was that that act
> of meaning the order had in its own way already traversed all
> those steps; that when you meant it your mind as it were flew
> ahead and completed all the steps before you physically arrived
> at this or that one.—Thus you were inclined to use such expres-
> sions as: The steps are *really* already taken, even before I take
> them in writing or orally or in thought [15] [§188].

They "are determined by the algebraic formula" [§189]. But how?
Surely thinking of the formula cannot help us [cf. §146], for one
and the same formula may be used for different purposes (think of
the different use which is made of the formula $a + b = b + a$ in
different parts of mathematics: in class theory it means the commutativity of class disjunction; in algebra it is used for expressing the
commutativity of algebraic addition; in number theory it is used
for expressing a general property of numbers; in lattice theory it has
still another meaning and likewise in group theory, etc). The imagining of the formula (if it ever does occur) must be connected with
a certain application of the formula in order to provide us with the
knowledge of its meaning and with the knowledge of the speaker's
intention in using it. And as it is always possible to apply a formula
in many different ways we have to observe how it is applied in a
particular case, by a particular mathematician, in order to determine
his way of using the formula and thus *what he means* when he utters

[15] Here is the core of Wittgenstein's criticism of the so-called Cantorian (cf. Poincaré,
loc. cit.) interpretation of mathematics. This criticism (it is developed in detail in his
mathematical writings, which are still unpublished—in the *Philosophical Investigations*
there are only a few passages, cf. §352) is another corollary of *T'*.

the formula. But the use of a formula is "extended in time" [§138]. And therefore, since following up this use is one of the criteria we employ to find out what is meant by A when he writes down a certain formula, we cannot say that meaning something is a mental event. "It may now be said: 'The way the formula is meant determines which steps are to be taken.' What is the criterion for the way the formula is meant? It is, for example, the kind of way we always use it, the way we are taught to use it" [§190].[16]

(D) Another criticism of the idea that meaning is a mental activity derives from the fact that sometimes it is calculation that decides the question whether a sentence is meaningful or not. Consider the sentence " 'I have n friends and $n^2 + 2n + 2 = 0$.' Does this sentence make sense?" [§513]. Assuming that a sentence is made meaningful by connecting its utterance with a certain mental content, we should conclude that there is no difficulty; we have only to look for the mental picture behind it, and that will teach us how to judge. But that is not the case, we are even inclined to say that we do not yet know whether anybody will be able to connect any meaning with the sentence, i.e., according to the theory we are discussing at present, whether anybody is justified in connecting an image with the utterance of this sentence. We have first to find out whether the sentence conforms to certain general rules (the number of friends can neither be negative nor imaginary) and we do so by calculating. We also cannot say at once whether we understand or not; we have first to find out whether there is anything to be understood; i.e., whether we understand or not can again be found out by a process of calculation only. One has, therefore, to realize that "we *calculate,* operate with words and in the course of time turn them sometimes into one picture, sometimes into another" [§449].

(E) Result: Meaning, understanding, intending, thinking (and, as we may add—remembering, loving, hoping[17]) are *not mental activities*. The criteria by which we decide whether or not A is thinking of . . . , intending to do . . . , meaning . . . , etc., do

---

[16] Cf. also §693: " 'When I teach someone the formation of the series . . . I surely mean him to write . . . at the hundredth place.'—Quite right; you mean it. And evidently without necessarily even thinking of it. This shows you how different the grammar of the verb 'to mean' is from that of 'to think.' And nothing is more wrong-headed than calling meaning a mental activity!"

[17] "What is a *deep* feeling? Could someone have the feeling of ardent love or hope for the space of one second—*no matter what* preceded or followed this second? What is happening now has significance—in these surroundings. The surroundings [the history of the event included—cf. the words "what preceded"] give it its importance." [§583; cf. §§572, 584, 591, 614 ff., esp. §638: "If someone says 'For a moment . . .' is he really only describing a momentary process?—But not even the whole story was my evidence for saying 'For a moment. . . .' "].

not relate only to the moment of the intention, the thought, the understanding. We cannot say "A intended . . . because" and point to a process which accompanies his utterances or his (apparently intentional) behavior. "For no *process* could have the consequences of [intending]" [cf. p. 218].

IX

†The last section was devoted to the discussion of a possible objection against an instrumentalist theory of language, as it seems to be suggested by Wittgenstein (cf. Sec. VII). The objection was founded on the idea that words are meaningful because we *mean* something when uttering them, and that quite independently of the way in which those words are used. But it turned out that in deciding whether somebody is really meaning something when uttering a sentence we are thrown back on observation of the way he uses certain elements of speech and that, therefore, an account of meaning can and must be given within the instrumentalist interpretation of language. Meaning is not something that needs consideration *apart* from the description of the way certain expressions are used by the speaker or by other people with whom he is trying to communicate. At the same time a tendency was discovered, namely the tendency "to hypostatize feelings where there are none" [§598].[18] No objection to the instrumentalist interpretation seems to be left, but one: When playing a language game we certainly obey certain *rules*. Thus the idea is suggested "that if anyone utters a sentence and *means* or *understands* it, he is operating a calculus according to definite rules" [§81], and the rules seem to be something which *directs* the activities within a language game, which therefore cannot be described in terms which are useful for describing the working of the language-game itself. It is this idea which we have to treat last. The discussion of this idea in the *Philosophical Investigations* is interwoven with the discussion of the other ideas treated in the book because there are arguments which apply to several ideas at once.†

Assuming that in talking, calculating, etc., we are acting in accordance with certain rules leads at once to the following question: "How am I able to obey a rule?" [§217]. For, on the one hand, it

[18] Cf. §295: "When we look into ourselves as we do philosophy, we often get to see just a picture. A full-blown pictorial representation of our grammar. Not facts; but as it were illustrated turns of speech."

seems to be the case that "the rule, once stamped with a particular meaning, traces the lines along which it is to be followed through the whole of space . . . all the steps are already taken" [§219]. But "if something of that sort really were the case, how would it help?" [§219]. For is there not always the possibility of interpreting the rule in a different way? And how are we to know which interpretation is the right one? Once the rule is separated from our activity it seems impossible that it can determine this activity any more. For it may try to make itself known to us by mental events ('grasping' the rule), by a book which contains all rules of the language game to be played, etc. In any one of those cases we can proceed in many different ways depending on how we interpret, i.e., how we use, the mental picture, the book, etc., in the course of our further activities [cf. §§73, 74, 86, 139, 237]. Thus it seems that "any course of action [can] be determined by a rule because every course of action [can] be made out to accord with the rule" [§201; "could" replaced by 'can'].

But "what this shows is that there is a way of grasping a rule which is *not* an *interpretation,* but which is exhibited in what we call 'obeying the rule' and 'going against it' in actual cases" [§201]. That will become clear from the following example [cf. §454]: "A rule stands there like a sign post. Does the sign post leave no doubt open about the way I have to go? Does it show which direction I am to take when I have passed it?" [§85]. How do I know which direction I have to go? "If that means 'have I reasons?' the answer is: My reasons will soon give out. And then I shall act, without reasons" [§211]. "When someone whom I am afraid of orders me [to follow the sign post], I act quickly, with perfect certainty, and the lack of reasons does not trouble me" [§212, with "to continue the series" replaced by 'to follow the sign post']. "When I obey a rule, I do not choose. I obey the rule *blindly*" [§219]. Let us now assume a land where everybody, on seeing a sign post: →, follows it in this direction: ←, where children are advised to follow the sign post in the way indicated, where foreigners who are in the habit of going → when they see a sign post like this: → are taught that they are acting wrongly, that '→' means 'go ←.' Should we say that the inhabitants of our imaginary country are misinterpreting the sign post? Obviously this would not be the right description of the situation, for without being related to human activities (language games included) the sign post is a mere piece of matter and the question as to its *meaning* (and therefore the question as to whether a certain interpretation is the right one) does not arise at all.

Now it is using the sign post in a certain way, i.e., behaving in a certain way in the presence of the sign post, that gives a meaning to it and that separates it from the other parts of nature which are meaningless in the sense that they are not parts of human language games. But *behaving in this way* is also called *obeying the rules.* "And hence also 'obeying a rule' is a practice. And to *think* one is obeying a rule is not to obey a rule. Hence it is not possible to obey a rule 'privately'; Otherwise thinking one was obeying a rule would be the same thing as obeying it" [§202].

Apply this to language games in general. It follows, that "to obey a rule, to make a report, to give an order, to play a game of chess, are *customs* (uses, institutions)" [§199] and "not a hocus-pocus which can be performed only by the soul" [§454]. "To understand a sentence means to understand a language. To understand a language means to master a technique" [§199]. And so we are back at the instrumental interpretation of language: "Every sign *by itself* seems dead. *What* gives it life?—In *use* it is *alive.* Is life breathed into it then?—Or is the *use* its life?" [§432]. And questions of meaning, of understanding, of following a rule are to be treated by taking into account the *use* of signs within a certain language game.

X

† Thus we arrive at the following result. According to *T* meanings are objects for which words stand. Rules are of a similar ethereal character. Understanding the meanings, grasping the rules, is an activity of the mind, which is the organ for finding our way about in the realm of meaning as the senses are organs for finding our way about in the physical world. We found that either there is no representation of the meanings or the rules in the mind or, assuming that a representation does exist, that it cannot determine the way in which we proceed because there are always many possibilities of interpretation. According to *T'* the meaning of the elements of a language game emerges from their *use* and that use belongs to a quite different category from a single mental event or a mental process, or any process whatever [cf. p. 196].

† Now a sign can be part of different language games just as a button can be used in a game of chess (instead of a pawn, e.g.,

which has been lost) or a game of draughts [checkers]. Do we try in this case to abstract from the differences between these two kinds of use in order to discover a common quality which will explain to us how it is possible for the button to function both as a pawn and as a piece in draughts? The question does not arise because it seems obvious that the button *changes* its function according to the game within which it is used. But in the case of a language game, theory *T* seduces us into thinking that the sign '2,' e.g., is in any case of its use within language connected with a single element, its meaning, and that the varieties of its use ('Give me *two* apples!'—as said in a grocery; $\int_0^2 x^3 dx = 4$; 'Two hours ago I met him in the street'; 'The number of solutions of the equation $x^2 + 5x + 4 = 0$ is *two*') are only a superficial aspect. Once this idea has been dropped, once it has been realized that the meaning of a sign is constituted by its use within a certain language game, words can be looked at as the button was above. And instead of trying to grasp the *essence* of a thing which is to explain the varieties of the use of the sign which stands for the thing we ought simply to describe the language game of which the sign is part. "We must do away with all *explanation,* and description alone must take its place" [§109]. "Our mistake is to look for an explanation where we ought to look at what happened as a 'proto-phenomenon.' That is where we ought to have said: *This language game is played*" [§654]. "Look at the language game as the *primary* thing. And look on the feelings, etc., as you look on a way of regarding the language game, as interpretation" [§656].[19]

† Wittgenstein's position has not yet been described correctly. Wittgenstein was said to hold a theory, *T'*, which emphasizes the instrumental aspect of language and which points to use in a language game as the essential thing. And describing the language game, so one is inclined to say, according to the presentation which has been given so far, is the task of philosophy. From that description quite a few philosophical problems will become clear which seemed hopelessly muddled when seen from the point of view of theory *T*. Philosophy, then, seems to be the theory of language games (a kind of general syntax or semantics in Carnap's sense) and *T'* seems to be its most important part. But according to

---

[19] Note that the idea of an ideal language becomes obsolete as soon as it has been recognized that all language-games are on a par. Vague concepts, e.g. [cf. §71], cannot be regarded as inadmissible any longer. They have a definite function, and that is all we can demand from them.

Wittgenstein this assumption would involve a misunderstanding. For the supposed theory of language games could do no more than enable people to run through the single moves of a game, as a player who is acquainted with the game runs through its moves. But for such a player there is no problem. If he asks, e.g., " 'How do sentences manage to represent?'—the answer must be: 'Don't you know? You certainly see it, when you use them.' For nothing is concealed" [§435]. Everything "lies open to view" [§92; §126]. "Philosophy" therefore "may in no way interfere with the actual use of language; it can in the end only describe it . . . it leaves everything as it is" [§124].

† Let us assume that somebody begins to construct a theory of language games. This theory, if formulated in the terms of T', will be thought to serve as an explanation of how meaning is conferred upon single signs by the way in which these signs are incorporated into a language game. The theory (or description, as it may also be called) will involve a new kind of use of terms such as 'sentence,' 'fact,' 'meaning.' But has a useful explanation or description really been found? We must realize that the supposed theory introduces a *new* use of 'meaning,' 'fact,' 'sentence,' etc. If this use involves even a slight deviation from the use of these words within the language games to be described (explained) the supposed description in fact involves a change in the phenomenon to be described. But if on the other hand the change is a considerable one (and that is to be expected if one is trying to develop a fully-fledged instrumentalist philosophy of meaning) a new language game for the expression 'sentence,' 'meaning,' etc., has been established and the task of describing the given language game is not fulfilled either. Thus "we must do away with all *explanation*" and with T' as well. The description, however, which Wittgenstein invites us to give instead of the explanation, consists only in "putting the things before us" [§126], and as "everything lies open to view, there is nothing to explain" [§126]. We might therefore say, rather hyperbolically, that the "language disguises thoughts" of the *Tractatus* [§4.002] is now replaced by "language is already thought, nothing is concealed."

† But the situation is not quite as simple as that. For there *are* philosophical systems, philosophical theories; and it needs to be explained how it is that they come into existence if "nothing is concealed."

† In describing how philosophical theories come into being, Witt-

genstein refers to the fact that "we *do not command a clear view* of the use of our words" [§122]. Given the answer that nothing is concealed, "one would like to retort: 'Yes, but it all goes by so quick, and I should like to see it as it were laid open to view' " [§435]. On the other hand, "we remain unconscious of the prodigious diversity of all the everyday language games because the clothing of our language makes everything alike" [p. 224]. "What confuses us is the uniform appearance of words when we hear them spoken or meet them in script and print. For their *application* is not presented to us so clearly" [§11]. Take the following example: The sentences 'Washington is a city' and 'Two is an even number' are of a similar structure. This suggests that just as in the first case 'Washington' is the name of a real thing, 'two' is the name of a more abstract object, notwithstanding the fact that the uses of the two signs are "absolutely unlike" [§10].

> In the use of words one might distinguish "surface-grammar" from "depth-grammar." What immediately impresses itself upon us about the use of a word is the way it is used in the construction of the sentence, the part of its use—one might say—that can be taken in by the ear. And now compare the depth-grammar, say of the word "to mean," with what the surface-grammar would lead us to suspect. No wonder that we find it difficult to know our way about [§661].

This difficulty is the reason why we resort to philosophical theories. Why we invent theories of meaning. And why we try to conceive an ideal form behind the complexities of our language games.

† But it is clear "that every sentence in our language 'is in order, as it is.' That is to say, we are not *striving after* an ideal, as if our ordinary vague sentences had not yet got a quite unexceptionable sense . . . there must be perfect order even in the vaguest sentence" [§98]. It should also be clear that the "philosophy of logic speaks of sentences and words in exactly the same sense in which we speak of them in ordinary life, when we say, e.g., 'Here is a Chinese sentence' or 'No, that only looks like writing; it is actually just an ornament' and so on" [§108]. Thus the proper task of philosophy will be to unmask philosophical theories, to "bring words back from their metaphysical to their everyday use" [§116], to destroy the "houses of cards" and to clear up "the ground of language on which they stand" [§113]. And philosophy becomes a "battle against the bewitchment of our intelligence by means of language" [§109]. This

battle is carried through by "assembling remainders for a particular purpose" [§127]—for the purpose of "seeing connexions" [§122]; and "different therapies" [§133], not "*a* philosophical method" [§133], are used in order to finish it victoriously.

† But in these therapies the statement of T' (or rather of the several corollaries of T' which have been mentioned so far) plays the most important part. So far we have interpreted the statement of T' as the exposition of a new (instrumentalist, nominalist, or whatever you like to call it) *theory of meaning*. This interpretation is not unreasonable in itself and taken as such it is a very interesting contribution to traditional philosophy (actually I think that everything that is interesting in the book attaches to the treatment of T' in this way). But this interpretation would go against the way in which his book is meant to be used by Wittgenstein. That may be seen from the following considerations: In Section IV the idea was criticized that reading is a mental process. If we stick to T' and interpret it as a theory we cannot understand why the discussion in Section IV should be a *criticism*. For we could argue in the following way: Wittgenstein says that the meaning of a word becomes clear from the way in which it is used within a specific language game. Let us, therefore, look at the language game which contains both of the expressions 'reading' and 'mental process.' Wittgenstein's presentation—so one would be inclined to say—is a description of certain features of this language game and includes, of course, the remark that 'mental process' as used *in this language game* has nothing whatever to do with toothaches.

† But that is not the right account of what Wittgenstein does. Wittgenstein does criticize—but his criticism is of a particular kind. It is not the kind of criticism which is directed, e.g., against a wrong mathematical calculation. In the latter case the result of the criticism is that a certain sentence is replaced by its negation or by a different sentence. But Wittgenstein does not want his reader to discover that reading is *not* a mental process. For if 'mental process' is used in a metaphysical way in 'reading is a mental process,' it is used just as metaphysically in "reading is not a mental process" [cf. §116]. For him "the results of philosophy are the uncovering of one or another piece of plain nonsense and of bumps that the understanding has got by running its head against the limits of language" [§119], and his aim is "to teach you to pass from a piece of disguised nonsense to something that is patent nonsense" [§464]

and in this way to clear up "the ground of language" [§119]. But that can only mean that "the philosophical problems should *completely* disappear" [§133]; for if the aim has been reached, "everything lies open to view and there is nothing to explain" [§126]. This implies that the formulation of T' as used within the critical procedure cannot be interpreted as a new theory of meaning, for it is applied with the intention of making the language games (e.g., that with 'reading') "lie open to view," i.e., lead to a situation where language games are simply played, without any question arising as to how it is that words become meaningful as part of a certain language game, etc. That being so, the formulation of T' loses its function as soon as *"complete clarity"* has been arrived at. But without a function the signs which are part of the formulation of T' are without meaning. Thus one could say of the sentences which are part of T': These sentences "are elucidatory in this way: he who understands me finally recognizes them as senseless . . . (He must so to speak throw away the ladder, after he has climbed up on it.) He must surmount these [sentences] . . . ; then he sees the world rightly" [*Tractatus* §6.54]. And seeing the world rightly means playing the language games without being troubled by philosophical *questions* or by philosophical *problems*.†

XI

* Note, now, that in the preceding section the idea of the essence has been reintroduced. In traditional philosophy the essence was hidden beneath the various ways of describing it. Now it is the "everyday use" [§116] that "has to be accepted," "is given" [p. 226]; but this everyday use is likewise hidden, beneath the "houses of cards" of philosophical theories [§118],[20] and it too has to be brought to light. Just so, traditional philosophers (i.e., the adherents of theory T) tried to bring to light the clear and sharp meanings which were hidden beneath the "muddied" use of the words which stand for them [§426]. If we assume, now, that in removing those philosophical coverings we finally arrive at *"complete* clarity" [§133], we assume that there is a *sharp line* between the "houses of cards" on the one hand and the language games on which they are built on the other. Now while Wittgenstein usually

---

[20] "Language disguises the thought" is the position of the *Tractatus* [§4.002]. One could say that according to the *Investigations*, the (philosophical) thought disguises language.

criticizes the idea that, e.g., "there *must* be something common [to games], or they would not be called 'games' " [§66; cf. IV A above] and points to the fact that if we "look and see" [§66] we find a "complicated network of similarities overlapping and criss-crossing" [§66], he seems to assume, nonetheless, that at least philosophical difficulties have something in common, that there is a definite boundary between the card houses of philosophy and the solid ground of everyday language, such that it becomes possible to "bring words back from their metaphysical use to their everyday use" [§116].

* To Wittgenstein we can apply the comment (which he used to characterize the adherents of *T*) that "A *picture* held [him] captive" [§115]. For if it is the use, the practice, which constitutes meaning, if "what has to be accepted, the given, is . . . *forms of life*" [p. 226], then one may ask why Wittgenstein tries to eliminate theory *T*, which certainly must be regarded as a form of life if we look at the way in which it is used by its adherents. Nevertheless Wittgenstein tries to eliminate this theory as well as other philosophical theories. But this attempt can only be justified by assuming that there is a difference between using a sign (playing a language game) and proceeding according to theory *T*. The procedures which are connected with theory *T* are supposed not to be taken as parts of a language game, they constitute a sham game which is to be destroyed. How is this attitude to be understood?

* I think we can understand it by looking at the ideas which Wittgenstein has about philosophy (at his *"picture"* of philosophy as one might call it, using his own word). This picture is the picture of the *Tractatus:* "The word 'philosophy' must mean something which stands above or below, not beside the natural sciences" [*Tractatus* §4.111]. In the *Investigations* we may replace "natural sciences" by "language games," and we arrive at: "Philosophy must be something which stands above or below, not beside the language games"; philosophy *cannot* be a language game itself; e.g., it cannot be theory *T'*. I submit that this idea is still present in the *Investigations* and that it makes it clear why Wittgenstein, having found that a sign can only be meaningful if it is incorporated into a language game, cannot admit that there are philosophical theories.[21] This

---

[21] There are some passages which seem to contradict this interpretation of Wittgenstein's views, e.g., "If one tried to advance *theses* in philosophy it would never be possible to question them, because everyone would agree to them" [§128], according to which philosophical theses are not meaningless, but *trivial.*

observation (as well as others which have not been mentioned [22]) suggests that the *Investigations* (apart from their substitution of language games for the one language of the *Tractatus*) are after all not as different from the *Tractatus* as they seem to be at first sight. I am even inclined to say (without being able to substantiate this contention at the moment) that the *Investigations* basically contain an application of the main ideas of the *Tractatus* to several concrete problems, the only difference being the use of language games instead of the language of the natural sciences which formed the theoretical background of the *Tractatus*.

* Trying to evaluate the book, we might say that the criticisms of *T* and the statement of *T'* which it contains, as well as the application of this theory to the discussion of concrete problems (remembering, obeying an order, the problem of sensation, etc.), are a great achievement, which, however, has its predecessors.[23] *Here we are within traditional philosophy*. But Wittgenstein wants us to see his criticisms in a different light. In the end we should forget them as well as *T*, we should forget philosophy entirely. Although the formulation of what can be regarded as a *theory* (theory *T'*) led us to the proper understanding of our difficulties, it must not be taken as the formulation of a *theory* but only as a proper means of getting rid of our philosophical troubles. *T'* has, therefore, to disappear together with those troubles. This new idea, which is Wittgenstein's own and which can be found in the *Tractatus* as well, is due, first, to the *picture* that philosophy must be something quite extraordinary and, second, to certain difficulties, already mentioned, which could be solved by taking into account the difference between object-language and meta-language (used by Tarski to get rid of similar difficulties, but never recognized by Wittgenstein [cf. §121]). Using this device we find that the philosophical language games do not necessarily disturb the language games they are supposed to describe. We also find that philosophy is not necessarily on a level with the language games it is about. On the contrary, the assumption that the philosophical language games are on a level with the language games they deal with leads to contradictions. This solution would not agree with Wittgenstein's, but it would retain several

---

[22] Cf. the similarity of "shows itself" in the *Tractatus* and "lies open to view" in the *Investigations*.

[23] Cf., e.g., H. Gomperz, *Weltanschauungslehre*, Vol. II, where further references are given; E. Mach, *Erkenntnis u. Irrtum*, 3rd ed., pp. 126 ff.; D'Alembert, *Traité de dynamique* (1743); the tenets of the various nominalistic schools, old and new, etc. Cf. also K. Popper's criticism of essentialism, developed as early as 1935.

elements of his philosophy: (1) his criticisms of T; (2) his statement of T'; (3) his observation, that language games may be disturbed by other language games which are supposed to explain or to describe them. It would, however, interpret the statement of T' as a special theory of meaning and formulate it by taking account of the difference between object-language and meta-language. It would be possible still to have philosophical theories and philosophical problems without being open to Wittgenstein's criticisms, except perhaps the one criticism, that the distinction introduced is purely artificial.*

Wittgenstein's Builders

BY RUSH RHEES

1

WHEN WITTGENSTEIN SAYS that an account of what "language" means would be something like explaining what "game" means, he is not thinking of an explanation you would give to anyone in an ordinary way, but of the explanation you might give in philosophy. And then the trouble is to know what that is: what kind of explanation does one look for here? He gives an analogy when he refers to the explanation of "game," but it is never more than an analogy, and at times we may feel unsure just how to take it. There is the analogy between speaking and playing a game too, of course. But I am thinking of the analogy in the idea of "explanation": the analogy which should show what "explaining what it means" or "explaining what it is" may be.

Wittgenstein did not always distinguish between "language" and "speaking," and sometimes this brings trouble. Suppose you say that "speaking" covers a family of related cases, just as "game" does. And suppose you then say that language—or the language we speak—*is* a family of language games. Here you would not be saying simply that the games are various instances of what we call language; but that *a* language is a family of language games: that this is the kind of unity a language has. And this distinction is important, especially in connection with the ideas of "a common language" and "something said in the same language." I will return to this.

If we consider "speaking," especially, there are certain ways in which the analogy with an explanation of "game" is hard to use. I suppose you might try to tell someone what "game" means by describing various games to him. (You must have come to the conclusion that he had never played one.) We could say then that he

251

learns what "game" means in this way, or that he has come to understand what a game is. But if you were trying to explain to someone what "speaking" means, it could not go like that at all. If you think he has never even played a game, you begin by describing the various cases. But if you thought he had never learned to speak . . . you would not begin by describing how it goes.

He cannot understand what speaking is, unless he can understand what is said. And if he can understand what is said, what is the explanation supposed to do? (The question of how a foreigner learns the English word "speaking" would not be relevant.)

"You may have played games often enough without ever having tried to say what playing a game is. And you may have spoken for years without ever having tried to say what speaking is." But these cases are not really parallel. If you try to say what playing a game is, you try to show in a general way what people are doing when they play games: you describe examples enough to give an idea of it, and say "and so on." But although "what people are doing when they play games" is all right here, a description of what people are doing when they speak would not do as an illustration of what speaking is.

Suppose I describe what the two men are doing while they are building, as Wittgenstein does in the *Investigations* [pp. 3 and 5]. If this does illustrate speaking for you, then you must not only understand what they are doing, but you must understand what they say. My description must show that they speak a language which each of them understands, and which you also understand, if the illustration is to help you. (Wittgenstein imagines them using German words. He would say this was of no consequence, I think.)

If anyone says anything, he says it in a language. If he says anything he can speak with people, and for this they must speak a common language. I can understand what is said, or at least I can try to, if I speak the language.

This is one of the reasons why it is so hard to see clearly what "a general account of language" would be. The difficulty is not simply in wondering whether "Those are all examples of language" means that they must have some general features in common, since we use the same word. That would be the sort of thing we might ask about the generality of "game." The trouble is in this idea of "the same language," when I say we speak the same language, for instance. As if the remarks that are made in the same language have something in common, so if you know the language you can understand them.

When Wittgenstein was writing the *Tractatus* he might have said that "being in the language" meant simply being language or being a proposition. "Die Gesammtheit der Sätze ist die Sprache." And anything meant by a *common* language was covered, if at all, by this notion of being language or being intelligible. For he argued that all propositions must have a kind of common intelligibility or commensurability simply through being propositions or having sense.

That idea of "all propositions" was extremely troublesome, and when Wittgenstein was writing the *Investigations* he had dropped it. The idea of "belonging to language," like the idea of "human language" (cf., "ein bestimmtes Bild der menschlichen Sprache") was difficult too, though in different ways. But Wittgenstein has kept this. He is still interested in "human language" rather than in the language or languages which people speak. When he says that any language is a family of language games, and that any of these might be a complete language by itself, he does not say whether people who might take part in several such games would be speaking the same language in each of them. In fact I find it hard to see how on this view they would *ever* be speaking a language. But these questions are complicated.

2

If I say something like "I may know well enough what a game is and still be unable to *tell* you in any general way what a game is," I am thinking about the word and of certain difficulties one sometimes feels about it: the question perhaps of what guides people when they call one thing a game and another not, or perhaps of the kind of generality the word has. For there might be misunderstandings about this, even when no one had misunderstood the word. And if we could get clear on these questions, then at any rate we should have a better understanding of how we used it.

But if we were trying to get a better understanding of language it would be different. There are misunderstandings here and that is why we ask, but they are not like the misunderstandings people may have about their use of the word "game." If you did say that our trouble is in finding a satisfactory account of the way the word "language" is used, then I have tried to show that this trouble is peculiar, and it cannot be dealt with in the way the trouble about the word "game" might.

The misunderstandings here are what Wittgenstein used to call "misunderstandings of the logic of our language," which give rise to the problems of philosophy. I think the point is: one is perplexed as to whether something can be *said* or not. Or more commonly, what one is trying to say shows that one is confused about this. It is a confusion or uncertainty connected with being able to speak, and so perhaps with learning to speak: a confusion in connection with what it is that one was learning as one learned to speak: with what saying something is and what understanding is. This sort of confusion or uncertainty (which is not just a confusion of the grammars of particular expressions) has led men to the scepticism which runs in one way or another into all the big questions of philosophy. And the understanding which philosophy seeks is in some sense an understanding of language or of what language is.

When Wittgenstein wrote the *Tractatus* he might have said that you understand the logic of language when you understand the syntax of a symbolism—or perhaps of *symbolism* as such. And in his later view he still would say that the logic of language is concerned with how words mean—which covers much of what he had meant by "how signs symbolize." But there is not the same idea of the *laws* of symbolism now, nor of the essential nature of signs. And he no longer thinks it important to find a symbolism which would show unambiguously the logical forms of the various statements; whereas in the *Tractatus* he thought that without this we cannot show their relations to reality. Unless we can find their logical forms we cannot find "how they mean": we cannot understand what it is that makes them statements at all.

In the earlier view, then "understanding the logic of language" and "understanding the relation of logic to language" seem to coincide.

In the later view it is not so. He still says that "we learn logic as we learn the language," but this is more important for what it tells you about logic than for what it tells you about language. But when we try to understand the logic of language, we are generally not concerned with the logical forms of statements, nor with the logical structure of language. In fact that idea of "the logical structure of language" would illustrate what he would now call a *misunderstanding* of the logic of language. The whole idea of a structure or system, like the idea of a logical connection, depends on what speaking is. But this is hardly even a statement, because speaking is not one thing, and "having meaning" is not one thing either. This is perhaps the hardest thing to understand about language, and it is for this that he refers to the language games.

When he says that a child learns various language games as it learns to speak, he is thinking partly of how the parents teach the child to use the different expressions. But he is also explaining what "teaching him expressions" *is:* what it is to be an expression or to mean something, and what it is to have a language. This is nothing that would help you in teaching a child and in one sense it says nothing about language: nothing that would interest philologists, for instance. But if you explain to me the various games, if you explain what we do with the various color words, or how we use "good" or "continuity" or "mind"—the games we play with them— you will have shown me how it is that they have meaning. In this way you will have shown me what makes it possible for language to have meaning, even though you have not referred to any general form or structure. You will have shown what it is for people to talk about things.

I think that is roughly Wittgenstein's position. But it takes for granted that it is the same language that is spoken in the various games. Much of what he says about the dangers in philosophy of being confused about the game we are playing when we talk about sensations and the game we are playing when we talk about physical objects, for instance, depends on that. And if we do say we are speaking the same language in the various games, then what does "speaking the language" mean here? We cannot give an explanation of this by describing the game that is played.

It seems to me the trouble lies still in some unclarity about what the explanation is supposed to do.

3

It is especially difficult when Wittgenstein speaks as though we might regard the different language games as different languages. He speaks so in the beginning of the *Brown Book,* for instance, and in the early examples like that of the builders in the *Investigations,* too. And the comparison of "game" and "language" fosters it, when this is meant to show what is meant by "make up a family of cases."

For the "cases" of games are all games themselves; and of course they do not *make up* a game. Different languages would not make up a language either. This shows that I am pushing the analogy in a way that it was not meant to go. And I admit I am puzzled. Suppose we say that we are playing a different language game when we are talking about our feelings and when we are talking about physical objects like motor cars. Obviously these different language games are not different languages in the sense in which French and English are, because for one thing it would seem from some accounts as though people might be said to be playing the same language game either in French or in English, but more especially because it would make no sense to talk of translating from the one language game into the other. On the other hand, Wittgenstein did say in the *Brown Book,* for instance, that the various language games he had mentioned as making up a language were to be regarded "not as incomplete parts of a language, but as languages complete in themselves, as complete systems of human communication" (p. 81). In this he is warning against the mistaken idea that a language may be found to be "incomplete," and against a view like that of the *Tractatus* that it should be possible to calculate all the possible forms of proposition. There is a great deal in the philosophy of logic that is connected with that, and the criticism Wittgenstein is developing in what he says about language games go deeper, probably, then any others have. But they also raise new issues themselves.

In the builders example in the *Investigations* Wittgenstein describes two men working with building stones. At various points in their work one of them shouts orders, for which he has a very limited number of expressions, and the other reacts to the orders by, for instance, bringing a slab when the first one shouts "Slab!" He then says that these men might have no other speech or language except this; and even that this might be the entire language of a tribe. It would be used, presumably, only in this kind of building work. But I feel there is something wrong here. The trouble is not to imagine a people with a language of such a limited vocabulary. The trouble is to imagine that they spoke the language only to give these special orders on this job and otherwise never spoke at all. I do not think it would be speaking a language.

When Wittgenstein suggests that in this tribe the children might be *taught* these shouts and how to react to them, I suppose this means that the adults would be using the expressions in giving the instruction, and this would be different from using them on the actual job. If they belong to a language, this is natural enough, just as it would be natural for the builders to use them in referring to the job when they had gone home. But then using the expressions and understanding the expressions would not be simply part of the building technique. Understanding "slab" would not be just reacting correctly on the job.

If it is an actual building job, it will not always go according to plan; there will be snags. But when these builders come on a snag which holds up the work and baffles them, then although they have been speaking to one another in the course of their routine, they do not speak while they are trying to find what the trouble is. What they have learned are *signals* which cannot be used in any other way.

In fact it seems as though Wittgenstein has described a *game* with building stones, and not the sort of thing people would do if they were actually building a house. In a game there are no snags of the sort you meet on a job. And the signals are part of the game, too. But this will not do what Wittgenstein wanted. It does not show how speaking is related to the lives which people lead.

In any case—and this is my chief difficulty—if they had learned only those shouts and reactions there would not be any distinction of sense and nonsense. They might be nonplussed by a shout to which they had not been trained. But this would be no different from their bewilderment if someone moved a stone in a way that was not part of the routine in which they had been drilled.

Wittgenstein might say that for these people there would be no distinction between "that is not what we generally do" and "That makes no sense." There might be some analogy to the example of the people who make no distinction between physical possibility and geometrical possibility (*Remarks on the Foundations of Mathematics,* page 189). These people notice that when you fold a paper in this way, you get this sort of construction; and they never ask whether this is a geometrical relation of the figures, or whether it is a result of the physical properties of the paper. Similarly, the people in our present example would simply disallow or take no account of certain expressions; and it is pointless for us to ask whether they are rejecting them as nonsense or rejecting them because they are not part of the routine. (As we might take no notice of an utterance in some language which we did not understand.)

But I do not think this would be satisfactory. Unless there were a difference between learning to move stones in the ways people always do, and learning what makes sense, then I do not think we could say they were learning to speak.

Wittgenstein used to wonder whether there might be a people who had only an applied mathematics and no pure mathematics. Could we still say that they calculated and had proofs, although their proofs were something of the order of showing you what you can get if you fold the paper in this way: showing you what you will get if you use this method in numbering and separating sheep, and so on. These proofs would have nothing to do with "concept formation," as the proofs of pure mathematics do. We might suppose the people used the proofs only for predicition: "You can get it in this way." The proofs would not then be normative, in the way the proofs of mathematics are. But just for this reason their whole position or rôle as proofs would become obscure. "What puzzles me," Wittgenstein said, "is how these proofs are *kept*." They are a set of techniques which are used in forecasts, but they do not form a system in which there is any kind of dependence. And it is not clear how people would be persuaded to adopt them or what force they would have.

"That is just the way we do things." Can we say that the sense or otherwise of what is said depends on that? Consider the question of whether he is using the words "in the same way" for instance. What decides this? Or what does the question mean, even? In our language as we speak it there are standards of what is correct or incorrect, and these come in when we say he is not using the word in the same way now, or when we say someone has misunderstood. But I do not see how there can be any such standard in the game Wittgenstein has described.

In the *Remarks on the Foundations of Mathematics* (p. 133) Wittgenstein says, "I want to say, it is essential to mathematics that its signs should also be used in civil life. It is their use outside mathematics, in other words the *meaning* of the signs, that makes the sign-game mathematics. Just as it is not a logical conclusion if I change one configuration into another (say one arrangement of chairs into another) unless these configurations have some use in language *besides* the making of these transformations."

You might ask why this should make such a difference—the fact that they are used elsewhere. And one reason is that then the ex-

pressions are not just part of one particular routine. Their uses elsewhere have to do with the point or bearing of them in what we are
saying now. It is the way in which we have come to know them in
other connections that decides whether it makes sense to put them
together here, for instance: whether one can be substituted for another, whether they are incompatible and so forth. The meaning
that they have within this game is not to be seen simply in what
we do with them or how we react to them in this game.

The builders are not supposed to be drawing conclusions or calculating. But if they speak to one another, the meaning of the expression they use cannot lie wholly in the use or the reaction that it
receives in this job. The point about the logical conclusion was that
if the signs had no use or meaning outside this transformation, then
the transformation itself would be without any significance and it
would not show anything. If people are speaking together, then the
significance of this or that remark is not like the significance of a
logical conclusion. But the remarks they make have something to do
with one another; otherwise they are not talking at all, even though
they may be uttering sentences. And their remarks could have no
bearing on one another unless the expressions they used were used
in other connexions as well.

4

If someone learns to speak, he does not just learn to make sentences and utter them. Nor can he merely have learned to react to
orders. If that were all he ever did, I should not imagine that he
could speak, and I should never ask him anything. When he learns
to speak, he learns to tell you something; and he tries to.

In learning to speak he learns what can be said; he learns, however fumblingly, what it makes sense to say. He comes to have some
sense of how different remarks have something to do with one another. This is why he can answer you and ask you things, and why
he begins to follow a conversation or to carry on a conversation
himself. Or rather, it is misleading to say this is *why* he does that, as
though what we had were a condition and what results from it. For
in beginning to carry on a conversation, in trying to tell you something and trying to understand your answer, he *is* getting a sense of
how different remarks have a bearing on one another. And because
he learns this, he can go on speaking or go on learning. If he can

speak with me or ask me something here, then he will be able to ask me something else later.

By "what it makes sense to say" I do not mean that he learns the correct way of using various expressions, although he does learn that. (He learns what pieces to call slabs and what to call beams, perhaps.) But "what it makes sense to say" is not "the sense these expressions have." It has more to do with what it makes sense to answer or what it makes sense to ask, or what sense one remark may have in connection with another.

He learns to tell you something. This is connected with the ideas of addressing you and greeting you. And you cannot teach it to him by putting him through the motions.

Nor is it like learning a game. We may *use* something like a game in teaching him. We say his sounds back to him, and in this way we bring him to imitate other sounds we make. And this is a game. But it is not what we are trying to teach him. And if all he learns is how to play like this, he will not have learned to speak. He will never tell you anything nor ask you anything either.

When he can speak we may be delighted because "he can say things himself now—not just repeat." But what is important is that he can *say* things: not that he can construct new sentences—as it were in an exercise. You may set him exercises if you want to test his vocabulary. But this is not how you find out whether he can speak.

You might test his knowledge of a foreign language by setting him exercises, too. And it would be something the same if you wanted to see whether he had mastered a particular notation. Or again, if you wanted to see whether he could do arithmetic. Wittgenstein used to speak of teaching a child to multiply by going through examples of multiplications for him, then getting him to go through these and through other exercises while you corrected his mistakes, and then saying "Go on by yourself now." But if you said anything similar about teaching a child to speak, you would have left out the most important thing. If he can speak, he has got something to tell you. In arithmetic it is different. Telling you things is not part of his achievement when he learns to multiply.

Learning to play a game is not just learning to do exercises either. And when Wittgenstein compared learning to speak with learning a game, one reason was that you generally play a game with other people. But this does not make it like conversation or like speaking. Not all speech is conversation, of course, but I do not think there would be speech or language without it. If there were someone who could not carry on a conversation, who had no idea of asking questions or making any comment, then I do not think we should say he could speak. Now one reason why a conversation is not like playing a game together is that the point of the various moves and countermoves is within the game. Whereas we may learn from a conversation and from what is said in it. Generally each of us brings something to the conversation too: not as he might bring skill to the game, but just in having something to say.

I want to contrast (*a*) the external relations of the moves in a game, and (*b*) the internal relations of the remarks people make to one another. "Internal relations" has a technical sense, so it may be misleading. But it does suggest "connections of meaning," and this is the point here. It cannot be reduced to connections in a game. This goes with the fact that we can learn from a conversation: that its point is not contained just in what happens there.

And that is connected with the idea of having something to say. The point about chess, for instance, is that the pieces are furnished to you—you do not have to find them or decide what they shall be.

If you are giving me lessons in a foreign language, we may carry on a sham conversation to give me the opportunity of constructing appropriate sentences and giving appropriate replies. Neither of us learns anything from what is said in this, because neither of us really tells the other anything. And unless there were the distinction between genuine speaking and sham or pretence, then speaking *would* be nearly like playing a game.

Once more: if I know you can speak, then it makes sense for me to ask you what you mean, to try to get you to say more clearly what you want, and to ask you questions about it: just as truly as it makes sense for me to answer you. The example of the builders does not seem to allow for any of these. Neither could reply to the other—there is no such thing and it would have no sense. And there can be nothing of the sort so long as the meaning of the utterance is confined to "what you do with it" in this particular connection.

5

We are back at the question of what it is to have a language or what it is to speak. This is the question Wittgenstein is trying to answer in his analogy with games. He speaks of the games we play with this or that expression—with color words, for instance, or with "meter" or with "good." And one might ask, "What is the objection to saying that the learning of these various expressions *is* learning to speak? There is not any *single* thing which is learning to speak— as though that were an operation too, or something over and above what we do with these various expressions. But knowing the use of such expressions—being able to use them on the occasions when they arise in connection with other people—that is speaking."

I could only answer what I have tried to say already. I do not want to suggest that there is some one thing which anyone learns when he learns to speak—especially if this means anything comparable to "some one operation." I have wanted to say that learning to speak is not learning *how* to speak or how to do anything. And it is not learning the mastery of a technique—although learning a foreign language might come nearer to that. (Not very near even then.) On the other hand, if it were really anything like what the paraphrase which I gave in the previous paragraph suggests—if that were all there were to it—then the child would not see the difference between a jumble of sentences and a sensible discourse. I have said that this is something that he learns, although it is not something you can teach him by any sort of drill, as you might perhaps teach him the names of objects. I think he gets it chiefly from the way in which the members of his family speak to him and answer him. In this way he gets an idea of how remarks may be connected, and of how what people say to one another makes sense. In any case, it is not like learning the meaning of this or that expression. And although he can go on speaking, this is not like going on with the use of any particular expression or set of expressions, although of course it includes that.

The remarks bear on one another. But not in the way in which parts of a technique do, nor as moves in a game might. If my remark has some bearing on yours, this is because of what I said and what you said: not just because our respective situations in this job have some bearing on one another, too. This is why the remarks have to be understood before you can see what they have to do with one another—in a way that moves in a game do not.

If we ask *how* they are connected with other things that are said, for instance, we shall be raising questions I can hardly begin to discuss here. Wittgenstein used to say that to imagine a language is to imagine a form of life. This idea was important in his later writings,

but he did not make it very explicit what was included in it. Some
times he speaks of it as a way of *working,* and it is hard to see the
difference between this and a language game. Or he speaks of an
institution like money, or an institution like buying and selling wood.
But I think this is confusing. There is clearly some important connection between the language a people speak and the life or culture
they develop. And it is important to emphasize, as Wittgenstein
was doing, that to understand what people are saying you must
understand more than the vocabulary and the rules of grammar.
But the differences between one form of life and another are not
like the differences between one form of institution (say, marriage
customs or financial institutions) and another. And the activity of
the builders does not give you an idea of a people with a definite
sort of life. Do they have songs and dances and festivals, and do
they have legends and stories? Are they horrified by certain sorts of
crimes, and do they expose people to public ridicule? The description of them on the building site, if you add "this may be all," makes
them look like marionettes. On the other hand, if they do have a
life, then to say that their speaking is part of that life would be different from saying that their speaking is part of this activity of
building.

Language is something that can have a literature. This is where
it is so different from chess. And if we include folk songs and stories,
then literature is immensely important in almost any language: important for the ways in which things said in the language are understood. It has to do with the "force" which one remark or another
may have in that language, for instance. And in this way it has to do
also with what is seen to make sense and what is not.

Of course there is much else that is necessary as well. If you
want to understand them you have to know what they are talking
about. And for this you need to know how they farm and build and
their marriage customs and the rest. I do not say this is less important than literature. I am saying only that it would be misleading to
describe language as a part of that—as a part of the way or ways
of doing things; especially if this leaves the suggestion that the language that belongs to building is no more closely connected with
the language that belongs to the routine of a local government office, than are the movements they make in building and the movements they make in the office. Or that the language they use at home
would have no other sort of connection with the language they use

at work than the way the home is run may have with the way the
job is organized or the way the office is run.

The boy learns to speak so as to make sense and to find sense,
and this is true in whatever job he happens to be or whatever he
happens to be doing. In other words, there is a distinction between
what we say and what we are talking about, and this goes with
the idea of a reason for saying what we do.

This does not mean that the remarks made in the language form
a system and that they get their sense from that. But it does suggest
something like a common understanding. To think of language as
a system, or as a kind of method (cf., "a method of representation,"
"method of projection"), almost as a kind of theory, is wrong if
only because language is something people speak with one another.
In this way it is not at all like mathematics. And it would be confusing to think that "the language" is related to applied mathematics. At the same time, the comparison does suggest something.
And when I speak of a common understanding I do not mean
simply what Wittgenstein used to call an "agreement in reactions"
which makes it possible to talk about using the word in the same
way or using it correctly. It has to do rather with what is taken
to make sense, or with what can be understood: with what it is possible to say to people: with what anyone who speaks the language
might try to say.

Wittgenstein on Some Questions in Foundations of Mathematics

BY ALICE AMBROSE

"PHILOSOPHY IS A BATTLE against the bewitchment of our intelligence by means of language." [1] This pronouncement in Wittgenstein's posthumously published book is an index to the philosophical outlook which prompted Wittgenstein to scrutinize with the greatest attentiveness the language in which philosophers have stated their problems. Each problem is according to him the product of an obsession—a linguistic obsession that is not recognized.[2] In consequence of this the philosopher envisages his task not as the elimination of the obsession, but rather as the solution of a scientific problem. It is as if he had to find out something new, as if he faced a question of fact about which we do not yet know enough.[3] "The real discovery," Wittgenstein says, "is the one that makes me capable of stopping doing philosophy when I want to.—The one that gives philosophy peace, so that it is no longer tormented by questions which bring *itself* in question." [4] The sign that this discovery has been made is that we cease to seek a *solution* of a particular philosophical problem. These problems are not the kind that have a solution, in the usual sense of "solution." They should *dis*solve, *"completely* disappear," [5] once clarity about our use of language is achieved.

Rather than launch into an extended discourse on method, I shall try here to exhibit Wittgenstein's procedure in dealing with certain philosophical problems, and I shall at the same time expound the

[1] *Philosophical Investigations* (New York: Macmillan, 1953), p. 47.
[2] Lectures, 1934–35.
[3] *Ibid.*
[4] *Philosophical Investigations*, p. 51.
[5] *Ibid.*

265

substance of what he had to say about them. The problems I have
chosen come from the foundations of mathematics. They were
treated by Wittgenstein in lectures I attended in Cambridge in
1934–1935 and in the 1939 lectures on foundations of mathematics of which I possess notes. Initially I shall set a question
which Wittgenstein did not formulate in precisely my fashion; but
my formulation provides a springboard for the exposition of his
treatment of problems intimately connected with it.

I shall begin with a question similar to Kant's question about
pure mathematics: How is applied mathematics possible? How is it
that *a priori* propositions have an application to matter of fact?
The puzzle suggested by this question is, more specifically, the
puzzle as to how an *a priori* proposition, e.g., $2 + 3 = 5$, can both
be true independently of matter of fact and be true of collections
of two apples and three apples. If *a priori,* such that its truth value
is unaffected by any theoretically possible state of affairs, it can
give no information about any actual state of affairs. How then can
it be about apples? Puzzlement about this may very well have been
one source of Mill's denial that "$2 + 3 = 5$" is anything more than
an empirical generalization. If it cannot both be true regardless of
fact and also imply a truth about apples or other observable objects
—in particular about objects which do not coalesce or reproduce
themselves in the course of being counted—one must discard one
of the two seemingly incompatible accounts of it. Mill discarded the
account of it as a necessity. And yet the arithmetic statement "$2 + 3
= 5$" seems obviously to possess all the properties ascribed to
necessary truths: it can be known without recourse to experience;
its opposite would be self-inconsistent; no state of affairs could possibly disconfirm it, nor would any be required to confirm it. How
then can one account for the harmony between the two quite different areas of logic and of empirical fact? How is it that we can
apply arithmetical calculations to physical objects, or trigonometric
calculations to physical lines and angles? Is there a genuine mystery
here or only a gratuitous puzzle?

The suggestion which my question makes, unlike that which
Kant intended by his, is that there is a difficulty in conceiving any
application of a proposition of logically incorrigible status to matter
of fact—that application is impossible. The question thus has what
Wittgenstein singled out as the earmark of every philosophical difficulty: the presence in its expression of the words "cannot" or

"must," or their equivalents. These are the words which signalize a philosophical obsession. How, we ask, *can* the statement "2 + 3 = 5," whose truth is independent of experience, apply to apples, i.e., be such that the numerical equality it asserts not only tallies with, but seems to be empirically established by, a count of the numbers of the two sets of apples, and seems even to *predict* the empirical result of counting? As Russell said, "We do not know who will be the inhabitants of London a hundred years hence; but we know that any two of them and any other two of them will make four of them. This apparent power of anticipating facts about things of which we have no experience is certainly surprising." [6]

But the applicability of mathematics is not surprising to common sense. That arithmetic, geometry, and trigonometry have an application is a commonplace, and no philosopher in his ordinary pursuits questions whether mathematical propositions can apply to matters of fact any more then he questions whether motion is possible. But one cannot as a philosopher dismiss the question by an appeal to common sense. The common-sense answer to "How can '2 + 3 = 5' imply a truth about collections of apples?.," namely, "It simply does," is true; but it is not the proper answer to the philosophical question. The proper answer should rid one of the puzzle. This, says Wittgenstein, is the business of philosophy: to rid one of puzzles which do not arise for common sense.[7] Doing philosophy according to him consists of three activities: first, seeing the common-sense answer to these problems; second, getting oneself so deeply into the problems that the common-sense answer seems unbearable;[8] and finally, getting oneself from that situation to the common-sense answer again. But the common-sense answer by itself is no solution; one must first allow oneself to be dragged into the mire and then get out of it.[9]

Were it proper to describe an arithmetic proposition as an empirical generalization having no exceptions, then its application to fact would present no puzzle. But tempting as it is to escape a difficulty in this way, I think it is clear that we should do violence to the current usage of the term "empirical generalization" were we to take this way out. For an empirical generalization can be falsified,

---

[6] B. Russell, *The Problems of Philosophy* (London: Oxford, 1912), p. 132.

[7] Lectures, 1934–35.

[8] In this connection, C. D. Broad's comment on common sense is worth remarking: "Let it go out and hang itself" (*The Mind and Its Place in Nature* [London: Routledge & Kegan Paul, 1925], p. 186).

[9] Lectures, 1934–35.

and it is clear that we will accept nothing as a counter-instance to "2 + 3 = 5." Mill's theory reclassifies arithmetic propositions, and furthermore, in such a way as to leave us with no proper use of the word "necessary." [10] For if arithmetic propositions are not necessary, we are at a loss to describe what would be necessary, just as we should be at a loss to say what would be a religious belief if the description "religious belief" were refused to "There is a God." Wittgenstein says that what he does under the name "philosophy" "may in no way interfere with the actual use of language." [11] "It is not our aim to refine or complete the system of rules for the use of our words in unheard-of ways." [12] "What *we* do is to bring words back from their metaphysical to their everyday usage." [13]

Let us begin then with acceptance of two facts: (1) that it is proper to describe mathematical propositions as necessary, and (2) that applied mathematics is possible. Whatever the philosophical difficulties involved, these are the facts which common sense dictates that we begin and end with. But philosophical difficulties in which it is easy to become mired do exist. I shall try to expound these difficulties as Wittgenstein envisaged them, together with the attempts he made to clarify them and, by clarification, to dissolve them. These are all intimately connected with whatever problem may be felt about the possibility of applied mathematics, though Wittgenstein did not make this particular problem central in the cluster of related problems he investigated. All of them concern the connection of mathematical propositions with experience, and in my opinion it would not be a misrepresentation of Wittgenstein to say they all arise directly or indirectly from the misleading question, "What are mathematical propositions *about?*"

It has sometimes been held that "2 + 3 = 5" is a proposition about numbers, necessarily true in virtue of the nature of numbers, whereas "2 apples + 3 apples = 5 apples" is a proposition about apples, which is factually true in virtue of the nature of the apples our world provides—nongenerating, noncoalescing apples. We can use arithmetic to count, and to predict the result of adding two apples to three, because, so it is claimed, it is a fact about apples that they do not either vanish or multiply when this operation is

[10] See M. Lazerowitz, *The Structure of Metaphysics* (London: Routledge & Kegan Paul), pp. 258–259.
[11] *Philosophical Investigations*, p. 49.
[12] *Ibid.*, p. 51.
[13] *Ibid.*, p. 48.

performed. The application of arithmetic thus depends on whether or not certain empirical conditions are satisfied. It will be true then to say, "If no apples disappear or multiply, 2 apples + 3 apples = 5 apples," but not unqualifiedly true that 2 apples + 3 apples = 5 apples. Now Wittgenstein says that whether this is a correct account of the proposition "2 apples + 3 apples = 5 apples" is to be determined by the *use* we make of it. It is not that the use is determined by whether the proposition states a contingent truth about apples or a necessary connection between concepts. If, unexpectedly, apples increase or diminish in number when addition is performed, and we accept this fact as constituting a falsification, then our statement is experimental. But if we excuse every case in which five apples fail to be present when three apples are added to two, i.e., if no such fact is accepted as disconfirming it, then our statement is necessary. One and the same sentence can be used in either of these two ways, and of course it is a fact that the latter way is by far the more usual.

If we examine this more usual use of "2 apples + 3 apples = 5 apples," i.e., to express a necessary proposition, we shall see its proper relation to the empirical fact that apples remain discrete when added. This fact is not an empirical condition of the truth of the proposition it is used to express; rather, that this proposition applies to apples is the criterion for their having remained discrete. And if in an imaginable case it did not apply, i.e., if the number of apples counted was not five, this would be the criterion, not for the equation's falsity, but for the number of apples not having remained constant during the process of their being counted. Similarly, that the equation "2 quarts + 3 quarts = 5 quarts" does not hold for the *physical* addition of two quarts of alcohol to three quarts of water indicates something about the mixture of these substances, but the behavior of these substances when mixed implies nothing about the truth of "2 quarts + 3 quarts = 5 quarts." Their behavior does imply the falsity of the statement "2 quarts physically added to 3 quarts yield 5 quarts," but it is logically irrelevant to the statement which asserts the arithmetic addition of units—as our usual use of this statement shows.

One likely source of the temptation to disregard how such a statement functions (as necessary rather than empirical) is the compulsion to ask, and to answer, the question, "What is the proposition about?" "About apples," "about discrete entities," etc., are the

natural answers. Similarly, "about numbers" is the natural answer
to "What is '2 + 3 = 5' about?"; and of course it cannot be denied
that it is proper to distinguish this proposition from empirical
propositions by characterizing it as being about numbers. But our
question, according to Wittgenstein, is misleading, since we thereby
treat "2 + 3 = 5" as analogous to empirical propositions, and
only differing from them in being about nonempirical, abstract
entities. Mathematics, according to this way of looking at it, becomes a sort of physics of mathematical entities, and mathematical
research an expedition of discovery. This is the conception which
Professor G. H. Hardy had. He writes: "I have myself always
thought of a mathematician as in the first instance an *observer,* a
man who gazes at a distant range of mountains and notes down his
observations. His job is simply to distinguish clearly and notify to
others as many different peaks as he can . . ." [14]

Wittgenstein says that philosophy arises out of prejudices in favor
of certain grammatical forms. We try always to work from one
paradigm, which operates as a grammatical obsession.[15] "What are
mathematical propositions about" is a question motivated by the
obsessional emphasis on the analogy of these propositions to empirical ones. To rid one of this obsession it has some point to say, as
Wittgenstein says in a number of places, that arithmetic propositions
are not about numbers, nor are geometric propositions about
geometrical figures. But this is also misleading, since, like Plato's
answer to this question, it seems to give information in the way in
which a scientific answer does. If we wish not to be misled we shall
do well to direct our attention away from the question as to what
they are about to the *use* we make of them. And by examining their
use the connection between their necessity and their application will
no longer appear puzzling.

Now what we do when we allow nothing to count against a proposition, when we enshrine it amongst the incorrigibles and refuse to
surrender it in the face of any conceivable facts, is to assign to the
expression for the proposition a special rôle in our language. According to Wittgenstein we have decided on using the sentence in
a certain way, namely, as a rule for the use of expressions, i.e., a
rule for the application of certain words.[16] To elucidate, let us consider an example similar to one he used: Suppose I multiply 25 by

[14] G. H. Hardy, "Mathematical Proof," *Mind,* Vol. XXXVIII (1929), p. 18.
[15] Lectures, 1934–35.
[16] Lectures, 1939.

17 in order to find out the number of squares in a rectangle 25 squares long by 17 squares wide. If the number of squares is found upon counting not to be 425, the result got by multiplying according to the rules, and I thereupon say "25 × 17 = 425" is false, I use it to express a proposition testable by experience. But if I say it is correct regardless of what number of squares I find on counting, and use it as a criterion of the correctness of my count, I thereby make it independent of experience. And to do this is to resolve on a certain use, namely, that it shall function analogously to a rule for the use of numerical terms—for one thing, that 425 can be substituted for 25 × 17, for another, that the two statements, "The number of roses I received is equal to the quotient 425/17" and "The number of roses I received is two dozen," may not describe the same fact. Similarly, the statement that it is impossible to construct a heptagon with straight edge and compasses functions as a rule which prevents my saying with sense, "I drew a heptagon on the board using only straight edge and compasses."

Mathematical propositions are *preparations* for the use of language, says Wittgenstein, almost as definitions are.[17] Note that he does not say they *are* either definitions or statements about symbols; but they function as explicitly formulated linguistic rules in fact function. Euclid's proof that a line can be bisected by a certain method serves to provide a rule for the application of "equal lengths," and arithmetic serves to give rules for the use of number words, whereas no nonverbal empirical proposition ever functions analogously to a rule governing the use of language. If, then, the function of mathematical propositions is to govern usage it is no more surprising that they have an application than that a knife should cut. The connection between them and their application is like that between a rule for the use of an expression and the occurrence of that expression in various verbal contexts.[18] For example, "exactly one straight line can be drawn between any two points" functions prescriptively: in understanding it we know it makes sense to say that one physical straight line, but not to say that more than one, is drawn between two points. One tends to look upon the geometrical proposition as asserting a truth about ideal lines which somehow also holds of coarse drawn lines. But the application of a geometrical proposition in an experimental con-

---

[17] *Ibid.*
[18] *Ibid.*

text is to show, not what is true or false, but what makes sense or nonsense.[19] It obscures an important difference between empirical generalizations and their purported instances and mathematical propositions and the things to which they apply to say that both kinds of propositions show what is true, or false. Necessary propositions about ellipses and circles show that "I cut an elliptical cake in eight equal parts" does not make sense, whereas "I cut a round cake in eight equal parts" does. The relation of the necessary propositions about circles to the physical circle is like that between a rule and its application, not between a generalization about ideal circles and a rough approximation.[20]

This account squares with the fact that mathematical propositions do not get confirmed or discomfirmed by experience: one does not confirm or disconfirm by seeing, feeling, etc., a proposition whose use is to show what makes sense rather than to assert what is in fact true, or false. Further, there are certain puzzles about the connection of mathematics with experience which this account helps clarify. One is that mathematical propositions when applied seem to make predictions whereas, being necessary, they cannot. Suppose we say that two crystals which separately weigh three grams each must together weigh six grams, or that six two-foot boards must fit into a space twelve feet wide. If these are predictions, then they can be false. It could happen that six two-foot boards cover more or less then twelve feet, and that the two crystals weigh more or less than six grams. But "$6 \times 2 = 12$" and "$3 + 3 = 6$" are not predictions. They function as criteria for judging when the boards do not fit or the scales read five, that something *must* have happened.[21] "$6 \times 2 = 12$" does not even assure us that, unless the boards change, six two-foot boards will fit into twelve feet, for the criterion of change is their not fitting. If we say they *must* fit, and cite "$6 \times 2 = 12$" as evidence while at the same time refusing to accept any other method of showing the width of the boards, then, says Wittgenstein,[22] we are not saying anything about measurement. The burden of what we are saying is that what is called two feet is what goes six times into twelve. Were we making an experiment to determine whether six such boards will fit the space, the result would not be fixed in advance, and prediction of the result would be appropriate.

[19] Lectures, 1934–35.
[20] *Ibid.*
[21] *Ibid.*
[22] *Ibid.*

The difference between a mathematical calculation and an experiment is that in fixing the rules of the calculation one fixes the result.[23]

What Wittgenstein says about the nature of mathematical propositions also has a bearing on the further puzzle, namely, that we sometimes seem to discover a fact of experience which we then go on to prove must be so. It looks as if a matter of fact has an *a priori* demonstration. Pythagoras' theorem is a case in point. But the puzzle is gratuitous. According to Wittgenstein what happens is that an empirical proposition, which experience discovers, is converted into a proposition which no experience could make us give up. The proposition which is made independent of experience is suggested by experience. For example, the proposition, "A pentagram is a pentagon plus five triangles," is certainly suggested by experience, but it functions as a rule because we allow no method of construction to invalidate it. To see a pentagram as this composite is an experience, but as Wittgenstein says, there is no comparable process of seeing that a rule holds.[24]

Now what may appear as a surprising harmony between mathematical propositions and their application is merely due to our assigning the functions of a rule to those propositions which conform to fact, other things being equal.[25] Because the specific gravity of iron is 7.86 it would be natural and might be useful to say "No matter what experiment shows, the specific gravity of iron is 7:86." By this token an empirical proposition would be given a status and function like that of a rule of language. But the matter of fact does not compel acceptance of this change of status. The kind of fact which persuades us to accept it is that it is useful; and that it has applications is a mark of its usefulness. Thus, if we had a world in which counting the members of two groups having 2 members and 3 members, respectively, *never* totaled up to 5, some other proposition than "$2 + 3 = 5$" would have been adopted as necessary. If circumstances made it practical to calculate differently than we do, e.g., because things multiplied or disappeared regularly upon being counted, we should adapt arithmetic calculation to the circumstances.[26] If we got different results every time we counted the squares of a rectangle 17 by 25,

[23] Lectures, 1939.
[24] Lectures, 1934–35.
[25] *Ibid.*
[26] Lectures, 1939.

we should probably not say the calculation, 17 multiplied by 25, was a proof that $17 \times 25 = 425$. We might still call the calculation a piece of arithmetic just as "it is not the case for all a and b that $a \times b = b \times a$" is a part of group theory. But we should either have different arithmetics, or we should have an arithmetic in which certain multiplications had different results. For example, as our world is now, there is no phenomenon for which "$23 \times 18 = 800$" has any use. But if these numbers were constants relating to all natural phenomena, says Wittgenstein,[27] we could imagine an arithmetic in which this multiplication, among all others, had two results. To the objection that it is in the nature of 23 and 18 to give 414, he replies that in giving a rule of multiplication we do not give an infinity of applications of it. Behind the use of a rule is a habit of reacting in a certain way. Given the rules of multiplication we do in fact agree in getting the result 414; to do this is natural. And it is this fact which makes us say this result is correct. But we can imagine having always agreed in getting 800. And if this were in fact the case, would not 800 be the *correct* result? What would it be like to say that we always had made a mistake in thinking $23 \times 18 = 800$? Our agreement, not that such and such a result *is* the case, but *in getting* that result, is what determines what is called a correct calculation. Thus arithmetical propositions, though independent of experience, are in two ways dependent upon experience: in being suggested by experience, and in having their special function rest on common linguistic habits.[28]

In the remainder of this paper I should like to examine certain things which Wittgenstein appears to be saying concerning the connection between the necessity of mathematical propositions and their origin in and application to matter of fact. He seems to be saying that it is by an arrangement of ours that, for example, the arithmetic proposition $2 + 3 = 5$ tallies with the empirical result of counting two groups of 2 and 3 things, respectively, and that if circumstances were different, so that counting the members of such groups never resulted in 5, we should adapt counting to the circumstances and accordingly have a different arithmetic. That is, if circumstances were different, we should have a different necessary proposition. A proposition can be "suggested by experience and then made independent of experi-

27 Lectures, 1934–35.
28 *Ibid.*

ence." [29] Thus an expression which is given a special place in our language by being used to denote a necessary proposition is somehow connected with fact. I should like to examine both the hypothesis and the consequent of the statement, "If circumstances were different we should have a different necessary proposition"; for there is an unclarity about both.

How are we to understand the words "circumstances such that the members of two groups of 2 and 3 things, resp., never total up to 5"? One possible interpretation of these words, though I advance it with hesitation and without intending to imply it was Wittgenstein's, is the following: that the juxtaposition of two groups of objects, each of which we correctly counted as having 2 and 3 members, respectively, should result in the creation or destruction of, say, one individual, so that subsequent counting of the combined sets showed more, or fewer, than 5 objects. It is of course perfectly conceivable that something like this should happen. Wittgenstein has said [30] that if, for example, things disappeared regularly in certain ways it might be practical to count differently, that one might adapt one's technique of counting to the circumstances. Our arithmetic might then include the statements "$2 + 3 = 4$," "$1 + 1 = 1$," etc. That is, we should adopt these as expressing necessary propositions, so that in the exceptional case when our final count was 5, or 2, we should say not that these propositions were false, but that the objects must have reproduced, just as now we say, when one object put in juxtaposition with another results in one, "the objects must have coalesced," or "one must have vanished." That we should say this sort of thing is a sign that we are in the two comparable cases taking "$2 + 3 = 4$" and "$2 + 3 = 5$," respectively, to be necessary: we accept nothing as a falsification.

Throughout this paper it will be noted that I am interpreting Wittgenstein to be taking arithmetic to consist of what are commonly called necessary propositions, i.e., propositions that are both nonempirical and *true*. The problem is to explain the connection of such propositions with matter of fact, with their application. Professor G. E. Moore, relying on lectures of the period 1930–33, points out [31] that Wittgenstein characterized "$2 + 3 =$

[29] Lectures, 1939, 1934–35.
[30] Lectures, 1939.
[31] G. E. Moore, "Wittgenstein's Lectures in 1930–33," II, *Mind*, Vol. LXII (1954), no. 251, pp. 298–308.

5" and the like as "rules of grammar," "treating only of the symbolism," and as being neither true nor false. This Wittgenstein undeniably did; "2 + 3 = 5" was said to be a rule specifying a possible manner of speaking or writing (which one might adopt or not). But he also stated at various times that "2 + 3 = 5" is not a definition, nor *about* the symbolism in the way " '2 + 3' is interchangeable with '5' "is about the symbolism, although it is used analogously to the way we use such a rule. For example, it prevents our saying such things as "I augmented my savings of three hundred dollars by two hundred more but did not have a total of five hundred." Moore thought he might be using such an expression as "2 + 3 = 5" in two different ways, to express a necessary proposition and to state a rule for using words or sentences, and even that when he used it in the first way it expressed something neither true nor false.[32] But it is obviously self-contradictory to describe necessary propositions as being neither true nor false; and one can find support in Wittgenstein's lectures (e.g., in his comparison of necessary and empirical propositions) for his supposing them to be *true,* though of course not true in the sense in which an empirical proposition is true. It may be no consistent account is to be had. I am going to assume that though he holds that such expressions as "2 + 3 = 5" are *used* to proscribe certain linguistic combinations,[33] he also holds that they do nonetheless express necessary truths, and hence that in a world of coalescing objects what is expressed by "2 + 3 = 4" is a necessary truth.

Now in this hypothetical world is it proper to say we should have a different *arithmetic*—in particular, that *arithmetical* addition of 2 and 3 would yield a different result than 5? We can easily conceive of "2 + 3 = 4" expressing a necessary proposition (it is easy to conceive of the involved symbols being used differently), but if we use "2," "3," and "4" as we do now, surely the meaning of some other symbol or symbols must change. The natural assumption is that "+" can no longer mean arithmetic addition of two numbers, nor "=" arithmetic equality. "2 + 3" must denote not the arithmetic sum of two numbers, but the physical combination of two sets, and "=" must mean something like "yields." "2 + 3 = 4" would be a shorthand for "$(x) . 2x +$

[32] *Ibid.,* p. 302.
[33] Note that such might be their use without their translating into rules "treating of the symbolism."

$3x = 4x$," interpreted as "2 things physically conjoined with 3 yield 4." But it describes this world paradoxically to say its arithmetic is different from ours. "$2 + 3 = 4$" only appears shocking if taken to express an equality between a number and an arithmetic sum of numbers, as it does now. If "$+$" had a different usage in this hypothetical world, and if we also had our arithmetic for sums of numbers, the expressions "$2 + 3 = 4$" and "$2 + 3 = 5$" both could without inconsistency express necessities, although confusion might result. And if there were but one arithmetic, what we might call the arithmetic of invariant coalescence, it is misleading to say that we have made "4" and "$2 + 3$" interchangeable as though *in preference to* "5" and "$2 + 3$," since "$2 + 3$" has two entirely different uses when equated with "4" and with "5." The sentence "In different circumstances some other proposition would be necessary" suggests that were facts different we should arrange that the *addition* of 2 and 3 would necessarily yield a different result. This is unobjectionable if we reinterpret "addition." What Wittgenstein says is then little more than that in a different world we might have a different language. What is interesting about his statement is the claim that a difference in the language of arithmetic is influenced by the exigencies of making application of arithmetic to fact.

There is reason to suppose that what I have described as possibly illustrating a circumstance in which we might have a different arithmetic, and the account I have given of it, is not in fact what Wittgenstein had in mind. It will be worthwhile to consider an example which Professor Moore reports in Wittgenstein's 1930–33 lectures,[34] in order to note differences and to elaborate what Wittgenstein has said. In this example I think it is clear that "$+$" continues to be interpreted as arithmetic addition, however puzzling this may be; and this is the main respect in which it differs from the case I have discussed. I shall alter the numerals so as to make comparison easier. Wittgenstein supposes the following imaginable circumstances: (1) that one has the two experiences of counting first up to 2, then up to 3 in the case of two groups of apples, and (2) then a third and subsequent experience of (correctly) counting *all* the apples and finding only 4. This is imaginable because it is a mere matter of experience that one usually finds 5, inasmuch as apples do not vanish with-

[34] Moore, *op. cit.*, pp. 302–304.

out cause. "2 + 3 = 5" makes no prophecy as to what experience one *will* have upon counting *all* the apples. But if one were
to find 4 apples, the most natural comment to make would be that
one must have vanished. By this comment Wittgenstein says we
can only mean "If we keep to the arithmetical rule '2 + 3 = 5'
we have to say 'one must have vanished.' " In analyzing this
latter statement and what he takes to be its consequences Moore
augments the circumstances (1) and (2) above by two further
ones which he supposed Wittgenstein to have had in mind as the
situation in which one made the comment "one apple must have
vanished": (3) that one knows, because one has kept watch, that
nothing has happened to account in any normal way for there
being only 4, (4) that one does *not* know, by counting done by
oneself or by someone else, that one has counted out a total of 5,
so that if one said there were 5 apples in all, this would be a deduction from the fact that one had counted out 2 + 3 of them.
It is important to keep circumstance (3) in mind in appraising
the consequences Moore draws from his analysis of Wittgenstein's
claim that by "one must have vanished" we can only mean "if
we keep to the rule '2 + 3 = 5' we must say 'one must have
vanished.' "

Suppose one says there are 5 in all. Moore claims that Wittgenstein's reason for explicating "one must have vanished" as he
did, is that "there are 5," if asserted under circumstances (1)
and (4), means something different from what it would mean had
one discovered by counting, rather than deduced, that there are
5, namely, B: "One keeps to the rule '2 + 3 = 5' if one asserts
there are 5 apples and violates it if one asserts anything inconsistent with saying there are 5." [35] And this is the only thing
meant by "there are 5" in circumstances (1) and (4). Now one
can keep to the rule, i.e., speak correctly, without saying what is
true: it can be correct but not true to say there are 5. Moore
concludes that Wittgenstein's insistence on proposition B as the
only thing that we mean by "there are 5" is intended to prevent
the mistake of supposing we mean "If one sets out 2 + 3 apples
then *necessarily* one sets out 5." This proposition Moore takes
Wittgenstein to suppose is false, which is to say he supposes it
imaginable that one should count 2 + 3 apples and that a correct
count of the total *at that very time* should show only 4. Further,

Moore thinks that whether or not this interpretation of Wittgenstein is correct, it is quite certain that he held that "2 + 3 = 5" is never used in arithmetic to express a proposition from which it follows that if one counts out 2 + 3 apples one necessarily counts out 5.[36] In this case I should take it that neither "2 + 3 = 5" nor "If one has 2 + 3 apples one has 5 apples" is a necessary proposition.

Wittgenstein has at various times certainly said things which support the account Moore has given, e.g., that "2 + 3 = 5" is "purely arbitrary," which suggests that there is no necessity about "If one counts out 2 + 3 apples the total is 5." I am not now in a position to judge whether this account of what Wittgenstein held is in fact correct, although I heard the 1932–33 lectures in which there was some discussion of the example under consideration. Nor for that matter am I sure that I am correctly reporting what he said in the lectures I heard in 1934–35 and in later lectures to which I have access at second hand. If Wittgenstein did commit himself to holding it to be imaginable that one should count out 2 + 3 apples and not at the same time have a total of 5, I think, with Moore, that he was surely mistaken. If he did, then "If one counts out 2 + 3 apples one has a total of 5" would be an empirical proposition. But I wish to make plain that I have not supposed him to imply this and my criticism will not presuppose thinking he does.

For one thing (*a*) when Wittgenstein said that "2 + 3 = 5" functions analogously to a rule of language, i.e., so that "I counted out 2 + 3 apples but did not at that time have a total of 5" does not make sense, I took it that what does not make sense could not express an imaginable state of affairs. Further, the reason for its not expressing an imaginable state of affairs is that the truth of "the total is not 5 apples" is inconsistent with the truth of "I counted out 2 + 3." That is, if I did count out 2 + 3 apples it necessarily is *true* that I counted 5. It is not merely that I must engage in this manner of speaking (and say there are 5) if I am to speak in accordance with a rule. This certainly seems to me to be correct, although I am not at all sure but that Wittgenstein held what Moore reports.

For another thing, (*b*) what makes convincing Moore's concluding that Wittgenstein held to be imaginable a logically in-

[36] *Ibid.*, pp. 307–308.

conceivable state of affairs is circumstance (3) of the example. (3) is to the effect that it is *known,* because one has kept watch, that nothing has happened to account in any normal way for there being only 4 apples, e.g., it is known that none has been removed, or has flown away. Only if Moore means that knowing this implies that *none has vanished* could it be inferred that one could set out 2 + 3 apples which total up to 4. But if we *know* that none has vanished, should we say, on counting 4, "one must have vanished"? I doubt that Wittgenstein intended this circumstance to figure in the example he was considering; rather, it seems to me that he supposed not that one knew an apple had *not* vanished, but that one did *not* know that it had, although it in fact had, by some process quicker than sense observation could detect. When Moore says he can imagine that one really has vanished, even under circumstance (3),[37] it appears that he also is holding not that one knows none has vanished but that one merely knows none has vanished *in any normal way,* though one has in fact done so. But then it could not be inferred from Wittgenstein's example that he held that one could set out 2 + 3 apples and have *at that time* 4. Rather, if one set out 2 + 3 apples and one vanished, one would have 4. And then we should have our present arithmetic—unless "2 apples + 3 apples = 4 apples" were interpreted as a statement about physical combination.

However, Wittgenstein made a comment on the example, according to my lecture notes of 1932–33, which might well have led Moore to suppose that Wittgenstein is committed to holding it to be imaginable that one should set out 2 + 3 apples and have a total of 4. The comment was that in circumstances (1) and (2) we can *either* say "one must have vanished" or we can *"change the rules."* [38] That is, we can choose either to say "I set out 5 apples" (and thereby speak in accordance with the present rule "2 + 3 = 5") or to adopt the rule "2 + 3 = 4"—and accordingly speak correctly in saying "I set out 4." Moore took it that since we can speak correctly without saying what is true, it could conceivably be false that one set out 5 apples when one set out 2 + 3. Wittgenstein's insistence that "there are 5" only means "If the rule '2 + 3 = 5' is adhered to one must say one put 5," Moore

[37] *Ibid.,* p. 309.
[38] Here is a clear case of Wittgenstein's characterization of "2 + 3 = 5," etc., as rules. I shall use his language in expounding what he said.

took to indicate that a proposition commonly held to be true was false, namely, "If one sets out 2 + 3 apples *necessarily* one sets out 5." And if this is false it would seem that one could set out 2 + 3 apples and not have a total of 5.

I have placed a different construction on what Wittgenstein said. Because he held that as language is used "I set out 2 + 3 apples but did not have a total of 5" does not make sense, I am supposing (as Moore does not) that he held that "2 + 3 = 5" is used in arithmetic to express a proposition from which it follows that if one set out 2 + 3 apples one necessarily sets out 5, that is, that if "2 + 3 = 5" is a necessary proposition so is "If I set out 2 + 3 apples I have a total of 5." And the latter *is* necessary because "2 + 3 = 5" expresses a necessity, as we use language now. When Wittgenstein says that under circumstances (1) and (2) one can either say "one must have vanished" or change the rules, I take him to be saying that either we can keep to our present arithmetic, whence "If I set out 2 + 3 apples I have 5" would be necessary, or we can have a different arithmetic, whence, for example, "If I set out 2 + 3 apples I have 4" would be necessary. Thus with present arithmetic "I counted out 2 + 3 but did not have a total of 5" would express a self-contradiction, and *with a different arithmetic* it would be a redundancy expressing a possible state of affairs. But what is expressed would be contingent on which arithmetic we chose. Now it is rather different to think (as I believe Moore did) that Wittgenstein is committed to holding it to be possible that one should set out 2 + 3 apples and have only 4 and to think him committed to holding that it would be possible *if* our arithmetic were different. It must be admitted, however, that the one position seems no whit better than the other. The example seems rather clearly to use "2," "3," "4," "+," and "=" precisely as we do now: the numerals to stand for the numbers we correlate with a couple, a trio, and a quartet, "+" to mean addition (not physical conjunction, as in my first interpretation), and "=" to mean "equals." But if this is their use it is difficult to know what could possibly be meant by saying "2 + 3 = 4" is necessary, or by saying that if our arithmetic were different (e.g., if this proposition were necessary) then it would be necessary that if I set out 2 + 3 apples I should have a total of 4.

The unclarity about this matter makes it unclear what is meant by saying that depending on the circumstances different propositions would be necessary. I should like now to examine this claim together with the view Wittgenstein apparently held that it is a matter of choice whether or not "2 + 3 = 4" expresses something necessary (whether we have "a different arithmetic"). According to Wittgenstein *we adopt* necessary propositions, and which ones we adopt is "suggested by experience." Present circumstances are such that we deduce "I set out 5 apples" from "I set out 2 + 3"; but we could choose to deduce " I set out 4 apples" instead. The fact that the arithmetic in use tallies with the result of counting is presumably explained by our choice being suggested by experience. Facts do not compel the choice, but they suggest it. Other things being equal, we take as necessary the proposition conforming to fact.[39] For example, were we to say "The specific gravity of iron is 7.86, no matter what experiment shows," we should thereby make independent of experience a proposition which experience suggests. Had we a different arithmetic, presumably the difference would be explained by what is suggested by experience: in our example, by the experience of always finding 4 apples when one counts out a couple and a trio.

But now *what* is suggested by experience? That it would be useful to adopt *these propositions* as necessary? *These* propositions are first of all factual truths, empirical propositions. Hence *they* cannot be made independent of experience, i.e., *these* propositions cannot be necessary. One and the same proposition cannot depend for its truth or falsity on matter of fact and also have its truth value quite independent of fact.

Suppose one maintains instead that because the proposition expressed by the sentence "2 + 3 = 4" is true as a matter of fact, this suggests making the *sentence* express something which no fact will falsify—something Wittgenstein possibly meant. The sentence, "2 + 3 = 4," which is first understood as expressing a generalization about sets of things in juxtaposition or about the number one arrives at by counting a couple and a trio, is made to express something to which the behavior of sets of things or the experience one has upon counting the total group comprised of 2 + 3 objects is irrelevant. It is made to do this by being made to serve an entirely different purpose—to function as a rule for the use of the expressions "2 + 3" and "4." What once served

[39] Lectures, 1934-35.

to express a generalization which a different world could confute comes to serve as a guide in the conduct of language, proscribing such statements as "I put 3 apples into a bowl containing 2, but there were in all more than 4." The proscription, of course, is not of a falsity but of a use of language—of the use of "2 + 3 but not 4" to characterize any set of objects. What experience "suggests" is then the *choice* of language—because such a choice would be useful.

Does this description of the change in status of the sentence "2 + 3 = 4" explain the harmony between the arithmetic proposition and the fact that 4 is the result got by counting a couple and a trio? Does it explain the connection of the necessary proposition with its application? The difficulty I find is in specifying any connection between the sentence expressing a necessity and the empirical proposition originally expressed in the same words. When the truth of the proposition "2 + 3 = 4" was verified by experience, the expression "2 + 3 but not 4" at that stage had a use, whereas at the stage where the sentence is taken to express what is necessary this same expression is thereby denied a use. And this is to say that "2 + 3" has different uses, i.e., different meanings, at the two stages. "2 + 3" means something in the one case which is inconsistent with "not 4," and in the other case not. If the sentence "2 + 3 = 4" has different meanings at the two stages, what connection is there between the sentence for the necessary proposition and the observed fact that when a couple and a trio are counted the result is found to be 4 —i.e., with the fact which verifies the empirical proposition which the sentence no longer expresses?

Wittgenstein's Philosophy of Logic

BY JOSEPH L. COWAN

> The people said, "The earth rests on
> the back of an elephant which rests
> on the back of a giant tortoise which
> rests on the face of a limitless sea."
> Yajnavalkya said, "The earth rests on
> nothing." The people said, "Your an-
> swer is so absurd as to be unintelligible,
> O Yajnavalkya, while ours is so obvi-
> ous as to be inescapable." And Yajna-
> valkya answered, "Your posterity will
> use *your* words in agreeing with me."
>
> —UPANISHADIC APOCRYPHA

LARGE AS THE NAME AND FAME of Ludwig Wittgenstein have
become in our day, the radical character and great power of Wittgenstein's criticism of the foundations of logic seem still inadequately appreciated. Wittgenstein has actually done for (or to)
deduction much the same sort of job Hume did with induction.
In both cases the problem is one of really fundamental philosophical importance. Both analyses result in conclusions so destructive as to seem completely unacceptable. But in neither
case is it easy to see how these conclusions can be avoided. By
this last remark I do not mean to deny, of course, that every
philosopher can produce a refutation satisfactory to himself. I am
suggesting only that it may well turn out to be the case with
Wittgenstein, as it most certainly is with Hume, that no one
seems to be capable of producing a refutation satisfactory to
anyone else.

Nor do I mean to deny that there are many who do appreciate
the force of Wittgenstein's work—or almost do, at any rate.

Wittgenstein's books have not fallen deadborn from the press. Michael Dummett's excellent discussion of Wittgenstein's philosophy of mathematics is a recent example of an appreciation of the difficulty both of accepting Wittgenstein and of finding any suitable alternative.[1] Yet it would seem that many—even of those who, like Dummett, have an excellent insight into Wittgenstein's position—are still not aware of the full stickiness of the situation.

In the paper referred to, for example, Dummett raised certain objections to Wittgenstein's conclusions. These seem to me to be good objections, the sort an informed and thoughtful person does have when confronted with Wittgenstein's philosophy of logic and mathematics. Yet I think answers even to objections such as these can be given from within the Wittgensteinian framework.

What I shall do in this paper, then, is simply object to some of these objections to Wittgenstein. In the process of so doing I shall recapitulate in summary fashion a few of the rather telling Wittgensteinian arguments which seem to have had even on Dummett less impact than they should and which have been for the most part simply ignored by those with a less firm grasp of the situation than his.

My first difference with Dummett is an apparently slight one, seemingly over nothing more than a choice of terminology. But the choice may have consequences. Dummett speaks of Wittgenstein's holding a form of conventionalism in logico-mathematical theory, indeed, a "full-blooded conventionalism." [2] But the issue of conventionalism as seen by a man like Carnap is as follows: "Are the rules on which logical deduction is to be based to be chosen at will and, hence, to be judged with respect to convenience but not to correctness?" [3] And if one is to be classified as a conventionalist by his affirmative answer to such a question as this (or, as with Carnap, his qualified affirmative) then Wittgenstein cannot be so classified. For Wittgenstein is rejecting (or ignoring) this whole question.

Wittgenstein's position, to put it with impossible brevity, is that each of our judgments is independent. A logical or mathematical proposition such as $2 + 2 = 4$ is true not because of

---

[1] Michael Dummett, "Wittgenstein's Philosophy of Mathematics," *Philosophical Review*, Vol. LXVIII (1959), pp. 324–348.
[2] *Ibid.*, p. 000.
[3] Rudolf Carnap, "Foundations of Logic and Mathematics," *International Encyclopedia of Unified Science* (Chicago, 1939), Vol. I, No. 3, pp. 26–27.

prior "meanings" or "rules," conventional or otherwise, much less some necessary correspondence with reality or whatever. Such a proposition is true simply because and in so far as we chose to regard it as true. "True" and "false" are words *we* use, and we always use the former in these cases and apply the latter only elsewhere. Indeed, our use of these propositions is so closely tied to our use of "true" and "false" that their being true is very much like the standard meter's being a meter long.

Dummett realizes all this. He is perfectly well aware that Wittgenstein in asserting the complete independence of each individual judgment is asserting our independence of any rules at all, whether of inference or of meaning, whether conventional or otherwise. But he does not seem quite to realize how radical is Wittgenstein's conception of the source of that independence.

What Wittgenstein is asserting is that (in a sense) *there is no such thing as a rule*. There is no such thing as (or state or condition of) understanding a rule, or knowing a rule, or meaning a rule. There is no such thing as behavior guided by, or even according to, a rule. There is none of these things in spite of the fact that there are many perfectly good and correct uses of the expressions "rule," "understanding a rule," "being guided by a rule," and so on.

Wittgenstein is arguing that what is going on here is just exactly the process which occasions so many other, perhaps most, philosophical confusions, exactly the process which the greater portion of *Philosophical Investigations* is designed to combat: we have significant words—"rule," "understanding," "knowledge," "meaning," "intention," and so on. So we assume, usually without quite realizing we are doing so, some thing (or state or condition) which they signify. How, we ask ourselves, can they be significant if they do not signify anything? And this is a question which seems difficult to answer—until we look at the ways the words in question are actually used.

Consider again an example like one of Wittgenstein's: "add two each time" or "$a_n = a_{n-1} + 2$." [4] Now we might be watching someone writing down a series of numerals, and I might ask for the rule involved, and you might give me in reply either of these two sets of signs, and I might be satisfied. Yet we must admit that the sign is not (is not identical with) the rule. For one thing,

[4] Wittgenstein, *Philosophical Investigations*, pt. 1, §§185–190; see also §§143–155.

we have two different signs (we could have many more) but only one rule. Or the same marks might denote some very different rule in another language, or might even have been natural phenomena of some kind, signifying nothing.

But perhaps all this is too obvious. Of course the rule is not the signs, but their meaning. And what is meaning?

Again, consider how we *teach* the meaning of the signs, that is, according to our present hypothesis, the rule. We write bits of the series for the learner, have him try, rebuke and congratulate, and so on. After he has done it correctly (as it seems to us he should have) for awhile, we will say, "Now he knows (understands, can follow) the rule."

But if when he gets to 100, he goes on, "104, 108, 112, . . . ," we may very well say, "So he didn't know the rule after all." And we should be saying this without denying any of the data on which we based our previous assertion that he did know the rule. Thus his previous behavior cannot have been identical with his understanding the meaning of the sign or, what we have postulated as equivalent, the rule.

But again, perhaps this too is too obvious. Of course behavior is not understanding. Behavior is something which is (or may be) first the source and then the result of understanding.

Is understanding something like grooves in the brain, then (or patterns of electrical impulses, to use a more current phrase)? Or is it some sort of image or feeling or the like? It can be neither, since we will want to say that someone understands the rule if he keeps on *doing* the series correctly in spite of having the wrong grooves, images, feelings, or whatnot.[5]

Let us be more actual. There are cases where we would say, "I thought I knew how to go on, but I was wrong" (behavior criterion over feeling). And there are other cases where we would say, "I did know how to go on, but I forgot" (feeling criterion over behavior). Thus there are many different criteria the application of which might lead us to say, "He understands" or "I understand." But there is no one criterion which always takes precedence. There is nothing (no state, behavior, and so forth) which is identical with (essential to) understanding the meaning of the signs, the rule.

It is important to note here that what is involved is *not* an ambiguity in our terms. Wittgenstein is sometimes accused of hav-

[5] See also *ibid.*, §199.

ing done nothing more than note that the same word is sometimes used in different ways—which of course everyone always knew. We must, as a matter of fact, be using our terms in the *same* way in the different cases considered above. For when, for example, we say, "I understand" on the basis of a feeling, and then are unable actually to perform in spite of a lack of excuses, we do not say, "Yes, I understand (in one sense), but no, I don't understand (in another sense)." We say, "I was wrong. I did not understand."

This might also be a good point to express astonishment at another fundamental misunderstanding of Wittgenstein's position. Wittgenstein and those who agree with him in these matters are sometimes said to be advocating some sort of physicalism, to be denying the existence of psychic events, and to be reducing understanding, meaning, and so on to behavior.[6] Yet of course Wittgenstein does not want to deny mental processes, or feelings, or sensations, or the like. And it is exactly his point that understanding and so on *cannot* be reduced to behavior or anything else.

We have a word—for example, "understanding." There are many things which may lead us to use the word—bits of behavior, feelings, and so forth. But understanding is *reducible to none* of these. None of them *is* understanding. For we are always prepared to withdraw the term on the basis of *other* bits of behavior, feelings, and so forth, without denying that the original behavior or feeling was exactly the behavior or feeling we originally thought it to be. ("Yes, he *did* say '8, 10, 12,' but it was just by chance." Or "Yes, he said it, but he turned out to have been following a *different* rule.")[7]

The objector is still unsatisfied. But why? Perhaps he wants to say that we would be surprised if our pupil went on, "104, 108, . . . ," and that we would not if he wrote instead, "102, 104, , , ," The latter, the objection might continue, is what *we* would have done. And this is because we *meant* "102, 104, . . . ," when we said, "Add two each time."

But again, what do these strange statements mean? Did we think of these numbers? Did we have any particular thought or feeling or do anything that *is* meaning them? Must not anything in our heads at that moment be no better than *another* sign—which could mean anything? Thus presumably our statements as to our

[6] See, for example, Clyde Laurence Hardin, "Wittgenstein on Private Languages," *Journal of Philosophy*, Vol. LVI (1959), p. 519.
[7] See again especially Wittgenstein, *op. cit.*, pt. 1, §§153–155.

surprise or our potential actions are very much like our statement that we would jump into the river to save someone if he fell in. We might, but then again we might not. And the superstition that through the act of meaning we can cross our bridges before we come to them is again revealed as a superstition, and double so. There is no act of meaning, and we cannot cross our bridges before we come to them (and sometimes not even when we *do* come to them).[8] "The prophecy does *not* run, that a man will get this result when he follows this rule in making a transformation—but that he will get this result, when we *say* he is following the rule." [9]

Turning now to a more specific consideration of some of Dummett's objections we can see how they have drifted somewhat from the mark. One objection Dummett mentions is that Wittgenstein's criticisms do not apply where a strict formalization of our principles of inference has been made.[10] But now we can see that this completely begs the question. Formalization of what? This objection is based on the assumption of exactly what Wittgenstein is denying— that there is something there, the rule, and that it is just a matter of describing it accurately enough. Yet any sign is still just a sign and never the rule itself. There is no rule.

But this cannot be so, the objection continues. We could even devise a machine which could form from an Arabic numeral the successor of its successor.[11] Then the device could mechanically and automatically crank out our series indefinitely. Surely there must be a rule built into such a machine. How can we say there is no rule when we here have one solidified in metal and glass?

The answer to this objection is that we should undoubtedly say that the machine was following our rule—unless, of course, we said it was not. An actual machine, that is, may come up with results we can agree to, or it may not. If it does not, we will probably say it is out of order and try to adjust it until it does. We may succeed and we may not. Even success, however, may be no more than temporary. Thus the machine, too, is only another sign. It is not that the human being possesses a freedom the machine lacks, but that the machine does not lack a freedom the human possesses. The idea that these gears should *compel* the machine to do such and such is

[8] *Ibid.*, §§187–188; also *The Blue and Brown Books* (London: Oxford, 1958), p. 143.
[9] Wittgenstein, *Remarks on the Foundations of Mathematics*, ed. by G. H. von Wright, R. Rhees, and G. E. M. Anscombe; trans. by G. E. M. Anscombe (London: Oxford, 1956), pt. II, §66.
[10] Dummett, *op. cit.*, p. 330.
[11] *Ibid.*, p. 331.

just as *ideal,* and ignores to as great an extent what may actually happen, as the idea that the formula should compel the man.[12]

But surely, the objection might continue, the machine will produce its correct results unless some specific thing goes wrong, a rod bends or melts, or some such thing? Surely the machine which goes wrong is not the *same* machine. And so we could say that the rule *was* built into our machine.

We *might* say something like this, even though we are aware that even with fairly simple machines we sometimes cannot find anything in particular wrong when they give us trouble. Sometimes not even when we manage to get them going right again are we able to see what it was that was amiss and was corrected—if anything. I shall return to this point in another context. Here, however, it seems better to point out that even were we to admit that some definite thing must have gone wrong, we should still not have resolved the difficulty. For if the original gears and wires which later went wrong were a rule, what rule was it? They were not, as it turned out, a rule for actually *producing* the desired results. We might just as well say that they were a rule for producing molten gears or whatever else it was that actually happened. A rule which turns out to be a rule for whatever happens to happen is hardly much of a rule. Presumably the only reason for calling our gears a rule for producing the series is that this is what we intended the machine to do. Thus we are thrown back on our own devices after all. Or, to put it more accurately, our own devices are thrown back on us. The conception of a machine is indeed related to that of a rule, but seems not to be more solidly based for purposes of explanation. In Platonic terms the machine, like the circle, is a creature of the ideal world. It may receive more or less partial and temporary embodiment. But its primary home is not, as we tend to suppose, the brute realm of necessity and chance.

Dummett considers in a different context the point raised above, the question of whether when we say, "Something has gone wrong," some definite thing has gone wrong.[13] His example is designed to show that we cannot simply accept or reject at will "$5 + 7 = 12$," since this is related to other things such as counting. Dummett argues as follows: If a man counted (as we do) five boys and seven girls and thirteen children, then he has made some definite mistake

---

[12] Wittgenstein, *Foundations,* pt. I, §122.
[13] Dummett, *op. cit.,* pp. 333 ff.

which he would have recognized as such had he noticed it—even though he does not know that $5 + 7 = 12$.

But how can we be so sure that he has made some definite mistake? Is this an inductive argument? Have we seen so many people counting five boys and seven girls and thirteen children and always finding their mistake? Even if we had so observed, would this make another outcome impossible? There would seem to be no way we could be so sure of a mistake as we are unless we had simply decided to count the assertion as true come what may, since, after all, $5 + 7 = 12$.

Yet, Dummett's objection continues, if we are to say (correctly) that a mistake has been made, then the disjunction of possible mistakes must be true (he counted one boy twice, or . . .). But if such a disjunction is true, then one of its disjuncts must be true. And if a statement is true, there must be something which, if we knew it, we would regard as criterion of that truth. God must know which of the disjuncts is true, one might say.

But where is God going to get his data? Uses of the words "true" and "mistake" are surely even less laid up either in our heads or in heaven then uses of "$a_n = a_{n-1} + 2$." Dummett is still laboring under the assumption that there *are* rules, so that if we grant such and such, something else *must* (objectively and independently of us) *follow*. He still tends to feel that there *are* such entities as meanings we give terms, and that these are sufficiently corporeal, in fact, to weigh down and so control the future coursings of the terms in question. Dummett is, in short, still using in attacking the Wittgensteinian position exactly the assumptions questioned by Wittgenstein.[14]

Furthermore, there seems to be no particular reason why the world could not work in a way Dummett says it cannot. Suppose, for example, that things happened *as though* we always skipped the numeral "12" when counting children (somewhat as hotels and apartment houses do not have thirteenth floors). I am not saying that we *actually* skipped, and in fact part of the supposition is that there be no direct evidence that we do: we never catch ourselves or others, and so on. Now none of this seems impossible. In fact one can almost see it unfolding before one's very eyes.

When we counted five boys and seven girls we would *always* (except when we did not count the total at all or when we made

14 *Ibid.*, p. 340.

a mistake) count thirteen children. And we would *never* be able to find any particular mistake. There would be other peculiar consequences, of course. When we counted thirteen boys and thirteen girls, we would count only twenty-five children. Our thirteen children could divide into six couples and dance happily away without any wallflower being left over. We could give twelve cookies to thirteen little boys without generating quite such intense conflict as would now obtain. And so on.

So long as the problem was confined to children it would presumably remain within the province of students of child behavior, and, these being rather unimaginative people in the main, no striking scientific results would ensue. We nontechnicians already realize that children just do behave oddly and are notorious for not obeying the rules. And we would have to help us along such useful phrases as "Boys will be boys." "This younger generation!" "Children aren't what they used to be in my day," and the like.

If the phenomenon were more general, on the other hand, if it happened with other things than children, the physicists might get into the game. They might, indeed, be provided with years of joyous employment in discovering the laws of combinatory-appearance-disappearance. Then, with these laws fairly comprehensively formulated, the next step, especially were the phenomenon quite widespread, would presumably be for some Einstein to come along with the suggestion that we modify our mathematics. His principle of relativity tells him that we can, it is true, explain our observations by *ad hoc* laws about the appearance and disappearance of objects. But we can get the same results in a much simpler and therefore aesthetically more satisfactory manner simply by abandoning the numeral 12 and shifting those which follow it down one place. Then our calculations would agree with our observations, and we would have no appearances and disappearances to explain. This suggestion would inevitably be greeted with shocked indignation. Some philosophers would demonstrate its utterly paradoxical character. Other philosophers would demonstrate the utterly paradoxical character of every other possibility. Scientists would balk at the complexity of the newfangled mathematics involved and be surprised that their students found the doctrine easier to handle than they. But it would prevail in the end.[15]

[15] Since the effect was not postulated as universal, the use in microphysics of whatever statistics work best for the problem at hand—Bose-Einstein *versus* Fermi-Dirac, for example—is perhaps an even better analogy than relativity. Compare also "particles vanishing backward in time" and so on.

One of Dummett's objections which is difficult to answer directly is to the effect that Wittgenstein's conception is especially hard to swallow when looking at a particular actual proof.[16] The best reply to this which I can offer is to ask the reader to look not at one but at several proofs. Is the same thing going on in one's perusal of each? Is the same thing going on as one moves to different points in the same proof, or over the same point at different times? Here one is puzzled, looks up the rules again, studies the step over in comparison with the formulation of the rule and with other exemplifications of the rule, and suddenly sees with a start how it works. Or one goes through a similar process but without the start, the acceptance dawning gradually this time. Or one moves along routinely, without doubt or its release. Does one always have a feeling of familiarity unless there is a feeling of unfamiliarity? Do we want to say that we feel the "because" here? Is there *a* feeling of being compelled by the rule? It is true that we do not think of any alternative, but what does this show? Look at all the monstrosities which have been accepted as conclusive proofs, or still are. Those fooled by them saw no alternative, but we can. Perhaps tomorrow we shall find an alternative where we now find none. Perhaps the next man to come along will find one.

These considerations slide into the last of the Dummett objections which I should like to examine. That objection lies simply in pointing out that if Wittgenstein were right, human communication would be in constant danger of breaking down. If there were no such things as rules, more or less objective entities which we more or less objectively follow, we would be in as great danger of simply wandering away in all directions as trains without tracks. Without meanings substantial enough for us to share the same one with one another, how could communication be possible at all? [17]

Perhaps the best approach to this sort of objection would be just that taken above. One could point out that there are no such things as communication, agreement, and so on, to be explained. Here again we have families of situations any two members of which may actually be entirely different from one another. Presumably there are reasons why we apply the words "communication" and "agreement." But presumably these reasons are different in different cases. And in any case reasons must come to an end. Then we shall

16 Dummett, *op. cit.*, p. 333.
17 *Ibid.*, p. 337.

simply act. Thus the desire for *an* explanation must inevitably be a fruitless one.

But if this approach has not allayed objections up to this point, it may well fail again here. So perhaps a somewhat different approach, granting the objector some of his rather dubious assumptions, should now be tried. Another answer, then, might simply be to point out that communication very often does break down. But such a reply is not enough. It is also true that communication sometimes does not break down.

A third approach might be to suggest that agreement may have other sources. The argument that there must be rules since there is agreement strikes one as being rather like the argument that there must be a God since mankind could scarcely have been deposited just by chance on the only planet in the whole solar system capable of sustaining human life. Wittgenstein points out that if mathematicians did disagree we would not have what we call "mathematics." One could put it even more strongly. Mathematicians *cannot* disagree very strenuously since people who do disagree very strenuously are not called "mathematicians."

This argument is still not good enough, however. It might seem from these considerations that we were selecting the ones with corresponding grooves in their brains. And as we have seen, Wittgenstein's doctrine is more radical than this. Thus a final answer to Dummett in this matter must be simply to say that he is entirely correct. This is exactly what Wittgenstein is driving at. There is no foundation for human communication. Disagreement is possible at any point. This is what Wittgenstein presumably means when he says that if language is to be a means of communication there must be agreement not only in definitions but in judgments. In other words, only agreement can guarantee agreement.[18] There is no foundation for this agreement. The judgment hangs in the air. The danger is that we should think otherwise and mislead ourselves by trying to give a justification, a foundation, instead of simply saying, "That's how we do it, that's how it is." It would not really supply any more support for, or explanation of, communication's not breaking down to say that a rule does it than it would to say that a god does. We should merely be deceiving ourselves in either case.[19]

It is true that we agree—sometimes—with each other and with

---

[18] Wittgenstein, *Philosophical Investigations*, pt. I, §§241–242.
[19] See, for example, *ibid.*, §§482–485; and *Foundations*, pt. II, §74.

our machines. The term "rule" has useful functions as things happen. Most philosophers of logic and mathematics begin with this agreement and move on from there. Thus Wittgenstein's philosophy of logic and mathematics is in a sense simply irrelevant both to logic and mathematics and to most philosophizing about them. For Wittgenstein is not concerned either to deny or to go on from the agreement from which the others start, but to look behind it, below it, and to show that it is based on, explained by, nothing more fundamental.

This, I may conclude—or almost conclude—is another and even more important reason for not calling Wittgenstein's philosophy of logic a brand of conventionalism and thus making it seem in opposition to the work of those such as Carnap. In so far as a man like Carnap is simply assuming our ability to agree and going on from there—doing what he calls "philosophy" but what Wittgenstein would probably call "mathematics"—there is no conflict between the two. They are doing very different sorts of jobs. This is undoubtedly one of the reasons many have felt Wittgenstein's work in philosophy of logic and mathematics to be unfruitful. It is simply not the sort of thing they call "philosophy of logic and mathematics." A conflict could arise only if we regarded one such as Carnap as having shown us some kind of ground or foundation for logic where Wittgenstein seems to have shown that there is and can be none.

Before I close, however, a final caveat must be entered about the use of such phrases as "communication is in constant danger of breaking down" to describe our situation. In the sense explained such phrases are perfectly all right. In other senses they are less all right.

Suppose we were on a small island and our sole communication with the mainland was by means of a telephone wire strung on buoys to the shore. Now someone asks us why the wire does not break. What answer could we really give except that it might, of course, but in general stout copper wire like this under conditions like these just does not. There are many things we do not understand about molecules and all that, but even if we knew them all would we not have to say at some point, "Well, molecules just *are* that way!"? With no better answer than this, no explanation of why everything happens just as it does, without a reason or ground for it *all,* our inquirer might choose to say, "Communication is in constant danger of breaking down." But we would usually reserve that phrase for special occasions, storms and such, when unusual things were happening, and some situation of a sort in which wire does frequently break was occurring or seemed imminent. And it seems useful to save some phrases to mark such eventualities.[20]

It is not that we always feel the necessity of a ground or support for a phenomenon. But we usually do so when we think we have one. In those cases habit has made it seem necessary. Show such a supposed support to be no support whatsoever, and we will cast about desperately for another. But this tendency should not affect our judgment as to whether or not a support is really necessary. For habit can also accustom us to doing quite well without any such grounds at all.

[20] These remarks also apply, of course, to the problem—or, better, problems—of induction.

Wittgenstein and Logical Laws*

BY ARNOLD LEVISON

I

THE NOTES AND WRITINGS posthumously published as *Remarks on the Foundations of Mathematics* [1] have been subjected to a variety of interpretations and accusations in the short time that they have been before the general public. Wittgenstein has been represented in these comments as urging upon us the theory that logical laws and rules of inference have a merely "normative" character;[2] as showing that "there is no such thing as a rule" and "no foundation for human communication";[3] and as expressing a "full-blooded conventionalism" or the view that "the logical necessity of any statement is always the *direct* expression of a linguistic convention." [4] While these interpretations differ in detail, they seem to agree in the consequence that Wittgenstein's aim or the result of his teaching (so far as that was consistent) was to overthrow the usual account according to which the logical necessity of a statement is not merely a matter of our own devising. To explain: the concept of logical necessity may be held to arise from reflecting on what we mean when we say that one statement can be "derived"

[1] L. Wittgenstein, *Remarks on the Foundations of Mathematics*, ed. by G. H. von Wright, R. Rhees, and G. E. M. Anscombe; trans. by G. E. M. Anscombe (London: Oxford, 1956); hereafter referred to as *RFM*. All references are by paragraph number to Part I. Thus "§112" means "*RFM, I, §112*."
[2] Edward J. Nell, "The Hardness of the Logical 'Must,'" *Analysis*, January, 1961.
[3] Joseph L. Cowan, "Wittgenstein's Philosophy of Logic" [included in this volume].
[4] Michael Dummett, "Wittgenstein's Philosophy of Mathematics," *Philosophical Review*, Vol. LXVIII (1959), pp. 324–348. [This article is discussed by Mr. Cowan in this volume.]

* This article is a revision and synthesis of two papers on this subject which originally appeared in *The Philosophical Quarterly*, Vol. 14, No. 57, pp. 345–355, and *Inquiry*, Vol. 7, 1964, pp. 367–373. I am grateful to the editors of these journals for permission to reprint this material and to Mr. Fann, editor of the present book, for providing me with the opportunity to make these alterations.

from another statement or set of statements such as a set of postulates or definitions. While these postulates and definitions may be arbitrarily stipulated and thus be a matter of choice or convention, what they *imply* is a question that cannot be determined in the same way, so that the derivability of a statement from the postulates and definitions is a matter which must be independent of any "normative" or "conventional" considerations.[5] That is, the principles which regulate the derivability of a statement are not modified or affected by our choice of initial postulates or definitions—in other words, by our choice of what "game" we wish to play in a given instance. These principles, then, are not "rules of a game" but "rules of the rules of a game"; they lay down the conditions for playing any game whatsoever. It is these principles which are the logical laws and rules of inference, and given any statement, the statement of what that statement implies is a "necessary" statement in the sense that its truth value depends on nothing but those logical principles which remain unmodified however frequently we modify or change our initial statement.

Now according to the interpretations of Wittgenstein's comments indicated above, these comments have the effect of reducing logical principles to the same sort of status as that which is usually accorded to postulates and definitions. But it seems implausible to suggest that Wittgenstein wished to deny the validity of the distinction between the grounds for making a statement and the grounds for making a statement as to what that statement implies. For this distinction, as far as it goes, is perfectly clear and does not give rise to any problems of a philosophical nature. If we say, for example, that the rules of chess lay down the conditions which must be accepted in order to play that game, then we do not mean that someone cannot refuse to accept those rules and still behave rationally, nor even that he cannot modify them and still have a game which, if he pleases, he can call "chess." But the rules of inference, by contrast, appear to lay down conditions which must be accepted in order to play any game at all, however Pickwickian its concep-

---

[5] See W. V. O. Quine, "Truth by Convention," in *Philosophical Essays for A. N. Whitehead* (New York: Longmans, Green & Co., 1936). Reprinted in Feigl, H., and Sellars, W., *Readings in Philosophical Analysis* (New York: Appleton-Century-Crofts, 1949), p. 273. ". . . It is not clear wherein an adoption of . . . conventions, antecedently to their formulation, consists; such behavior is difficult to distinguish from that in which conventions are disregarded. . . . We may wonder what one adds to the bare statement that the truths of logic and mathematics are *a priori*, or to the still barer behavioristic statement that they are firmly accepted, when he characterizes them as true by convention in such a sense."

tion; and to refuse to accept *these* rules—whatever we may want
to say about such a refusal—is certainly not of the same order as
refusing to accept the rules of chess or any other special game. The
distinction, therefore, between the rules of inference or logical laws,
on the one hand, and what may be called "rules of the game" on
the other, is one which must be presupposed before any genuine
philosophical problems about logical laws and rules of inference
can arise.

What is often perplexing in talk that involves an appeal to logical
laws or rules of inference is the nature of the relation which is being
presupposed between the logical rules and particular steps in reasoning, or between the logical laws and particular statements which are
held to be "instances" of such laws. In many of his comments on
logical laws, Wittgenstein is concerned with the nature of this relation rather than with the distinction between logically necessary
statements and other kinds of statements or between logical rules
and other kinds of rules.[6] For we can easily see that there must be
a distinction between the two kinds of rules and between the two
kinds of statements; it is only when we have accepted this distinction that we become puzzled and go on to ask why logical laws and
rules of inference should have their sacrosanct status. For example,
we want to ask what it means to say that anyone who rejects the
rules of inference is "incapable of playing any game at all." A man
who was suddenly seized with a disease of the nerves which prevented him from sitting upright in a chair or from taking part in any
other kind of activity involved in playing a game might be said to
be "incapable of playing any game at all" and no puzzles would
arise. But why should a man who refuses to accept the rules of
inference be in this plight? How precisely, if at all, would his behavior be affected? It is often said, furthermore, that a man "can't
refuse" to accept the rules of inference and still reply rationally, that
a man "can't think" a contradiction,[7] and that logical rules "com-

[6] "How is it established which pattern is the multiplication 13 × 13?—Isn't it *defined*
by the rules of multiplication—But what if, using these rules, you get a different result
today from what all the arithmetic books say? Isn't that possible?—'Not if you apply the
rules as *they* do!' Of course not! But that is a mere pleonasm. And where does it say
how they are to be applied—and if it does say somewhere, where does it say how *that* is
to be applied?" [§§112 ff.] In this passage, Wittgenstein is concerned with what it
means to follow a rule, such as an ordinary rule of arithmetic. But this remark applies,
mutatis mutandis, to following rules of inference.

[7] Compare: ". . . If you say that, while he may indeed *say* it, still he can't *think* it,
then I am only saying that that means, not: try as he may he can't think it, but: it is
for us an essential part of 'thinking' that—in talking, writing, etc.,—he makes *this sort*
of transition" [§116].

pel" us to follow them in a certain way.[8] Surely, however, we have
to ask what is the meaning of the word "can't" and the meaning of
the word "compel" in these cases. To ask this question is not to
suggest that we would not be justified in making such assertions;
it is rather to ask what making such assertions amounts to; it is to
seek clarification and the removal of puzzlement, not the creation
of new puzzlement. What is implicitly puzzling must be made explicit before it can be removed, of course, and Wittgenstein employs
various devices and examples to bring the puzzlement forth; but
his aim in providing such examples is still to resolve rather than to
create occasions for philosophical perplexity.

In order to deal adequately with perplexities such as Wittgenstein's comments raise, we have to be able to speak precisely about
the relations between logical laws and what we would call "correct
thinking." If the "logical 'must' " is as hard as it is usually made
out to be,[9] then it ought to be able to withstand any attempt to
make its content more precise. If, however, it cannot, then merely
reiterating its "hardness" in the face of Wittgenstein's very carefully
wrought possible cases is just so much hot air.

Traditionally, it would seem, logical laws have been supposed to
regulate and determine the actual processes of valid thought, so
that it would be literally impossible for anyone to "break" a logical
law. Aristotle, for example, says in Book IV of his *Metaphysics*
that the law of contradition is one "regarding which it is impossible
to be mistaken," and that "it is impossible for anyone to believe the
same thing to be and not to be" [W. D. Ross trans., 1005b 12, 23].
Aristotle's point may be modified and made more plausible, perhaps, by disengaging the logical law from any direct influence on
psychological processes of thought and holding instead merely that
it is impossible for anyone to violate such a law without making an
excursion into nonsense. Whether we take Aristotle's view or one
of its modifications, we are nevertheless apt to use language in a
peculiarly misleading way when we appeal to a logical law or a rule
of inference in evaluating a step in reasoning. For the way we often
speak suggests the following picture: there is some entity we can
understand, called the "logical law" or "rule," which exists inde-

---

[8] "But am I not compelled, then, to go the way I do in a chain of inferences?"—Compelled? After all I can presumably go as I choose!—"But if you want to remain in accord
with the rules you *must* go this way."—Not at all, I call *this* "accord."—"Then you have
changed the meaning of the word 'accord,' or the meaning of the rule."—No;—who says
what 'change' and 'remaining the same' mean here?" [§113].
[9] As, for example, by Nell, *op. cit.*

pendently of any occasions for using it; and determining the correctness of a step in reasoning is a process of "applying the rule" and having the answer given *automatically,* as it were, or "yielded" by the rule, as if we who do the reasoning were cogs in a celestial logical machine and as if the logical law were written on high in imperishable letters. It is against this *picture* of logical laws and their relation to reasoning that Wittgenstein's comments [§§112 ff.] are mainly directed. I believe that the effect of his comments is to show that we can maintain everything that a logician needs to say about the distinction between logical rules and other kinds of rules, without committing ourselves to such a picture.

In order to see this, we have to review what could be meant by the terms "logical law" and "rule."

By a "logical rule" we may mean, e.g., the rule of detachment, that if a statement is true and that statement implies another, then the latter is a valid consequence of the former, or in other words that we may validly infer a statement from a premise which is true and implies it. Thus a logical rule is a recipe for taking correct steps in reasoning. But sometimes the phrase "logical law" is used to mean the same thing, e.g., as in the phrase "the *law* of detachment." Now it may be that, when people speak of a "law" in this sense, what they have in mind is an assertion which might be offered as the ground or justification of the rule. In this instance such an assertion might take the form "Whatever is implied by a true statement is true." The "logical law" in this sense has either an equal or a prior status to the rule. On the other hand, a "logical law" is sometimes spoken of in contexts where what is meant is the truism corresponding to an application of the law. If this is what we mean by a "logical law," then the "law" would have a derivative status with respect to the rule.

From this I would draw the conclusion that there just *isn't* any clear distinction between a logical law and a rule beyond the fact that it is more natural to use "rule" in the context of "following" (i.e., reasoning), and "law" in the context of asserting, and beyond the fact that a law can be said to be "true" whereas a rule cannot.

Now it is often said that a "logical law" in the sense of a truism is *entailed* by the logical rules we have adopted. For example, the logical law "No statement is both true and false" might be said to be entailed by the rules for conjunction and negation, namely (*a*) the rule that whenever we negate a true statement a false one must result, and vice versa; and (*b*) the rule that the result of joining statements by "and" is to be counted true if and only if the component statements are true. However, saying that the rule *entails* the law seems to presuppose acceptance of a "higher" law in virtue of which the entailment relation holds, and is going in a circle. For if there corresponds to every valid inference a statement which is necessarily true, then the inference of the law from the rule must have a corresponding necessary truth. It does not extricate us from the circle to hold that there is in fact such a necessary truth, only one of a higher order; for if it is possible to hold in the first place that a necessary truth is so because it is entailed by the rule, then we are justified in asking, What is the rule in *this* case which entails the second-order necessary truth? Suppose we call this second-order necessary truth the "Law of Consistency"; then it will be entailed in turn by some second-order set of rules, say the "Rules of Harmony and Dissonance." But then there would still have to be prior laws and rules in virtue of which the ascription of an entailment relation in *these* cases would be justified. Now it is usual to put a halt to this regress by simply taking a stand on either a law or a rule and refusing to be budged. The rule or law on which we choose to take our stand is then denominated "self-evident"; and anyone who questions this procedure is advised that he is imperiling rationality. But the question arises, why not just call the *original step in reasoning,* if it is a valid one, "self-evident"? What is to be gained by going up the ladder from steps in reasoning to rules, from rules to laws, from laws to rules, and so on? To echo Frege, surely such a procedure is the very reverse of rational!

In order to make any sense out of "appeals to rules" we must say not that such appeals can *justify* the step in reasoning but rather that we employ this device when we want to show that the step in reasoning *conforms to,* or is an *instance of,* or *accords with* the rule that we accept, which it is assumed we know how to apply.[10]

But now the question arises, what is it that determines when a step in reasoning *is* in accord with the rule? Is it the rule itself? Does the rule of detachment, for example, determine when an inference conforms to it? The answer seems to be that it is not the rule so much as *we* that determine when a step in reasoning is in accord with the rule.[11] That is, we have a standard way of interpret-

---

[10] In other words, a rule is not a *premise.* Cf. Lewis Carroll, "What the Tortoise Said to Achilles," *Mind,* N. S. Vol. 4 (1895), pp. 278 ff.

[11] §§112 ff.

ing patterns of symbols which we call rules and other patterns which we call steps in reasoning, and we do not count any deviations from this standard interpretation as an exception to the rule, but as a *failure* of some sort. If we have a recipe for making soup, for example, which when correctly followed always produces good soup, then if our soup turns out to be bad, we do not blame the recipe but say that something must have gone wrong in applying it. It is possible, however, that the soup should turn out to be bad, or perhaps merely different from what we expected, even though we followed the recipe correctly.

Wittgenstein says that when we follow a rule, then "following" means not only knowing what is the pattern of symbols which we call the rule, but also knowing how this pattern is intended to be used, and that knowing how to apply or use a rule is not something that is derived from a preexistent rule.[12] This last point seems to be offered as a matter of fact, but to deny it certainly involves one in an infinite regress of rules. The problem, then, is to get at the precise sense in which steps in reasoning can be regarded as "results" of applying logical rules, when the rules by themselves do not determine the results of applying them, and when the citation of the rule does not justify [13] the step which is taken. Wittgenstein offers the example of an obstinate individual who stubbornly refuses to concede that he is not applying the logical rule in the same way that we are, despite the fact that he gets deviant results.[14] Confronted with such behavior we should want to say: "He doesn't know how to apply the rule; he thinks he does but he doesn't." The question arises, however, whether we can take a stand on the rule when someone challenges our claim that a deviant result is not in accord with the rule. Since, as we have seen, a rule does not certify its own

---

[12] *Ibid.*

[13] I mean "justify" here in the sense of "giving a reason for" or "tending to establish a fact," *not* in the sense of "vindicating the rightness of." In saying that citing the rules does not "justify" the reasoning, I mean that the rule does not certify its own correct application; the reasoning is as much *self*-justifying as it is justified by the rule, although one may *vindicate* a particular move in reasoning by citing a rule to which the move conforms, provided that all parties concerned are interpreting the rule in a standard way. The rule does not "justify" the step in reasoning because to say that it does involves one in a regress of rules. Cf. Carroll, *op. cit.*

[14] " 'But you surely can't suddenly make a different application of the law now!'—If my reply is: 'Oh yes, of course, *that* is how I was applying it!' or: 'Oh! *That's* how I ought to have applied it—!'; then I am playing your game. But if I simply reply: 'Different?— But this surely isn't different!'—what will you do? That is: somebody may reply like a rational person and yet not be playing our game" [§115]. That Wittgenstein is here concerned with inference rules rather than rules of a specified game is indicated by the preceding comment: ". . . When we *follow* the laws of inference (inference rules) then following always involves interpretation too" [§114].

correct application—for to say that it does, or to appeal to other rules, definitions or laws for certification is merely to go in the circle noted above—and since a rule neither determines nor justifies a step in reasoning, it follows that so long as we confine ourselves to appealing to rules and definitions we can never dislodge such a man from his position, that is, a man who is resolute in his behavior and who refuses to concede that what he is doing, though deviant, is not in accord with the rule. He may *be* mad, but to call him so merely on the basis that he refuses to admit that his result is not in accord with the rule is to concede the point. For he is not necessarily *defying* logic; rather, he is standing on logic in the sense that his behavior is logically possible in virtue of the circularity inherent in any attempt to justify a step in reasoning by appealing to a rule, or a rule by appealing to a definition or a law.

Is Wittgenstein right in suggesting that such a person, despite his peculiar behavior, might be rational? The point is, I think, that this man's refusal to admit that his behavior fails to conform to the rule does not *make* him irrational; that is, we cannot on the grounds given exclude the *possibility* that he is rational. Although we cannot say that he is rational, neither can we say that he is irrational, for he replies "*like* a rational person." One imagines that ultimately the verdict as to whether he is rational or not will depend on how we get on with him, what further use he makes of words like "following," "remaining the same," "in accord with," and so on. Perhaps he will eventually respond to a simple imperative such as: "Don't talk that way! ," or "Infer *this* way!" It is possible, of course, that we will *never* be able to make a satisfactory judgment in his case; perhaps we will commit him to an institution with vague feelings of uneasiness.

As we have noted, the procedure of formal logic is to justify a step in reasoning by citing a corresponding rule which gives a recipe for taking the step, and to justify the rule by appealing to logical laws or necessary truths, from which the rules are said to be generated. But if we challenge the laws, we find that these are held to follow from the rules, either the same or other. Of course it is possible to give up any reference whatever to "laws" and confine oneself to rules,[15] which, however, *it must be assumed that we*

---

[15] As in "natural deduction" procedures. In doing logic from this standpoint one has to get over the feeling that the rules should apply themselves. The same is true when we are dealing with "axiom schemata" which have an "infinite number" of substitution instances.

know how to apply. I do not wish to question the acceptability of any of these procedures [16]—nor does Wittgenstein, if I am right—but merely to bring out the fact that they are not *justifications*. To cite a criterion, i.e., a logical rule, is different from giving a justification or stating that an entailment relation holds. When we justify a claim we engage in reasoning, and the reasoning in such a case either conforms or fails to conform to a logical rule, but it is not justified in its turn by the rule nor by any other rule or law. Whether the reasoning in a given case conforms to the rule is a problem of interpretation, and requires sophistication in the use of symbols. It is a question which is not *closed* by citing a rule, unless, that is, all parties concerned already accept the rule and apply it in a standard way. Although the distinction between rules of inference and other kinds of rules ought not to be muddled, nevertheless what it is to follow a rule is the same with regard to both classes of rules. That is, for both classes of rules, "following" means "being able to recognize deviant results, refusing to regard them as exceptions to the rule, and counting them always as failures or errors in applying the rule." The man in Wittgenstein's example is "following" the rule to the extent that he admits that his result, though deviant, is not an exception to the rule. What is peculiar in his behavior is that he refuses to count his deviant result as a failure or an error in applying the rule. Thus his behavior neatly cuts across our usual criteria for "following."

In the context of a formalized language,[17] the thesis that we are compelled to conform to logical rules and laws is *prima facie* true because adequate definitions are provided and rules explicitly laid down. If we attempt to test the possibility of accepting the definitions and rules and denying the theorems, a sense of bewilderment arises which becomes transmuted into the feeling that we are compelled to accept the theorems if we accept the rules and definitions. If this is what we mean when we say that logical rules or laws

---

[16] A regress of rules is not necessarily vicious; it usually comes to an end because we reach a rule which everyone in fact accepts. Introducing the rule for negation, e.g., causes very little trouble; if we can then get someone to accept a rule for alternation or conjunction, we can proceed to widen the circle in such a way that the regressiveness is not obvious.

[17] But the difference between a formalized language and a natural language cannot be a difference in essential kind; for what would it be like to have a formalized *language* that we couldn't possibly understand, couldn't possibly do anything with at all? Furthermore, formalizing languages doesn't make superfluous the attempt to characterize more precisely the relation between logical rules and particular steps in reasoning, for this is a relation that has to occur in *any* case of using such rules, whether within or outside the context of a formalized language.

"compel," then we need not deny that logical rules compel. But if this kind of event is offered as an explanation of what we *mean* by saying that a statement is necessarily true—i.e., that what we mean is that accepting the rules and definitions compels us to assert the statement—then we must object, if only because it confuses a logical concept with a psychological event. On the other hand, if the claim that logical rules "compel" is construed to mean that the logical rules themselves *cause* us to behave in a certain way, i.e., to draw the theorems from the rules and definitions, then again we must object, if only because rules are not the sorts of thing which are causally efficacious, much less compelling, in this world. It is one thing to say that we are compelled to follow a rule, but quite another to say that the rule itself compels.[18] If someone wants to say that logical rules have an objective reference to necessary states of affairs, and it is the latter that compel, then there is nothing so far *logically* wrong with his view, but it brings us back to the picture of the universe as a celestial logical machine which does our reasoning for us.

II

Although Wittgenstein's philosophy of logic has been called a species of conventionalism, it is interesting that Wittgenstein explicitly repudiates the suggestion that following logical rules is merely a matter of choice based on an arbitrary definition or convention.

"Then according to you everybody could continue the series as he likes; and so infer *any*how!" In that case we shan't call it "con-

---

[18] Admittedly this depends on what you mean by a "rule." It seems to me that the most correct way to use the word "rule" is in the context of a pattern of symbols or formulae. It might be objected, however, that there is no meaning in the concept of a "rule" which is utterly devoid of any interpretation, i.e., is a *mere* formal pattern; and that for something to be a "rule," something we can "follow" in a particular case, it must already contain or involve an interpretation. The "rule," therefore, would be not merely the abstract pattern conveyed in the symbols, but a complex of behavior, and to "apply a rule" would be not merely to interpret a pattern of symbols but to conform to a certain way of talking or behaving. However, to admit that it is incorrect to speak of a "rule" as existing apart from a knowledge of how to use it is already to give up the "theological" view of logic. Furthermore, even if we give up *this* misleading way of speaking about "rules," it is still unilluminating to say that we are compelled *by the rule.* If we are compelled, it is not by the meaning or indication of the words "conforming to the rule," unless, that is, we are prepared to say that temporally antecedent cases of behavior *compel* those which follow merely because they *are* temporally antecedent. Presumably, if our behavior is an instance of a regularity, it is not the case that it is *caused* by this regularity. If, on the other hand, it is *caused* by the past instances of this regularity, it still does not follow that it is *compelled* by them. There just does not seem to be any clear sense in the phrase, "compelled *by* the rule," i.e., whether by "rule" is meant the formula or the regularities of behavior which the formula may reflect.

tinuing the series" and also presumably not "inference." And thinking and inferring (like counting) is of course bounded for us, not by an arbitrary definition, but by natural limits corresponding to the body of what can be called the role of thinking and inferring in our life. [§116]

Correct inference, then, for Wittgenstein, is evidently not a matter of "arbitrary definition" or convention, nor is it true that we can correctly call anything we please "inferring." Inferring, he says, is bounded *for us (für uns)* not "by us" or by an arbitrary definition; there are *natural limits (natürliche Grenzen)* to what we call "thinking and inferring."

In Wittgenstein's discussion of logical necessity the terms "logical compulsion" *(logische Zwang)* and the "inexorability" *(Unerbittlichkeit)* of logical laws gradually come to replace occurrences of "logical necessity" *(logische Notwendigkeit)*. The reason for this is perhaps that the concept of logical necessity is merely the abstract and formal reflection of the "role" that "thinking and inferring play in our life," this role being much better expressed by the terms "compulsion" and "inexorability." For example:

> But doesn't it follow with logical necessity *[logische Notwendigkeit]* that you get two when you add one to one, and three when you add one to two? and isn't this inexorability *[diese Unerbittlichkeit]* the same as that of logical inference?—Yes! it is the same. . . . [§5]

It is as if Wittgenstein were suggesting by this shift in terminology that the concept of logical necessity has been so thoroughly dried out and dissected by philosophers that nothing is left of it but bare bones, and any connection between it and the *Lebensform* of reasoning and thinking is beyond recovery. Thus he says:

> . . . We talk of the "inexorability" of logic; and think of the laws of logic as inexorable, still more inexorable than the laws of nature. We now draw attention to the fact that the word "inexorable" is used in a variety of ways. There correspond to our laws of logic very general facts of daily experience. They are the ones that make it possible for us to keep on demonstrating those laws in a very simple way (with ink on paper for example). They are to be compared with the facts that make measurement with a yardstick easy and useful. This suggests the use of precisely these laws of inference, and now it is *we* that are inexorable in applying these laws. Because we "measure"; and it is part of measuring for everybody to have the same measures. . . . [§118]

Among the things worth noting in this passage are Wittgenstein's unabashed use of the phrase "logical law" and his willingness to indicate a connection between logical laws and "very general facts of daily experience," in addition to his recognition that we tend to think of logical laws as "more inexorable" even than laws of nature. This is a clear reference both to ordinary usage and philosophical tradition; it cannot be said that this passage seeks to repudiate such usage; on the contrary, it seeks to *understand* it, or rather, to understand what there is behind it that is sound.

Now we often carelessly speak of both logical laws themselves and the results of applying such laws as "necessary truths" and "truths by convention" or "legislation." However, this usage invites confusion, for there is considerable difference between a formal truism such as "not both p and not p" and, e.g., the logical law of noncontradiction, which says that *for every proposition p,* it is not the case that p is both true and false. The logical law is a statement about every statement or proposition, whereas the formal truism is simply a statement which is true by virtue of its form or arrangement of parts. Thus it is logically necessary that the conjunction of admittedly contradictory statements be false; this result is guaranteed by the logical law of noncontradiction. But what of the law of noncontradiction itself? This law, by whose application the conjunction of contradictory statements is judged necessarily false, is not itself *logically* necessary; it is not true merely by virtue of the arrangement of its parts. Thus if the law of noncontradiction is "necessary," its necessity must be of a different order from that of the formal truisms which it certifies.

Instead of seeking a higher or "celestial" necessity to account for the inexorability with which we apply logical laws such as the law of noncontradiction, Wittgenstein turns to such mundane considerations as "very general facts of daily experience," and an analogy between laws and rules of measurement.

Wittgenstein's discussion of the "inexorability" of logical laws is his way of accounting for what is customarily regarded as their *a priori* status. His explanation finds a middle path between "necessary facts" or "celestial necessity" on the one hand, and mere convention on the other. The connection which Wittgenstein sees between logical laws and very general facts of daily experience is not one of descriptive correspondence, however, and does not account for *logical* truth, nor does it suggest any descriptive function for the laws of logic. The appeal to facts of daily experience is made in order to account specifically for the *formation* of logical laws, *not for the fact that we refuse to allow them to have exceptions*. Our experience of the world, Wittgenstein says, suggests to us the use of the logical laws which we have; these *laws* are not inexorable; rather, it is *we* who are inexorable in applying them—because we want them to do a job and because we see that in order to get the job done everyone has to do it by the same rules. The logical laws are thus indeed *a priori* in the way that they are *applied* but not in the way that they *originate*. Experience plays a role in the formation of logical laws, but the need for having unambiguous, common rules of inference, the need that Wittgenstein elsewhere calls "the deep need for the convention," means that convention must play a role also. The element of convention guarantees uniformity of application of the laws, i.e., that they shall be exceptionless, but it does not supply the laws themselves, which come to us rather partly through our experience of the world and partly through our projected needs and interests, the ends we have in view. Such, then are the "natural limits corresponding to the role of thinking and inferring in our life."

The "inexorability" of logical laws arises partly out of our observations of and conditioning with respect to "very general facts of daily experience," partly out of the "deep need for the convention" and our apprehension of our own purposes. Just as it is part of "measuring" for everybody to have the same measures, Wittgenstein says, so it is part of "thinking" for everybody to have the same rules of inference, whose application results in the same moves by everyone. These needs are understood by us, and then it is "*we* that are inexorable in applying these laws," i.e., we supply the convention that such laws shall be exceptionless.

That this is the correct interpretation, at least in essentials, of what Wittgenstein is saying, is brought out in the following passages from the *RFM*:

> . . . It never in fact happens that somebody who has learned to calculate goes on obstinately getting different results, when he does a given multiplication, from what comes in the arithmetic books. But if it should happen, then we should declare him abnormal, and take no further account of his calculation. [§112]

What is at stake here is a general fact of daily experience, which is a basis for regarding the deviant case as abnormal, as something which we can disregard. We could also appeal to such a general fact in justification of such claims as "He doesn't know how to use the rule," or "He is misusing language." However,

> It might be practical to measure with a ruler which had the property of shrinking to, say, half its length when it was taken from this room to that. A property which would make it useless as a ruler in other circumstances. [§139]

Thus conditions might occur under which a "rule" would be useful which is not so in ordinary or standard cases. While we cannot always anticipate or describe such circumstances, we cannot exclude the possibility of their occurring. To say that we would be justified in declaring someone "abnormal" who obstinately gets results other than those which normally follow when we apply a logical rule does not mean that no conditions can possibly occur under which we would accept the result of the deviant as a legitimate application of the rule. But our standard rules and interpretations would not be falsified or made useless in the event that such circumstances arose. Thus the "inexorability" of logical laws is not incompatible with our changing, revising or rejecting them in possible circumstances.

> The steps (in reasoning) which are not brought in question are logical inferences. But the reason they are not brought in question is not that they "certainly correspond to the truth"—or something of the sort,—no, it is just this that is called "thinking," "speaking," "inferring," "arguing." There is not any question at all here of some correspondence between what is said and reality; rather is logic *antecedent* to any such correspondence; in the same sense, that is, as that in which the establishment of a method of measurement is *antecedent* to the correctness or incorrectness of a statement of length. [§155]

The analogy that Wittgenstein is drawing here between, on the one hand, logical rules and true descriptive statements, and on the other, rules of measurement and correct statements of length, brings out what is the use of having logical rules, what role they play in a language. This passage obviously suggests that their function is the regulation of descriptive discourse, i.e., discourse capable of being evaluated by the standards of empirical truth or falsehood. Antecedent logical rules are presupposed in any attempt to determine a correspondence between descriptive statements and reality, just as antecedent rules of measurement are presupposed by statements of length. Logical rules do not, however, themselves describe anything, any more than rules of measurement describe. It is possible, of course, to make up "necessary truths" out of statements which taken by themselves are descriptive, and that this is so is what enables us to go validly from one descriptive truth to another, without intervening observations. The point is that we must be prepared to talk about "necessary truths" if we are prepared to talk about logic being "antecedent" to any correspondence, and, consequently, that Wittgenstein is not repudiating the correctness, so far as it goes, of standard talk about "necessary truths." What Wittgenstein is saying is that logical necessity arises out of language rather than the reverse, and that explicit logical rules are conventionalized transcriptions of standardized behavioral forms which have arisen naturally and "unconsciously" from the kind of world in which we find ourselves.

It might be thought that there is an inconsistency in allowing "necessary truth" while denying that logical rules or laws *compel* us to go in a certain way in a chain of inferences, or while admitting that we can distinguish between ambiguous and unambiguous rules of inference. That there is in fact no inconsistency here is shown by the following observations:

> Frege calls it "a law about what men take for true" that "It is impossible for human beings . . . to recognize an object as different from itself."—When I think of this as impossible for me, then I think of *trying* to do it. So I look at my lamp and say: "This lamp is different from itself." (But nothing stirs.) It is not that I see it is false, I can't do anything with it at all. . . . [§132]

Now it is obviously possible for one to *say,* "This lamp is different from itself."

> And if you say that, while he may indeed *say* it, still he can't think it, then I am only saying that that means, not: try as he may he can't think it, but: it is for us an essential part of "thinking" that—in talking, writing, etc.,—he makes *this sort* of transition. [§116]

Wittgenstein is thus not denying that, for example, someone "cannot think" a contradiction, but rather is attempting to understand what it means to say this. Is it out of our power to "think" a contradiction as it is out of our power, for most of us, to lift a 500-pound weight, i.e., in the sense that we are too weak to do it? Is it out of our power in some broader sense of being contrary to laws of nature or psychology? Or is it rather that the question whether or not someone can "think" a contradiction is not to be tested in the way that one would test ordinary claims about what is or is not "in our power"? If someone says, "It is impossible for us to jump twenty feet high by our own unaided muscular power," and this is denied, then we can by testing clearly see that the denial is false, at least with respect to ourselves and at the present time. But when someone tries to think, "This lamp is different from itself," it is not that he sees it is false: "He can't do anything with it at all." So there is the sense in which something is impossible when the utterance that it is possible or that it is the case can be clearly seen to be false, and the sense in which something is impossible when the utterance to the contrary is not so much testably false as it is queer, puzzling, inappropriate. Hence, to attempt to prove the "necessity" of a logical truth by testing the possibility of thinking its denial is to give an argument which consumes itself, like the serpent swallowing its own tail. That we cannot in a given case "conceive the opposite" is presumably a question of empirical fact which, even if true, would fail to establish the logical impossibility of the opposite being the case. *Thus, to deny that we are always compelled to think in conformity with a logical rule does not imply that there are no necessary truths, nor is it to deny that appeals to the rule or to the meaning of a word have a useful role in language.* What is at stake here, Wittgenstein is saying, is not so much what are the limits of our *powers,* but what are the limits of what we call "thinking." We don't call it "thinking" or "reasoning correctly" unless it is consistent or follows the rule. And since appeals to rules are things that *do* have a useful role to play in language, we have to distinguish between ambiguous and unambiguous formulations of rules. But such distinctions are a matter of degree in a natural language, for:

> . . . the line between what we include in "thinking" and what we no longer include in "thinking" is no more a hard and fast one than the line between what is still and what is no longer called "regularity." [§116]

III

In this paper I have criticized the growing tendency among commentators to interpret Wittgenstein as teaching in the *Remarks on the Foundation of Mathematics* that logical laws and rules of inference have a merely "normative" foundation. According to this interpretation of Wittgenstein's teaching we could, if we wished, break logical laws in serious argument without being necessarily mistaken or irrational, and if we do not do this, it is solely because of *practical* considerations, such as facility of communication, avoidance of punishment, and so on. I have tried to show that this way of interpreting Wittgenstein greatly oversimplifies what he is saying and must be regarded in the end as a serious distortion of his views. I have tried to show that Wittgenstein is better understood not as denying that a person who deliberately violates a logical law or rule is being necessarily irrational, but rather as attempting to discover what it means to say that such a person is being necessarily irrational. If I am right, however, Wittgenstein *does* wish to deny that saying that logical laws cannot be rationally controverted is to say that they express "eternal and immutable truths," or that there are no possible conditions under which we might rationally change, revise, or reject a formulation of what we now accept as a logical law. The reason for this is not that "there is nothing irrational about breaking a logical law" but that our concept of what is a logical law and what it is to follow a rule of logic is fuzzy and blurred at the edges, with the result that we cannot always tell when we are "following" a logical rule and when we are not. The view that according to Wittgenstein we can break logical laws in serious argument without being necessarily irrational seems to be a misinterpretation of those comments in the *Remarks* in which he discusses the question whether being rational means being compelled to behave in a certain way by a law of logic, which he denies is the case. However, while Wittgenstein denies that our feeling of "logical compulsion," of being "compelled to go as we do in a chain of inferences," is what we mean by "logical necessity," he does not deny that we often have a feeling of logical compulsion which guides our thinking. His point seems to be that this feeling is a mixture of many factors, normative, psychological, and logical, and has no simple or *essential* explanation. At the same time Wittgenstein is surely right to stress the element of indeterminacy in our concept of "following the rule," so far as this affects our concept of rational behavior, and he is surely right also in saying that any rule requires an act of interpretation before it can be applied, an act which is not itself determined by the rule. This is not to say that a proof cannot be rigorous, nor that we can rationally reject a conclusion which we admit is validly derived from the conjunction of a set of premises. Rather, what is involved is the question, "What is it to derive validly a conclusion from a premise?" or "What is it to follow a logical rule?" In his discussion of such questions Wittgenstein is not proposing a reductionistic explanation of logical laws, but rather attempting to resolve the familiar perplexities into which questions about the nature of the relation between logical rules and rational conduct have thrown us. What makes his discussion worth careful study is his attempt to do this without being driven into giving "metaphysical" explanations that in the end only intensify or increase our perplexities.

Thus Wittgenstein's later philosophy of logic is not an expression of the kind of conventionalism which has been ascribed to him. On the contrary, Wittgenstein gives expression to a "mixed" theory which genuinely tends to resolve the perplexities usually associated with the thesis of the *a priori* character of logical truth. Although my argument has been exegetical, the point is, I think, of more than exegetical interest. For the argument shows that the analysis of what it is to appeal to a logical rule, and what it means to say that the results of applying such a rule are necessary, can be carried through without having to deny that there are such things as logical rules or that they have a useful role to play in contexts of evaluating reasoning. It shows that we can discover the limits of the concept of logical necessity without having to repudiate the logician's standard talk of "necessary truth" and "logical form," or the usual assumption that this kind of talk has a bearing on ordinary contexts of reasoning utilizing natural languages. If Wittgenstein's comments imperil rationality, that is because rationality is often imperiled, but his intent is to challenge us to make precise the nature of the relationship which we tend to presuppose between logical rules and particular steps in reasoning.

Wittgenstein, Nonsense, and Lewis Carroll

BY GEORGE PITCHER

THE PHILOSOPHER LUDWIG WITTGENSTEIN (1889–1951) was always concerned, one way or another, about nonsense; and much more so in his later writings than in the early ones. Nonsense is construed in the *Tractatus*[1] in a narrow technical way: a combination of words is nonsensical when it cannot possibly be understood, because no sense is or can (except trivially) be accorded it.[2] As an example of a nonsensical question, Wittgenstein gives that of "whether the good is more or less identical than the beautiful" [*T,* §4.003].[3] He thinks that "most of the propositions and questions to be found in philosophical works are not false but nonsensical" [*T,* §4.003], not even excepting, sadly, those found in the *Tractatus* itself [*T,* §6.54]. One of his main objectives is to devise and justify a method for distinguishing sense from nonsense, so that the latter may be consigned, as it should be, to silence [*T* §7]. Nonsense is thus viewed as the major target for the philosopher's destructive weapons.

In the later *Philosophical Investigations,* Wittgenstein still finds that philosophers—including the author of the *Tractatus*—are professionally given to uttering nonsense. Not obvious nonsense, but hidden nonsense: and he conceives the job of *good* philosophy to be that of revealing it for what it is. "My aim," he wrote, "is: to teach you to pass from a piece of disguised nonsense to something

---

[1] Wittgenstein completed the *Tractatus Logico-Philosophicus* in 1918; it was published in the original German in 1921, and a year later in a German-English parallel text.
[2] Wittgenstein distinguishes nonsensical utterances from those which simply lack sense: "Tautologies and contradictions lack sense" [*T,* §4.461], but they are not nonsensical. They are *sinnlos,* but not *unsinnig.*
[3] The following abbreviations will be used in giving references to Wittgenstein's works: *PI, Philosophical Investigations; BB, The Blue and Brown Books; T, Tractatus Logico-Philosophicus; RFM, Remarks on the Foundation of Mathematics.*
    The following will be used for Carroll: *AW, Alice's Adventures in Wonderland; TLG, Through the Looking Glass; SB, Sylvie and Bruno; SBC, Sylvie and Bruno Concluded.*

that is patent nonsense" [*PI,* §464; *see also* §119]. Disguised nonsense has a surface air of plausibility and naturalness about it, so that it can take in even a sensible man. It has the semblance of sense. But when one examines it carefully and follows out its consequences, its inherent absurdity becomes manifest. Wittgenstein is still as concerned as ever to exorcise nonsense from philosophy; he wants to cure us of the puzzlement, the deep disquietude, it engenders in our soul. But now he also *uses* it[4] like a vaccine that cures us of *itself.* He may, for instance, describe some state of affairs that, according to a certain harmless-looking view or picture which he is criticizing, ought to be perfectly unexceptionable: but in fact the alleged state of affairs is radically odd, inherently absurd. The hidden nonsense is thus uncovered.

It is through the bond of nonsense that Wittgenstein is closely linked with Lewis Carroll. What I shall seek in general to demonstrate is the remarkable extent and depth of the affinity between these two great writers with respect to nonsense. Since I do not want to embroil myself in controversies about matters that would be excessively difficult to establish with anything approaching certainty, I shall not draw the further conclusion that Carroll exerted a profound influence on the later Wittgenstein. That he did, is one of my firm convictions;[5] but I shall content myself with pointing out what I believe to be the extraordinary and illuminating parallels between their treatments of nonsense.

What I aim to show in particular is, first, that some of the important general kinds of nonsense that the later Wittgenstein finds

---

[4] To be sure, even in the *Tractatus, some* nonsense—namely, Wittgenstein's own—was deemed to be profoundly useful:

> My propositions serve as elucidations in the following way: anyone who understands me eventually recognizes them as nonsensical, when he has used them—as steps—to climb up beyond them. (He must, so to speak, throw away the ladder after he has climbed up it.) [*T,* §6.54]

But whether this doctrine is a legitimate one or not—I think it is not—it still claims a radically different kind of use for nonsense from those uses found in the *Investigations.*
[5] Quite apart from the fact that anyone who lived in England, and particularly Cambridge, during the time that Wittgenstein did, could not fail to have read Lewis Carroll—especially the *Alice* books—it is known with certainty that Wittgenstein did read and admire Carroll. Miss G. E. M. Anscombe, Mr. R. Rhees, and Prof. G. H. von Wright, all friends of Wittgenstein, have kindly provided me with information about his acquaintance with the works of Carroll. All confirm that he read at least some of the works. Miss Anscombe and Mr. Rhees both report that Wittgenstein used to cite, as a good grammatical joke, the Mock Turtle's remark "We called him Tortoise because he taught us" [*AW,* ch. 9]. Mr. Rhees recalls a conversation in 1938 in which Wittgenstein referred admiringly to a passage in *Sylvie and Bruno;* but he adds that in the last eight or ten years of his life, Wittgenstein no longer thought as highly of Carroll as he had earlier. Carroll is mentioned by name in *PI,* §13 and p. 198; and it is a safe bet that the nonsense poems referred to in *PI* §282 are those of Carroll.

in the doctrines of philosophers are found also in the writings of Lewis Carroll. By "kinds of nonsense," I mean nonsense that has its source in certain fundamental confusions and errors. I shall try to show that the very same confusions with which Wittgenstein charges philosophers were deliberately employed by Carroll for comic effect. Second, I want to show that some quite specific philosophical doctrines that the later Wittgenstein attacks are ridiculed also by Carroll. (Certain of these specific doctrines will embody, naturally, some of the general *types* of nonsense just mentioned.) Third, I shall cite several examples used by Wittgenstein to illustrate his points that resemble, in varying degrees, examples that are found in the works of Carroll.

Does it seem paradoxical, or even perverse, to assert that philosophy and humor—especially *nonsense* humor—are intimately related? If so, I hasten to add that Wittgenstein himself was keenly aware of the connection:

> Let us ask ourselves: why do we feel a grammatical joke to be *deep?* (And that is what the depth of philosophy is.) [*PI*, §111].

And Malcolm reports that

> . . . Wittgenstein once said that a serious and good philosophical work could be written that would consist entirely of *jokes* (without being facetious).[6]

Wittgenstein undoubtedly had the works of Lewis Carroll in mind when he made those remarks.

Nor is it really very surprising to find some affinity between the nonsense of Carroll and that which bothered Wittgenstein: for both men were professional logicians and much of their nonsense, as we shall see, is grounded in just those matters connected with language that a logician must concern himself with—such matters, for example, as the meanings of terms and sentences, as the logical) differences that exist amongst various sort of terms, as the fact that sentences having the same (or at least *apparently* the same) grammatical form sometimes express propositions of radically different logical forms, and so on.

I SHALL PRESENT MY CASE by starting with items of less importance and proceeding in the rough direction of those of more importance.

---

[6] N. Malcolm, *Ludwig Wittgenstein: A Memoir* (London: Oxford University Press, 1958), p. 29.

1. Wittgenstein makes the point that one must not be seduced into thinking that one understands a certain sentence simply because it is grammatically well-formed and consists entirely of familiar words: the sentence may, in fact, make no sense whatever, or be at least "fishy" in some important respect.

> "These deaf-mutes have learned only a gesture-language, but each of them talks to himself inwardly in a vocal language."—Now, don't you understand that?— . . . I do not know whether I am to say I understand it or don't understand it. I might answer, "It's an English sentence; *apparently* quite in order—that is, until one wants to do something with it; it has a connection with other sentences which makes it difficult for us to say that nobody really knows what it tells us; but everyone who has not become calloused by doing philosophy notices that there is something wrong here." [*PI*, §348]

The same point is made in *The Blue and Brown Books:* there, instead of saying, "It's an English sentence; *apparently* quite in order," he says, "It sounds English, or German, etc., all right" [*BB,* p. 56]. This point and even the forms of words in which it is expressed are reminiscent of Carroll. After the Hatter had said something (viz., "Which is just the case with *mine*") that he seemed to have thought answered Alice's criticism of his watch,

> Alice felt dreadfully puzzled. The Hatter's remark seemed to her to have no sort of meaning in it, and yet it was certainly English. "I don't quite understand you," she said, as politely as she could. [*AW,* ch. 7.]

A similar scene occurs in *Sylvie and Bruno Concluded.* The Professor said:

> "I hope you'll enjoy the dinner—such as it is; and that you won't mind the heat—such as it isn't."
> The sentence *sounded* well, but somehow I couldn't quite understand it. . . . [*SBC*, ch. 22.]

2. Just as there are remarks that are nonsense, or nearly so, because one can "do nothing" with them, so there are acts which make little or no sense because nothing of the right sort follows from them; they do not have the consequences or connections that are needed to make them into the kinds of acts they purport to be. Two examples that Wittgenstein gives of such acts find parallels in Carroll:

(a) Why can't my right hand give my left hand money?—My right hand can put it into my left hand. My right hand can write a deed of gift and my left hand a receipt.—But the further practical consequences would not be those of a gift. . . . [*PI*, §268.]

When Alice, after having eaten a piece of magical cake, grew so tall that she could hardly see her feet, she contemplated the possibility of having to send presents to them.

> And she went on planning to herself how she would manage it. "They must go by the carrier," she thought, "and how funny it'll seem, sending presents to one's own feet! And how odd the directions will look!
>
> Alice's Right Foot, Esq.
>   Hearthrug,
>   near the Fender
>   (with Alice's love).

Oh dear, what nonsense I'm talking!" [*AW*, ch. 2.]

(b) Imagine someone saying: "But I know how tall I am!" and laying his hand on top of his head to prove it. [*PI*, §279.]

Putting your hand on top of your head does not demonstrate that you know how tall you are, because it has no conceptual connections with anything beyond itself—for example, with acts of measuring with foot rules, or of standing back to back with another person of known height. The same (vacuous) act could be performed by anyone, no matter how tall he was and whether or not he knew how tall he was. Similarly, if you should ever have occasion, like Alice, to wonder whether you are rapidly growing or shrinking, it will avail you nothing to put your hand on top of your head to find out: the same results will be achieved in either case—namely, none.

> She ate a little bit, and said anxiously to herself "Which way? Which way?", holding her hand on the top of her head to feel which way it was growing; and she was quite surprised to find that she remained the same size. [*AW*, ch. 1.]

Alice's procedure would not be fruitless, of course, if she had reason to think that *only* her head and/or neck were stretching or shrinking while the rest of her body was remaining the same size. But she had no such reason, nor, as far as I can tell, did she think she had. Her surprise, therefore, is entirely unwarranted.

3. I can detect no intimate connection between Carroll and the early Wittgenstein, and so virtually all my examples are drawn from the later Wittgenstein. Still, there is one point in the *Tractatus* with which Carroll would presumably agree. Wittgenstein maintains that tautologies, including the Law of Excluded Middle, say nothing.

> (For example, I know nothing about the weather when I know that it is either raining or not raining.) [*T.* 4.461.]

Carroll relies on this truth for his laughs when he has the White Knight describe the song he intends to sing.

> "It's long," said the Knight, "but it's very, *very* beautiful. Everybody that hears me sing it—either it brings *tears* into their eyes, or else—"
> "Or else what?" said Alice, for the Knight had made a sudden pause.
> "Or else it doesn't, you know." [*TLG*, ch. 8.]

4. In both the *Tractatus* and the *Investigations,* Wittgenstein heaps scorn on the (alleged) proposition that "A thing is identical with itself."

> Roughly speaking, to say of *two* things that they are identical is nonsense, and to say of *one* thing that it is identical with itself is to say nothing at all. [*T,* 5.5303.]

> "A thing is identical with itself."—There is no finer example of a useless proposition, which yet is connected with a certain play of the imagination. It is as if in imagination we put a thing into its own shape and saw that it fitted. [*PI,* § 216.]

Carroll, too, saw that there is something very peculiar about such propositions:

> "I'm sorry you don't like lessons," I said. "You should copy Sylvie. *She's* always as busy as the day is long!"
> "Well, so am *I!*" said Bruno.
> "No, no!" Sylvie corrected him. *"You're* as busy as the day is *short!"*
> "Well, what's the difference?" Bruno asked. "Mister Sir, isn't the day as short as it's long? I mean, isn't it the *same* length?" [*SB*, ch. 12.]

5. One of the points that Wittgenstein makes over and over again in his later writings is that certain words which seem to denote something momentary and fleeting—usually, a feeling or thought or

sensation—actually signify something quite different—perhaps a disposition or ability, or at least a longer-range pattern of events. At one point, he uses the example of "grief": one is tempted to think that this word simply denotes an inner feeling which, although it usually endures for some time, may happen on occasion to last for only a few seconds or even for only one. To cast doubt on this whole idea, Wittgenstein asks:

> Why does it sound queer to say: "For a second he felt deep grief?" Only because it so seldom happens?
> But don't you feel grief *now?* ("But aren't you playing chess *now?*") The answer may be affirmative, but that does not make the concept of grief any more like the concept of a sensation. [*PI*, p. 174.]

Carroll, too, appreciates the absurdity of supposing that someone could feel deep grief for only a second. In Knot VIII of *A Tangled Tale,* we read:

> "But oh, agony! Here is the outer gate, and we must part!" He sobbed as he shook hands with them, and the next moment was briskly walking away.
> "He *might* have waited to see us off!" said the old man piteously.
> "And he needn't have begun whistling the very *moment* he left us!" said the young one severely.

6. Two points that are constantly stressed in the later writings of Wittgenstein are the following: (*a*) that "an ostensive definition can be variously interpreted in *every* case" [PI, §28],[7] and (*b*) that from the fact that a person knows what a word *W* denotes in one linguistic construction, it does not follow that he knows what *W* denotes in a different construction. (This latter point is, of course, intimately related to point 1, above.) To illustrate point (*b*), Wittgenstein uses the example of "measuring": one may know very well what it is to measure distance or length, but from this it does not follow that he knows what it is to measure *time* [see *BB,* p. 26, and N. Malcolm, *Ludwig Wittgenstein: A Memoir,* p. 47 f.]. In Carroll, there are passages in which these two points seem to play an essential part. During the trial of the Knave of Hearts,

---

[7] Giving an *ostensive definition* of a general term (e.g., "two") consists in pointing to, or otherwise indicating, something to which the general term is applicable (e.g., two nuts) and saying, "That is called 'two'," or something equivalent to it. Wittgenstein shows that the person to whom an ostensive definition is given *may* always interpret it wrongly: in our example, for instance, the person may think that "two" denotes that particular pair of nuts, or that *kind* of nut, or the color of the nuts, or their size, or any number of other things.

one of the guinea-pigs cheered, and was immediately suppressed by the officers of the court. (As that is rather a hard word, I will just explain to you how it was done. They had a large canvas bag, which tied up at the mouth with strings: into this they slipped the guinea-pig, head first, and then sat upon it.)

"I'm glad I've seen that done," thought Alice. "I've so often read in the newspapers, at the end of trials, 'There was some attempt at applause, which was immediately suppressed by the officers of the court,' and I never understood what it meant till now." [*AW*, ch. 11.]

This was not, to be sure, a paradigm case of an ostensive definition, since no one pointed to the proceedings and said to Alice "That is what is known as 'suppressing a guinea-pig' "; but it was just like one, since Alice guessed, from her previous reading of the newspapers, that it was in fact a case of suppressing a guinea-pig. Although not explicitly stated, it seems clear enough that Alice thought the phrase "suppressing a guinea-pig" refers to the beast's being put head first into a large canvas bag and being then sat upon, rather than to its being restrained and its cheering quelled, by whatever means. She thus misinterpreted the "ostensive definition" (point (*a*)). It is not so clear what is to be made of the second paragraph. Did Alice think she understood what the phrase "suppressing the *people*" (i.e. those who attempt to applaud at the end of trials) means? If so, she was wrong—for such people are not generally put head first into large canvas bags and sat upon— and then the point of passage would be to show just how drastic her misinterpretation of the ostensive definition was. Or, to read the passage more literally, did Alice rather think she understood what "suppressing an *attempt*" (e.g., at applause) means? If so, she was wrong again: for even if she knew what suppressing a *guinea-pig* was, it would not follow that she knew what suppressing *an attempt at applause* was (point (*b*)). Indeed, on her understanding of the phrase "suppressing a guinea-pig," the phrase "suppressing an attempt at applause" is nonsensical, for attempts cannot be put into bags and be sat upon.

The following passage from *Sylvie and Bruno Concluded* is, however, more clearly relevant to point (*b*):

"You seem to enjoy that cake?" the Professor remarked.
"Doos that mean 'munch'?" Bruno whispered to Sylvie.
Sylvie nodded. "It means 'to munch' and 'to *like* to munch.' "
Bruno smiled at the Professor. "I *doos* enjoy it," he said.

>   The Other Professor caught the word. "And I hope you're enjoying *yourself,* little Man?" he enquired.
>   Bruno's look of horror quite startled him. "No, *indee*d I aren't!" he said. [*SBC*, ch. 23.]

Sylvie's analysis of "enjoy cake" seems to me to be masterful; at any rate, Bruno may be assumed to know what it is to enjoy *cake*. But he mistakenly thought this knowledge entailed a knowledge of what it is to enjoy *himself*. Hence the Other Professor's kindly enquiry, which Bruno wrongly construed as containing the imputation of auto-cannibalism, badly shocked him.

7. Wittgenstein shows that one cannot always with sense "make the easy transition from some to all" [*PI,* §344]: for example, although it certainly makes sense to say that people sometimes make false moves in some games, it does not make sense to suggest that everyone might make nothing but false moves in every game [*PI,* §345]. Carroll also realizes the absurdity of such transitions from *some* to *all*. After Alice has recited the poem called "You are old, Father William" to the Caterpiller, the latter is highly critical:

>   "That is not said right," said the Caterpillar.
>   "Not *quite* right, I'm afraid," said Alice, timidly: "some of the words have got altered."
>   "It is wrong from beginning to end," said the Caterpillar; and there was silence for some minutes. [*AW*, ch. 5.]

During the silence, Alice was doubtless wondering just what was fishy about the Caterpillar's accusation. (Alice's "ear" for nonsense is infallible; but she is never able to locate the source of the trouble.) The answer is that the charge was much too harsh to be intelligible: for although it is quite possible to recite a poem and get some of the words wrong, it is not possible to recite a given poem and get *all* of the words wrong—for then one is not reciting *that poem* at all.[8] Similarly, when the Dodo announced that *everyone* had won the Caucus-race [*AW* ch. 3], he was speaking nonsense. One of the contestants can win a race, or some of them can, but not all. All can be given prizes, or even *win* prizes, for running so well or just for taking part in the race at all or for some other reason; but they cannot all receive prizes for *winning the race*—for

---

[8] Under these conditions, in fact, one is not reciting any poem whatever. Even if the (wrong) words that come out should happen, by chance, to constitute a poem, the speaker would not be *reciting* that poem.

to *win* a race is to come out *ahead* of the other. There is one at least apparent exception to this rule—namely, a race in which all the contestants arrive at the finish line in a dead heat; but even then, it is not obvious that they all *win* the race—and anyway, the Dodo's Caucus-race was not like that. (Carroll, of course, delighted in ridiculous extremes of all sorts. In chapter 11 of *Sylvie and Bruno Concluded,* for example, Mein Herr argued that since a map is better the larger its scale, the best map must be one drawn on the scale of a mile to the mile. His countrymen actually produced such a map, but they were unable to unfold it for fear of shutting out the sunlight; so they had to be content to use the country itself as its own map.)

8. Some of the later Wittgenstein's investigations were concerned with the relationship between, as we may put it, what a thing (quality, process, etc.) *is* and what it is *called*. One absurd extreme view is that a thing really *is* what a certain group of people (e.g., English speakers) call it, so that speakers of other languages are flatly wrong to call it by some other name ("How peculiar you Germans are to call it a 'Tisch' when it is so obviously a *table*"). But another extreme view is equally absurd—the view, namely, that *in all cases* what a thing really *is* is altogether different from, is wholly independent of, what it is *called*. Wittgenstein, as might be expected, maintains that the way the relation is to be characterized varies from case to case:

> First I am aware of it as *this,* and then I remember what it is called.—Consider: in what cases is it right to say this? [*PI,* §379. See also §§ 380 and 381, and the illuminating discussion of colors and color words at the beginning of Part II of *The Brown Book,* especially *BB,* pp. 133–5.]

There are two passages in Carroll in which the absurdity of the second extreme view, above, is demonstrated. In the first, the Cheshire-Cat explains to Alice why he is mad. After getting Alice to agree, reluctantly, that a dog is not mad, he goes on:

> "Well, then," the Cat went on, "you see a dog growls when it's angry, and wags its tail when it's pleased. Now *I* growl when I'm pleased, and wag my tail when I'm angry. Therefore I'm mad."
> "*I* call it purring, not growling," said Alice.
> "Call it what you like," said the Cat. [*AW,* ch. 6.]

The second is the famous passage in which the White Knight tells Alice what song he is about to sing to her:

"The name of the song is called *'Haddocks' Eyes'*."

"Oh, that's the name of the song, is it?" Alice said, trying to feel interested.

"No, you don't understand," the Knight said, looking a little vexed. "That's what the name is *called*. The name really *is* *'The Aged Aged Man'*."

Then I ought to have said, 'That's what the *song* is called'?" Alice corrected herself.

"No, you oughtn't: that's quite another thing! The *song* is called *'Ways and Means'*: but that's only what it's *called*, you know!"

"Well, what is the song, then?" said Alice, who was by this time completely bewildered.

"I was coming to that," the Knight said. "The song really *is* *'A-sitting On A Gate'*: and the tune's my own invention." [*TLG*, ch. 8.]

If it is absurd to think that what a thing *is* is in every case *wholly* independent of what it is *called*, it is equally, and even more evidently absurd to suppose that the entire nature of a thing is *completely* dependent on what it is called. In Carroll, of course, we find just this absurdity beautifully exploited. Alice came to a forest where nothing had a name: she met a fawn which then walked trustingly by her side.

So they walked on together through the wood, Alice with her arms clasped lovingly round the soft neck of the Fawn, till they came out into another open field, and here the Fawn gave a sudden bound into the air, and shook itself free from Alice's arm. "I'm a Fawn!" it cried out in a voice of delight. "And, dear me! you're a human child!" A sudden look of alarm came into its beautiful brown eyes, and in another moment it had darted away at full speed. [*TLG*, ch. 3.]

9. As is well known, the later Wittgenstein wages war against essentialism, the doctrine that there is a unique set of characteristics—constituting an essence—that is shared by all and only those individuals to which a certain general term (e.g., "table," "tree," "serpent") applies. Carroll pokes gentle fun at essentialism when he describes the Pigeon's interview with Alice, whose neck had just stretched to an alarming length:

"Serpent!" screamed the Pigeon.
. . . .
"But I'm *not* a serpent, I tell you!" said Alice. . . . "I—I'm a little girl." . . .

"A likely story indeed!" said the Pigeon, in a tone of the deepest contempt. "I've seen a good many little girls in my time, but never *one* with such a neck as that! No, no! You're a serpent; and there's no use denying-it. I suppose you'll be telling me next that you never tasted an egg!"

"I *have* tasted eggs, certainly," said Alice, who was a very truthful child; "but little girls eat eggs quite as much as serpents do, you know."

"I don't believe it," said the Pigeon; "but if they do, then they're a kind of serpent: that's all I can say." [*AW*, ch. 5.]

The Pigeon had very peculiar ideas about the essences of little girls and of serpents: indeed, her conceptions of these two essences represent two extremes. On the one hand, she thought that the essence of little-girlness contains a great many characteristics, including that of having a neck considerably shorter than poor Alice's stretched one. Since Alice lacked that essential characteristic, the Pigeon judged that she could not possibly be a little girl, despite the fact that she presumably had all the other required characteristics. On the other hand, the Pigeon seemed to hold that the essence "serpenthood" consists of only one characteristic—that of eating eggs: therefore, if little girls eat eggs, they must be a kind of serpent.

10. A variety of problems connected with *rules* occupy the later Wittgenstein's attention as much as anything else. Carroll, too, has something to say about these matters. In the well-known article, "What the Tortoise Said to Achilles," for example, Carroll attacks the problem of what it is to accept a rule of inference. He tries to show that, if accepting a rule of inference is considered to be the same thing as accepting a premise of an argument, then absurdity, in the form of an infinite regress, results. As soon as the rule is added to the premises of an argument, it no longer applies to the argument, and new rules must forever be appealed to.[9] The issue raised here by Carroll is a near cousin to Wittgenstein's intimately connected worries about obeying or following a rule, applying a rule to a particular case, and interpreting a rule.

There are many other difficulties connected with rules. For example, suppose that one or more persons are engaged in something that may be called a rule-governed activity. How can an

[9] I *think* this is what Carroll tried to show. I also think he does not succeed: see J. F. Thomson, "What Achilles should have said to the Tortoise," *Ratio*, Vol. III, No. 1 (1960), pp. 95–105.

external observer determine what rules the participants are following? If it is a game, can he "read these rules off from the practice of the game—like a natural law governing the play?" [*PI*, §54.] But then "how does the observer distinguish in this case between players' mistakes and correct play?" [*PI*, §54.] Or, more troubling still: how can the outside observer—or the participants themselves, for that matter—determine the difference between the participants' acting (merely) *in accordance with* a rule and their (knowingly) *obeying* or *following* the rule. (See *BB*, p. 13. Kant, as everyone knows, stressed the importance of this distinction in the realm of morality.) That Carroll was also aware of these problems is clearly demonstrated in the following scene, in which the Red Knight and the White Knight fight to determine whose prisoner Alice shall be:

> "I wonder, now, what the Rules of Battle are," [Alice] said to herself, as she watched the fight, timidly peeping out from her hiding-place. "One rule seems to be, that if one Knight hits the other, he knocks him off his horse; and, if he misses, he tumbles off himself—and another Rule seems to be that they hold their clubs with their arms, as if they were Punch and Judy. . . ." Another Rule of Battle, that Alice had not noticed, seemed to be that they always fell on their heads; and the battle ended with their both falling off in this way, side by side. [*TLG*, ch. 8.]

11. One of the most deeply Wittgensteinian—or perhaps I should say "anti-Wittgensteinian"—characters in all of Lewis Carroll is Humpty Dumpty. Wittgenstein attacks the idea that what a person means when he says anything is essentially the result of his performance of a mental act of intending (or meaning) his words to mean just that. If this view were correct, it would seem to follow that a person could utter a word or group of words and mean *anything* by them, simply by performing the appropriate act of intention. Wittgenstein concedes that the possibility exists of a person's giving a special meaning of his own to a word or words which mean something quite different in the language; but to do that is not to perform a special mental act:

> But—can't I say, "By 'abracadabra' I mean toothache"? Of course I can; but this is a definition; not the description of what goes on in me when I utter the word. [*PI*, § 665.]

(See the principle of point 5, above, of which this is a special case.) But generally—and this is a necessary truth—what a person means by the words he utters is just what those words *do mean*. We do not have to wait for the speaker to tell us what, in virtue of the mental act of meaning he performed while he spoke, he meant by them: and indeed, if we did, we could *never* discover what he meant—for we would be in no better position to understand his explanation than we were to understand his original utterance! One could almost say that it is precisely Humpty Dumpty whom Wittgenstein is here opposing.

> "There's glory for you!"
> "I don't know what you mean by 'glory'," Alice said.
> Humpty Dumpty smiled contemptuously. "Of course you don't —till I tell you. I meant 'there's a nice knock-down argument for you!' "
> "But 'glory' doesn't mean 'a nice knock-down argument'," Alice objected.
> "When *I* use a word," Humpty Dumpty said, in rather a scornful tone, "it means just what I choose it to mean—neither more nor less."
> "The question is," said Alice, "whether you *can* make words mean so many different things."
> "The question is," said Humpty Dumpty, "which is to be master —that's all." [*TLG*, ch. 6.]

Some of Wittgenstein's examples sound extremely Humpty-Dumpty-ish, in fact:

> Can I say "bububu" and mean "If it doesn't rain I shall go for a walk"?—It is only in a language that I can mean something by something. This shows clearly that the grammar of "to mean" is not like that of the expression "to imagine" and the like. [*PI*, p. 18.]

Underlying the Humpty Dumpty view of the use of language is the following picture: a person's ideas (which are nonlinguistic) are formulated, more or less clearly, in his mind; in order to express them, he need only find some suitable words—and, if Humpty-Dumpty is right, *any* old words will do. And so, as the Duchess saw, if you are sure that the idea itself is clearly formulated, the matter of translating it into words is no great problem:

> "Take care of the sense, and the sounds will take care of themselves." [*AW*, ch. 9.]

Wittgenstein describes the picture as follows:

> The phrase "to express an idea which is before our mind" suggests that what we are trying to express in words is already ex-

pressed, only in a different language; that this expression is before our mind's eye; and that what we do is to translate from the mental into the verbal language. [*BB,* p. 41.]

Wittgenstein regards the picture with suspicion, since it is dangerously apt to mislead the philosopher; Carroll, on the other hand, simply has fun with it.

We sometimes—and mothers of young children, quite often—speak of saying something and meaning it ("I told you to put on your overshoes and I *meant* it!"). This form of expression inevitably gives rise to the idea that the *saying* is one thing and the *meaning it another*—a mental act or private feeling or whatever, that accompanies the saying. Wittgenstein argues against this idea (see, for example, *BB,* p. 34f. and p. 145): in doing so, he is defending Alice—at least up to a point—against the March Hare and the Mad Hatter:

> ". . . You should say what you mean," the March Hare went on.
> "I do," Alice hastily replied; "at least—at least I mean what I say—that's the same thing, you know."
> "Not the same thing a bit!" said the Hatter. "Why, you might just as well say that 'I see what I eat' is the same thing as 'I eat what I see'!"
> "You might just as well say," added the March Hare, "that 'I like what I get' is the same thing as 'I get what I like'!" [*AW,* ch. 7.]

12. Of the several techniques Wittgenstein uses to make his philosophical points, two that are especially conspicuous are that of describing worlds (or possible situations) in which "certain very general facts of nature" are different from what we are used to, and (perhaps a more special case of the first) that of describing tribes of people whose institutions and practices are quite different from our own. What he says in the following passage would apply to *both* of these methods:

> I am not saying: if such-and-such facts of nature were different people would have different concepts (in the sense of a hypothesis). But: if anyone believes that certain concepts are absolutely the correct ones, and that having different ones would mean not realizing something that we realize—then let him imagine certain very general facts of nature to be different from what we are used to, and the formation of concepts different from the usual ones will become intelligible to him. [*PI,* p. 230.]

Thus, for example, Wittgenstein makes important points by considering the possibility of pain patches [*PI*, §312]; of one mathematician's always being convinced that a figure in another's proof had altered unperceived—presumably where there is no way of ascertaining whether it had or not [*PI*, p. 225]; of a chair's suddenly disappearing and reappearing [*PI*, §80]; of all peoples' "shape, size and characteristics of behavior periodically undergo[ing] a complete change [*BB*, p. 62]; and so on. And here are some examples of the second method: Wittgenstein imagines tribes of people who measure things with elastic footrules made of very soft rubber [*RFM*, p. 4]; or who have slaves that they think are automatons, although they have human bodies and even speak the same language that their masters do; [10] or who have no common word for (what we call) light blue and dark blue [*BB*, p. 134f.]; or who show no outward signs of pain [*PI*, §257]; and so on.

I do not think it overly speculative to suggest that Wittgenstein *might* have gotten the original idea of these devices from his reading of Carroll: for what are any of Carroll's worlds but worlds in which certain "very general facts of nature" are radically different and in which people (or at least *beings*) act in very strange ways? One or two of Carroll's actual fancies, indeed, closely resemble some of Wittgenstein's: the ontological behavior of the Cheshire-Cat [*AW*, chs. 6 and 8] is like that of Wittgenstein's disappearing and reappearing chair; and in *Sylvie and Bruno,* Bruno measures garden beds with a dead mouse [*SB*, ch. 15], which, although not elastic, shares some salient characteristics with foot rules made of very soft rubber. Countless other of Carroll's fancies are Wittgensteinian in spirit: for example, the White Queen screamed in pain *before* she pricked her finger [*TLG*, ch. 5]; and the Other Professor described certain people who do not feel pain when burned by a red-hot poker until years later, and who *never* feel it if they are (merely) pinched—only their unfortunate grandchildren might feel it [*SB*, ch. 12].

13. I have saved until last the respect in which Wittgenstein and Carroll are most deeply "at one," in which they become true spiritual twins. If any theses can be said to lie at the heart of Wittgenstein's later philosophy, one of the plausible candidates would certainly be the doctrine that much of the nonsense and puzzlement to be found in philosophy is the direct result of one fundamental

---

[10] See N. Malcolm, "Wittgenstein's *Philosophical Investigations*" [included in this volume].

kind of mistake—namely, that of wrongly treating a word or phrase as having exactly the same kind of function as another word or phrase, solely on the basis of the fact that they exhibit superficial grammatical similarities.

> When words in our ordinary language have prima facie analogous grammars we are inclined to try to interpret them analogously; i.e., we try to make the analogy hold throughout. [BB, p. 7. See also *PI*, § 90.]

We thus "misunderstand . . . the grammar of our expressions" [*BB*, p. 16], and fall victim to misleading analogies [*BB*, pp. 26 and 28.] Numerous examples of this pernicious, but completely natural, tendency are presented by Wittgenstein. Quite as many are scattered throughout the works of Carroll: indeed, I venture to suggest that the single major source of Carroll's wit lies precisely in his prodigious ability to exploit this particular human frailty. I do not propose to burden the reader with long lists of examples drawn separately from Wittgenstein and Carroll: I content myself with giving a handful (five, in fact) that I have chosen from among those found in *both* authors.

(*a*) Wittgenstein would maintain that the absurdity of Humpty Dumpty, already discussed, stemmed from his being misled by grammatical similarities.

> . . . What tempts us to think of the meaning of what we say as a process essentially of the kind which we have described is the analogy between the forms of expression:
> "to say something"
> "to mean something,"
> which seem to refer to two parallel processes. [*BB*, p. 35.]

So Humpty Dumpty treated the phrase "to mean such-and-such" as if it meant something very like what the phrase "to say such-and-such" means, and hence as though it referred to a private process going on in his mind while he spoke, just as "to say such-and-such" seems to refer to the observable public process. (Humpty Dumpty was inordinately given to this vice: thus he treated the sentence "I can make words mean what I want them to mean" as though it were perfectly analogous to "I can make workers do what I want them to do.")

(*b*) The temptation to assimilate phrases with radically different uses to one another is especially great, of course, when one or more of the words involved are the same (or at least appear to be the same). Hence it is treacherously easy to confuse empirical and logical necessity, since words like "must" or "can't" or "won't" occur typically in expressions of both:

> . . . It is somewhat analogous to saying: "3 x 18 inches won't go into 3 feet." This is a grammatical rule and states a logical impossibility. The proposition "three men can't sit side by side on a bench a yard long" states a physical impossibility; and this example shows clearly why the two impossibilities are confused. (Compare the proposition "He is 6 inches taller than I" with "6 foot is 6 inches longer than 5 foot 6." These propositions are of utterly different kinds, but look exactly alike.) [*BB*, p. 56.]

Both Alice and the White Queen are guilty of this very confusion:

> "I'm sure *my memory* only works one way," Alice remarked. "I can't remember things before they happen."
> "It's a poor sort of memory that only works backwards," the Queen remarked. [*TLG*, ch. 5.]

Alice thought that the statement "I can't remember things before they happen" stated an empirical necessity; that is, she thought it was like "I can't break twigs before they are dry." She thus supposed that if she had a better memory, she might have been able to manage remembering things *before* they happened. But clearly it is not an empirical, but rather a logical, or conceptual, necessity that one can't remember things before they happen. Since the White Queen thought that Alice's inability to remember things before they happen was due to the poor quality of the girl's memory, she too confused empirical with logical necessity. The White Queen fell into this confusion because in her world (if it *is*, in fact, a conceivable world), time ran backwards, and in that kind of world it would presumably make sense to speak of remembering "things that happened the week after next" [*TLG,* ch. 5]. But she forgot that her own memory, too, worked in only one direction (albeit in the opposite direction from that which Alice's memory worked [11]), and had she remembered it, she would have been blissfully unaware that this, too, was a matter of logical necessity.[12]

   (*c*) Wittgenstein points out that many of our forms of expres-

[11] Let us leave unasked the question: How could the White Queen, for whom time ran backwards, converse with Alice, for whom time ran forwards?
[12] Ignoring some minor qualifications, we can say that in Alice's world it is logically necessary that one can remember only things in the past, while in the White Queen's world, it is logically necessary that one can remember only things in the future. Here we may begin to see, if only dimly, the (very important) connections between (*i*) the distinction between logical and empirical necessity (point 13) and (*ii*) certain very general facts of nature being what they are (point 12).

sion seduce us into thinking of time as "a *queer thing*" [BB, p. 6] of one sort or another—for example, as a ghostly kind of stream or river:

> . . . We say that "the present event passes by" (a log passes by), "the future event is to come" (a log is to come). We talk about the flow of events; but also about the flow of time—the river on which the logs travel.
>
> Here is one of the most fertile sources of philosophic puzzlement: we talk of the future event of something coming into my room, and also of the future coming of this event. [*BB*, p. 107f.]

We would not expect Carroll to pass up the opportunities presented by this sort of confusion—and he doesn't.

> Alice sighed wearily. "I think you might do something better with the time," she said, "than wasting it in asking riddles that have no answers."
>
> "If you knew Time as well as I do," said the Hatter, "you wouldn't talk about wasting *it*. It's *him*."
>
> "I don't know what you mean," said Alice.
>
> "Of course you don't!" the Hatter said, tossing his head contemptuously. "I dare say you never even spoke to Time!"
>
> "Perhaps not," Alice cautiously replied; "but I know I have to beat time when I learn music."
>
> "Ah! That accounts for it," said the Hatter. "He won't stand beating. . . ." [*AW*, ch. 7.]

> "In *your* country," Mein Herr began with a startling abruptness, "what becomes of all the wasted Time?"
>
> Lady Muriel looked grave. "Who can tell?" she half-whispered to herself. "All one knows is that it is gone—past recall!"
>
> "Well, in *my*—I mean in a country *I* have visited," said the old man, "they store it up: and it comes in *very* useful, years afterwards! . . . By a short and simple process—which I cannot explain to you—they store up the useless hours: and, on some *other* occasion, when they happen to *need* extra time, they get them out again." [*SBC*, ch. 7.]

(*d*) Although it is not a very easy trap to fall into, someone might conceivably construe "nobody" as if it were a proper name, because of certain grammatical similarities, some of which are indicated in the following passages from Carroll:

> "Just look along the road, and tell me if you can see either of them."
>
> "I see nobody on the road," said Alice.
>
> "I only wish *I* had such eyes," the king remarked in a fretful

tone. "To be able to see Nobody! And at that distance too! Why, it's as much as I can do to see real people, by this light!" [*TLG*, ch. 7.]

"Who did you pass on the road?" the King went on, holding out his hand to the Messenger for some hay.

"Nobody," said the Messenger.

"Quite right," said the King: "this young lady saw him too. So of course Nobody walks slower than you."

"I do my best," the Messenger said in a sullen tone. "I'm sure nobody walks much faster than I do!"

"He can't do that," said the King, "or else he'd have been here first." [*TLG*, ch. 7.]

Wittgenstein imagines a language in which it would be much easier to succumb to this temptation:

Imagine a language in which, instead of "I found nobody in the room," one said "I found Mr. Nobody in the room." Imagine the philosophical problems which would arise out of such a convention. [*BB*, p. 69.]

(*e*) Finally, Wittgenstein warns us that just as "now" is not a "specification of time," despite the apparent similarities between such utterances as "The sun sets at six o'clock" and "The sun is setting now" [*BB*, p. 108], so

the word "today" is not a date, but isn't anything like it either. [*BB*, p. 108.]

The White Queen needs to learn this lesson—or else she has learned it very well and is not above applying it for her own advantage. She offers to engage Alice as her maid at wages of "Two pence a week, and jam every other day":

"It's very good jam," said the Queen.

"Well, I don't want any *to-day*, at any rate."

"You couldn't have it if you *did* want it," the Queen said. "The rule is jam to-morrow and jam yesterday—but never jam *to-day*."

"It *must* come sometimes to 'jam to-day'," Alice objected.

"No, it can't," said the Queen. "It's jam every *other* day: to-day isn't any other day, you know."

"I don't understand you," said Alice. "It's dreadfully confusing!" [*TLG*, ch. 5.]

WITTGENSTEIN AND CARROLL, AS WE HAVE SEEN, were both professionally concerned with nonsense—and with very much the same sort of nonsense. It is the kind of nonsense that results from the very natural confusions and errors that *children* might fall into, if only they were not so sensible. It is nonsense, in any case, that can delight and fascinate children. It is significant, I think, that both Wittgenstein and Carroll understood the way children's minds work: this is obvious in the case of Carroll, and as for Wittgenstein, one must remember that he spent six years (1920–1926) teaching in village elementary schools. (Note, too, that this period came *between* his earlier and later phases—that is to say, just *before* his conception of nonsense took a Carrollian turn.)

Wittgenstein's and Carroll's nonsense both produce extreme puzzlement: Alice is constantly bewildered and confused by the nonsense she hears in the course of her adventures, just as philosophers, according to Wittgenstein, are puzzled and confused by the nonsense that they themselves unknowingly utter. In both cases, the nonsense takes on the form of something like madness. Alice's world is a mad one, and she is a victim of it: she is utterly powerless against the nonsense of the mad ones she encounters—she *never* wins! The philosopher's mind, on Wittgenstein's view, is just Alice's mad world internalized.

> The philosopher is the man who has to cure himself of many sicknesses of the understanding before he can arrive at the notions of the sound human understanding.
> If in the midst of life we are in death, so in sanity we are surrounded by madness. [*RFM*, Part IV, § 53.]

Like Alice, the philosopher is a helpless victim of the madness (the nonsense)—until, also like Alice, he awakens, or is awakened, into sanity.

To be sure, Wittgenstein and Carroll had radically different attitudes towards nonsense: it tortured Wittgenstein and delighted Carroll. Carroll turned his back on reality and led us happily into his (wonderful) world of myth and fantasy. Wittgenstein, being a philosopher, exerted all his efforts to drag us back to reality from the (horrible) world of myth and fantasy. But the two men cover much the same ground: we may even look upon Wittgenstein as conceptualizing and applying to philosophy many of the points that Carroll had simply *intuited*. But the attitude, certainly, is fundamentally different. The same logical terrain that is a playground for Carroll, is a battlefield for Wittgenstein. That is why, although standing very close to one another, they may appear to the superficial eye to be worlds apart.

Wittgenstein on Universals

BY ALICE AMBROSE

> Consider the geography of a country for which we have no map or else a map in tiny bits. The difficulty about this is the difficulty with philosophy: there is no synoptic view. Here the country we talk about is language and the geography grammar. We can walk about the country quite well but when forced to make a map we go wrong.

IN THIS ANALOGY, which gives the gist of Wittgenstein's introduction in his lectures of Michaelmas term 1933 [1] to problems connected with understanding, thinking, meaning, lies the hint of an important and original conception of what the philosopher's task should be. To "command a clear view of the use of our words" so as to "see connections" [2] was the way Wittgenstein expressed this task some years later. But the *point* of such activity in connection with traditional philosophical problems is what differentiates it from the investigation other philosophers have made of language. Bertrand Russell, for example, set himself the problem of determining "whether anything, and if so, what, can be inferred from the structure of language as to the structure of the world." [3] And G. E. Moore attempted to show the falsity of views running counter to common sense, e.g., "Space is unreal," "Time is unreal," "Causation in self-contradictory," by "translating them into the concrete," that is, by considering the views in terms of concrete applications of space-denoting words, time-denoting words, etc. The philosophical investigations of the later Wittgenstein were aimed neither at obtaining information about the world nor at refuting the positions of philosophers who claimed to have succeeded in this. According to

---

[1] Preceding the dictation of the *Blue Book*. My notes.
[2] *Philosophical Investigations* (Oxford: Basil Blackwell & Mott, Ltd., 1953), p. 49. References to this work to be abbreviated as *PI*.
[3] *Inquiry into Meaning and Truth* (London: George Allen & Unwin, 1940), p. 429.

him philosophical "solutions" arise as the result of an initial linguistic muddle: "A philosophical problem has the form: 'I don't know my way about.' " [4] We lack the map which clearly sets out the grammar of the language we use, and get into difficulties which are quite unlike ordinary difficulties. We can neglect philosophic difficulties, says Wittgenstein, in a way we can't neglect those of the engineer, because philosophers' difficulties, unlike the others, are due to misunderstanding: [5] "misunderstandings concerning the use of words, caused, among other things, by certain analogies between the forms of expression in different regions of language." [6] We can become obsessed by a certain language form, and if we can remove the obsession we can dissolve the difficulty—make it disappear as would an illness with proper treatment.[7] The task then is to recognize the linguistic obsessions, for like other obsessions they are not recognized as such. Philosophical questions sound as if they were questions about fact of which we do not yet know enough, rather than questions about language, and accordingly they are approached as a scientific problem would be.[8]

Now in virtue of Wittgenstein's conception of philosophical puzzles as arising from the philosopher's use of language it is to be expected that the word "meaning" would play a preeminent role in his investigations. It is not, he insists,[9] that it is of more importance to talk about meaning than to talk of chairs or time—there are many problems in philosophy not concerned with the meaning of "meaning." But a cluster of inherited problems are associated with the term "meaning," several of central importance in the history of philosophy. Here I wish to present Wittgenstein's treatment of the metaphysical position that there are universals—abstract objects that are the meanings of general words. Parmenides said that one cannot think of what is not, that thought must have an object. The Platonist counter to this claim is that thinking must indeed be about something but that what does not exist can be thought of *via* a universal; to think that something of a given kind, ϕ, does not exist is to believe with regard to an apprehended object, ϕ-ness, that it has no instances. Similarly, to think of what does exist is to

4 *PI*, p. 49.
5 Discussion in the intervals between dictation of the *Blue Book*, 1933–34. Notes taken by Margaret Masterman and Alice Ambrose. Hereafter to be referred to as the *Yellow Book*. Abbreviation, *YB*.
6 *PI*, p. 43.
7 *Ibid.*, p. 91.
8 Lectures, 1934–35. My notes.
9 Lectures, 1932–33. My notes.

think of a thing or things that exemplify what is common to everything called by the same name. "Wherever a number of individuals have a common name," says Plato, "we assume them to have also a corresponding idea of form. . . ." [10] ". . . The things to which the term 'many' is applied . . . may be brought under a single idea, which is called the essence of each. . . . The many, as we say, are seen but not known, and the ideas are known but not seen." [11] "These, unlike objects of sense, have no separate organ, but . . . the mind, by a power of her own, contemplates the universals in all things." [12] The picture created by these excerpts of what understanding a general word consists in is that of a refined object being apprehended by an inner vision. This object is the word's meaning, something in virtue of which the word is applied to a number of things. Hearing or uttering a general word has as its accompaniment a mental process of laying hold of the element common to things the word designates. This common element, like an essential ingredient, makes them what they are. ". . . Nothing makes a thing beautiful but the presence and participation of beauty. . . . By beauty all beautiful things become beautiful." [13] *What* it is could theoretically be specified by a complete analysis, for its boundaries are exact. Any uncertainty over whether a thing possesses a property ϕ is due to our imperfect grasp of the perfectly definite essence, for a thing must have either ϕ or non-ϕ.

This, now, is the view from whose spell Wittgenstein sets out to free us, an enchantment "which forms of expression exert upon us." [14] For the germ of the verbal malady finding expression in every philosophical view lies in the language of everyday use.[15] Not that our language is not perfectly adequate to its job. No reform of language on the part of a philosopher is necessary.[16] In fact, says Wittgenstein, we are going to find out that everything is all right except what the philosophers say. What the bed-maker says is all right, but what they say is all wrong.[17] This is because in doing philosophy they are inclined to view our language as much simpler

[10] *Republic,* Book X, Sec. 596. Jowett translation.
[11] *Ibid.,* Book VI, Sec. 507.
[12] *Theaetetus,* Sec. 185.
[13] *Phaedo,* Sec. 100.
[14] *Blue Book* (Oxford: Basil Blackwell & Mott, Ltd., 1958), p. 27. Abbreviation, *BB.*
[15] Note also G. E. Moore's complaint that "language should have grown up just as if it were expressly designed to mislead philosophers." *Philosophical Studies* (London: Macmillan & Co., Ltd., 1922), p. 217.
[16] *PI,* p. 51; *BB,* p. 28.
[17] *YB.*

than it is.[18] (Cf. St. Augustine's description of learning Latin by learning the names of things.) Similar structures in language—verbally analogous forms—can mislead; for example, the noun form of "understanding" and "walking," and of "the meaning of a word" and "the man sitting next to me." "The cases in which particularly we wish to say that someone is misled by a form of expression," says Wittgenstein, "are those in which we would say: 'he wouldn't talk as he does if he were aware of this difference in the grammar of such-and-such words.' " [19] Several misinterpretations of what Wittgenstein does when he takes up the Platonic view, or, for that matter, any philosophical position, should be noted at once, in advance of fuller discussion. These misinterpretations are understandable, for there is no doubt that his language often encourages them. One misinterpretation is to suppose he is holding that we are misled by a form of expression into pronouncing a *false* view. Another is to think that because his investigations often are empirical, they are directed to *denying* what some philosophers assert to be true.

I turn now to an account of his procedure in dealing with various of the claims comprised in the Platonic view on universals, presenting first the kinds of investigations he engages in and then the interpretation, consonant with his own statements, which is properly to be placed on them. The following, all of which look to be empirical directives, are some of the lines he invited his pupils to pursue: (1) look at what understanding a general word comes to; (2) try thinking of the meaning of a word without thinking of the word; (3) look and see whether you find something common to all the things having a common name; (4) look at how "understanding" is used, at how "meaning" is used.

(1) Is understanding a word or sentence a mental accompaniment of a sign, and is the difference between understanding and not understanding an expression constituted by the presence in the one case and the absence in the other of meanings in addition to the verbal expressions? Wittgenstein's answer is "No." "When I think in language, there aren't 'meanings' going through my mind in addition to the verbal expressions." [20] Nor does one always discover a mental event or process happening concomitantly with a heard or spoken word which is understood. If the two were concomitants,

[18] Lectures, 1933–34.
[19] BB, p. 28.
[20] PI, p. 107.

then presumably the one could be found in divorce from the other, like the melody and words of a song. Yet thinking "seems to be an accompaniment of speech. A process, which may accompany something else, or can go on by itself." [21]

To see that thinking the meanings is not an activity independent of or in addition to the activity of using an expression, nor the meanings independent of symbols, Wittgenstein suggests (2) our "mak[ing] the following experiment: Say and mean a sentence, e.g.: 'It will probably rain tomorrow.' Now think the same thought again, mean what you just meant, but without saying anything. . . ." [22] One can, of course, speak without thinking. "Speaking a sentence without thinking consists in switching on speech and switching off certain accompaniments of speech. Now ask yourself: Does thinking the sentence without speaking it consist of turning over the switch (switching on what we previously switched off and vice versa); that is, does thinking the sentence without speaking it now simply consist in keeping on what accompanied the words but leaving out the words? Try to think the thought of a sentence without the sentence and see whether this is what happens." [23]

It certainly seems to be correct to describe the proposed investigation here as an experiment conducted for the purpose of justifying an empirical statement about understanding. It looks as though a point of psychology has been raised, to be settled by introspection, and that Wittgenstein has simply denied a factual claim about "the eye of the mind" and its objects. It is important therefore to take note of Wittgenstein's remark in this connection: "This, of course, doesn't mean that we have shown that peculiar acts of consciousness do not accompany the expression of our thoughts! Only we no longer say that they *must* accompany them." [24] There may be nothing at all going on in the mind; ". . . the experience of thinking *may* just be the experience of saying." [25] What I shall try to make clear is the philosophical point of citing facts which will remove the temptation to say that understanding a word, or having a general idea, *must* be a mental event. A hint is given by Wittgenstein in the following comments: [26]

. . . Philosophy arises out of prejudices—prejudices in favor of

[21] *Ibid.*, p. 107.
[22] *BB*, p. 42.
[23] *Ibid.*, p. 43.
[24] *Ibid.*, p. 42.
[25] *Ibid.*, p. 43.
[26] Lectures, 1934–35.

one form of description. Every philosophical problem contains one particular word or its equivalent, the word "must" or "cannot." When you ask yourself what happens in your mind when you hear or use a sentence in which the word "plant" occurs, you immediately tend to say that there must be an image before your mind, either an image of a particular plant or, if not this, then a Galtonian composite photograph. But on examination you find there is often no image. When you discover this you tend to say that you must have something like it: "If it is not an image it must be something more subtle." There must be some idea, else what do we mean when we say a man understands the word "plant"? Understanding must be some process in his mind. This "must" is a sign of a philosophical problem.

(3) Parallel comments apply to his injunction to look and see whether there is anything common to all the things having a common name. To revert to our consideration of understanding a word, it comes natural to suppose that the phrase "having a general idea" stands for one kind of phenomenon (else why use the same phrase for each of the cases we call "having a general idea"?), and that *what* is grasped in the act of having a general idea is the element common to all entities subsumed under it. Socrates' search for the definition of virtue, knowledge, and so on, was avowedly a search for such a common element, an essence. Wittgenstein comments that "the idea of a general concept being a common property of its particular instances . . . is comparable to the idea that *properties* are *ingredients* of the things which have the properties, e.g., that beauty is an ingredient of all beautiful things as alcohol is of beer and wine. . . ." [27] People who try to find something common to all applications of the word "good" maintain: "There is one word, therefore there must be one thing." [28]

The kind of fact Wittgenstein wants to point out in this connection he illustrates in several places [29] by using the example of games: "We are inclined to think there must be something in common to all games, say, and that this common property is the justification for applying the general term 'game' to the various games; whereas games form a *family,* the members of which have family likenesses," [30] for example, build, gait, temperament, mannerisms. Instead of one common feature, one finds overlapping similarities. These form a series in which adjacent members resemble each other

[27] *BB*, p. 17.
[28] Lectures, 1934–35.
[29] *BB*, p. 17; *PI*, pp. 31–32.
[30] *BB*, p. 17.

and things at later points in the series may have no similarity to those at earlier points. Socrates fails in his search for what is common to all instances of knowledge because there is no one property possessed by *everything* to which the term "knowledge" applies. We use the term "knowledge" in all sorts of ways.[31]

It might be supposed that Wittgenstein was simply denying the truth of the Platonic claim that here is something common to all things having a common name. My exposition thus far leaves it open whether he intended to conclude with a counter *position* such as Locke intended by his challenge: "For I demand, what are the alterations [which] may or may not be in a horse or lead, without making either of them to be of another species? . . . [We] will never be able to know when anything precisely ceases to be of the species of a horse or lead." [32] Locke, like Wittgenstein, is saying that were there a common property ∅ which if lacking to a thing made it cease to be what it is, it would be possible to know, as it gradually transformed into something else, *exactly* the point where this happened. But we know that when a change proceeds by imperceptible gradations, this is not possible. The difference between Wittgenstein and Locke is in the *point* of calling attention to such a fact. Actually it is a way, on Wittgenstein's part, of calling attention to our use of language. He explicitly denies that he is attempting to ascertain what the facts are that are described by language. ". . . Our considerations could not be scientific ones. . . . Philosophical problems . . . are, of course, not empirical problems; they are solved, rather, by looking into the workings of our language. . . ." [33] "The work of the philosopher," he says, "consists in assembling reminders for a particular purpose." [34] The question is, reminders of what? and for what purpose?

The answer, as it bears on the questions, expressed in the factual idiom, "What is the meaning of a word?," "Is understanding a general word for the mental activity of apprehending an abstract object?," exhibits what his conception of a philosophical problems and its solution is, and the therapy by which the *dis*solution of a problem may be effected. This brings us to his injunction (4), look at how "understanding" and "meaning" are used in the language. The question this injunction naturally raises is whether Wittgenstein is

[31] Lectures, 1934–35.
[32] *Essay Concerning Human Understanding*, Bk. III, Ch. III, Sec. 13.
[33] PI, p. 47.
[34] *Ibid.*, p. 50.

not, after all, proposing an investigation of matter of fact—of linguistic fact as against the nonlinguistic facts philosophers believe themselves to be dealing with. Linguists and grammarians have this kind of interest. What is the difference between Wittgenstein's and the linguist's study of grammar? Wittgenstein denies that he is interested in the natural history of human beings.[35] He is no more interested in recording linguistic conventions than in investigating psychology [36]—he wishes to give neither a definition of the word "understanding" nor a psychological description of what usually goes on in understanding. What then is his concern with the "grammar" of a word? If he states what is correctly substitutable for a word,[37] does this not duplicate the work of the lexicographer? Wittgenstein admits that what he as a philosopher does under the heading of "grammar" often departs from what is generally called "grammar." [38] For example, ordinary grammar does not preclude substantives which in their occurrence in sentences appear to have a use to denote objects when in fact they do not: the word "sake" is such a spurious substantive. Nor does ordinary grammar tell us that the use of "time" in "time flows" cannot be explained by ostensive definition (in the usual sense of pointing to a thing) as can the use of "water" in "water flows." [39] It is part of the "grammar" of "time," "or," "perhaps," "one" that they do not have a definition of this kind. Now such facts we all know as well as he. I cannot teach you any new fact, he says, but I can help you to recognize certain facts which otherwise you would not recognize.[40] Sometimes I have to describe the actual use of a word if you have forgotten it,[41] and sometimes to construct new uses of a word which differ from any actual use. And what is the point of this? The answer distinguishes Wittgenstein's and the linguist's interests, and more important, makes clear a new conception of what traditional philosophical problems and solutions are, and the means Wittgenstein conceives as the only ones relevant to dealing with them.

Wittgenstein states he is interested in language only insofar as it produces certain puzzles that we want to get rid of. He describes the actual use of a word only in order to remove certain troubles.[42]

[35] Lectures, 1934–35.
[36] Lectures, 1933–34.
[37] Lectures, 1934–35.
[38] Lectures, 1932–33.
[39] Lectures, 1932–33.
[40] YB.
[41] Lectures, 1934–35.
[42] Lectures, 1934–35.

The questions to which Platonic, and other, answers have been given, "what is the meaning of a word?," "what is understanding a word?," seem merely to be transferred to a verbal plane when one puts them in the form "what is the meaning of 'meaning'?," "what does 'understanding' mean?" However significant this step may appear, it seems quite another matter to adopt the procedure Wittgenstein recommends, of replacing "meaning of a word" by "use of a word," and correspondingly, "understanding a word" by "knowing the use of (being able to use) a word." He seems to move even further from the question when instead of examining "meaning of a word" he examines "explanation of the meaning of a word." In the *Blue Book*,[43] he argues the relevance of the latter procedure as follows: Suppose you were asked to explain what "length" means, or to explain "to know." It helps us in answering these questions to consider what we call "measuring a length" and what we call "getting to know." Similarly with the phrase "explanation of meaning," "for, surely, to understand the meaning of 'meaning' you ought also to understand the meaning of 'explanation of meaning.' Roughly, 'let's ask what the explanation of meaning is, for whatever that explains will be the meaning.' " [44] These questions concern the "grammar" of the words "length," "to know," "meaning." The phrases in which they occur provide the contexts in which it makes sense to use these words; the fact that "to explain a length" and "to explain a meaning" are not parallel usages and that "to measure a meaning" has no use at all shows up the differences between "length" and "meaning."

Wittgenstein says: All I can give you is a method; I cannot teach you any new truths.[45] The method is, in part, a therapy for curing one of the fascination of certain linguistic molds in which one's thinking is habitually channelized. The virtue of replacing "meaning of a word" and "understanding a word" by "use of a word" and "being able to use a word" is that the latter do not suggest pictures that block our seeing the use of these expressions in their "original home," [46] i.e., in a nonphilosophical setting. When the philosopher says, "understanding a general word, like having a pain, is a private inner process," "thought must have an object, as surely as must the senses," he has succumbed to the enchantment of a spurious picture.

[43] *BB*, pp. 1, 24.
[44] *Ibid.*, p. 1.
[45] Lectures, 1934–35.
[46] *PI*, p. 48.

And although he does not express his position as an account of a word ("understanding," "meaning"), he has fixed his own boundary around its use and supposes himself to have delineated the essence of what the word applies to. This implies a certain blindness to other criteria for the use of a word. Wittgenstein reminds him of these criteria, so as to destroy the preeminence of the preferred criterion. Of understanding he says:[47]

> The characteristic of words like "understanding" is that they are used alternately for (*a*) something happening in a person's mind as a conscious event and (*b*) a disposition. Actually, very often words in sentences are accompanied by something or other, images and whatnot. (It is this which gives rise to the notion of a general idea.) When you say "I said so-and-so while thinking of something else," we take it that two activities are going on at the same time, saying and thinking. But does it follow that understanding, thinking, etc., are activities accompanying speaking? Is there something in our minds like a set of bells, so that when a word is heard one chimes, and when a sentence is heard, several chime one after the other? (Cf. William James, who took understanding to consist in impressions made by every word.) Now it may be the case that whenever anyone hears a word a peculiar mental event occurs. I do not wish to deny this. Perhaps when a word is heard something like a bell sounds. But is this what we mean by "understanding a word"? [48]

The fact that we use the phrase "understands a word" in cases where no one kind of mental event occurs and even when none at all occurs shows that the presence of a mental event cannot be the criterion for its use. (This is the linguistic point of what looked to be a psychological investigation of what goes on in our minds when we are said to understand an expression.) Yet the model for describing the use of "understanding a word" which attracts philosophers is "experiencing a mental image." Understanding and imagining are assimilated to each other by treating each as having a content, the one a meaning and the other an image, both being determinants under the determinable "mental." But "meaning" and "image" are not related as "red" and "blue." [49] One can have a parade of images, but in making the ordinary use of words one does not have a parade of their meanings.[50] Of course it cannot be doubted that there *is* a similarity between the expressions "grasping

[47] Lectures, 1934–35.
[48] See also *PI*, p. 107, and the *Brown Book*, p. 157.
[49] *PI*, p. 176
[50] *Ibid.*, p. 176.

a meaning" and "having an image." Their similarity, however, is only skin deep, no deeper than school grammar. But like beauty it is capable of casting a spell over our minds. Preoccupation with the similarity prevents one's recognizing that an important criterion for anyone's understanding a word is his being able to use it. We do use "understanding a word" for this disposition; whether or not a conscious inner process takes place, "understanding a word" will not be correctly applied if the ability to use the word is the only test for determining that its meaning has been grasped. This is what justifies Wittgenstein's replacing the verbal noun "understanding" by "being able to use." Further, the replacement has the advantage that "being able to use" does not stand for an activity. It makes us aware of the difference between the functioning of the word "understanding" and that of "walking" and "having an image." "The scrutiny of the grammar of a word weakens the position of certain fixed standards of our expression which . . . prevent us from seeing the facts with unbiased eyes. Our investigation trie[s] to remove the bias, which forces us to think that the facts must conform to certain pictures embedded in our language." [51]

The Platonic picture of the mind's grasp of general notions as a vision of "the colorless, intangible essence" [52] incorporates two pictures which arise from our obsessions with one linguistic model. One is to take "understanding" as the name of an activity ("the mind, by a power of her own, contemplates the universals in all things"), the other is to take "meaning of a word" as the name of an object. I have already indicated how Wittgenstein loosens the hold of the first obsession. I now turn to the other. That "meaning of a word" is a noun form is already a potential trap. Consider any general word: ". . . you think of [its] meaning as a thing of the same kind as the word, though also different from the word. Here the word, there the meaning." [53] If a philosopher asks, "What is meaning?," we feel we ought to be able to point to something. "We are up against one of the great sources of philosophical bewilderment; we try to find a substance for a substantive." [54] Now it is quite true that many substantives do have a naming function, e.g., proper names, like "John," names of specific colors, like "cerise," general names, like "chair" (though amongst these there are important

[51] *BB*, p. 43.
[52] *Phaedrus*, Sec. 247.
[53] *PI*, p. 49.
[54] *BB*, p. 1.

differences). But not all words stand for things that can be pointed to, any more than what money buys can always be pointed to, e.g., permission to sit in a theatre, a title, one's life.[55] This is to say that it is part of their grammar that they cannot be explained by pointing to something. "Meaning" is such a word. Yet there is a great propensity upon hearing the substantive "meaning" to think of it as naming an ethereal entity. We speak of meanings as abstract objects, in contrast to the concrete things of sense, and the difference is treated as analogous to that between the solid and the gaseous, rather than between a chair and the permission to sit in a chair.[56]

The temptation to do this is especially evident in connection with number words. "What is the number 3?" prompts us to look for an object which it names, for since "3" is not the general name of a number of things, each of which is three, nothing seems more natural than to take it to be the special name of a single object. Arithmetic becomes "the natural history of the domain of numbers." [57] Disputes then arise as to what kind of objects numbers are. Numerals are one candidate, but since, for one thing, the infinity of numbers and the finitude of the set of actual numerals precludes their identification, the argument is that inasmuch as there *must* be something numerals stand for, the objects denoted are ideal. Wittgenstein says: " 'The symbol *"a"* stands for an ideal object' is evidently supposed to assert something about the meaning, and so about the use, of *'a.'* And it means of course that this use is in a certain respect similar to that of a sign that has an object, and that it does not stand for any object. But it is interesting what the expression 'ideal object' makes of this fact." [58] What the expression does is to suggest that "ideal" and "real" are adjectives functioning like "red" and "blue" to distinguish amongst objects. It is a step in the right direction to note that no object corresponds to "the number 3" in the sense that there is one corresponding to "Smith," but it is not enough.

There are several traps we constantly fall into, because we are inclined to look at language as something much simpler than it is. (1) One primitive feature is that we look for an object when we see a sign of the language. (2) We think of anything we mention as falling under one genus only. (3) We compare the qualities of a thing with the ingredients of a mixture. . . . This is difficult

[55] Lectures, 1932–33.
[56] Lectures, 1932–33.
[57] *Remarks on the Foundations of Mathematics* (Oxford: Basil Blackwell & Mott, Ltd., 1956), p. 117. Abbreviation, *RFM*.
[58] *Ibid.*, p. 136.

to avoid because it is embodied in our language. The genus, as
being something in common, is treated as if this common element were an ingredient. . . . There is a great difficulty in philosophy because all words look so much alike. The dictionary, in
which they are united, is like a box of tools which do look alike
but which have enormously different uses.[59] The use of words
differs in the way beauty differs from a chair. They are entirely
incomparable. . . . When we talk of words and their meanings we
tend to compare these with money and the things bought rather
than with money and its use.[60]

There is a certain spell exercised by the phrase "meaning of a
word," which results in such notions as that there must be a single,
perfectly definite property meant by each noun and adjective, that
this object is the meaning of the word, and is named by it analogously to the way an individual is named by a proper name. To
break this spell Wittgenstein urges speaking, not of the meaning of
words, but of the use of words. For in ordinary, nonphilosophical
contexts, "meaning of a word" can be replaced without loss by "use
of a word," e.g., in "knowing the meaning of a word," "explaining
the meaning," and so on. One advantage of this replacement is that
"use" carries with it no suggestion of an object corresponding to a
word. Wittgenstein's analogy of language with a box of tools aptly
illustrates the point of the replacement: one is not tempted to speak
of the use, say, of a hammer, as something independent of a tool
and as itself an object. How misleading it is to construe every noun
as standing for an object shows up if we contrast "meaning of a
word" with cases where no one could contest that it is proper to say
a noun has an object corresponding to it; when we can give an
ostensive definition, i.e., point to an object in order to explain a
word's meaning. It is never the case that we explain or give a word's
meaning by pointing to a meaning. Explaining its meaning consists
in explaining its use, and though in some cases this may be done by
pointing to things the word applies to, if the meaning were merely
a different kind of object than its denotata, it should make sense to
ask that it too be pointed out. The retort that, being abstract, it
cannot be pointed out but can only be seen by the eye of the mind
simply sidesteps the question why the meaning of a word can be
given by describing its use, in some cases without ostensive definition and in all cases without providing a procedure for becoming
acquainted with a universal. If it is maintained that both ostensive

[59] See also *PI*, p. 6.
[60] Lectures, 1933–34.

and verbal definition *are* such procedures, we have reached the kind of stalemate characteristic in philosophy where a matter under dispute is "treated perfectly hopelessly, as if it were a scientific problem about which we had to find out something new." [61] It is one of Wittgenstein's most original insights that an examination of the *philosopher's* use of language, in relation to the uses in non-philosophical contexts of the words figuring in a problem, will show what a philosophical position is.

It is obvious that Wittgenstein has a reason for urging our attending to the uses of words, and a reason for equating "for a *large* class of cases" [62] "meaning of a word" and "use of a word." [63] I shall try now to show the bearing of his procedure on the dissolution of the position that a shadow world of universals stands between names and the things named. For some connection needs to be made between a view not explicitly about any verbal matter and the thesis that it is the result of a linguistic muddle. As a first step, we should discover the linguistic point of certain investigations Wittgenstein engages in which seem not to be linguistic. Although he recognizes that the phrases "meaning of a word" and "use of a word" are not precisely intersubstitutable,[64] the fact that he nevertheless treats them as such has a direct bearing on what he has to say about the meaning of the word "meaning," namely, that it is not related to "meaning" as an object to its name. We can understand his directive to try thinking of the meaning of a word without thinking of the word as a graphic way of inviting us to look at the use of the substantive "meaning." For the result of the "experiment" is to find that this substantive is without a substance, that it does not have a naming function. In our language, some words are *general* names of objects, such as "chair," "man," "planet," and some are *special* names (i.e., proper names) of objects, such as "John," "Saturn." "Meaning" is neither a general name like "chair" nor a proper name like "John." It does not have a name use, although its use in sentences is namelike.

When in philosophy we ask such questions as "What is time?," "What is number?," "What is beauty?," evidently what we want is an analysis of the meanings of the words "time," "number," "beauty." It is taken for granted that there is *a* meaning which an

61 Lectures, 1934–35.
62 *PI*, p. 20.
63 See also *RFM*, p. 40.
64 When one understands a word "in a flash" the whole use does not come before one's mind [*PI*, pp. 54, 80].

analysis will explicate, that there are features which must be had in common by things covered by the term, and that a complete analysis will attain a completely exact delineation of essence. Wittgenstein's challenge, "Look and see whether you find anything common to the things having a common name," and his assertion that there need not be anything common to all things for which a word is used, but only a number of overlapping resemblances, do not on the surface place him in a different light from other philosophers, say the nominalists. But if we heed his injunction to look at the use of words, the linguistic point of his assertion becomes clear: that general words may have a number of related uses that gradually merge into one another, so that it is a mistake to try to find a boundary to use when none has been drawn in our language. When he says there is no one thing common to all things said to be good, no single strand running the length of the rope, he is making the linguistic point that "good" is used in a variety of related ways. The Platonist says there *must* be something common to things called by a common name, and he tries to state the boundaries of the concept by an exact definition. But "can you give a boundary? No. You can *draw* one; for none has so far been drawn." [65] ". . . The boundary will never entirely coincide with the actual usage, as this usage has no sharp boundary." [66] Inexactness is commonly taken as a defect, either in our grasp of a perfectly definite concept or in our language: "Frege compares a concept to an area and says that an area with vague boundaries cannot be called an area at all." [67] But this is "like saying that the light of my reading lamp is no real light at all because it has no sharp boundary." [68] The fact that a word has a family of uses does not trouble us when we use it, for example, when we use "beautiful" to describe things so different as a face, a sonata, and a mathematical proof. When we need a more restricted use we redefine (cf. the physicist's redefinition of "work").

The philosopher who is puzzled about the nature of goodness and seeks for its essence is asking that a boundary be drawn. What he puts forward as a theory shows the boundary that he wishes to draw. But it is not apparent that "an assertion which the metaphysician makes expresses discontentment with our grammar. . . . He is not aware that he is objecting to a convention." [69] When a phi-

[65] *Ibid.*, p. 33.
[66] *BB*, p. 19.
[67] *PI*, p. 34.
[68] *BB*, p. 27.
[69] *Ibid.*, p. 57.

losopher says "thought must have an object" he has already made his boundary decision, but it looks to be a decision about fact rather than about language. In the "disputes between Idealists, Solipsists and Realists . . . the one party attack the normal form of expression as if they were attacking a statement; the others defend it, as if they were stating facts recognized by every reasonable human being." [70] Suppose one said, "Everyone is really going to Paris; true, some don't get there, but all their movements are preliminary." [71] The form of idiom here is factual; but the use of the statement is to exclude from language, from descriptive use, "He is going no further than the market." (This is like "All lines in a plane meet, parallel lines as well, but they meet at infinity.") The words "really," "must," "cannot" are the signals that a philosopher "wish[es] for a notation which stresses a difference more strongly, makes it more obvious, than ordinary language does, or one which . . . uses more closely similar forms of expression than our ordinary language." [72] By means of these words he expresses his refusal to depart from a notation to which he is attracted, or his decision to reject another which repels him. But he appears not to be doing this at all. Nor is it what he supposes himself to be doing. He has the illusion, pervasive throughout philosophy, that a philosophical problem concerns a fact of the world instead of a matter of expression.[73]

The object of my bringing out the linguistic point of trying to think a meaning without thinking of a symbol and of looking to see whether anything common is to be found among things having the same name is to destroy a wrong notion of what Wittgenstein is doing. This is the notion, which has considerable currency, that he is simply denying the truth of the assertions "understanding a word is a mental accompaniment of the word," "meanings are definitely circumscribed objects." Wittgenstein's own words make clear what his intentions are: "What we deny is that the picture of an inner process gives us the correct idea of the use of the word. . . . We say that this picture with its ramifications stands in the way of our seeing the use of the word as it is. . . . Why should I deny that there is a mental process? . . . If I do speak of a fiction, then it is of a *grammatical* fiction" [74] Wittgenstein is not concerned to question

[70] *PI*, p. 122.
[71] Lectures, 1932–33.
[72] *BB*, p. 59.
[73] *YB*.
[74] *PI*, pp. 102–103.

matter of fact and is not to be construed as contesting the claimed truth value of any philosophical position, although he can be interpreted as concerned with removing the temptation to adopt one and defend it. Whenever we encounter a view in philosophy, "the thing to do . . . is always to look how the words in question *are actually used in the language*." [75] For this will weaken the obsessive hold of certain language forms, usually extremely simple forms taken as models in accordance with which everything is construed.[76] Another means to this end is the invention of artificially simple languages—"language games"—set up as "objects of comparison" [77] with our ordinary language whose words have a greater variety of uses. In these we may see the models to which we assimilate ordinary language, for the grammatical obsessions consist just in taking our language to be simpler than it is.

Although Wittgenstein did not explicitly develop the bearing of these general comments on the Platonic theory of universals, I shall try now to indicate briefly their application in a way consonant with what he has said on the subject. What specifically is the picture of language "which [holds] us captive" [78] when we picture thought as directed to the "invisible, intangible essences"? It is the picture of a very simple language in which all words are names—labels for things. "Meaning," "chair," and "John" have a superficial grammatical similarity; all are substantives. The philosopher who is impressed by their common grammatical form may be tempted to ignore their extraordinarily different uses and redraw the boundaries of the word "meaning" so as to stress the similarity. To treat it as a name is to recategorize it under a stretched use of "name." The appeal of viewing every general word as a proper name is the Platonic "grammatical obsession." Ordinary language encourages it, for "the clothing of our language makes everything alike." [79] But the Platonist who asserts that there must be common properties of things to account for the application of a single name does not recognize the presence of an obsession: "The philosopher is the man who has to cure himself of many sicknesses of the understanding before he can arrive at the notions of the sound of human understanding." [80]

[75] *BB*, p. 56.
[76] Lectures, 1934–35.
[77] *PI*, p. 50.
[78] *Ibid.*, p. 48.
[79] *Ibid.*, p. 224.
[80] *RFM*, p. 157.

A Feature of Wittgenstein's Technique

BY JOHN WISDOM

WILLIAM JAMES, at the beginning of his second lecture on *The Varieties of Religious Experience,* writes that "most books on the philosophy of religion try to begin with a precise definition of what its essence consists of"; and a little later says:

> The theorizing mind tends always to the oversimplification of its materials. This is the root of all that absolutism and one-sided dogmatism by which both philosophy and religion have been infested. Let us not fall immediately into a one-sided view of our subject but let us rather admit freely at the outset that we may very likely find no one essence, but many characters which may alternately be equally important to religion. If we should inquire for the essence of "government," for example, one man might tell us it was authority, another submission, another police, another an army, another an assembly, another a system of laws; yet all the while it would be true that no concrete government can exist without all these things, one of which is more important at one moment and others at another. The man who knows governments most completely is one who troubles himself least about a definition which shall give their essence. Enjoying an intimate acquaintance with all their particularities in turn, he would regard an abstract conception in which these were unified as a thing more misleading than enlightening.

And in his first lecture he says:

> To understand a thing rightly we need to see it both out of its environment and in it,

and

> it always leads to a better understanding of a thing's significance to consider its exaggerations and perversions, its equivalents and substitutes and nearest relatives elsewhere.

353

I

1. Wittgenstein said, "We have the idea that the meaning of a word is an object." He spoke of the craving for generality, of the contemptuous attitude towards the particular case. He said: "The idea that in order to get clear about the meaning of a general term one has to find the common element in all its applications has shackled philosophical investigation, for it has not only led to no result, but has also made the philosopher dismiss as irrelevant the concrete cases which alone could have helped him to understand the usage of the general term. When Socrates asks the question 'What is knowledge?' he does not regard it as even a preliminary answer to enumerate cases of knowledge."

These specifications and reformulations help us to know what he meant, but as he himself would have insisted, they don't take us far enough. The best way to teach a child the meaning of money is to show him what it will buy, and what it will not. We can't tell what a man means, we can't tell what Wittgenstein means, until we have faced the laborious job of finding what in innumerable incidents he refers to. This takes time.

2. A first and very natural response when someone says, "We have the idea that the meaning of a word is an object" is to reply, "Do you mean that we think that the meaning of a word is an object like a house, or a stone, or a cloud, or a block of ice? If so you are quite wrong. We haven't any such idea any more than we have the idea that the soul is a ghost or a bird, or the idea that causal connections are made of string. Or do you mean that we have the idea that the meaning of a word is an object, an entity, of a peculiar kind, not concrete but abstract, not subject to decay but timeless. If so, isn't that idea correct? We speak with the help of certain metaphors. We speak of the soul as within a body, as inhabiting a body, as leaving its tenement of clay; we speak of the likenesses between things in terms of the characteristics they *possess,* of the qualities *in* them. But what's the harm in these metaphors? What is the evidence that normal people or even philosophers are deluded by these metaphors?"

3. The first part of the answer is this. It is notorious that philosophers spend much time on certain questions, and that though it isn't

true that they make no progress with them, the whole business is or was in an unsatisfactory state. Philosophers, professional and amateur, often amaze, bewilder, and even alarm us and themselves by saying that we don't know things which we had all along thought we knew. We may, as soon as they stop talking, endeavor to smother our fears by saying, "It's all nonsense." And we can do this the better because among the philosophers are some who say this same thing, namely, "It's all nonsense." Besides, though there have always been sceptical philosophers who say that we don't know, there have always been others who say that what the sceptics say is false, and that we do know. And this dispute has gone on not merely for hours, not merely for years, but for centuries. Isn't that perhaps because the parties to the dispute don't know what they are talking about? And when one recalls philosophical controversy this suspicion is confirmed. A question in accountancy may baffle expert accountants for hours, a question as to the causes of malaria or of cancer may baffle expert investigators for years. Experts may differ and it may take time to settle which is right. But though experts often differ as to an answer, they don't differ as to what the general character of the procedure appropriate to their questions is, or not nearly as much as philosophers do. I mustn't exaggerate. Sometimes, especially of late years, when philosophers disagree they yet do proceed on the same lines in settling the issue. And then very often the issue is settled. Also, it isn't only philosophers who carry on disputes in a way which makes one feel that there is no agreement as to what is to count in favor of one answer and what in favor of another. Some political disputes smack of this—are they concerned with what *should* be so, or with what *would* be so if this or that were done? Still, it is especially among philosophers that one gets the impression of a game of cross questions and crooked answers. Among them, and I am one of them, one very often and very strongly gets the feeling "They aren't talking the same language, they aren't at all talking the same language."

4. Amongst the differences between players of the philosophic game which make one feel inclined to say they aren't playing the same game though they don't realize this is one very large one which I want to emphasize. It's this. Some philosophers have said in so many words that philosophical questions, or truly philosophical questions, are concerned with the meanings of words, or the logical

structure of the propositions we express by the sentences we utter. For instance, Professor Ayer said in *Language, Truth and Logic*, p. 50: "If the philosopher is to uphold his claim to make a special contribution to the stock of our knowledge, he must not attempt to formulate speculative truths. . . . He must, in fact, confine himself to works of clarification and analysis of a sort we shall presently describe." And of course many who say this sort of thing proceed accordingly. Philosophers of this sort have been or might be called "logico-analytical philosophers," or "logico-mathematical philosophers," or "philosophers of the linguistic school." There are sometimes differences between philosophers who say that philosophical questions are concerned with the meanings of words, and those who say that philosophical questions are logical, and you may feel that you are not very clear about what either of them means. But at least they agree in this, and at least this much is clear: both wish to insist on a close affinity in a certain respect between philosophical questions and logical and mathematical questions. Both wish to insist that philosophical questions are akin to logical and mathematical questions in a certain respect very characteristic of logical and mathematical questions. It is this. Without denying for a moment that logical and mathematical truths in some way help us when we are trying to learn and to grasp the way things happen, we must remark that the truth and falsehood of mathematical and logical statement does not depend on what happens to come about. Come what may, $2 + 2 = 4$. Come what may, $2 + 2$ will never equal 5. It never has, and it never will, and it never could. Maybe in some golden age when you put into a basket two eggs and then two more you could then pull out five. Maybe. But tall stories don't interest the mathematician; anyway they don't alarm him, they only amuse him. For his point is that while, when, and in so far as, there are two things of a certain sort and two more then there couldn't but be four, it's nonsense to talk of there being five. And it's the same with logic. Come what may, if all men are mortal and you and I are men, then we are mortal too. The inevitable is unshaken by the accidental, the timeless untouched by the temporal.

5. Now are philosophical questions like that? Are they questions as to what could or would not have been so and not at all questions as to what has been, is, or will be so though it might not have been? Take, for instance, the famous question "Can one ever really, directly, know what is in the mind of another?" Is this question like a

logical, mathematical question in that it is a question as to whether something conceivably could happen, if not in this world, then in a better? Or is it a question as to what actually happens, like the question "Can one live for four days without water?"

6. One might hope that this seemingly simple question as to the character of a certain question would be easy to answer. But it is not. There are two sources of difficulty. Suppose someone asks, "What is the character of the Englishman? Is he simple and honest like a bulldog, or is he very foxy?" It is not easy to answer this question. In the first place, there are Englishmen and Englishmen and Englishmen. Some are comparatively simple and honest like dogs, some are *very* foxy, and many are mixed. In the second place, even in the case of an individual Englishman it is not as easy to say what character he possesses as it is to say whether he possesses a watch of gold or any other object. We may, of course, guess that a man possesses a watch from the many occasions on which he arrives on time for pleasant appointments and ten minutes late for unpleasant ones. But besides observing and remembering those incidents in a man's life which may well be due to his possession of a watch, there is a quicker and surer way of telling whether he has a watch or any other object, namely, looking to see. But with his character, his motives, and his meaning, there is not. There is no better and surer way of ascertaining what character a man possesses or what motives drive him than that of observing and remembering those incidents in his life which are due to his possession of that character. To study these is to study his character and the driving forces of his life.

We could the better cope with the first difficulty, namely, the varieties among Englishmen, if though numerous, they fell into one or two definite types, like the horses of a county where there are only heavy draft horses and racehorses, and nothing betwixt and between. But they don't, any more than Frenchmen or Americans do. The consequence is that we have to keep in mind certain real or imaginary individuals such as Bull-Dog Drummond and Mr. Sherlock Holmes or perhaps Mr. Lloyd George, who was, I think, called the Welsh fox, and describe other individuals as being like, very like, rather like, or unlike, far from or near to these fixed stars who exhibit certain traits in extreme or in purity. Of course, the manifold of human nature, and even of the Englishman's nature, has innumerable dimensions, and consequently the frame of reference calls for many pairs of stars. The study of human nature is endless. But this doesn't mean that nothing can be done, and novelists and psychoanalysts and others who study mankind keep on at the job.

Fortunately, questions about the characters of questions are not quite so difficult to deal with. But the same sort of difficulties arise. Our question was "Is the question 'Can one know what is in the mind of another?' a question as to what actually happens like the questions 'Can one last four days without water?' or 'Are there people with clairvoyant powers?' or is it a question as to what conceivably could be the case like 'Could one square the circle?' ? "

Having in mind the first difficulty in dealing with questions about the Englishman we are ready to notice much variety in the manifold of occasions which may be referred to by one who speaks of "the question whether one can ever really know the mind of another." There are many occasions on which someone says, "One can't really know or can't directly know what is in the mind of another" and explains why he says what he does, and these occasions may differ not merely in what is meant by the words used but in the type of statement which is being made. It may be that they are sometimes used to make a statement as to a matter of fact which might have been otherwise, and sometimes used to make a statement which if true could not have been false and if false could not have been true. In order to grasp the character of the question raised or statement made on any *one* of these occasions we have to review the course of the discussion which forms what one might call the life history of that question on that occasion. In order to learn a man's character or his motives we cannot rely on his appearance or even on what he says. In order to learn what a man means we cannot rely on the form of words he uses nor even on what he says he means. The proof of the pudding is in the eating.

Suppose that when a person *A* asks, "Can one ever know what is in the mind of another?" it turns out that he is concerned with the correctness of all those stories, accounts, and figures which bear on the matter of whether it sometimes happens that one person knows what is in the mind of another without being able to see him or hear what he says or observe what he does, and that he is concerned to investigate these phenomena and add to this evidence. It seldom happens, I think, that a discussion which centers round the question, "Can one ever really know the mind of another?" proceeds purely as if the question were the question of fact, "Are there people with telepathic powers?" But *sometimes* such discussions approach this. The more they do, the more they are scientific and concerned with what actually happens.

Sometimes, however, one who says, "One can never know what is in the mind of another" is not concerned with the exotic facts which support the claim that there are people with telepathic powers. For instance, when Matthew Arnold in *Isolation* says, "We mortal millions live alone," he is not concerned with exotic facts which support the claim that there are people with telepathic powers. He is concerned with facts familiar to us all even though we ignore them. He is much less calling upon us to investigate incidents we have never come upon than to reflect upon those we have. And here we may think of Newton. Here we may remember how Einstein, when astronomers were hurrying to check his theory, remarked to Bertrand Russell, "Whatever they find, it's a damn good theory." Further observation was not irrelevant to the theories of Newton and Einstein, but we are apt to forget how much they called for thought, for reflection upon phenomena which had already been observed. What is more, their theories called for reflection involving a modification in our ideas, our idea of space and time, our idea of the action of one thing upon another. They spoke paradoxically. And so of course did Arnold when he said that each of us is alone really. He was concerned with something more difficult to remedy than what we usually count as being alone, with something more difficult to reach than what we usually count as meeting other people at a large luncheon party or a family breakfast. Because what he says is at once reflective and paradoxical, so that the thought it calls for runs counter to our usual habits, we may perhaps call his words philosophical. But if we do we must remember that, like one who says that nothing is really solid or that everything is bound to everything by invisible bonds, he is still concerned to show us the actual in contrast with what is conceivable. He speaks in *The Buried Life* of times when, as he puts it, "a hand is laid in ours . . . and what we mean we say and what we would we know." This is why I say that even though that of which he speaks is seldom or never attained, it is not something which, like parallel lines that meet, *could* not have been.

Even Proust is not plainly and definitely concerned only with what is absolutely inevitable when he writes:

> . . . It was she who first gave me the idea that a person does

not (as I had imagined) stand motionless and clear before our eyes with his merits, his defects, his plans, his intentions with regard to oneself exposed on his surface, like a garden at which, with all its borders spread out before us, we gaze through a railing, but is a shadow, which we can never succeed in penetrating, of which there can be no such thing as direct knowledge, with respect to which we form countless beliefs, based upon his words and sometimes upon his actions, though neither words nor actions can give us anything but inadequate and, as it proves, self-contradictory information—a shadow behind which we can alternately imagine, with equal justification, that there burns the flame of hatred and of love.

In his words we detect the influence of professional philosophers. But in his words we feel still the air of an old regret, regret for what might have been.

Does it ever happen that one who says, "One can never know what is in the mind of another" is concerned with what it would be as senseless to lament as it is to lament that one cannot draw a circle that is square? Are there among the discussions which center round the words "Can one ever really know what is in the mind of another?" some in which the issue in no way depends on what could conceivably have been otherwise?

The answer is: Yes. For some such discussions approximate to the following model:

A. How odd is mind.

Q. What's so odd about mind?

A. It's so accessible and at the same time so elusive.

Q. How d'you mean?

A. Well, one can know very well what's in one's own mind, and know well enough what's in the outside world, but one can't really know what's in the mind of another.

Q. How d'you mean?

A. When there is a question as to whether one feels cold, one can answer better than anyone else. When there is a question as to whether it is cold, one can answer as well as anyone else. But when there is a question as to whether someone else feels cold, one can't answer as well as he.

Q. How d'you mean?

A. When there is a question as to whether one feels cold, one's feeling of cold gives one better reason to answer Yes than does a like feeling give to anyone else. When there is a question as to whether it is cold, one's feeling of cold gives one as good reason to answer Yes as does a like feeling give to anyone else. But when there is a question as to whether someone else feels cold, one's feeling of cold does not give one as good reason to answer Yes as does a like feeling give him.

Q. When is a question a question as to whether one feels cold, when is a question a question as to whether it is cold, and when is a question a question as to whether someone else feels cold?

A. A question is a question as to whether one feels cold when one's feeling of cold gives one better reason to answer Yes than does a like feeling give to anyone else. A question is a question as to whether it is cold when one's feeling of cold gives one as good reason to answer Yes as does a like feeling give to anyone else. A question is a question as to whether someone else feels cold when one's feeling of cold does not give one as good reason to answer Yes as does a like feeling give him.

Q. Is it then so odd that mind is so accessible and so elusive?

In this discussion it comes out that the so-called Sceptic does not at any point refer to anything which could have been otherwise. Mind indeed is odd, but there is no more anything odd about its oddity than there is about the oddity of irrational numbers or of odd numbers. The asymmetrical logic of statements about the mind is a feature of them without which they would not be statements about the mind, and that they have this feature is no more a subject suitable for regret than the fact that lines if truly parallel don't meet.

More than this comes out of this discussion. For in it there emerges not merely the result that what the Sceptic means could not have been false, but also what it is he means. And both these results are obtained not by asking him to define his terms, to reformulate what he says, but by a process which leads him to illustrate in instances what it is he refers to. A person who says, "One can never really know the mind of another" may add, "I mean, one can never know directly the mind of another, never observe, never be acquainted with, his experiences, his sense data, his own immediate experience." But these reformulations leave us still in difficulties. And if he coins a phrase and speaks of "the asymmetrical logic of statements about minds," then, though his words make it clear that he is concerned to remark some inevitable feature of statements about minds, we are still not clear what this feature is without instances of statements which are about minds contrasted with instances of statements which are not about minds but about the material world, pairs of statements which are as like as possible except in the feature to be illustrated.

Take another instance. The statements of pure mathematics have a familiar but remarkable feature: they are true no matter what happens. The feature I refer to in this way has been referred to in many other ways. The truths of mathematics, it has been said, can be known by thought alone, can be derived from self-evident principles. The questions of pure mathematics, it has been said, can be answered from an understanding of the terms involved. And, more paradoxically, it has been said that the statements of pure mathematics are not really statements but rules as to the use of words, or again that they all tell us nothing.

The very variety of these descriptions of the peculiar character of the questions and statements of pure mathematics suggests that though we have always had some appreciation of their character, that appreciation has not been quite satisfactory. And isn't it true that we may be puzzled by such questions as "What is it for the answer to a question to be self-evident, or obtainable by thought alone? How can one know that what a person says is true merely by knowing what he means by the words he uses? And if the statements of mathematics could not be false no matter what happened, how can they tell us anything as to what happens? And if they tell us nothing as to what happens, how can they help us in any everyday or scientific enquiry as to what happens?"

In spite of the inadequacy and even deceptiveness of the various descriptions which have been given, we must allow that in the course of time an apprehension of the difference between armchair questions which can be answered by thought alone, and those questions which can be answered without experiment and observation, has improved. And I admit, I hope that what philosophers have said in trying to describe the nature of mathematical questions has contributed to our better apprehension of that nature. What I want to do here is only this: to recall with emphasis what I think no one will deny, that the final testing of the merits of these descriptions lies always in applying them to instances.

But now if no one would deny this, why do I assert it; if everyone would admit it, why do I try to emphasize it? Because I believe that though everyone will admit that descriptions of the nature of mathematical enquiry should be tested by the consideration of instances of such enquiry, and even puts this advice into practice, nevertheless the consideration of instances is often *very perfunctory*. Too often the response to a proffered description of the nature of mathematical enquiry consists less in vigorous review of the instances that description purports to cover than it does in argument such as the following: "You say that mathematical statements are not really statements. But surely they may be wrong or right, true or false." Or "You say that mathematical statements all say the same thing, namely, nothing. But then (*a*) how is it that they differ from one another, and (*b*) how can they be wrong or right?"

Without saying that this ratiocination gets us nowhere, I do submit that it doesn't get us far, and certainly not where we want to be, namely, at an understanding of what was really meant by the philosopher who said these paradoxical things as to the place of mathematical enquiry in the manifold of all enquiry. In order to see whether his metaphor, his extravagant words, illuminate that position, we need to bring before the mind in lively detail pictures, moving pictures, of people engaged upon a mathematical enquiry, and compare it with a film of one engaged upon an enquiry as like as possible yet still not mathematical—an enquiry perhaps about the actual habits of beads, pulleys, dice, not the habits of perfect celestial, timeless dice, pulleys, beads, but of their terrestrial, temporal copies. In this way we may come to see how misleading it is to describe statements about mathematical, perfect, pulleys and their faultless performance as statements about a species of pulley, and why one should represent mathematical statements as far nearer than we had realized to such statements as "If a being were perfect he would be sinless." And should we for a moment be tempted by the paradox "Mathematical statements say nothing" to consider them all as bringing no more light than "Sinless beings don't sin," then revival of instances will correct this misplacement, and still leave us the insight we won when instances reminded us how immune are mathematical statements, whether about the integers or the performance of systems of perfect pulleys, to all that happens in space and time.

The same procedure by instances which is needed when we are faced with such paradoxes as "Mathematical statements say nothing" or the paradoxical pronouncement "One can never know the mental, inner, world of another," is needed again when we are faced with the old metaphysical paradoxes: "One can never know the external physical world, but only our sensations of it," "One can never know the past," "One can never know anything beyond one's own sensations of the moment."

I believe that if, faced with the extraordinary pronouncements of metaphysicians, we avoid asking them to define their terms, but instead press them to present us with instances of what they refer to contrasted with instances of what they do not refer to, then their pronouncements will no longer appear either as obvious falsehoods or mysterious truths or pretentious nonsense, but as often confusingly presented attempts to bring before our attention certain not fully recognized and yet familiar features of how in the end questions of different types are met. These are features without which the questions or statements of the type in question would not be themselves. And they are features which can seldom or never be safely or vividly brought to mind by the use of general terms.

When Wittgenstein said, "We have the idea that the meaning of a word is an object," when he spoke of our craving for a definition and of our contempt for concrete cases, he was not saying that these habits of "abstract" thought always and everywhere mislead us. But he was claiming that too often when what we need is to come down towards the concrete, we don't, and that this especially hinders our philosophy, our metaphysics.

Others before Wittgenstein had warned us of "abstract" thought. But Wittgenstein *showed* the danger of it in instance after instance. Kant said that examples are the go-cart of the human understanding. But this is not enough. Examples are the final food of thought. Principles and laws may serve us well. They can help us to bring to bear on what is now in question what is not now in question. They help us to connect one thing with another and another. But at the bar of reason, always the final appeal is to cases.

And this has application beyond the sphere of metaphysics. For if we now turn from the remote sphere of metaphysics and think of more normal enquiry directed upon the actual events in nature, in life, we shall find on occasion questions which cannot be answered, statements which cannot be tested, either by experiment and observation or by reasoning in general terms. And amongst them are some of those questions and statements which mean most to us, and most call for thought. When, for instance, Sartre says that love is a condition in which one person consumes another, or when someone says that devotion is an explosive mixture of hate and love, or that we are all much more haunted by what is past than we recognize, and more bankrupt of the power to live or to love than we allow, then these words call less for experiment than for thought. But thought too will fail us here if we think that all thought which carries us to the truth must be thought on lines as definable or at least as conventional as the thought of an accountant who assesses a firm's financial position, and forget how much it may be a matter of giving our minds to incidents and incidents, whether they be as familiar as the fall of an apple or as recondite as the Michelson-Morley experiment, or the disorder of a madman like poor Dr. Schreber.

Wittgenstein as Dialectician

BY ALBERT W. LEVI

I

THUS FAR, I think, there has been no book or extended essay written on the philosophy of Wittgenstein as a whole. We have David Pole's *The Later Philosophy of Wittgenstein,* and we have (among others) Erik Stenius' "Critical Exposition" and Alexander Maslow's "Study" of the *Tractatus,* but to date no one seems to have been interested or able to provide a synthetic or synoptic gospel demonstrating that our philosopher is one and not two; that the "early" and the "later" Wittgenstein are a single and coherent mind at work which should command the same philosophical audience for a sympathetic reading alike for the *Tractatus* and the *Philosophical Investigations.*

This absence is striking and significant. It shrouds a perplexity and it masks a problem. And if we turn to its consideration on the basis of evidence internal to the work of Wittgenstein himself, we may, I think, not only provide an interesting footnote to one type of philosophizing in the modern world, but also demonstrate in passing how the eternally controversial question of philosophical method is inseparable from those personal factors which determine the development of a philosopher's thought.

Problems of transformation and development haunt the history of philosophy. Lutoslawski's study of the "Socratic" versus the "essential" Plato; Jaeger's brilliant conjectures about the fundamentally tripartite development of Aristotle's metaphysics; Vaihinger's, Erdmann's, and Adickes' hypotheses about the relation of Kant's "precritical" to his "mature" writings are standard examples of theories of philosophic transformation. But such transformations characterize the work of Russell, Wittgenstein, and Carnap no less than that of Plato, Aristotle, and Kant. Any logical empiricist will

366

be interested in three basic themes: "logic," "perception," and "language," but their intrinsic order may be precisely what differentiates his historical thrust. Russell begins with *Principia Mathematica,* turns to *Our Knowledge of the External World,* and ends with *An Inquiry into Meaning and Truth.* Carnap begins with *Der Logische Aufbau der Welt,* turns to *The Logical Syntax of Language,* and continues with *Foundations of Logic and Mathematics.* Thus one might say that Russell begins with logic, turns to perception, and ends with language, whereas Carnap begins with perception, turns to language, and continues with logic. How is it with Wittgenstein?

But before turning to this question I should like to point to one interesting difference between Russell and Carnap which is immediately relevant to our problem. Russell, like Picasso, has had many "periods," and he has never been timid about changing his mind. But although the early Platonic realism, the logical atomism, the neutral monism, and the later speculative grammar are far from mutually consistent, the changes are so frequent and come with such quantum regularity as to provide a macroscopic view of continuity rather than acute disharmony. Carnap's case is almost the reverse. Between the phenomenalist constructionism of the *Aufbau* and the syntactics of the immediately following work lies a methodological chasm to which Carnap's own uncompromising repudiation of the *Aufbau* [1] has called dramatic attention. Carnap responds to his own earlier work by wishing that it did not exist; Russell's inconstancies work out into the higher consistency (and permissiveness) of a maturing philosophical consciousness.

The difference between Carnap and Russell is immediately relevant to Wittgenstein in this respect: there is an underlying assumption that the philosophy of Wittgenstein is as disjunctive as that of Carnap, that between the *Tractatus* and the *Philosophical Investigations* exists the same type of incongruity as between the *Aufbau* and *The Logical Syntax of Language.* And this effect is heightened by the fact that Wittgenstein, like Carnap, is a father who has ungratefully disinherited his first-born. ("I have been forced," he says in the Preface to the *Investigations,* "to recognize grave mistakes in what I wrote in that first book.")

And yet this curious discrepancy in the work, this disjunctive

[1] "Die physikalische Sprache als Universalsprache der Wissenschaft," *Erkenntnis,* 2 (1931).

strangeness between the *Tractatus* and the *Philosophical Investigations,* loses its point when we add to the picture the intermediate evidences of the *Remarks on the Foundations of Mathematics.* For a close reading of this will show, I think, that the development of Wittgenstein's philosophy is closer to the paradigm of Russell than of Carnap, and that what we have here is an inherently dialectical mentality, momentarily stunned by the systematic vision with which for three decades *Principia Mathematica* had dazzled the European mind, until, rudely jarred awake again by the monstrous but cogent representations of Gödel, it could resume the dialectic that had always been the deepest direction of its spirit.

II

Let us consider the literal evidence of the titles (as we might seek a clue to the Kantian system through the names of the three Critiques). Wittgenstein begins with a *Logisch-Philosophische Abhandlung* (*Tractatus Logico-Philosophicus*). He passes to *Bemerkungen über die Grundlagen der Mathematik* (*Remarks on the Foundations of Mathematics*), and he concludes with *Philosophische Untersuchungen* (*Philosophical Investigations*). The titles are of the greatest interest. For they have been carefully chosen, and they are structurally alike. Each one suggests both a content and a form, a *subject matter* and a *method.* And they therefore present two questions concerning Wittgenstein's philosophical development: (1) Why, beginning with the notion that philosophy and logic are co-implicative, did Wittgenstein's considerations of the foundations of mathematics lead to a notion of philosophy in which strict logic has been eliminated? and (2) Why, beginning his philosophic work with a formal "treatise" (*Abhandlung*), did Wittgenstein turn to mere "remarks" (*Bemerkungen*) as a way of passing to the final enterprise of "investigations" (*Untersuchungen*)? The two questions ask essentially the same thing. And they have, I think, a common answer. For whether we attempt an analysis of Wittgenstein's content or a critical examination of the formal elements of his literary style, we shall be forced to the same conclusion.

Two conceptions of philosophic procedure have dominated the Western tradition. The first is classically illustrated in the earlier dialogues of Plato; the second is outlined in Aristotle's *Posterior Analytics.* The first, originating in a crisis of intelligibility, symbolized in the activities of the Sophists and rhetoricians of the fifth century, and contemporaneous with a loss of faith in the adequacy of language, proceeds toward a sustained, if piecemeal effort toward the establishment of meaning. The second, stemming from the practice of Euclidean geometry and Greek mathematics, uses axiomatic procedures to establish the chain of implications.

Wittgenstein's *Tractatus* lies under the acknowledged spell of Russell and Whitehead. Both in its systematic pretensions and in its almost obsessive preoccupation with elementary propositions and their truth functions, it registers a faith in the necessity for and in the possibility of logical formalization. But for all that it is an emblem of man's life. It begins with the world, and it ends with silence! Here, however, the analogy ends. For, while human life is prey to the fortuitous, the *Tractatus* carries the tokens of logical necessity in each of the numbers carried to four decimal places that introduce its propositions. I do not know whether Wittgenstein ever attempted the explicit formalization of the *Tractatus* that Carnap provides in the famous Chapter IV ("Entwurfeines Konstitutionssystems") of the *Aufbau,* or even whether such formalization could be successful, but the spirit of its method, like Carnap's, remains nonetheless that of Euclid and the *Posterior Analytics.* Its pretension is that of systematic order, and its arrangement is according to a canon of descending generality. At the same time its vocabulary pretends to exhaust the elements by which philosophic levels are defined: things, ideas, words—metaphysics, epistemology, logic. "1. The world is everything that is the case." "2. What is the case, the fact, is the existence of atomic facts." "3. The logical picture of the facts is the thought." "4. The thought is the significant proposition." "5. Propositions are truth functions of elementary propositions." World becomes facts; facts become thoughts; throughts become propositions; propositions become governable by truth functions. And now "world" has been left far behind; only "truth functions" remain, and the trickery of reductionism larded with the trappings of logical inevitability has persuaded us that logic is our entire philosophic landscape, bounded at the dim horizon only by mysticism or by silence. Now our minds are free. Now the air is fresh. Now we can begin to move. I do not deny that desert air can be bracing. The curious thing, I think, is that Wittgenstein himself found it intolerable to live in this desert.

Plato conceived of dialectic as a device by which words, despite their treacheries and ambiguities, might give intimations of their models and thus might be illumined by a truth unstatable in words. The Platonic operation may begin anywhere, as the Dialogues indicate—in a chance statement uttered by a Sophist, a slave, a successful businessman, or a poet—and it will continue as long as the words of the discussion offer adumbrations of the truth. But there is no ultimate faith in literal propositions. In fact, since the meaning of terms shifts, and definitions themselves are therefore variable, Platonic discourse is inherently drifting and analogical. But the sense of the *Posterior Analytics* is quite different. It attempts to found a science of demonstration; its presupposition must, therefore, be that ambiguity is a disease of language that can be cured. If unambiguous answers are to be provided, literal terms—terms univocal and with fixed meaning—must be distinguished. The Aristotelian philosophy of science thus requires a categorical scheme, devices for distinguishing systematic ambiguity, and a method of syllogistic reasoning. Thus the logical essence of the Aristotelian spirit is the adequacy of univocal language and a confidence in the products of demonstration, and in both respects Wittgenstein, in the Preface of the *Tractatus,* shows himself to be an Aristotelian. "This book," he says, "deals with the problems of philosophy and shows, as I believe, that the method of formulating these problems rests on the misunderstanding of the logic of our language. Its whole meaning could be summed up somewhat as follows: *What can be said at all can be said clearly. . . .*" Here is the faith in the possibility of univocal language, and the confidence in the products of demonstration is not slow to follow: ". . . The *truth* of the thoughts communicated here seems to me unassailable and definitive. I am, therefore, of the opinion that the problems have in essentials been finally solved."

Wittgenstein's *Tractatus* is indeed Aristotelian in spirit: in its concern for a symbolism in harmony with the conditions that would have to be fulfilled by a logically perfect language, in its belief that the essential business of language is the assertion or denial of facts, in its insistence (to which Russell called attention in his Introduction) that a logically perfect language must have both rules of syntax that prevent nonsense and single symbols that always have definite and unique meaning. So far it expresses a semantic orientation not unlike that of the Vienna Circle, and in fact Carnap in *The Logical Syntax of Language* [sec. 73] expressed both a personal debt to the argument of the *Tractatus* and appreciation for a syntactical emphasis which holds that the rules and proofs of syntax should have no reference whatsoever to the meaning of symbols. Yet Carnap adds that there are two points upon which he is in disagreement with Wittgenstein—what he terms Wittgenstein's two "negative theses"—and these two "negative theses" will well repay our brief attention. For Carnap's reservations are perceptive indeed; they are the very points at which an unrepentantly dialectical strain betrays its paradoxical presence within the framework of a systematic treatise.

Dialectic in its essence is purely an affair of discourse. It is not about actuality as science is, and can therefore neither produce empirical propositions nor strive after their species of truth. Indeed the two realms are logically disjunctive, with the consequence that the very relation between them (discourse and actuality) cannot be treated discursively, and that at precisely this point dialectic must give way to silence. Wittgenstein expresses it in proposition §4.121: "Propositions cannot represent the logical form: this mirrors itself in the propositions. That which mirrors itself in language, language cannot represent. That which expresses *itself* in language, *we* cannot express by language. The propositions *show* the logical form of reality. They exhibit it." This is the first negative thesis to which Carnap objects.

But the second is even more critical and paradoxical. For it is nothing less than the equation of philosophy itself with dialectic! This is the famous proposition §4.112: "The object of philosophy is the logical clarification of thoughts. Philosophy is not a theory but an activity. A philosophical work consists essentially of elucidations. The result of philosophy is not a number of 'philosophical propositions,' but to make propositions clear. Philosophy should make clear and delimit sharply the thoughts which otherwise are, as it were, opaque and blurred."

What Wittgenstein has recaptured is merely the ancient wisdom of Plato: that the peculiarities of language form a set of limiting conditions for the realization of logical values in discourse; that, since argument depends on language, the "meaning" of propositions and the "significance" of terms become crucial for the resolution of dialectical opposition; that, since natural language is already a vast assemblage of meanings before dialectic impinges upon it, dialectical definition can do little more than organize or

isolate meanings already caught in the common stock of verbal
references. What is paradoxical is to find a rationalization of
Socratic method in a treatise whose formal thrust implies an appeal
to the axiomatic method, an igneous intrusion of Platonic insight in
a sedimentary formation composed of layers of Aristotelian structure. But what is staggering is to find that this Platonism has the
last word. "My propositions," says Wittgenstein [§6.54] "are elucidatory in this way: he who understands me finally recognizes them
as senseless, when he has climbed out through them, on them,
over them. (He must so to speak throw away the ladder, after he
has climbed up on it.) He must surmount these propositions; then
he sees the world rightly." One can imagine the aged Plato reading
over the Dialogues of his youth and attempting to put himself back
into the Socratic atmosphere to sum up the intention of their
therapy; he could have chosen no better words than these.

III

On a memorable afternoon in Paris Gertrude Stein said to Ernest
Hemingway: "Hemingway, remarks are not literature." The question is, Are they philosophy? and, perhaps more to the point, why
did Wittgenstein so obviously think so? Why, after the systematic,
almost austere pronouncements of the *Tractatus,* did Wittgenstein
abandon this spare, cleansed style for the rambling, obsessive
dialectic of the *Remarks on the Foundations of Mathematics?* Why
did a "treatise" on philosophical logic turn into "remarks" about
mathematics?

It will be well to remember that *Principia Mathematica,* by
turning formal logic into a science of order, at once abolished the
distinction between logic and mathematics and demonstrated the
continuity between general procedures of implication and the
axioms of cardinal arithmetic. Wittgenstein's *Tractatus,* nevertheless, never ranges far from the earlier sections of *Principia Mathematica.* But in 1931 appeared in the *Monatsheft für Mathematik
und Physik* Kurt Gödel's famous paper "Uber formal unentscheid-
bare Sätze der Principia Mathematica und verwandter Systeme."
Its disturbing significance was not immediately recognized, but
within six years its revolutionary implications for the unreliability
of the axiomatic method that had dominated Western thinking since
Euclid and the *Posterior Analytics* had become the scandal of
advanced mathematical thought. Between 1929 and 1932, so his

editors tell us [*Remarks,* p. vi], Wittgenstein had written a great deal on the foundations of mathematics—the published version itself dating from 1937–1944. In some ways this is an agonizing reappraisal of the position held in the *Tractatus*. It is my belief that this agonizing reappraisal was forced upon Wittgenstein by the representations of Gödel.

Gödel's paper attacked a central presupposition of the foundation of mathematics—the tacit assumption that each branch of mathematics can be furnished with a set of axioms sufficient to generate the enormous totality of its true propositions. And it indicated the disquieting fact that axiomatic method has certain intrinsic limitations which make it ultimately impossible to establish the internal consistency of any deductive system such as that of cardinal arithmetic without assuming principles of reasoning so complex that their mutual consistency is as difficult to establish as that of the systems themselves. Thus the conclusions are two: (1) that for much of mathematics no final axiomatization is possible, and (2) that for many important branches of mathematics there exists no indubitable proof that they are free of internal contradiction. But, on the other hand, Gödel's paper suggests that mathematical theorems, recalcitrant as they are to strict axiomatization, may nevertheless be "established" by less formal metamathematical reasoning. Wittgenstein's transition from the crisp propositional dogmatism of the *Tractatus* to the informal methods and conversational meanderings of the *Remarks* indicates the methodological and stylistic repercussions of the Gödelian revolution—in Wittgenstein's case from a formality of expression learned from the example of *Principia Mathematica* to the permissive informality of a naturally dialectical bent.

What is the evidence for this interpretation? It can lie only, I think, in the basic way one construes the *Remarks on the Foundations of Mathematics* as a whole. What does it mean? what is Wittgenstein's intention here? what is the entire enterprise about? And I think a careful examination of this work will provide the following inescapable conclusions. It is haunted by the specter of Gödel; it is a dramatic presentation of the writhing struggle in which Wittgenstein as logical Laocoön tries to escape annihilation by the Gödelian serpent. Less histrionically stated, it provides a living demonstration of how Wittgenstein, through a reinterpretation of the nature of mathematics made necessary by Gödel, is forced before our very eyes to pass from the "logistic" to the "linguistic" point of view. And the vehicle of this passage is nothing else than the substitution of a Platonic for an Aristotelian theory of mathematics—I mean the reluctant admission that arithmetic is not completely formalizable in an axiomatic system, and a resultant attempt to found not a "deductive" but a "dialectical" mathematics.

Let me turn briefly to these two conceptions: "the Laocoönian struggle" and "a dialectical mathematics." In Appendix I to Part I of the *Remarks* Wittgenstein turns specifically to the issue of "truth and provability in the system of *Principia Mathematica*"—to a discussion of any proposition P that asserts its own unprovability. And unerringly he puts his finger upon the crucial question, namely, that of the role and importance of the principle of contradiction in what he now wants to call "the language game." For if mathematics is a deductive system, the principle of contradiction is central and, as Gödel has shown, ominous. But if mathematics is *dialectical,* that is, merely an arrangement of discourse, *only a language game,* then perhaps we need no longer take seriously a consistency postulate which functions as the reef against which the hope of any ultimate mathematical systematization will be dashed to pieces. Let us watch Wittgenstein writhing and squirming against the Gödelian serpent. [*Remarks,* 51e]:

> §11. Let us suppose I prove the unprovability (in Russell's system) of P; then by this proof I have proved P. Now if this proof were one in Russell's system—I should in that case have proved at once that it belonged and did not belong to Russell's system.—That is what comes of making up such sentences.—But there is a contradiction here!—Well, then there is a contradiction here. Does it do any harm here?

> §12. Is there harm in the contradiction that arises when someone says: "I am lying.—So I am not lying.—So I am lying.—etc."? I mean: does it make our language less usable if in this case, according to the ordinary rules, a proposition yields its contradictory, and vice versa?—the proposition *itself* is unusable, and these inferences equally; but why should they not be made?—It is a profitless performance!—It is a language game with some similarity to the game of thumb-catching.

And now let us see how childishly he dismisses Gödel [52e]:

> §13. Such a contradiction is of interest only because it has tormented people, and because this shows both how tormenting problems can grow out of language, and what kind of things can torment us.

And now an example of the Wittgenstein bravado:

> §14. A proof of unprovability is as it were a geometrical proof;
> a proof concerning the geometry of proofs. Quite analogous, e.g.,
> to a proof that such-and-such a construction is impossible with
> ruler and compass. Now such a proof contains an element of
> prediction, a physical element. For in consequence of such a proof
> we say to a man: "Don't exert yourself to find a construction (of
> the trisection of an angle, say)—it can be proved that it can't be
> done." That is to say: it is essential that the proof of unprovability
> should be capable of being applied in this way. It must—we might
> say—be *a forcible reason* for giving up the search for a proof
> (i.e., for a construction of such-and-such a kind).
>
> A contradiction is unusable as such a prediction.

Finally let us listen as he tries to reassure those childish mathematicians who have taken Gödel so seriously [53e]:

> (The superstitious fear and awe of mathematicians in face of
> contradiction.)

But I suspect that, despite the facade, Wittgenstein *has* taken
Gödel more seriously than he would like to have us believe, and
that the language of §13 above is as indicative of his own state as
of that of others. For one so deeply committed to the presuppositions of *Principia Mathematica* as Wittgenstein, Gödel must indeed
have made the principle of contradiction into a "torment." There
is a curious recurring metaphor which appears both in the *Remarks*
and in the *Philosophical Investigations*—"to show the fly the way
out of the fly-bottle." It is a metaphor of desperation and frustration, and, as it appears in the later work, Wittgenstein stands as
the emancipator and not the victim. But the Laocoönian struggle
memorialized in the *Remarks* exhibits him in the other role. Here
he is less the savior than the fly!

And yet, the *Remarks* does recommend a *via salvationis:* it
suggests the principles of what I have called "a dialectical mathematics." This conception deserves a much more extended treatment
in its own right, but here I can only suggest the ideas that Wittgenstein puts forward in the *Remarks* to give it point and substance.
They are as follows. A dialectical mathematics in Wittgenstein's
terms denies (1) the "geometrical" conception of proof, (2) that
logic is the foundation of mathematics, and (3) that there is any
need for a "mechanical insurance" against contradiction. On the
contrary, it affirms (1) that the propositions of mathematics are

merely "instruments of language," (2) that what we call "proof" is chiefly a "memorable picture," and (3) that at bottom mathematics is essentially merely "a *motley* of calculating techniques" rather than a deductive system. It is perhaps the case that the conception of a dialectical mathematics will make its own quaint niche in the history of mathematical thought. But it is not for this that I have made it the center of our attention here. Rather it has been to show its place in the evolution of Wittgenstein's thought— that we may use it as the vehicle whereby we may pass from the suppressed dialectic of the *Tractatus* to the fullblown dialectic of the *Philosophical Investigations*.

IV

One of the most interesting aspects of the work of Wittgenstein is the problem of his philosophical style. If he is sometimes unintelligible, he is almost always exciting, and the reason for this lies both in the terse epigrammatic manner of the *Tractatus*, which, for all the system of its inner connectedness, sometimes suggests the formlessness of a Nietzsche or a Pascal, and in the meandering, episodic treatment of the *Philosophical Investigations*, which, for all its apparatus of outwardness and pedagogy, so frequently permits us to glimpse the inwardness of a meditative mind at work, as in the case of an Augustine or a Proust. For stylistically the *Tractatus* and the *Philosophical Investigations* are, I think, at opposite poles, and this contrast does suggest a difference of mood emblematic of two entirely different modes of philosophical procedure.

The style of the *Tractatus* presents a literary atomism completely congruent with the logical atomism of its underlying epistemic position. Here *the single proposition is the element of discourse,* and it is made to stand out independently both by the strategies of punctuation and by the definiteness of the assertoric act. "The total reality is the world." "The pictures is a fact." "What is thinkable is also possible." "The propositional sign is a fact." "Objects I can only name." "The thought is the significant proposition." "A proposition is the description of a fact." "What *can* be shown *cannot* be said." "Mathematics is a logical method." The propositions bark out like pistol shots, and like pistol shots they are severally clear, unmuffled, and emphatic.

The style of the *Philosophical Investigations* is very different, but, again, completely congruent with the dialectical method of philosophizing that has now become Wittgenstein's acknowledged procedure. Here, not the single proposition but the lengthy paragraph, even the complex linkage of many paragraphs bears the burden of communication, as if we must get a clear view of the *situation,* of the whole context or language game in which the problem or the expression is set, and so the mood also has clearly shifted from the assertoric and the apodictic to the *problematic* and the *hypothetical:*

> Suppose, however, that not merely the picture of the cube, but also the method of projection comes before our mind?—How am I to imagine this?—Perhaps I see before me a schema showing the method of projection: say a picture of two cubes connected by lines of projection.—But does this really get me any further? Can't I now imagine different applications of this schema too?—Well, yes, but then can't an *application come before my mind?*—It can: only we need to get clearer about our application of *this* expression. [55e]

Not merely here, but throughout, the style of the *Investigations* is suppositional and interrogative: "Consider how . . . . " "But imagine the following case . . . ." "Which sensation does one mean by . . . ?" "In what circumstances should I say that . . . ?" "Suppose I gave someone the order . . . ." "Was I justified in saying . . . ?" "If it is asked . . . ." "What does it mean to say . . . ?" And this is entirely appropriate and right for an enterprise concerned not with an Aristotelian *assertion of propositions within a system* but with a Platonic *entertaining of propositions within a situation.* For while the former has as its goal the establishment of truth, the aim of the latter is the examination of meaning. "Dialectic," says Aristotle in a famous passage of the *Metaphysics* [1004b], "is merely critical, where philosophy claims to know," and this fits perfectly the distinction between Wittgenstein's two major philosophical works. The *Investigations* is "merely critical," while the *Tractatus* "claims to know."

The consequences are apparent in the forms. In the *Tractatus* it is as if one had a manual of war produced by the German general staff, where the formations are explicit, and the battle order is drawn up with logic and dispatch; whereas in the *Investigations* our concept of war is something akin to what one derives from the historical plays of Shakespeare where there are only "alarums and excursions," and the skirmishes are brief and episodic, but no less suggestive and definitive for that fact. There is some evidence that even in the *Investigations* Wittgenstein had hopes of producing a manual which might be worthy of the general staff. "It was my intention at first," he tells us in its Preface, "to bring all this together in a book whose form I pictured differently at different times. But the essential thing was that the thoughts should proceed from one subject to another in a natural order and without breaks." But this, as he so perspicuously tells us, became increasingly impossible:

> After several unsuccessful attempts to weld my results together into such a whole, I realized that I should never succeed. The best that I could write would never be more than philosophical remarks; my thoughts were soon crippled if I tried to force them on in any single direction against their natural inclination.—And this was, of course, connected with the very nature of the investigation. For this compels us to travel over a wide field of thought criss-cross in every direction.—The philosophical remarks in this book are, as it were, a number of sketches of landscapes which were made in the course of these long and involved journeyings. [ixᵉ]

The failure to weld the results into a successful whole is, as Wittgenstein so clearly sensed, not the result of incompetence, but of a limitation intrinsic to the dialectical mode of procedure. For what we have here is less the devotion of sustained attention to the solution of a series of philosophical problems, be they those of solipsism, dualism, phenomenalism, or indeed any other of the enduring perplexities that constitute the standard coin of traditional philosophical exchange, but rather a constantly exploratory investigation of the linguistic media in which philosophical activity finds the conditions of its operation. Controversial discourse has always been an expression of the life of reason, but its dialectical examination has always had "understanding" rather than "belief" as its aim. Insofar as the dialogues of Plato exemplify the cognitive qualities of human discourse, they found that tradition of which the *Philosophical Investigations* serves as only the most recent exemplar.

Systematic thinking—the structural presentation of a coherent and compendent body of propositions *in ordine geometrico,* of which *Principia Mathematica* is perhaps our most brilliant contemporary example and under whose spell even Wittgenstein's natively dialectical bent fell victim in the *Tractatus*—is one legitimate model upon which the philosophical quest for certainty can pattern itself, but it is neither the only nor the oldest possibility of our philosophical expressiveness. For conversational argument came first, and, as conversational argument grows more philosophical, it becomes reflexively an object as well as an activity. Since argument lives in language, linguistic "understanding," the "significance" of terms, the "meaning" of propositions become increasingly relevant, and dialectic turns to discourse itself as its domain. This is, of course, the meaning of the rhetorical and Sophistic revolution of the fifth century—into whose whirlpool Socrates himself descends.

Generally, at the beginning, it seems as if the realm of discourse were a single, unified matrix in which conflicts are generated out of the oppositions of simple, atomic propositions, but, as argument develops and presuppositions emerge, it becomes slowly clear that conflicts are less between isolated propositions than between alternative, perhaps even qualitatively different, universes of discourse. When this is the case, dialectic either proceeds by the production of a transformation formula that will convert one set of propositions into the matrix from which they were originally excluded, or, by denying the possibility of such transformation, will assert the local autonomy of alternative and mutually recalcitrant linguistic matrices. It is precisely within this tradition of the adjustment of interpretive contexts that Wittgenstein can describe the program of the *Philosophical Investigations* [43e]:

> Our investigation is therefore a grammatical one. Such an investigation sheds light on our problem by clearing misunderstanding away. Misunderstandings concerning the use of words, caused, among other things, by certain analogies between the forms of expression in different regions of language.

Dialectic is that activity within which meanings compete for mastery and control. Therefore "What does it mean to say, that . . . ?" is perhaps the distinctively dialectical question. Any age that suffers a crisis of communication will of necessity turn to a dialectical examination of intrinsic speech. This is the meaning of the *Philosophical Investigations* for our time.

The Unity of Wittgenstein's Thought

BY DENNIS O'BRIEN

J. O. URMSON's historical account of the development of philosophical analysis in Britain between the two World Wars casts Wittgenstein as the founder of two opposed views of the notion of philosophical analysis—a "metaphysical" reductive analysis akin to Russell's "logical atomism," and an "ordinary language," descriptive analysis akin to the analyses of Austin or Ryle.[1] The *Tractatus Logico-Philosophicus* [2] is the cornerstone of atomism; the *Philosophical Investigations* [3] is a rejection of the Tractatus in favor of a new mode of philosophy. Urmson notes, however, that new interpretations of the *Tractatus* in the light of the later *Investigations* appearing at the time his book was written tended to question the radical disparity between early and late Wittgenstein, but he justifies his own account on the ground that his reading of the development of analysis was the one held by the philosophers of the period. There is no doubt that Urmson reports correctly on the general opinion current until very recently that Wittgenstein rejected and even disparaged his early work.[4] Interpreters of the *Tractatus* have had to work in the face of Wittgenstein's own seeming rejection. Still, Wittgenstein did want the *Tractatus* published as a background to the *Investigations* [5] and Stenius expresses the

---

[1] J. O. Urmson, *Philosophical Analysis: Its Development between the Two World Wars* (Oxford: Clarendon Press, 1956).

[2] Ludwig Wittgenstein, *Tractatus Logico-Philosophicus*, newly translated by D. F. Pears and B. F. McGuiness (New York: Humanities Press, 1961). All references to the *Tractatus* will be to this edition.

[3] Ludwig Wittgenstein, *Philosophical Investigations*, translated by G. E. M. Anscombe (New York: Macmillan, 1953). Afterward cited as *PI*.

[4] David Pole, *The Later Philosophy of Wittgenstein* (London: University of London, 1958) is an account of the philosophy of the *Investigations* which regards it as a wholly independent endeavor totally divorced from the rejected *Tractatus*.

[5] "It suddenly seemed to me that I should publish those old thoughts [*Tractatus*] and the new ones [*Investigations*] together: that the latter could be seen in the right light only in contrast with and against the background of my old way of thinking." *PI*, p. x.

"newer" view when he says, "I share the often-expressed feeling that Wittgenstein overshoots the mark when in his later work he criticizes his earlier thought." [6]

On some of the most crucial points of seeming change the record is unclear. Is it the espousal of ordinary language that marks the new philosophy? *Tractatus* §5.5563 reads: "In fact, all propositions of our everyday language, just as they stand, are in perfect logical order." [7] Clearly the *Investigations* rejects the notion of sense data, but according to Anscombe so does the author of the *Tractatus*.[8] In this article, I should like in a very brief and sketchy way to indicate a fundamental unity that runs through all of Wittgenstein. It will be seen that the unity is most clear in what is uniformly *rejected* by both the *Tractatus* and the *Investigations*. On the more "positive" side, a fundamental unity or at least continuity can be discerned in Wittgenstein's notion of the task and method of philosophy. Bringing out this unity is not simply a hollow meta-philosophical victory, since in a philosophy which offers no theses the notion of how to philosophize is central.

1. How to Reject Nonsense

An historian of philosophy writing as a Wittgensteinian faces great difficulties describing the relation between the *Tractatus* and the later works. He says of the propositions in the *Tractatus*: [§6.54] "My propositions serve as elucidations in the following way: anyone who understands me eventually recognizes them as nonsensical, when he has used them—as steps—to climb up beyond them." He contrasts philosophical propositions with propositions of the natural sciences [§6.53] on the ground that the propositions of the sciences say something, while philosophical propositions do not and are without meaning. If Wittgenstein is serious here, and I believe he is, as I will show below, then it does not seem that he could *refute* the *Tractatus* by showing that the propositions in it were false. Scientific theories say something, they make a claim about how the world is, and these theories can be verified or

[6] Erik Stenius, *Wittgenstein's Tractatus* (Ithaca, N. Y.: Cornell U. Press, 1960), p. 16.
[7] Frank Ramsey objected to Russell's claim that the *Tractatus* was concerned with "ideal languages" on the basis of this statement. See the reprint of Ramsey's review of the *Tractatus* in F. Ramsey, *Foundations of Mathematics* (New York: Harcourt, 1931).
[8] G. E. M. Anscombe, *An Introduction to Wittgenstein's Tractatus* (London: Hutchinson Univ. Library, 1959), Ch. 1. Anscombe criticizes Popper's sense-data interpretation of "atomic facts" which she cites as "the most common view of the *Tractatus*" (p. 25).

refuted. It is the misfortune of philosophical statements that they
are neither verifiable or refutable. Wittgenstein does say, that "the
truth of the thoughts that are here [in the *Tractatus*] set forth seems
to me unassailable and definitive" [p. 5]. Just how that claim is to
be interpreted is very puzzling since it hardly seems possible that
propositions which he characterizes as "nonsense" can be "true."
The simplest way of accounting for this discrepancy is to hold that
what he says in a general way about the *Tractatus* in the Preface
does not conform to the strict conventions of the text itself. Strictly,
philosophical propositions are elucidations and Wittgenstein's are
true elucidations, i.e., the right and proper elucidations, but we
should not think that an elucidation is itself a statement of *fact*
which conforms to the canons of verification. It is no inconsistency,
no matter how paradoxical it sounds, to say that the *Tractatus*
gives the true elucidation of philosophical problems while offering
no truths. As we shall see, this notion of elucidation is critical.

If no truths are offered by the *Tractatus* then there is no possibility of showing their falsity at a later date. Of course one could
abandon this purely elucidatory notion of philosophy and conclude
that philosophy really *does* offer truths. From such a standpoint
one could say that it was a philosophical *truth* that purely elucidatory conceptions of philosophy are misconceived in some fashion.
Wittgenstein, of course, does not criticize the *Tractatus* in this
fashion, and he says in the *Investigations,* §128: "If one tried to
advance *theses* in philosophy, it would never be possible to question them, because everyone would agree to them." This statement
implies that philosophy does not, in fact, advance theses—statements that could be taken as truth claims—and *if* it did, they would
be very odd claims, since they would seem so unassailable that
everyone would agree right off and wonder why any claim needed
to be made at all. This general agreement to philosophical "theses"
is comparable to the "truth" of the propositions of the *Tractatus*
which is definitive and unassailable—and for that reason not properly comparable to even the most well verified scientific statements.
We will have to choose from the category of rejection some notion
other than "false" or "refuted" to describe Wittgenstein's attitude
toward the *Tractatus* or else we will undercut his own notion that
philosophy does not offer theses. The statement, "I have refuted a
philosophical thesis," is anomalous for Wittgenstein throughout.

Just how to characterize the undoubted rejection of the *Tractatus*
is very puzzling. If we were to state it in ways suggested by the

Investigations it would seem that the earlier work was too *narrow*. Whatever "truth" it contained was restricted to only one very limited problem, the meaning of declarative sentences in the context of the strict sciences. In the later work we are asked to consider the whole variety of language games from giving orders to guessing riddles, making jokes, thanking, cursing, greeting, praying, of which scientific claims are only a small group [*PI, §*23]. As Wittgenstein comments after listing these various language games: "It is interesting to compare the multiplicity of the tools in language and the ways they are used, the multiplicity of kinds of word and sentence, with what logicians have said about the structure of language. (Including the author of the *Tractatus Logico-Philosophicus.*)" What is "false" about the *Tractatus* may be mistaking part for whole. Even in ordinary cases, decisions about parts and wholes are not straightforward empirical matters. It is clearly a mistake to say that an arm is the whole of what we know as the body, but it is not like the mistake of describing an arm as if it worked by steel springs. Perhaps the *Tractatus* should be looked on as a wrong *decision,* which, like a wrong decision about parts and wholes in a scientific case, proved unfruitful—though not in the scientific sense of unfruitful.

2. *"The Meaning of* P *Is ———."*

The simplest key to the whole of Wittgenstein's philosophy lies in the evaluation of sentences of this type. It is a perfectly ordinary type of sentence which is used everyday and, like St. Augustine's problems with the notion of time, it never bothers us unless we are asked to explain it. (Wittgenstein, of course, uses Augustine's famous query about time as an illustration of a *philosophical* problem: *PI,* 89.) Philosophers have taken the explanation of this sentence as their particular task and have produced various theories of meaning, behavioristic, mentalistic and so on. To understand Wittgenstein properly we must realize that he consistently holds that *all* these attempts are beside the point. The notion of a *theory* of meaning is empty or an instance of language on a holiday. "Theory" is a perfectly comprehensible word and so is "meaning" despite our temptation to think of it as queer [*PI, §*93]; but the two gears don't mesh. When the two notions are brought together neither one does its proper work and so the machine idles.

To state in summary fashion what will be developed below, the

sentence, "The meaning of p is————," has been wrongly interpreted by philosophers as a statement admitting truth values. It
looks like a declarative sentence, like "The color of the rug is
blue," and so philosophers have tried to indicate what sorts of facts
could be used to substantiate a claim that the meaning of something
was such-and-such. In the *Tractatus,* Wittgenstein holds that such
sentences *about* meaning are themselves meaningless since they do
not, as meaningful sentences do, picture any facts. Sentences about
meaning and theories of meaning in general are not *theoretical* because they do not have any factual basis; they are part of "the
mystical." There is a *prima facie* case that there is an analogous
position in the *Investigations* where we are told to completely
abjure looking for the meaning of words and sentences and to concentrate on how they are used. The heart of the misinterpretations
of the *Tractatus* and the *Investigations* lies in assuming in various
ways that some theory of meaning is being presented. For the
Tractatus it has been sense data which are the *facts* which substantiate the claim that the meaning of p is ————, while in the
Investigations it is a behavioral criterion. Both notions are fundamentally misconceived.

3. Psychological and Logical Theories of Meaning

In order to understand the *Tractatus* it is necessary to remind
ourselves of Russell's views on the nature of meaning from which
Wittgenstein was attempting to escape. It is a well-known fact,
which Russell himself gratefully acknowledged, that Wittgenstein's
criticism caused him to change his mind on certain issues. Yet in
his introductory remarks to the *Tractatus* Russell managed to
suggest a way to reading that book which was much closer to his
own views than Wittgenstein's. Russell's views we can fairly characterize as a psychological theory of meaning, while Wittgenstein's
we can call a logical theory for lack of a better term, though we
must realize that in the last analysis it is not a theory. That Russell's
theory of meaning was psychological *even after* the impact of Wittgenstein's ideas is testified to by this remark from the lectures on
logical atomism in which he publicly acknowledged his debt to
Wittgenstein: "The notion of meaning is always more or less psychological, and . . . it is not possible to get a pure logical theory of

meaning." [9] It is a psychological theory of meaning via sense processes that Russell suggested as a proper reading of the *Tractatus*. As Anscombe tries to show in her commentary—and I agree with her in this—no such reading can be supported by the text.

We will fail to appreciate the radical nature of Wittgenstein's proposals in the *Tractatus* unless we are caught by the plausibility of Russell's views about meaning. A word is only a noise, a fact like any other, but as a word it has the capacity to *stand for something,* to be a sign. How does this marvelous capacity arise? Russell's account is straightforward and seemingly correct. The noise attaches itself to the object which it stands for through some process in the brain. As red objects cause red sensations, so the word "red" can cause, bring to mind, red sensations and thus make us turn to consider the world. It is obvious why such a view is labeled "psychological"; it is also clear that it is a straightforward *theory* since like all theories it describes a factual or causal connection. There is nothing mysterious about the claim that "red" has a meaning; it amounts to the factual claim that this sound "red" causes a psychological event which in turn is or has been causally related to certain facts in the world. To say that "red" has a meaning is to make a factual claim about the relation of a certain sound to the brain and through the brain to the world. This gives a picture of how words have meaning that seems inescapable; yet if we pursue it we run into grave problems.

As a theory of meaning this psychological view offers a convenient way of handling meaninglessness. A word is meaningless if the causal connection fails to obtain. If words have meaning when they refer to objects in the world, then a noise which cannot be traced to the world via sensations will be empty noise, meaningless. Words like "god" must be analyzed into sense qualities in order that they can be given meaning; if they cannot be so analyzed they are vacuous. If a word has meaning ultimately via a connection to objects through sensations, our ordinary names of objects like "dog" will need analysis into sense qualities, and finally even the normal sense words like "red" prove insufficient. The sound "red" may cause some sensation in my brain—no doubt "god" causes some vague images to swim into view—but I can only be sure that a sound has a meaning if the quality of the sensation is

9 Bertrand Russell, "The Philosophy of Logical Atomism," reprinted in B. Russell, *Logic and Knowledge*, ed. R. C. Marsh (London: Allen & Unwin, 1956), p. 186.

the kind caused by the world. If not, then my language hooks on
to nothing. The only way of finally verifying that a sensation is
caused by the world is in present experience. There is no *real* way
of doubting that this present impression is from the world, so the
word which signifies via this sensation has a meaning.[10] Thus
Russell felt it imperative to replace the ordinary names of our
language like "dog" or "Socrates" with logically proper names like
"this" whose function is clearly directed toward what is immediate
in experience. Sentences compounded out of logically proper names
which indubitably had a meaning guaranteed by present experience
were the end point of analysis. It was in this way that those strange
sounds that we call words could hook onto a world and have
meaning. If meaning consists in the factual connection of sound,
sensation, and object, then, like all factual assertions, it must
ultimately be grounded in the immediate observation of just such
a connection.

If basic or atomic propositions are compounded of logically
proper names construed in the fashion suggested, then it follows
that not only must they be meaningful, since they stand at the point
of causal linkage between the brain and the world, but they must
also be *true*. Any proposition formed out of such logically proper
names directs us at once to the present reality which gives them
meaning by hooking them on to the world *and* presents us with the
data which will confirm the proposition. We are to imagine a
proposition like "This is thus" in which the words definitely have
a meaning because they hook onto the world in our immediate
awareness. But, if this is the case, while I am gathering in the
meaning of the names I will also inspect the very data which will
confirm the judgment. Indeed, I will always discover that such
judgments are true. If I look about and see that this is *such,* not
thus, I am in no position to say that the original proposition is false.
I can reply, "But what do you mean? I see a this that is such, is
that what you mean by 'thus'? If so then your proposition is surely
true, if not then I don't know what I am to look for." Russell did
maintain just such a view of basic propositions even as late as the
Inquiry into Meaning and Truth.

> A basic proposition must have two properties: (1) it must be
> caused by some sensible occurrence; (2) it must be of such a form
> that no other basic proposition can contradict it.

[10] I pass by as irrelevant the problem of the existence of the external world as the cause
of these direct sensations.

As to (1): I do not wish to insist upon the word "caused," but the belief must arise on the occasion of some sensible occurrence, and must be such that, if questioned, it will be defended by the argument, "why, I see it" or something similar.

As to (2): . . . No previous or subsequent occurrence, and no experience of others, can prove the falsehood of a basic proposition. . . . When we have analyzed a judgment of perception in this way we are left with something that cannot be *proved* to be false.[11]

There are many anomalies about this theory, including the fact that such basic propositions cannot be uttered because by the time the words are formulated the experience has flitted by. But the most striking for our purposes is that a basic proposition is a factual statement that cannot be *proved* to be false. Indeed, it would turn out on Russell's view that if we had an ideal language, not only would all propositions have clear empirical meanings, but there would be no false propositions. Any molecular proposition either can be analyzed into a compound of basic propositions all of which *must* be true so that the equivalent complex must be true, or it simply cannot be analyzed at all and is meaningless. Ironically, it is precisely on the matter of atomic propositions that Russell and Wittgenstein differ so radically and yet where they were interpreted as basically identical. Russell's basic propositions are defined by certain *factual* considerations, psychological immediacy, and causal relation to the world; Wittgenstein's are defined by the *logical* property of having one and only one way of being falsified. This point is made in very different ways by Anscombe [12] and by Stenius in his account of how an atomic proposition determines a "yes-no space." [13]

We shall discuss Wittgenstein's notion of atomic propositions below. Yet we should emphasize the striking contrast between two theories which rest on atomic propositions, but for one of which these propositions must be true, where for the other they must always be univocally falsifiable. The misunderstanding is vividly pointed up in the correspondence between Russell and Wittgenstein about the *Tractatus*. Russell asks, "But a *Gedanke* (thought) is a *Tatsache* (fact): what are its constitutents and components, and what is their relation to those of the pictured *Tatsache?*" Wittgenstein replied;

11 B. Russell, *Inquiry into Meaning and Truth*, (London: Allen & Unwin, 1940), pp. 138-39.
12 Anscombe, *op. cit.*, pp. 34-36.
13 Stenius, *op. cit.*, ch. IV.

I don't know what the constituents of a thought are but I know *that* it must have constituents which correspond to the words of our language. Again the kind of relation of the constituents of the thought and of the pictured fact is irrelevant. It would be a matter of psychology to find out.[14]

And as Wittgenstein says in the *Tractatus:* "§4.1121 Psychology is no more closely related to philosophy than any other natural science." If you have a psychological and causal theory of meaning, as we claim Russell has, then it is absolutely vital to find out the constituents of the thought-fact. How else will you make the causal connection which defines meaning? For Wittgenstein, however, the relation of the factual constituents of a thought and a pictured fact are "irrelevant." A psychologist might discover what they were but it would not assist the philosopher in his task of elucidating meanings. As he says in the *Investigations,* "Try not to think of understanding as a 'mental process' at all" [*PI,* §154].

There is no doubt that at first blush one could imagine that Wittgenstein and Russell had the same notion of meaning. For Russell, language hooks onto the world via logically proper names which must have meaning, which are guaranteed to stand for things in the world. And Wittgenstein says:

§2.1514 The pictorial relationship consists of the correlations of the picture's elements with things [*Sachen*].

§2.1515 These correlations are, as it were, the feelers of the picture's elements, with which the picture touches reality.

The elements of the picture are the names out of which it is concatenated, these names are correlated to things, and by this means language hooks onto the world. But the contrast can be brought clearly into focus by looking at the difference in the two men's "doctrine" of *objects.* For Russell, if I know that "red" has a meaning then I know as a *fact* that red objects exist or have existed. In the final analysis if a word has a meaning it is because a causal connection can be traced to the world which entitles us to make some sort of true existence statement. Meaning is a *factual* relation between a sound fact and some occurrence of a sense object. These objects which stand as the meaning of the sounds are quite concrete, positive existents—if they weren't they could hardly enter into the factual claim involved in saying that some sound had a meaning. The essence of basic objects is that they are directly

[14] Quoted in Anscombe, *op. cit.,* p. 28.

observable qualia. In Wittgenstein, on the other hand, objects are not positive concrete entities at all. What exist are facts. "§1.1 The world is the totality of facts, not things." When I know an object I am not directly acquainted with a sense quale; rather,

> §2.0123 If I know an object I also know all its possible occurrences in states of affairs.
> (Everyone of these possibilities must be part of the nature of the object.)
> §2.0124 If all objects are given, then at the same time all *possible* states of affairs are also given.

At least for the purposes of meaning analysis, objects are defined as the *possibilities* of states of affairs. Wittgenstein doesn't deny that they may have positive qualities, perhaps like Russell's basic sense qualia, but "§2.01231 If I am to know an object, though I need not know its external properties, I must know all its internal properties." Knowing the internal properties of an object is knowing its possible occurrences in states of affairs. If, then, propositions do touch reality via the names which are correlated with objects, it is not actual reality, to existents, but to possible states of affairs.[15]

Because Russell's objects, which are the meanings of words, are positive existents, it follows that any time we know the meaning of the word we also know some truth about the world, or conversely, for any word or proposition to have meaning some other proposition must be true, viz., the one which asserts the factual connection which is the meaning of the words. Since Wittgenstein's objects are not concrete existents, when we know the meaning of a word via its relation to objects we do not know any facts, since the relation of the picture-fact to a *possibility* can hardly be a fact. Thus Wittgenstein can make precisely the opposite claim about what we can "know," given the relation between names and objects.

---

[15] The fact that for purposes of analysis "objects" are defined by their internal properties as possible states of affairs rather than any positive, external characteristics, calls into question a common interpretation of the famous opening section of the *Investigations*. There Wittgenstein criticizes Augustine's notion that we learn the meaning of words by an association between the concrete objects pointed at by parents and teachers and the sounds which they utter—a virtual paradigm of the psychological theory we have been discussing. It has been widely taken as an attack against the *Tractatus*, where meaning was supposedly the correlation of names and object. But Augustine, like Russell, is talking about concrete, existent objects and a factual association between a sound and a thing, while the positive characteristics of objects are quite beside the point in the *Tractatus*, where their whole function seems to be as something that enters into possible states of affairs. There is an enormous difference between a theory in which a sound has meaning in virtue of a straightforward factual relation to some concrete object, and one in which a word has meaning because it is seen as relating to a possible state of affairs. Clearly the *Investigations* is attacking sense data and psychological theories of meaning, but so, it seems to me, is the *Tractatus*.

§2.021 Objects make up the substance of the world.
That is why they cannot be composite.

§2.0211 If the world had no substance, then whether a proposition
has sense would depend on whether another proposition was
true.

§2.0212 In that case we could not sketch out any picture of the
world (true or false).

One of the paradoxes of *any* position which maintains that the
sentence, "The meaning of p is ————," is a truth claim of some
sort (about sensations, behavior and so on) is that *simply* from
admitting that some sign has a meaning we can derive a true factual
statement about the world. Indeed, we seem to be able to derive an
infinite set of true statements from the admission that a sign S has
a meaning. If S has a meaning, then the proposition " 'S' is related
to s (the object which is its meaning)" must be true. And if this
proposition is true, it must have a meaning—how could a meaningless proposition be true?—and some further true propositions
stating this meaning must be derivable and so on. We are involved
in an infinite regress in which to know that a proposition is meaningful we must know the truth of another meaningful proposition
which involves the truth of another meaningful proposition and so
on. Either we accept the infinite regress or stop the process by
means of some propositions in which truth and meaning are identical, as Russell does in his basic propositions. To Wittgenstein it
seemed preferable to simply deny that ascertaining meaning involved the truth of any proposition, in particular, the proposition
"the meaning of p is ————." But if "the meaning of p is ————"
cannot be true or false it does not share the "logic" of sentences
which have sense. §4.5 says, "The general form of a proposition is:
This is how things stand." Our claims about the meaning of p do
not express how things stand, they are neither verifiable or falsifiable, and thus are strictly without sense. If we cannot make truth
claims about the meaning of this or that word or sentence, then
we must also lack any factual basis for a theory of meaning which
would describe in a general way the factual process by means of
which sounds get associated with the world. Wittgenstein believed
that past philosophies had in various ways attempted such theories
and hence were not simply false but nonsense.[16]

[16] This belief seems to me substantially false. Stenius has already pointed out the resemblance between Wittgenstein and Kant: see Stenius, *op. cit.*, ch. XI. Philosophers
have been remarkably ingenious in distinguishing their metaphysical or critical endeavors
from scientific theory.

We have so far used the blanket term "meaning" to cover the notion of what it is that a word as distinguished from a mere sound accomplishes. Before proceeding to a further discussion of Wittgenstein we must take note of the distinction between sense (*Sinn*) and reference (*Bedeutung*) which Wittgenstein borrowed from Frege. Words are distinguished from mere noises in that they are *means* by which we take account of something. A proper name like "Socrates" is used to refer to someone but normally we do not think it has any sense, i.e., that it describes some quality. I can call my cat "Socrates," and that may be odd, ironic, and funny but it isn't false. On the other hand, "wise," has sense, so that referring to my cat as wise would be false. As Anscombe points out, Russell uses only one notion of meaning and "holds that the meaning of words must always be objects that one is directly acquainted with." [17] All meaning is finally referential; that is why the ultimate constituents of meaning must be logically proper names, i.e., just those words which fail to function if they have no reference. The attempt to ground meaning in factual relations requires just this reduction of all meaning to referential meaning because a sound has a meaning only when it directs us toward an object in the world. Just as "Socrates" is simply a noise if it isn't used to refer to some object, so, Russell thinks, all words fail to have "meaning" if they cannot be grounded in an object referred to. Wittgenstein's position is at first sight closer to common sense since he holds that names have reference but no sense, while propositions have sense but no reference. The "meaning" of a proper name is to pick out the bearer, but the meaning of a proposition does not pick out any object; it conveys a sense which we can see is either confirmed or not confirmed by reality.

This distinction between sense and reference seems obviously correct *at first sight,* but we must credit Russell with showing that on deeper reflection it is puzzling. Russell, after all, consciously rejected the distinction which he knew from Frege. Why? Well, we are back at our initial problem: How do these noises hook onto the world? If the names out of which a proposition is compounded do not serve to pick out objects in the world, how can propositions ever have meaning or be verified? If names which direct us to present experience in the fashion that "Socrates" directs us to its bearer are not the ultimate meaningful units out of which every-

17 Anscombe, *op. cit.*, p. 17.

thing else is compounded, then how does language direct us to the world at all? Referential meaning is *the* sense of meaning because it involves this necessary linkage between a noise and something for which that noise is a sign. Nevertheless, if we are bewitched by Russell's solution we will have to accept all of its paradoxes. Let us turn, then, directly to Wittgenstein's treatment of these questions.

A proposition has sense but no reference. "§3.3 Only propositions have sense [*Sinn*]." Or, as Russell put it after accepting Wittgenstein's criticism, propositions are not names of facts.

> It is quite obvious as soon as it is pointed out to you, but as a matter of fact I never realized it until it was pointed out to me by a former pupil of mine, Wittgenstein. It is perfectly evident as soon as you think of it, that a proposition is not a name of a fact, from the mere circumstance that there are *two* propositions corresponding to each fact. Suppose it is a fact that Socrates is dead. You have two propositions: 'Socrates is dead' and 'Socrates is not dead.' And these two propositions corresponding to the same fact, there is one fact in the world that makes one true and one false.[18]

The point can be made clear by reversing Russell's example. Let us ask ourselves what makes the name "Socrates" work (have a meaning) and the proposition "Socrates is white" work. "Socrates" works when there is a Socrates to which it refers, but, curiously enough, "Socrates is white" works when there is a white Socrates *or* when there is a black, yellow, or red Socrates. Using the blanket notion of meaning, we say that "Socrates" has no meaning if it doesn't actually function to pick out somebody, but "Socrates is white" becomes false, not meaningless when it serves to pick out the red Socrates. If we were to say that our *proposition* had *referential* meaning, then we would have to say that the "objects" to which it referred were a white Socrates or a red Socrates or a yellow Socrates, etc. This would have to be the case, since it is the existence of any of these states that makes the proposition meaningful, although frequently false. When we know that a proposition has sense we know nothing about the world one way or the other. If *p* is meaningful then either P or not-P; if "Socrates is white" is meaningful, then either Socrates is white or Socrates is not white.

---

[18] Russell, "The Philosophy of Logical Atomism," *op. cit.*, p. 187. Either the point didn't sink in deeply enough or Russell forgot these good words when he came to treating "basic propositions," which certainly appear to function as names of atomic facts.

And of course this doesn't tell me anything: "§4.461 I know nothing about the weather when I know that it is either raining or not raining."

If p is meaningful when a p or a non-p state of affairs obtains in the world, we could still wonder why there isn't a sort of factual check on whether a proposition has meaning. Imagine a universe U consisting of two objects, a and b, and two predicates, blue and red. Now consider the propositions "a is green" or "c is blue" or "c is green": are they meaningful in U? It would seem so. For U it is certainly the case that these propositions are false. All these propositions are meaningful in U because they are all false in U; and if a proposition can be false, it must be meaningful. Whatever the state of the facts in U, whether a is red or blue, b is red or blue, we can see that "a is green" is false, so that in a backhanded fashion a knowledge of the facts in U tells us that these propositions which seem to have nothing at all to do with U are meaningful. This is a paradoxical result. Wittgenstein's answer is the notion of atomic propositions. If we wish to see whether any proposition is meaningful we must analyze it into atomic propositions. Complex propositions have an indefinite sense. "§3.24 When a propositional element signifies a complex, this can be seen from an indeterminateness in the propositions in which it occurs. In such cases we *know* that the proposition leaves something undetermined." As Anscombe suggests, "One kind of indefiniteness in a proposition might be that there was more than one way of its being false." [19] In U we know *the* meaning of "a is red" when it is false, viz., that a is blue. The two opposed colors form an analogy of a yes-no space of possibilities such that the recognition that "a is red" is false can mean only one thing, that it is blue. In contrast, "c is blue" is false in U not because c is red, but because c just isn't. When I am told that "c is blue" is false, I would normally think that this was because c was red or some other color, but it appears that there are two ways in which it could be falsified, namely, when c is some other color or when there isn't any c at all. This shows that, when I know that the proposition is false, I do not yet know what is being asserted—I don't know whether I am to conclude that c is another color or that c is nonexistent. An atomic proposition is one in which no such ambiguity exists.

---

[19] Anscombe, *op. cit.*, p. 34. My discussion at this point is particularly indebted to Anscombe's analysis of the *Tractatus*.

Adopting Anscombe's terminology, we say that "*c* is blue" is not meaningful in respect to *U* because it is radically false.[20] If it were meaningful, it could be analyzed into atomic propositions which, if they were false, would be false in the ordinary way i.e., "*a* is red" is false because *a* is blue.[21] If we assumed that the assertion of the color predicates of *a* or *b* exhausted the atomic propositions in *U,* then "*c* is blue" must be analyzed in terms of these—in which case its falsehood will be ordinary falsehood—or else it cannot be so analyzed and it will be meaningless in *U.* Thus when we say that a proposition *p* is meaningful, we tacitly affirm that either a P or a non-P state of affairs obtains in the world, which, we say, tells us nothing, just as the fact that it is raining or not raining tells us nothing about the weather—except of course that raining is a *possible* state of the weather. The insistence on analysis to atomic propositions is meant to rule out having to hold that *p* is meaningful because it is radically falsified as an impossible state of affairs. The "non-P" state of affairs that falsified an atomic proposition is simply the non-holding of the state of affairs pictured. "§4.25 If an elementary proposition is true, the state of affairs exists: if an elementary proposition is false, the state of affairs does not exist [*so besteht der Sachverhalt nicht*]."

To recapitulate: for Russell, if *p* has a meaning then some other proposition *q* (which states the factual relation constituting the meaning of *p*) must be true. For Wittgenstein, if *p* is meaningful, then I must admit the truth of either *p* or not-*p*. From the fact that a proposition has meaning I can conclude nothing about the world, *except* either *p* or not-*p* which is a tautology supposedly true of every situation. But Wittgensein says in §6.124:

> The propositions of logic describe the scaffolding of the world, or rather they represent it [*darstellen*]. They have no "subject

---

[20] *Ibid.,* p. 49.

[21] My example is only an analogue of an atomic proposition intended to suggest the sense of "ordinary" as opposed to "radical falsehood." § 6.3751 rules out statements like "*a* is red" as atomic propositions. In *U* "*a* is red" and "*a* is blue" are possible propositions and I am imagining that they are atomic. In fact they can't be because their logical product is contradictory and "the logical product of two elementary propositions can be neither a tautology nor a contradiction." One of the real anomalies about Wittgenstein's atomic propositions is that, from the falsity of such a proposition, we can make no *positive* inferences. If "*a* is red" is false, we would normally imagine it was blue or some other color, but for Wittgenstein it would simply be "not-red" if it were atomic. My example in which there are only two possible color predicates comes closer to Wittgenstein's thought than our ordinary world in which the falsity of "*a* is red" leaves a great deal undetermined. Wittgenstein believed when writing the *Tractatus* that determinate meaning required this yes-no space as opposed to a multivalued logical space. This is clearly one of the things on which he changed his mind. *PI*, § 88: "If I tell someone 'Stand roughly there'—may not this explanation work perfectly? And cannot every other one fail too?"

matter." They presuppose that names have meaning and elementary propositions sense; and that is their connection with the world. It is clear that something about the world must be indicated by the fact that certain combinations of symbols—whose essence involves the possession of a determinate character—are tautologies. This contains the decisive point.

The "fact" that when I say p has a meaning I am admitting that either p or not-p is true does indicate something about the world: it indicates the "scaffolding" of the world, the framework of possibilities. In U, "c is blue or c is not blue" not only does not convey any information about U; it is totally useless, not part of any symbolism for U. The tautology which follows from the admission that an atomic proposition is meaningful excludes the case in which p is false because p-conditions are impossible. Propositions hook onto the world when we see that either p or not-p is true. Meaning determines no facts in the world but it determines "the limits of the world." As we pointed out above, Russell and Wittgenstein both have the proposition touch reality via names of objects, but where Russell's objects function as existent termini of a causal relation, for Wittgenstein, "Objects contain the possibility of all situations." [§2.014] Propositions relate to reality via the scaffold of possibilities which is given by the objects. "§2.0124 If all objects are given, then at the same time all *possible* states of affairs are also given." [22]

4. *"Don't Ask for the Meaning, Ask for the Use."*

The whole discussion of the *Tractatus* can be summed up by reminding ourselves that under no conditions can a sentence of the form "The meaning of p is ————" be meaningful. In order to be meaningful it would have to determine some truth conditions, but statements about meaning are "true" only if the fact pictured exists *or* doesn't exist, i.e., that p is meaningful determines no truth conditions, only a tautology. "§4.461 Propositions show what they say: tautologies and contradictions show that they say nothing. A tautology has no truth conditions, since it is unconditionally true." From this very simple consideration the mysticism of the *Tractatus* and its conclusions about a proper philosophical method follow.

[22] The fact that "logic" and a "knowledge of objects" presents us with the scaffolding of the world suggests that even in the *Tractatus* "logic" does not mean simply a formal study of inference but is being conceived of more broadly, or more concretely, in the direction of the later sense of "logic" in which certain *subject matters* determine a "logic." In Kantian language it is more like transcendental logic than formal logic.

If the philosopher's job is one of analysis, getting meanings clear, not settling factual problems like a scientist, then the function of his sentences cannot be to *describe* anything. The philosopher elucidates; he tries to make clear how a sentence is meaningful, what possibilities it sketches out. Wittgenstein thinks of this as an activity rather than a *theory* because theory suggests that we are offering truths, factual statements, in philosophy.

Russell was rightly disturbed by the mystical turn of the *Tractatus* since it implicitly categorized Russell's philosophy as nonsense, and he suggested that a hierarchy of language might allow us to formulate sentences of the type "The meaning of *p* is ————" in a proper manner. This suggestion was taken up by Carnap:

> According to [Wittgenstein], the investigations of the logic of science contain no sentences, but merely more or less vague explanations which the reader must recognize as pseudo-sentences . . . when in what follows [i.e., in Carnap's own work] it is shown that the logic can be formulated not in senseless, if practically indispensable pseudo-sentences, but in perfectly correct sentences.[23]

He then goes on to add that, if we follow Wittgenstein, we will be unable to distinguish between the useful logic of science and the sentences of the speculative metaphysician. A Wittgensteinian rejoinder to Carnap's suggestion offers a convenient bridge between the *Tractatus* and the *Investigations*.

Wittgenstein thought that the only "correct sentences" were like the propositions of the natural sciences, i.e., propositions which pictured a fact and stated a truth claim [§6.3]. If statements about meaning are to be formulated in "perfectly correct sentences," then they will have to picture a fact and make truth claims, and we will be right back in all the paradoxes of Russell's psychological theory of meaning with its infinite regress and/or basic propositions in which the distinction between meaning and truth collapses. And as far as the distinction between metaphysical statements and Wittgenstein's elucidations are concerned, it is not Wittgenstein who confuses the point but Russell. The *Tractatus* is anti-metaphysical because it opposes factual statements that are *necessarily* true.

We could distinguish three kinds of sentences in connection with the *Tractatus:* (1) *Factual sentences:* the propositions of the natural sciences that picture a fact and make a truth claim. Sentences like

[23] Carnap, *Logical Syntax of Language* (London: Routledge and Kegan Paul, 1937), p. 283.

"The cow is brown." (2) *Elucidatory sentences:* sentences which *show* something by the fact that we accept them. "If *p* is meaningful then either P is the case or P is not the case: If 'Socrates is white' is meaningful then either Socrates is white or he isn't." These sentences clearly picture no fact; they do not make any truth claims and hence "say nothing." But "It is clear that something about the world must be indicated by the fact that certain combinations of symbols—whose essence involves the possession of a determinate character—are tautologies" [§6.124]. (3) *Metaphysical sentences:* factual propositions which are true because their falsehood would be impossible or inconceivable. Russell's basic propositions are an excellent example. Russell said that "a judgment of perception . . . cannot be *proved* to be false." Now of course any verified factual claim cannot be proved to be false bacause it is, in fact, true, but Russell's basic propositions cannot be proved false because their falsity is inconceivable. If we understand the meaning of "This is thus," it must be true, or, conversely, we could not understand the proposition and say that it was false. A Russellian basic proposition we can say is "radically true" because its negation is "radically false"—but it is just such sentences that Wittgenstein declares are meaningless. Metaphysics is a pseudo-science because it offers synthetic *a priori* judgments, factual propositions which are necessarily true. Metaphysical sentences fail because they *appear* to make factual claims, but when we examine their truth conditions we discover that their truth rests on a question of meaning, not fact. Wittgenstein's elucidatory sentences, he is very careful to note, are *not* factual claims at all.

In the light of this rejoinder to Carnap's charge of metaphysics, consider the following passage from *The Blue Book:*

> We have been told by popular scientists that the floor on which we stand is not solid, as it appears to common sense, as it has been discovered that the wood consists of particles filling space so thinly that it can almost be called empty. This is liable to perplex us, for in a way we know of course that the floor is solid, or that if it isn't solid, this may be due to the wood being rotten but not to its being composed of electrons. To say on the latter ground that the floor is not solid, is to misuse language. . . .
>
> As in this example the word "solidity" was used wrongly and it seemed that we had been shown that nothing really was solid, just in this way in stating our puzzles about the *general vagueness* of sense experience, and about the flux of phenomena, we are

using the word "flux" and "vagueness" wrongly, in a typically
metaphysical way, namely without an antithesis; whereas in their
correct and everyday use vagueness is opposed to clearness, flux to
stability, inaccuracy to accuracy, and *problem* to solution. The
very word "problem," one might say, is misapplied when used
with our philosophical troubles. These difficulties, as long as they
are seen as problems, are tantalizing, and appear insoluble.[24]

It is obvious that the criticism of "metaphysics" made in these
preliminary studies for the *Investigations* has a close *family resemblance* to the criticism of metaphysics we have extracted from the
Tractatus. Why is the statement "All floors are unsolid" metaphysical and meaningless? Not because the words in it lack sense content—Carnap and Russell's criterion for "metaphysical." Not only
is the sentence perfectly sensible but it could conceivably be true.
What makes the sentence metaphysical is that in trying to *prove*
its truth, the scientist construes the word "unsolid" in such a way
that the solidity of a floor would be inconceivable.

> For even if the particles were as big as grains of sand, and as
> close together as those in a sandheap, the floor would not be solid
> if it were composed of them in the sense in which a sandheap is
> composed of grains. Our perplexity was based on a misunderstand-
> ing; the picture of the thinly filled space was wrongly *applied.*[25]

In *Tractatus* §6.1232 Wittgenstein distinguishes between the
"essential general validity" of logical propositions and the "accidental general validity" of such propositions as "All men are
mortal." The statement "All floors are unsolid" looks like a statement of accidental general validity. There is no reason why careful
investigation might not establish this fact, but the truth of the
statement offered has "essential general validity." It is "metaphysical" because it appears to make a factual claim whereas the
truth conditions suggested leave no way for the claim to be falsified
—it is a paradigm case of a factual statement whose meaning
guarantees its truth, of a synthetic *a priori* judgment, of a necessary
fact, in short, of metaphysics.

Wittgenstein labels the fault "metaphysical" and adopts his later
terminology when he calls it a misuse of language. We should note
how close the notion of "misuse" is to "metaphysical meaninglessness" as construed in the *Tractatus.* Words fail to have a use or are
meaningless when they are used "without antithesis." The great

[24] L. Wittgenstein, Preliminary Studies for the "Philosophical Investigations," known as
The Blue and Brown Books (Oxford: Blackwell, 1958), pp. 45–46.
[25] *Ibid.*

shift that has come since the *Tractatus* is that Wittgenstein is willing to consider a range of possible antitheses, states which could be positively characterized and would exclude the truth of the judgment offered, where before we were asked to believe that atomic propositions, the ultimates on which all determinate meaning rested, involved only one negation which was not equivalent to any state of affairs that could be described positively. No matter how necessary atomic propositions may have seemed to Wittgenstein he was not able to suggest any example and we have no cases of analysis actually being carried out to the level of atomic propositions. If the requirement is loosened so that meaning does not depend on a yes-no space but on a multivalued space—a series of possible alternatives—then actual examples of analysis can be offered.[26] Once a *range* of antitheses is opened up, we will no longer be able to give *the* analysis of the meaning of a proposition, but we can construct various language games specifying various possible antitheses and request the auditor to show us which game he is playing.

> Now it looks as if when someone says "Bring me a slab" he could only mean that expression as *one* long word corresponding to the single word "slab"—then can we mean it sometimes as four? And how does one usually mean it?—I should think that we would be inclined to say when it is used in contrast with other sentences such as "Hand me the slab," etc.; that is in contrast with other sentences containing the separate words of our command in other combinations [*PI*, §20].

"Bring me a slab" will have a range of meanings depending on how you lay out the contrasts. Metaphysical utterances can be rejected because there is *no* game being played with them, no contrasts are suggested. We dissolve metaphysical "problems" by treating them *as if* they made factual claims, i.e., as if the words had antitheses, and if the metaphysician says he is playing the suggested language game we can show that his judgment is false or harmlessly true.

5. *"And Don't Ask for the Use Either!"*

The fact that most of Wittgenstein's interpreters have been brought up in the British philosophical tradition has produced a

---

[26] Not only is a range of possible states of affairs which would falsify a declarative sentence allowed, but all sorts of other linguistic entities like commands, thanking, cursing, praying can be seen to function contrastively.

characteristic misinterpretation of both the *Tractatus* and the *Investigations*. Hume's simple impressions updated as sense data were seen as the key to the earlier book, and the later studies seemed to be part of the "common-sense" tradition most recently exemplified by Moore. When we are told [*PI*, §124], "Philosophy may in no way interfere with the actual use of language," it may appear that this common-sense interpretation is proper. Nevertheless there is a fundamental difference between Moore and Wittgenstein.[27] Moore was interested in defending the *truth* of common sense against metaphysical *doubts*. Can any metaphysician really make me doubt the truth of the judgment that this is my hand in front of me? And if not, in what way can I have any doubts about the existence of the external world? Moore's technique was to take some common-sense judgment supposedly rendered dubious by a metaphysician and just ask us to examine it in the light of present experience to see if we could really sense this doubt. As Paul correctly points out, Wittgenstein's technique was quite different. Where Moore invited his auditor to concentrate his attention on some present fact which could scarcely be doubted, Wittgenstein used his language games to assemble cases.

> Instead of concentrating into a gaze, I am to make a wide survey; and it is not that cases just come before me in their arrangement, for there are cases to be invented by me and arrangements of them to be made by me. Here is why Wittgenstein produces no method in philosophy, there is no method for inventing cases, no method of arranging them.[28]

And a passage in *The Blue Book* is almost a direct attack on Moore and the techniques of common-sense philosophy:

> There is no common-sense answer to a philosophical problem. One can defend common sense against the attacks of philosophers only by solving their puzzles, i. e., by curing them of the temptation to attack common sense; not by restating the view of common sense.[29]

Wittgenstein continues to hold as he did in the *Tractatus* that the philosopher has no direct interest in the *truth* of common sense, or science or whatever. Common sense cannot be defended against metaphysical attack by attempting a *verification* of the truths of

---

[27] This difference is pointed out in an excellent chapter by G. A. Paul on Wittgenstein in A. J. Ayer, et al., *Revolution in Philosophy* (London: Macmillan, 1956) [Included in this volume].

[28] *Ibid.*, p. 96.

[29] *The Blue Book*, p. 58.

common sense in present experience or by a more subtle view of the facts, but by showing the metaphysician that he has failed to make any claim, true or false, and hence his utterance is meaningless. "What *we* do is to bring words back from their metaphysical to their everyday use" [*PI,* §116].

I think we should take this last statement quite literally: Wittgenstein is interested in the everyday *use* of language, not in the truth which may or may not be conveyed in everyday judgments. If, using his own criterion, *"ordinary language"* is to have a meaning, we must search for the contrast that is being pointed to. It is obvious that the contrast is "metaphysical language." The ordinary use of language is to point up something *rather than* something else: "Go left!" also says "Don't go right!" But metaphysical language is language on a holiday because it *seems* to be saying something, rather than another, but we can try to show that in fact it is not functioning at all. The virtue of "everyday" is that language *functions* there, not that it always states truths. And if the espousal of "ordinary language" is not an espousal of common-sense truths, it is also not clearly a rejection of technical language. Technical languages like mathematics or psychology have an ordinary use. Thus he says: "An investigation is possible in connection with mathematics which is clearly analogous to our investigation of psychology. It is just as little a *mathematical* investigation as the other is a psychological one" [*PI,* pt. II, p. xiv]. Technical studies like mathematics and psychology may be subject to a philosophical analysis if their language functions metaphysically and not in the ordinary way.[30] "Ordinary language," then, points neither to everyday truths nor prosaic vocabularies, but to the ordinary way in which language has meaning as against the extraordinary and metaphysical ways that philosophers misuse language.

The task of the philosopher rémains, as it was in the *Tractatus,* one of elucidating meaning—and how do we do that? In a broader and looser fashion we are right back to the same "meaningless" statements about meanings that we saw in the *Tractatus.* Under

---

[30] Much of the *Foundations of Mathematics* (Oxford: Blackwell, 1956) is concerned with "metaphysical claims" that mathematicians make about what they are doing. A metaphysical claim always involves the notion of a *necessary* truth. Wittgenstein held in the *Tractatus* and later that "necessary" was a matter of our chosen meanings for terms and we should never think that because we have chosen to make certain patterns meaningful that we have therefore established a truth. FM I, 5: " 'But doesn't it follow with logical necessity that you get two when you add one to one?' . . . The proposition: 'It is true that this follows from that' means simply: this follows from that." Mathematicians like to think that "One plus one is two" is a necessary truth—but if it is necessary, it is not a truth and if it is a truth it is not necessary.

what states of affairs is the command "Go left!" meaningful? When the person who hears the command goes left—or when he goes right, just stands there or lies down or something, i.e., that the command if meaningful is compatible with seemingly any state of affairs. I always find myself saying that he understood my command if he did it or if he didn't do it—he disobeyed, forgot, and so on. But if "Go left!" is meaningful when he goes left or he doesn't go left, then the "fact" that it is meaningful determines no state of affairs at all. Rather, we say that the command is meaningful if the person knows how to play the game of obeying directions. The noise "Go left" does not have meaning like a conditioned reflex— a casual connection between a sound fact and a behavioral fact— but because it is seen as a move in a game. We say that the command has meaning, not because it determines any behavior or state of affairs, but because the person who understands it fits it into a game where there is obeying orders *and* disobeying orders, forgetting them, mishearing them, and so on. That an order is meaningful determines the limits of my world, my language game—it determines a range of possible behavior that would be regarded as obeying and disobeying and so on.

The notion that the *Investigations* substitutes a behavioristic psychological theory of meaning for the *Tractatus'* sensationalist psychology is clearly incorrect. Wittgenstein is perfectly clear in the *Investigations* that philosophy offers no theses, and clearly behaviorism offers a *theory* of meaning based on factual data. One can reconstruct the paradoxes of a psychological theory of meaning for behaviorism. For example, if noises become commands by causal association to behavior, then commands must always be infallibly obeyed, as in any causal process: if you topple the first domino they all come down necessarily. The behavior we call "disobeying" is really obeying some other (possibly internal) command. The only thing that can interfere with a causal process being carried through is another causal process. One is tempted to construct the notion of "atomic commands" in which disobedience is simply not doing what you are told, rather than obeying some other command. It becomes metaphysical in a behavioristic theory to say that the subject "obeys" the command since "disobeying a command" has no function. The subject can *only* obey commands and, if the commands are incompatible, he must of course do one and not the other, but there is no disobedience involved. Commands subject only to "radical obedience" are not linguistic entities having a meaning any more than atomic propositions which cannot be proved false.

If admitting that some sound has a meaning is a matter of seeing it as a piece in a game, then we should see that the motto "Don't ask for the meaning, ask for the use!" should be amended, "And don't ask for the use either!" Behavioristic misinterpretation of the *Investigations* assumes that the intent of this new slogan is to direct us away from something going on inside the subject's head, the unobservable psychic process, to the observable behavior associated with the word. Behaviorism, however, assumes that "The meaning of *p* is ———" is a statement setting forth truth conditions, when all a statement about meaning does is show forth a language game. For behaviorism the meaning of "Go left!" is that the subject goes left (no other causes interfering): for Wittgenstein the meaning of "Go left" is that the subject goes left or he doesn't go left *but* he sees his behavior as a move in a language game. Meaning is not a factual connection between sound and behavior; it is seeing a fact *as* a piece in a game. The second part of the *Investigations* discusses the notion of "seeing *x* as" at length in order to point out that seeing something *as* is not a matter of discovering a new fact about it. " 'Seeing as . . .' is not part of perception" [*PI*, §197]. For a psychological theory of meaning, grasping the meaning of a sound is ultimately *seeing* the sound in connection with another fact (sense object or action), so that meaning becomes a perceptible fact.

The slogan "Ask for . . . the use!" can mislead us, then, if we think that this asking will be settled by a declarative reply, "The use is. . . ." The reason that there is no reply is not only that we cannot say what *the* use is since there are many games that could be played with this counter—a point sufficiently emphasized by interpreters of Wittgenstein—but that we could not *say* what a use is since noting that a word has a use is seeing it as a piece in a game and *that* a mark is a piece in a game is not a describable fact about the mark. We can, however, try to *show* what the meaning or use of a word is by assembling a variety of language games that could be played with the word. Failure to understand the meaning of a word is failing to see how it directs us one way and not another —we don't understand what contrasts are being pointed to by the scientist who claims the floor is unsolid because it is made of elec-

trons. In order to appreciate the range of contrasts in a particular
game we may surround it with other games which vary slightly in
certain ways. Our interest will not be in games actually played but
in imaginary and even bizarre cases, since they point up more
sharply the contrasts in the game under investigation.

> A main source of our failure to understand is that we do not
> *command a clear view* of the use of our words.—Our grammar
> is lacking in this sort of perspicuity. Hence the importance of
> finding and inventing *intermediate cases* [*PI*, §122].

We see what we *do* mean by showing what we could mean if we
played different games with different contrasts being pointed to.
We come to understand the game we are playing by appreciating
what games we aren't playing; this gives us the perspicuous aspect
that allows a clear view of our use of words.

Wittgenstein's advocacy of ordinary language differs markedly,
in my judgment, from that of many contemporary philosophers who
would claim his blessing. He is not interested in the truths of everyday discourse. He would find no *philosophical* assistance in the
surveys of the descriptive linguist or the compilations of the *O. E. D.*
of what is or has been uttered. He clearly thinks the philosopher's
job lies in *inventing* intermediate—even absurd—cases, not toting
up actual uses. And how can we be sure that the utterances of the
linguist's informant or the quotations from F. H. Bradley in the
O. E. D. are not metaphysical "uses" of language? The philosopher's task of elucidating meaning remains logical, i.e., nonfactual.
He neither establishes facts, nor can he depend on facts from physiology, psychology, or the history of language to reveal meanings.

In this steadfast contrast between the philosopher's concern with
meaning and the scientist's concern with facts lies a key to the unity
of Wittgenstein's philosophy. Philosophy is not a theory offering
truths about meanings, because meanings are not truths about the
world. Philosophy must be an *activity,* because its "subject matter,"
meaning, is not factual. The notion that meaning is *use,* not fact,
seems to me implicit in the *Tractatus.* If coming to understand a
meaning is a matter of engaging in an activity, rather than coming
to know a truth, then the language games of the *Investigations* fit
into the overall conception of philosophy outlined in the *Tractatus.*

SELECTED BIBLIOGRAPHY[1]

The following abbreviations are used: *A* for *Analysis*; *AJP* for *Australasian Journal of Philosophy*; *APQ* for *American Philosophical Quarterly*; *B.B.* for *The Blue and Brown Books*; *BJPS* for *British Journal for the Philosophy of Science*; *D* for *Dialogue*; *DR* for *The Downside Review*; *I* for *Inquiry*; *IPQ* for *International Philosophical Quarterly*; *M* for *Mind*; *Me for Methodos*; *MS* for *Modern Schoolman*; *NS* for *New Scholasticism*; *NSt* for *New Statesman*; *PACPA* for *Proceedings of the American Catholic Philosophical Association*; *PAS* for *Proceedings of the Aristotelian Society*; *P.B.* for *Philosophische Bermerkungen*; *P.I.* for *Philosophical Investigations*; *PPR* for *Philosophy and Phenomenological Research*; *PQ* for *Philosophical Quarterly*; *PR* for *Philosophical Review*; *PS* for *Philosophical Studies*; *PSc* for *Philosophy of Science*; *R* for *Ratio*; *R.F.M.* for *Remarks on the Foundations of Mathematics*; *RM* for *The Review of Metaphysics*; *S* for *Spectator*; *SJP* for *The Southern Journal of Philosophy*; *TLS* for *The Times (London) Literary Supplement*; *U.P.* for *University Press*.

I. Works by Ludwig Wittgenstein
(In Order of Composition)

Notebooks 1914–16. Edited by G. H. von Wright and G. E. M. Anscombe, with an English translation by G. E. M. Anscombe. Oxford: Blackwell, 1961.

Tractatus Logico-Philosophicus (finished in 1918), with an introduction by Bertrand Russell. The first English translation by C. K. Ogden. London: Routledge & Kegan Paul, 1922. A new English translation by D. F. Pears and B. F. McGuinness. London: ibid., 1961.

"Some Remarks on Logical Form," *PAS*, supp. Vol. 9 (1929), pp. 162–71.

"A Lecture on Ethics (1930)," *PR*, Vol. 74 (1965), pp. 3–12.

Philosophische Bemerkungen (1930). Edited by R. Rhees. Oxford: Blackwell, 1965. English translation by Anscombe, forthcoming.

The Blue and Brown Books (1933–35). Edited with a Preface by R. Rhees. Oxford: Blackwell, 1958.

Lectures and Conversations on Aesthetics, Psychology and Religious Belief (1938). Compiled from notes taken by R. Rhees, Y. Smythies, and J. Taylor; edited by Cyril Barrett. London: Blackwall, 1966.

Remarks on the Foundations of Mathematics (1937–44). Edited by G. H. von Wright, R. Rhees, and G. Anscombe with an English translation by G. Anscombe. Oxford: Blackwell, 1956.

Philosophical Investigations (Part I finished in 1945; Part II written be-

---

[1] An extensive bibliography compiled by the editor is forthcoming in *The International Philosophical Quarterly*.

tween 1947 and 1949). Edited by G. Anscombe and R. Rhees with
an English translation by G. Anscombe. Oxford: Blackwell, 1953.
Zettel (1945–48). Edited by G. Anscombe and G. H. von Wright with
an English translation by G. Anscombe. London: Blackwell, 1966.

II. Writings on Wittgenstein

BOOKS

ANSCOMBE, G. E. M. *An Introduction to Wittgenstein's "Tractatus."*
London: Hutchinson, 1959.

BLACK, MAX. *A Companion to Wittgenstein's "Tractatus."* Ithaca:
Cornell U. P., 1964.

COPI, I. M., and R. W. BEARD (eds.). *Readings in Wittgenstein's
"Tractatus."* New York: Macmillan, 1966.

FAVRHOLDT, DAVID. *An Interpretation and Critique of Wittgenstein's
"Tractatus."* Copenhagen: Munksgaard, 1964.

FEIBLEMAN, JAMES. *Inside the Great Mirror* (Examination of the
Philosophy of Russell, Wittgenstein, and their followers). The
Hague: Martinus Nijhoff, 1958.

GRIFFIN, J. *Wittgenstein's Logical Atomism.* London: Oxford U. P.,
1964.

HARTNACK, JUSTUS. *Wittgenstein and Modern Philosophy.* Translated
by Maurice Cranston. (Orig. publ. in Danish, 1962). New York:
Anchor Books, 1965.

KIELKOPF, CHARLES. *An Investigation of Wittgenstein's "Remarks on
the Foundations of Mathematics."* The Hague: Martinus Nijhoff,
forthcoming.

MALCOLM, NORMAN. *Ludwig Wittgenstein: A Memoir.* London: Oxford U. P., 1958.

MASLOW, ALEXANDER. *A Study in Wittgenstein's "Tractatus."* Berkeley:
University of California Press, 1961.

PITCHER, GEORGE. *The Philosophy of Wittgenstein.* Englewood Cliffs,
N.J.: Prentice-Hall, 1964. (Ed.) Wittgenstein: *The Philosophical
Investigations.* New York: Anchor Books, forthcoming.

PLOCHMANN, G. K., and J. B. LAWSON. *Terms in Their Propositional
Contexts in Wittgenstein's "Tractatus": An Index.* Carbondale:
Southern Illinois U. P., 1962.

POLE, DAVID. *The Later Philosophy of Wittgenstein.* London: The
Athlone Press, 1958.

RAO, A. P. *A Survey of Wittgenstein's Theory of Meaning.* Calcutta:
Indian U. P., 1965.

SPECHT, ERNEST KONRAD. *Die Sprachphilosophischen und Ontologischen Grundlagen im Spätwerk Ludwig Wittgensteins. Kantstudien,*
Ergänzungsheft 84. Kölner Universitätsverlay, 1963.

STENIUS, E. *Wittgenstein's "Tractatus."* Oxford: Blackwell, 1960.

Wittgenstein Schriften/Beiheft: Arbeiten über Wittgenstein. Mit Beit-ragen von I. Bachmann, M. Cranston, J. Ferrater Mora, P. Feyera-bend, E. Heller, B. Russell, und G. H. von Wright. Frankfurt: Suhrkamp Verlag, 1960.

ARTICLES AND CHAPTERS

AARON, R. I. "Wittgenstein's Theory of Universals," *M*, Vol. 74 (1965), pp. 249–51.

ALBRITTON, R. "On Wittgenstein's Use of the Term 'Criterion'," *JP*, Vol 56 (1959), pp. 845–57.

ALDRICH, V. C. "Pictorial Meaning, Picture-Thinking, and Wittgen-stein's Theory of Aspects," *M*, Vol. 67 (1958), pp. 70–9.

ALLAIRE, E. B. "Tractatus 6.3751," *A*, Vol. 19 (1959), pp. 100–5. "Types and Formation Rules: A Note on *Tractatus* 3.334," *A*, Vol. 21 (1961), pp. 14–6. "The *Tractatus:* Nominalistic or Realistic," in Allaire and others (eds.), *Essays in Ontology.* The Hague: Martinus Nijhoff, 1963.

AMBROSE, A. "Proof and the Theorem Proved," *M*, Vol. 68 (1959), pp. 435–45. "Review of *P. I.*," *PPR*, Vol. 15 (1954), pp. 111–5. "Review of *R.F.M.*," *PPR*, Vol. 18 (1957), pp. 262–5. "Review of Pitcher's *The Philosophy of Wittgenstein*," *PPR*, Vol. 25 (1965), pp. 423–5.

ANDERSON, A. R. "Mathematics and the 'Language Game'," *RM*, Vol. 11 (1958), pp. 446–58.

ANSCOMBE, G. E. M. "Mr. Copi on Objects, Properties and Relations in the *Tractatus*," *M*, Vol. 68 (1959), p. 404. "What Wittgenstein Really Said," *The Tablet* (April 17, 1954).

AYER, A. J. "Can There Be a Private Language?," *PAS*, Supp. Vol. 28 (1954), pp. 63–76.

BAMBROUGH, J. R. "Universals and Family Resemblances," *PAS*, Vol. 61, (1960–61), pp. 207–22.

BENNETT, J. "On Being Forced to a Conclusion," *PAS*, Supp. Vol. 35 (1961), pp. 15–34.

BERGMANN, G. "The Glory and the Misery of Ludwig Wittgenstein" in his *Logic and Reality*, Madison: University of Wisconsin Press, 1964. "Stenius on Wittgenstein's *Tractatus*" in his *Logic and Reality*.

BERNAYS, P. "Comments on Wittgenstein's *R.F.M.*," *R*, Vol. 2 (1959), pp. 1–22.

BERNSTEIN, R. J. "Wittgenstein's Three Languages," *RM*, Vol. 15 (1961), pp. 278–98.

BLACK, MAX. "Critical Notice of Wittgenstein's *Notebooks 1914–1916*," *M*, Vol. 73 (1964), pp. 132–41. "Some Problems Connected with Language," *PAS*, Vol. 39 (1938–39), pp. 43–68. Reprinted as "Wittgenstein's *Tractatus*" in his *Language and Philosophy*. Ithaca: Cornell U. P., 1949.

BOGEN, J. "Was Wittgenstein a Psychologist?," *I*, Vol, 7 (1964), pp. 374–8.

BRITTON, K. "Review of Malcolm's *Ludwig Wittgenstein: A Memoir*," *P*, Vol. 34 (1959), pp. 277–8.

BUNTING, I. A. "Some Difficulties in Stenius' Account of the Independence of Atomic States of Affairs," *AJP*, Vol. 43 (1965), pp. 368–75.

CAMPBELL, K. "Family Resemblance Predicates," *APQ*, Vol. 2 (1965), pp. 238–44.

CARNEY, J. D. "Is Wittgenstein Impaled on Miss Hervey's Dilemma?," *P*, Vol. 38 (1963), pp. 167–69. "Private Language: The Logic of Wittengstein's Argument," *M*, Vol. 69 (1960) pp. 560–5.

CASSIRER, EVA. "On Logical Structure," *PAS*, Vol. 64 (1963–64), pp. 177–98. "Review of Anscombe's *An Introduction to Tractatus*," *BJPS*, Vol. 14 (1964), pp. 359–66.

CASTANEDA, H. N. "The Private-Language Argument," A symposium with comments by Chappell and Thompson, in C. D. Rollins (ed.): *Knowledge and Experience*, U. of Pittsburgh Press, 1962.

CAVELL, S. "The Availability of Wittgenstein's Later Philosophy," *PR*, Vol. 71 (1962), pp. 67–93.

CHARLESWORTH, M. J. "Wittgenstein: The Limits of Language and Language Games," in his *Philosophy and Linguistic Analysis* (pp. 74–125). Pittsburgh: Duquesne U. P., 1961.

CHIHARA, C. "Mathematical Discovery and Concept Formation," *PR*, Vol. 72 (1963), pp. 17–34. "Wittgenstein and Logical Compulsion," *A*, Vol. 21 (1961), pp. 136–40. C. C. and J. A. Fodor. "Operationalism and Ordinary Language," *APQ*, Vol. 2 (1965), pp. 281–95.

CHIODI, P. "Review of Hartnack's *Wittgenstein und die moderne Philosophie*," *BJPS*, Vol. 15 (1964), pp. 166–8.

COLLINS, J. "Review of *R.F.M.*," *MS*, Vol. 35 (1957), pp. 147–50.

COOK, J. W. "Wittgenstein on Privacy," *PR*, Vol. 74 (1965), pp. 281–314.

COPI, I. M. "Objects, Properties, and Relations in the *Tractatus*," *M*, Vol. 67 (1958), pp. 145–65. "Review of E. Stenius' *Wittgenstein's "Tractatus*," *PR*, Vol. 72 (1963), pp. 382–90. "Review of *Notebooks 1914–1916*," *JP*. Vol. 60 (1963), pp. 765–8. "*Tractatus* 5.542," *A*, Vol. 18 (1958), pp. 102–4.

CORNFORTH, M. C. "The Philosophy of Wittgenstein," in his *Science and Idealism*, New York: International Publishers, 1947.

CRANSTON, M. "L. Wittgenstein," *World Review*, (Dec. 1951), pp. 21–4.

DAITZ, E. "The Picture Theory of Meaning," *M*, Vol. 62 (1953), pp. 184–201.

DAVIE, I. "Review of *P. I.*," *DR*, Vol. 72 (1954), pp. 119–22.

DUMMETT, M. "Wittgenstein's Philosophy of Mathematics,"*PR*, Vol. 68, No. 3 (1959).

DUTHIE, G. D. "Critical Study of *R. F. M.*" *PQ, Vol.* 7 (1957), pp. 368–73.

EICHNER, H. "Review of Pears and McGuinness' translation of *Tractatus*," *D*, Vol. 1 (1962), pp. 212–6.

EVANS, E. *"Tractatus* 3.1432," *M*, Vol. 64 (1955), pp. 259–60. "About 'aRb,' " *M*, Vol. 68 (1959), pp. 535–8.

FAVRHOLDT, D. *"Tractatus* 5.542," *M*, Vol. 73 (1964), pp. 557–62.

FERRE, F. "Colour Incompatibility and Language Games," *M*, Vol. 70 (1961), pp. 90–4.

FEYERABEND, P. K. "Review of E. K. Specht's *Die sprachphilosophischen und ontologischen Grundlagen im Spätwerk Ludwig Wittgensteins*," *PQ*, Vol. 16 (1966), pp. 79–80.

FINDLAY, J. N. "Wittgenstein's *Philosophical Investigations*," *P*, Vol. 30 (1955), pp. 173–9.

GARDINER, P. "Schopenhauer and Wittgenstein," in his *Schopenhauer*. Baltimore: Penguin Books, 1963.

GARVER, N. "Review of *B.B.*," *PPR*, Vol. 21 (1961), pp. 576–7. "Wittgenstein on Criteria," A symposium with comments by Ginet, Siegler, and Ziff; in Rollins (ed.): *Knowledge and Experience* (ibid.) Englewood Cliffs, N.J.: Prentice-Hall, 1963. "Wittgenstein on Private Language," *PPR*, Vol. 20 (1960), pp. 389–96.

GARVIN, J. N. "Review of *R. F. M.*," *NS*, Vol. 32 (1958), pp. 269–71.

GASKING, D. A. T. "Anderson and the *Tractatus*," *AJP*, Vol. 27 (1949), pp. 1–26.

GILL, J. H. "Wittgenstein's Concept of Truth," *IPQ*, Vol. 6 (1966), pp. 71–80.

GOODSTEIN, R. L. "Critical Notice of *R. F. M.*," *M*, Vol. 66 (1957), pp. 549–53.

GRUENDER, D. "Wittgenstein on Explanation and Description," *JP*, Vol. 59 (1962), pp. 523–30.

HALLIE, P. P. "Wittgenstein's Grammatical-Empirical Distinction," *JP*, Vol. 60 (1963), pp. 565–78. "Wittgenstein's Exclusion of Metaphysical Nonsense," *PQ*, Vol. 16 (1966), pp. 97–112.

HAMPSHIRE, S. "Out of the World," (A review of *P.B.*), *NSt*, Vol. 71 (Feb. 4, 1966), pp. 163–64. "The Proper Method," (A review of *B.B.*), *NSt*, Vol. 56 (Aug. 23, 1958), pp. 228–9. "Review of *P. I.*," *S*, (May 22, 1953), pp. 682.

HANNAY, A. "Was Wittgenstein a Psychologist?" *I*, Vol. 7 (1964), pp. 379–86.

HARDIN, C. L. "Wittgenstein on Private Language," *JP*, Vol. 56 (1959), pp. 517–28.

HARRISON, F. R. "Notes on Wittgenstein's Use of 'das Mystische'," *SJP*, Vol. 1 (1963), pp. 3–9. "Wittgenstein and the Doctrine of Identical Minimal Meaning," *Me*, Vol. 14 (1962), pp. 61–74.

HAWKINS, D. J. B. "Wittgenstein and the Cult of Language," *Aquinas Paper* No. 27. London: Blackfriars Publications, 1956.

HEATH, P. L. "Wittgenstein Investigated," *PQ*, Vol. 6 (1956), pp. 66–71.

HERVEY, H. "The Private Language Problem," *PQ*, Vol. 7 (1957), pp. 63–79. "The Problem of the Model Language Game in Wittgenstein's Later Philosophy," *P*, Vol. 36 (1961), pp. 333–51. "A Reply to Dr. Carney's Challenge," *P*, Vol. 38 (1963), pp. 170–5.

HINTIKKA, J. "On Wittgenstein's 'Solipsism'," *M*, Vol. 67 (1958), pp. 88–91.

HORGBY, I. "The Double Awareness in Heidegger and Wittgenstein," *I*, Vol. 2 (1959), pp. 235–64.

HUNTER, J. "Review of Griffin's *Wittgenstein's Logical Atomism*," *D*, Vol. 3 (1965), pp. 461–62. "Review of Pitcher's *The Philosophy of Wittgenstein*," *D*, Vol. 3 (1965), pp. 463–84.

HUTTEN, E. H. "Review of *P.I.*," BJPS,Vol. 4 (1953), pp. 258–60.

JARVIS, J. "Stenius on the *Tractatus*," *JP*, Vol. 58 (1961), pp. 584–96.

KAUFMANN, W. "Wittgenstein" and "Wittgenstein and Socrates," in his *Critique of Religion and Philosophy*. New York: Harper & Row, 1958.

KENNY, A. "Aquinas and Wittgenstein,"*DR*, Vol. 77 (1959), pp. 217–35. "Review of Black's *A Companion to* Tractatus," *M*, Vol. 75 (1966), pp. 452–3.

KEYT, D. "A New Interpretation of the *Tractatus* Examined," *PR*, Vol. 74 (1965), pp. 229–39. "Wittgenstein's Notion of an Object," *PQ*, Vol. 13 (1963), pp. 13–25. "Wittgenstein's Picture Theory of Language," *PR*, Vol. 73 (1964), pp. 493–511.

KHATCHADOURIAN, H. "Common Names and Family Resemblances," *PPR*, Vol. 18 (1958), pp. 341–58.

KOHL, H. "Wittgenstein Returns," in his *The Age of Complexity*. New York: Mentor Books, 1965.

KOLENDA, K. "Wittgenstein's 'Weltanschaung'," *Rice University Studies*, Vol. 50, No. 1 (1964), pp. 23–37.

KREISEL, G. "Review of *R.F.M.*," *BJPS*, Vol. 9 (1958), pp. 135–58. "Wittgenstein's Theory and Practice of Philosophy," *BJPS*, Vol. 11 (1960), pp. 238–52.

LEVI, A. W. "G. E. Moore and Ludwig Wittgenstein," in his *Philosophy and the Modern World*. Bloomington: Indiana U. P., 1959.

LIEB, I. C. "Wittgenstein's Investigations," *RM*, Vol. 8 (1954), pp. 125–43.

MALCOLM, N. "Knowledge of Other Minds," *JP*, Vol. 55 (1958), pp. 969–78.

MARGOLIS, J. "The Privacy of Sensation," *R*, Vol. 6 (1964), pp. 147–53. "The Problem of Criteria of Pain," *D*, Vol. 4 (1965), pp. 62–71.

MCBRIEN, V. O. "Review of *R. F. M.*," *NS*, Vol. 32 (1958), pp. 269–71.

MELDEN, A. L. "My Kinaesthetic Sensations Advise Me . . ." *A*, Vol. 18 (1957), pp. 43–48.

MUNDLE, C. W. K. " 'Private Language' and Wittgenstein's Kind of Behaviorism," *PQ*, Vol. 16 (1966), pp. 35–46.

MUNSON, T. N. "Wittgenstein's Phenomenology," *PPR*, Vol. 23 (1962), pp. 37–50.

NAGEL, E. "Impressions and Appraisals of Analytic Philosophy in Europe," *JP*, Vol. 33 (1936), pp. 5–53.

NAKHNIKIAN, G. "Review of *P. I.*," *PSc*, Vol. 12 (1954), pp. 253–4.

NARVESON, A. "The Ontology of the *Tractatus*," D, Vol. 3 (1964), pp. 273–83. "Review of Hartrack," *D*, Vol. 5 (1966), 101–2.

NELL, E. "The Hardness of the Logical 'Must'," *A*, Vol. 21 (1961), pp. 68–72.

NORTHROP, F. S. C. "Language, Mysticism and God," in his *Man, Nature and God*. New York: Simon & Schuster, 1962.

OLSCAMP, P. J. "Wittgenstein's Refutation of Skepticism," *PPR*, Vol. 26 (1965), pp. 239–47.

PASSMORE, J. "Wittgenstein and Ordinary Language Philosophy," in his *Hundred Years of Philosophy*. London: Gerald Duckworth, 1957.

PERKINS, M. "Two Arguments Against a Private Language," *JP*, Vol. 62 (1965), pp. 443–58.

PEURSEN, C. A. VAN "E. Husserl and L. Wittgenstein," *PPR*, Vol. 20 (1959), pp. 181–95.

PLOCHMANN, G. K. "Mathematics in Wittgenstein's *Tractatus*," *Philosophia Mathematica*, Vol. 2 (1965), pp. 1–12. "A note on Harrison's Notes on 'Das Mystische'," *SJP*, Vol. 2 (1964), pp. 130–2. "Review of Anscombe's *Introduction to Tractatus*," *MS*, Vol. 37 (1960), pp. 242–6. "Review of Pears and McGuinness' translation of *Tractatus*," *MS*, Vol. 39 (1962), pp. 65–7.

PROCTOR, G. L. "Scientific Laws, Scientific Objects, and the *Tractatus*," *BJPS*, Vol. 10 (1959), pp. 177–93.

RANKIN, K. W. "Wittgenstein on Meaning, Understanding, and Intending," *APQ*, Vol. 3 (1966), pp. 1–13.

RHEES, R. "Can There Be a Private Language?," *PAS*, Supp. Vol. 28 (1954), pp. 77–94. "Miss Anscombe on the *Tractatus*," *PQ*, Vol. 10 (1960), pp. 21–31. "Some Developments in Wittgenstein's View of Ethics," *PR*, Vol. 74 (1965), pp. 17–26. "The Tractatus: Seeds of Some Misunderstandings," *PR*, Vol. 72 (1963), pp. 213–20.

RICHMAN, R. J. "Something Common," *JP*, Vol. 59 (1962), pp. 821–30.

ROLLINS, C. D. "Review of Malcolm's *Ludwig Wittgenstein: A Memoir*," *JP*, Vol. 56 (1959), pp. 280–83.

RORTY, R. "Pragmatism, Categories, and Language," *PR*, Vol. 70 (1961), pp. 197–223.

RUSSELL, B. "The Impact of Wittgenstein," in his *My Philosophical Development*. New York: Simon & Schuster, 1959.

RYLE, G. "The Work of an Influential But Little-Known Philosopher of Science: Ludwig Wittgenstein," *Scientific American*, Vol. 197 (Sept., 1957), pp. 251–9.

SCHWYZER, H. R. G. "Wittgenstein's Picture-Theory of Language," *I*, Vol. 5 (1962), pp. 46–64.

SHAPERE, D. "Philosophy and the Analysis of Language," *I*, Vol. 3 (1960), pp. 29–48.

SHOEMAKER, S. "Logical Atomism and Language," *A*, Vol. 20 (1960), pp. 49–52. "Review of Pitcher," *JP*, Vol. 63 (1966), 354–8.

SHWAYDER, D. S. "=," *M*, Vol. 65 (1956), pp. 16–37. "Critical Notice of Stenius's *Wittgenstein's Tractatus*," *M*, Vol. 72 (1963), pp. 275–89. "Gegenstände and Other Matters: a review discussion of Griffin's *Wittgenstein's Logical Atomism*," *I*, Vol. 7 (1964), pp. 387–413.

SMART, H. *"Language-Games,"* *PQ*, Vol. 7 (1957), pp. 224–35.

STENIUS, E. "Wittgenstein's Picture-Theory of Language: A Reply to Mr. H. R. G. Schwyzer," *I*, Vol. 6 (1963), pp. 184–95.

STERN, K. "Private Language and Skepticism," *JP*, Vol. 60 (1965), pp. 745–59.

STIGEN, A. "Interpretations of Wittgenstein," *I*, Vol. 5 (1962), pp. 167–75.

STOCKER, M. A. G. "Memory and the Private Language Argument," *PQ*, Vol. 16 (1966), pp. 47–53.

STRAWSON, P. F. "Critical Notice of *P.I.*" *M*, Vol. 63, No. 249 (1954).

STROUD, B. "Wittgenstein and Logical Necessity," *PR*, Vol. 74 (1965), pp. 504–18.

TANBURN, N. P. "Private Language Again," *M*, Vol. 72 (1963), pp. 88–102.

THOMSON, J. J. "Private Languages," *APQ*, Vol. 1 (1964), pp. 20–31.

TODD, W. "Private Languages," *PQ*, Vol. 12 (1962), pp. 206–17.

[Unsigned]. "Obituary. Dr. L. Wittgenstein," *The London Times* (May 2, 1951). "The Limits of What Can Be Said," *TLS*, (December 23, 1960). "The Passionate Philosopher," *TLS*, (May 1, 1959). "Review of *B.B.*," *TLS*, (January 16, 1959). "Review of *P. I.*," *TLS*, (August 28, 1953). "Review of *P.B.*," *TLS* (December 9, 1965).

WARNOCK, G. J. "The Philosophy of Wittgenstein," in R. Klibansky (ed.), *Philosophy in the Mid-Century* (II of 4 vols.). Firenze, Italy: La Nuova Italia Editrice, 1961. "Review of *B. B.*," *M*, Vol. 69 (1960), pp. 283–4.

WEILER, G. "Review of *P. B.*," *AJP*, 43 (1965), 412–16.

WEINBERG, J. R. "Wittgenstein's Theory of Meaning," in his *An Examination of Logical Positivism*. London: Routledge & Kegan Paul, 1936.

WELLMAN, C. "Our Criteria for Third-Person Psychological Sentences," *JP*, Vol. 58 (1961), pp 281–93. "Wittgenstein's Conception of Criterion," *PR*, Vol. 71 (1962), pp. 433–47. "Wittgenstein and the Egocentric Predicament," *M*, Vol .68 (1959), pp. 223–33.

WHITE, A. R. "Wittgenstein's *P.I.*," in his *G. E. Moore, A Critical Exposition*. Oxford: Blackwell, 1958.

WHITE, M. "The Uses of Language: Ludwig Wittgenstein," in *The Age of Analysis*. N.Y.: Mentor Books, 1955.

WIENPHAL, P. D. "Wittgenstein and the Naming Relation," *I*, Vol. 7 (1964), pp. 329–47. "Zen and the Work of Wittgenstein," *Chicago Review*, Vol. 12 (1958), pp. 67–72.

WINCH, P. "Rules: Wittgenstein's Analysis," in his *The Idea of a Social Science*. London: Routledge & Kegan Paul, 1958.

WILLIAMS, C. J. F. "The Marriage of Aquinas and Wittgenstein," *DR*, Vol. 78 (1960), pp. 203–12.

WISDOM, J. "Mace, Moore and Wittgenstein," in Vida Carver (ed.), *C. A. Mace, A Symposium*. London: Methuen, 1962.

WOLGAST, E. H. "Wittgenstein and Criteria," *I*, Vol. 7 (1964), pp. 348–66.

WOLTER, A. B. "The Unspeakable Philosophy of the Later Wittgenstein," *PACPA*, Vol. 34 (1960), 168–93.

ZEMACH, E. "Wittgenstein's Philosophy of the Mystical," *RM*, Vol. 18 (1964), pp. 39–57. "Material and Logical Space in *Tractatus*," *Me*, Vol. 16 (1964), pp. 127–40.

and L. Ranjit Singh, etc. Oxford Clarendon, 1968. Trans. from 2nd German. B.V. Abhyankar, 1971.

Wild, K. W. "Intuition and the Indian System." Trans. . . . . Vol. XXXVII. . . . . . and the . . . W. M. "Intuition." Trans. . . . . Vol. IX. (1937), pp. 67–77.

. . . . . R. "Wittgenstein's Aesthetics" in his The Case of . . . . London: Routledge & Kegan Paul, 1973.

Wisdom, Ms. C. J. F. "The Marriage of Aquinas and Wittgenstein" . . . . Vol. 35 (1960), pp. 203–13.

Wisdom, J. "Gods, Moore and Wittgenstein" in his Other . . . . Vol. 34 Oxford, Oxford: London: Methuen, 1953.

Wisdom, J. O. "Wittgenstein and Certainty," A. Vol. 3 (1964), pp. 23–36.

Wuthnow, R. "The Limits of the Philosophy of . . . . Later Wittgenstein" XVIII, Vol. 21 (1961), 9–31.

Zemach, . . . "Wittgenstein's Philosophy of the Mystical," Vol. 18 (1963), pp. 19–37. "Meaning and Correspondence in Reference," . . . Vol. 71 (1964), pp. 137–40.